The Ideal Society and its Enemies

THE IDEAL SOCIETY AND ITS ENEMIES

The Foundations of Modern New Zealand Society 1850–1900

MILES FAIRBURN

AUCKLAND UNIVERSITY PRESS

First published 1989
Auckland University Press
University of Auckland
Private Bag
Auckland, New Zealand

ISBN 1 86940 028 3

Typeset in Garamond
by Saba Graphics Ltd, Christchurch
Printed in Hong Kong

Distributed outside New Zealand
by Oxford University Press

Contents

. . . colonies begin as crudely broken-off fragments of the parent society; the impulse behind their foundation generally includes an urge to realise more fully some part of the implicit ideal purpose of that society. The effort of settling new country, however, usually exhausts the urge, and the colony once established easily drifts into a stagnating existence as a dull provincial reflection of the parent society, with its own comfort as its chief concern.

[Charles Brasch] 'Notes', *Landfall*,
    June 1953.

Acknowledgements

During my long search for the defining characteristics of New Zealand settler society I have been assisted by a great many people without whom this book would never have been conceived, written, and published.

Amongst these are my Hist. 316 and Honours students whose research papers led to the accumulation of data which indicated when I was on the right track and when I was wrong. Their discussions in class, furthermore, allowed me to clarify my thoughts and gave momentum to my own research and writing.

I also must thank Graeme Davison, Professor of History, Monash University (Melbourne), for the interest he took in my work at a crucial time and for bringing to my attention various pieces of research on Australian social history which had interesting parallels to my own.

I count myself very fortunate in having a network of friends and academic colleagues whose intellectual stimulation and resistance to mediocrity has compensated for the provincialism of New Zealand university life. Amongst these is Peter Webster, of the Anthropology Department, Victoria University. Some also took the trouble to read earlier drafts of the book, in whole or in part, and gave me the benefit of their trenchant criticism and comments. These people include John Morrow of the Political Science Department, Victoria University; David Thomson and Colin Davis of the History Department, Massey University; Peter Munz, Emeritus Professor of History, Victoria University; Steve Haslett of the Institute of Statistics and Operations Research, Victoria University, who also collaborated with me on a project on violent crime and injected a rigour and sophistication into my research which I could never have achieved by myself; Richard Hill of the Historical Publications Branch, Department of Internal Affairs; Allan Levett, a social research consultant of Wellington; my father, G. E. Fairburn, of Hamilton; and my wife, Maria.

My debt to Elizabeth Caffin, the editor of Auckland University Press, is also acknowledged; she has processed the manuscript with

7

complete professionalism. Likewise I owe much to Dennis
McEldowney for the care and effort with which he edited the text.

Lastly I am obliged to Gloria Biggs and Kristen Downey for the
long hours they spent entering the text and the many changes to
it into the word processor.

Introduction

THE reader will probably find the content and form of this book
on the social history of 19th-century Pakeha New Zealand
unfamiliar and new. Hence some preliminary discussion is needed
to indicate why this might be so, and to prepare the reader for the
approach the book has taken.

Why will the content seem unfamiliar? The likely reason is that
of three common preconceptions of what social history is all about,
the book conforms to none.

The first is that social history is antiquarianism, unfocused
empiricism, the scrupulous compilation of facts about the everyday
experiences of the common people. The compilation should be as
voluminous as possible, its criteria of selection being everything
contained in the original sources. What is left out should be dictated
only by editorial considerations. The arrangement of the minutiae
is not by themes but according to the years when they were recorded
and the headings of the original sources. With this genre of social
history there is no testing of hypotheses, let alone an explicit
interpretation, for the assumption is that the facts speak for
themselves. Poor in technique, it will not know if the examples it
adduces are typical of the behaviour of large aggregations of people.
Interested only in little New Zealand, it may ascribe events to causes
without realising that in other societies the same causes had the
reverse effects or that comparable events stemmed from contrary
causes. It may rely on fine writing and entertaining anecdotes to
compensate for its lack of intellectual bite and coherence. Its undoubted

9

strength, if the research has been thorough, is to bring forth details which are intrinsically interesting and useful as references. These details may touch at random on the calorie and protein intakes of ordinary folk, their drinking habits, table manners, work practices, earnings, the yields of crops, land-tenure systems, the size of land-holdings, the relations between men and women, their sexual traits and child-raising methods, the role of women, the structure of households, leisure pursuits and communal celebrations, religious rites, the customary manner in which turning points in the life cycle are acknowledged, consumer preferences, the concept of social justice or the image of the social structure, ideas about the Deity and His agents, the code of morality, definitions of anti-social behaviour and madness, the punishment of wrong-doers, the forms of medicine, collective representations of extraordinary events, the basis on which status was allocated, relationship with authority and superior status groups, and so on, and on.

The reader will quickly find that this book's approach is different altogether. Although the writer agrees that social history is about the everyday experiences of the common people, he believes that the facts do not speak for themselves. To make sense they have to be interpreted; they are intelligible only if they are fitted into a pattern, related to some general principle.

The second preconception is that the literature must reflect professional developments in social history as an academic discipline. Internationally the discipline has become compartmentalised into many subject-areas. They include demography, women's history, history of the family, rural history, the history of popular culture, urban history and so on. Each has acquired its own theoretical orientations, issues, techniques, and standards and forms of evidence. With these developments in mind, it would be natural for the reader to assume that a book which purports to be a general interpretation of colonial social history by a professional social historian would address itself to all the sub-disciplines. Logically this would entail giving the sub-disciplines equal representation, excluding only those clearly irrelevant. In practical terms the book would have to be arranged as a series of topics, equating to the sub-disciplines and allotted a chapter apiece. Each chapter would begin with a discussion of overseas literature. New Zealand data would then be selected and assembled according to the conventions of the sub-discipline, and perhaps formally constituted as a case-study to determine whether a model devised for another society was applicable to New Zealand.

Now the author totally approves of any New Zealand social history which is informed by international professionalism. There could be no better way of opening up a field of research in New Zealand than by using the theory, techniques, and issues in the international literature. A general social history of New Zealand arranged as a series of topics would have far more penetration and purpose than unfocused empiricism. But it is not the best approach. Although it can tell us how the parts of a social system operated as separate entities, it shows nothing of how they meshed together. There is nothing built into it, either, that allows the historian to identify the most revealing parts of a particular society, the special collection of factors which are the ingredients of national character. What is missing from this approach is a governing category, a master variable, the concept most able to identify and integrate those things fundamental and distinctive to the colonial social pattern, while retaining the best qualities of international professionalism.

This brings us to the third reason why the contents of this book will probably seem unfamiliar. If asked what colonial New Zealand should have as its governing category, the reader would in all likelihood nominate one from the following list of five: gender, ethnicity, region, class, and possibly religion. Some of these (gender and ethnicity most of all) have become prominent issues in modern New Zealand. The literature on social history—whether on New Zealand or other countries—has dwelt disproportionately on all five categories. The reader will soon learn that this book is based on none of them. No doubt this will irritate those who think their favourite topic has not been accorded its primacy. It is up to them to demonstrate that their notion of the governing category is a superior one. So far such a demonstration has not been offered except by ideologues convinced that what is important in the present must have been just as important in the past.

The governing category employed in this book is the colony's social organisation—the fabric of interpersonal relationships, the sorts of ties people formed, the settings and institutions which bonded them together and through which they interacted. Pakeha New Zealand, to be sure, was not unique in having a social organisation; every society has one. It would not be a society otherwise. The first claim in this book is that New Zealand's social organisation was of a particular type. It was gravely deficient. Community structures were few and weak and the forces of social isolation were many and powerful. Bondlessness was central to colonial life. The typical colonist

was a socially independent individual. The other claim in this book
is that atomisation can account for a large cluster of the traits and
trends which characterise the colonial social pattern. Many of these
were pathological, others benign and healthy. The deficient framework
of association produced appalling social problems of a predictable
kind—loneliness, drunkenness, violence. The same want of
interpersonal ties, however, also helped to prevent social problems
of another sort, collective protest and group disorder, and so assisted
in maintaining Pakeha New Zealand's remarkable political stability.
Atomisation also contributed to the colonial's powerful attachment
to family life, to the rapid growth of coercive and beneficent state
institutions, and to the development of a deeply self-repressed
personality. It was connected to the society's high level of material
independence and prosperity. It ensured that 'jack and jill were as
good as their master and mistress', and led to the prevalence of the
'jack and jill of all trades'. It forged strong petit-bourgeois tendencies
and hence accounts for the peculiarities of New Zealand's
egalitarianism. Among its fundamental symptoms were irresistible
feelings of restlessness, displacement, and rootlessness. It aroused
a chronic moral panic over vagrancy, and was a major constraint
upon the anti-liquor cause and the feminist demand for women's
suffrage, the colony's two most powerful social movements. Connected
to atomisation also were the country's demographic imbalances, a
pattern of dispersed and thin settlement, poor communications, pork
barrel politics, limited opportunities for organised leisure, and
disproportionately large numbers of jobs which were inherently
impermanent. As the book unfolds the reader will see how all these
apparently disparate elements in the colonial social pattern were
interrelated.

It is true that many of the same elements have been observed
in other peripheral or new societies. This could mean that New
Zealand's particular type of social organisation should not be used
as its governing category, since a governing category in social history
must be able to discern characteristics in a society which were both
fundamental and distinctive. But, without totally dismissing this
possibility, it should also be said that the major theorists and historians
of new societies have explained the same characteristics differently,
and have seen in other new societies distinguishing features which
cannot be found in New Zealand and vice versa. For example, Alexis
de Tocqueville, the famous French observer of early 19th-century
America, thought that what was notable about American society was

the restless, acquisitive, rootless, and transient proclivities of its inhabitants—traits just as prominent in New Zealand. De Tocqueville attributed their presence in America not to a deficient social organisation but to the absence of a hereditary aristocracy; in fact De Tocqueville stated that another of America's distinguishing features was that its people were avid makers and joiners of voluntary organisations, the very reverse of the situation in New Zealand. There are also certain parallels between Frederick Jackson Turner's classic account of the role of the frontier in forging the American national character and the model of New Zealand colonial society offered in this book, particularly the emphasis both place on extreme individualism. But Turner's ideas diverge from the author's on several significant points. Whereas in New Zealand extreme individualism arose from a complex set of circumstances (including an imported ideology), Turner related it solely to environmental forces, the most important being the abundance of free land. While Turner postulated that extreme individualism co-existed with much informal community interaction and neighbourly collaboration, in New Zealand this was rare. And although Turner sees frontier influences as entirely positive and beneficial, in New Zealand atomisation had malign effects which were inextricably linked to the more desirable. Likewise the reader might discern common elements in Manning Clark's vision of mid-19th-century Australia and the concept of New Zealand society in this book. Both societies were deeply flawed and failed to live up to their contemporary image as ideal societies. Clark, however, concentrates on the dark side of mid-century Australia whereas this author avers that in some respects New Zealand went a long way in living up to its self-image. Moreover, according to Clark the defects of the new society in Australia were the result of something eschatalogical, the fall of man, the inherent corruption of human nature; this author, on the other hand, regards New Zealand's faults as the unintended consequences of the extreme individualism which colonists believed in so passionately.[1]

These then are the matters of content which may be unfamiliar. But what about the book's form? Is this likely to be as strange as the content to the reader? The answer is that it probably will be. The convention in historical writing is to delineate past events through narration, by telling a story in other words, and to fit these events into major divisions of time or periods. In New Zealand's case, a consensus has evolved amongst historians about what the periods should be. Those covered by the span of this book (1850–1900) are five in number. In the first, the 1850s, the salient events are the granting of responsible self-government, the establishment of the provincial system of government, and the 'golden age' of Maori agriculture. Marking the second, the 1860s, are the gold rushes and whole-scale race conflict. The abolition of the provincial governments and massive private and public expenditure of money borrowed overseas during the 1870s (the 'Vogelite era') are the common reference points for the third period. This usually gives way to the 'Long Depression' and the upsurge of social protest in the 1880s, culminating in the Maritime Strike and the electoral victory of the Liberal Party in 1890. The fifth period, the 1890s, centres on the reformist activities of the Liberals, the rise of small farming, and the ascendancy of Richard John Seddon.

The reader will be struck by the absence of this familiar structure. The author has no objection to the narrative technique as a matter of principle. History is about change through time and normally the narrative is an indispensable means for talking about change. Use of standard periods is also of unquestionable value in certain circumstances; it provides a language all New Zealand historians can understand, and it suggests the significant developments in the country's past which social historians should try to explain and illuminate. But narrative and standard periods do have limitations when writing social history. One is that atomisation does not have a history which can easily be discussed through story-telling and the five conventional periods. Another is that these tools are more suitable for biography and politics, where change occurs faster and more dramatically than it usually does in social history.

The main reason these conventional forms have been abandoned, however, is that they are not the most useful techniques with which to make a persuasive case. The interpretation the book advances is ambitious and outside the range of the received wisdom; thus it is bound to encounter more resistance than one which is less far-reaching and more orthodox. To take account of these problems the book is designed so that it proceeds as a systematic and formalised argument. Broadly speaking, the first two-thirds refutes a sequence of four alternative views; the last third draws on the data obtained from the process of refutation to set up the atomisation model and then tests it. The rationale behind the lengthy refutation is to enhance the book's rigour. Behind the methodological design is the assumption that the strength of a theory is the product not of its own merits alone but of the demonstrable weakness of its rivals. Without the refutation the author would lay the atomisation model open to the objection that other theoretical positions explain the social pattern just as convincingly, perhaps more so.

The first alternative interpretation occupies all three chapters in Part I. This is called the 'insider's view' of New Zealand's social organisation. It is the idealised picture European colonists had of their new society, a New Zealand with all kinds of marvellous features originating from naturally abundant resources and a minimal framework of associations. The three other conceptions of colonial society are the subject of Part II. These consist of implicit attacks levelled at the 'insider's view' by modern historians. Although each of these implied attacks has a different angle, they have the same basic premise. They assume that the associational framework instead of being minimal was powerful, excessive in fact, and that New Zealand was far from an ideal place precisely because of the baleful effects of its strong social organisation. Finally in the chapters of Part III the reader comes to the author's own view. It affirms that the associational framework was indeed minimal and spells out its predictable consequences, many of which were undesirable and chaotic.

The title of the book is a play upon a famous book by the philosopher Karl Popper, called *The Open Society and its Enemies*.[2] In it Popper condemned the representatives of a tradition in Western philosophy who, as the enemies of freedom, advocated a Utopian totalitarian state, and the cessation of individualism and the spirit of critical enquiry, to resolve human problems. The argument in the following chapters is not in any way intended to reject Popper's plea for social freedom. Rather, the underlying moral purpose is to indicate that minimally organised societies are the polar opposite of totalitarian societies in the whole spectrum of ideal societies, and these minimally organised societies unintentionally but inevitably produce contrasting enemies, the identity of which will be revealed as the argument builds.

The book starts roughly in 1850 and neglects the 1840s to offset the undue historical attention given to the Wakefield settlements. The author contends that these were untypical of colonial society and that any influence they exercised was swamped by social transformations from the 1850s onwards. Little attention is given to Maori society, but for quite dissimilar reasons. Its social organisation was obviously and markedly different and separate from the European; and although this suggests a fruitful comparison between the two within the context of the history of race relations, it would be beyond the scope of this book.

PART ONE

The 'Insider's View' of New Zealand as an Ideal Society

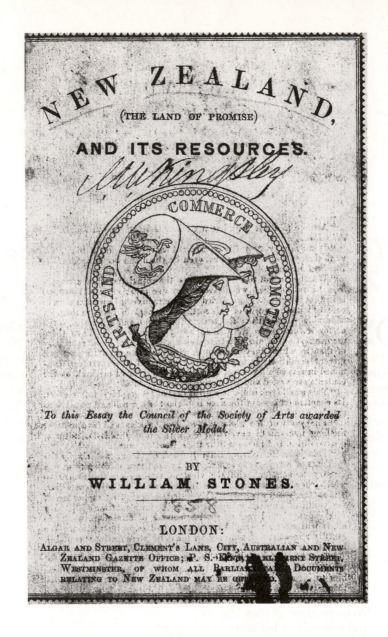

NEW ZEALAND,

(THE LAND OF PROMISE)

AND ITS RESOURCES.

To this Essay the Council of the Society of Arts awarded the Silver Medal.

BY

WILLIAM STONES.

LONDON:

ALGAR AND STREET, CLEMENT'S LANE, CITY, AUSTRALIAN AND NEW ZEALAND GAZETTE OFFICE; P. S. KING, PARLIAMENT STREET, WESTMINSTER, OF WHOM ALL PARLIAMENTARY DOCUMENTS RELATING TO NEW ZEALAND MAY BE OBTAINED.

The Land of Promise. A standard title for pamphlets idealising New Zealand to an Old World readership. This work won a Society of Arts medal. *Alexander Turnbull Library.*

Prologue

OVER the 19th century the most prominent image of New Zealand was as an ideal society for European settlers. In the first phase of its evolution the legend existed well in advance of the country's discovery by Europeans; it was implicit in the European linguistic convention prevailing from the 16th to the 18th centuries which attributed to many regions in the New World the characteristics of a particular kind of ideal society, Arcadia. Perhaps the most famous of these romantic projections, strongly influenced by the pastoral poetry of Virgil and other classical writers, is in Shakespeare's *The Tempest*, where Gonzalo fantasises about the island in the New World on which his ship has been wrecked:

I' the commonwealth I would by contraries
Execute all things; for no kind of traffic
Would I admit; no name of magistrate;
Letters should not be known; riches, poverty,
And use of service, none; contract, succession,
Bourn, bound of land, tilth, vineyard, none;
No use of metal, corn, or wine, or oil;
No occupation; all men idle, all;
And women too, but innocent and pure;
No sovereignty. . . .
All things in common nature should produce
Without sweat or endeavour: treason, felony,
Sword, pike, knife, gun or need of any engine,

Would I not have; but nature should bring forth,
Of its own kind, all foison, all abundance,
To feed my innocent people.[1]

Once New Zealand had been discovered and its colonisation began
the secondary stage of idealisation was set in train. A great flood
of literature published in Britain tended to focus the Arcadian image
of the New World more narrowly on specific British colonies and
possessions, including New Zealand. Simultaneously the linguistic
convention was shaped to fit contemporary British fears, attitudes
to social problems, popular ideas of a moralising kind. The imagery
suffused advice books to immigrants written by private individuals
and organisations, as well as provincial newspapers favourable to
emigration, novels, tourists' accounts, travellers' tales, memoirs of
former settlers, scientific and ethnographic works, letters and articles
from colonists and retired colonial officials printed in newspapers
and magazines.[2]

New Zealand figured strongly in this stream of idealising literature.
According to T. M. Hocken's famous *Bibliography of New Zealand
Literature* (1909), some 2,000 titles on all manner of subjects
concerning New Zealand appeared between 1840 and 1909. Not all
of these reached the British market and much had no idealising
element; on the other hand Hocken excluded multitudinous items
that both appeared in print in Britain and contained glowing references
to New Zealand, such as reviews in newspapers of advice books
to immigrants, reports of speeches by immigration agents, letters
to the editor, and statements and comments that Hocken failed to
pick up because their titles did not point to New Zealand. Publishing
houses such as the firm of Edward Stanford and periodicals like the
Australian Record and Emigration Journal (1841) or the *Emigration
Gazette and Colonial Settlers' Universal Guide* (1841), specialising
in promotional literature on the colonies, did much to spread idyllic
conceptions of New Zealand. So did the New Zealand government:
when the Agent-General's office was formed in 1870, a major function
was to distribute the government's publicity in Britain; in 1891 it
set up a library and information bureau in the office.[3] The Arcadian
tradition was obviously useful in boosting capital investment and
immigration, thus enhancing New Zealand's 'development'. As well,
a strong humanitarian influence drew upon the imagery as a means
of encouraging emigration to the New World in order to relieve
distress in the Old. Finally, a miscellaneous group of writers who
were neither colonial 'boosters' nor humanitarians borrowed the

linguistic convention chiefly to make money by catering for the book-buying public's insatiable appetite for tales about far-away lands, confirmations of British imperial greatness, factual information about the colonies, and so forth.

Although there has been no systematic research on the print runs of all these writings, there are several indications of their popularity. In the preface to his official *Handbook of New Zealand* (Wellington, 1883), James Hector noted that two earlier editions of the *Handbook* had sold rapidly, and he wrote his in response to the demand for information which could not be satisfied by 'many hundreds' of other tracts. In 1890, a bad year for immigration and therefore a slack year for requests for information, 12,000 handbooks were sent out from the Agent-General's office in London in response to enquiries.[4] Evidence that the readership was wide also comes directly from immigrants themselves, who say either that they had read the idealising literature before coming to New Zealand or that it had induced them to come. One man recorded that prior to leaving the Old Country in 1842 he had been given a book which told that the wild pigs of New Zealand 'grew fat on wild peaches, and waddled about helplessly, simply asking to be killed'. John Hall, who immigrated in 1853, said he came out under the spell of Charles Hursthouse's glowing portrait of New Zealand society. A Captain and Mrs Mace said they were allured to New Plymouth in the 1850s also after reading Hursthouse.[5] We can likewise tell the literature had an impact because newcomers occasionally grumbled that they found it misleading. In his memoirs published in 1922 Henry Scott said that before he left Britain in 1877 he had read pamphlets from Shaw, Savill and Co., which gave the false impression that New Zealand was a land of little or no snow. A notorious example comes from Nelson in 1843 when its 'workingmen' went on strike, and petitioned the New Zealand Company saying that they came to New Zealand under the deception that it was a 'Splendid country', one of 'Elysian fields and Groves adorned with every beauty of Nature'; 'Instead of the bread fruit tree there is the flax tree in a Swampy piece of Ground'. Another example is Edmund Sale, who testified to the Royal Commission on Land Settlement and Tenure of 1905 that before he left London his inquiries about the prospects of land settlement had left him with the impression that 'it was much easier to get land than I found it to be.' Furthermore, the Arcadian evocations must have had a wide currency because recent immigrants themselves utilised the language in their letters to people back home. H. A.

Atkinson wrote to Mrs Coster from Taranaki in 1854,

> I am entirely incompetent (not being a poet) to do justice to the Arcadian beauties of our luxuriant province. . . . I would refer you to Moore's *Utopia*, but people have got to consider it chimerical now a-days. I once thought so, poor foolish thing that I was, but I know better now that I have found the 'Island' and have lived in New Plymouth. . . . Upon landing you see at once that you mistake the country if you thought it aught but a land flowing with milk and honey. It is this in a literal sense, honey is most plentiful, and so indeed is everything that is good.

Finally, it seems reasonable to assume that the messages in the literature would have been spread widely in Britain by word of mouth when visiting colonists addressed public meetings, and by immigration agents in their lectures and talks during recruitment campaigns. The ideas were sufficiently common for the National Agricultural Labourers' Union (which collaborated with an army of immigration agents to send rural labourers to the colony during the 1870s) to state in the *Labourers' Union Chronicle*:

> Not a farm labourer in England but should rush from the old doomed country to such a paradise as New Zealand. . . . A GOOD LAND — . . . A LAND OF OIL, OLIVES AND HONEY;—A LAND WHERE IN THOU MAY'ST EAT BREAD WITHOUT SCARCENESS: THOU SHALT NOT LACK ANYTHING IN IT.[6]

The third stage of the evolution of New Zealand's identity as an ideal society proceeded after immigrants arrived in the colony carrying the images in their 'cultural baggage'. Powerful mechanisms prevented the formation of alternative and contrasting visualisations and led colonists to narrow the focus of the linguistic convention even further, to believe that their adopted country was uniquely Arcadian. Crucial here was the fact that, as we shall see, the realities of the colonial social pattern went some way in confirming the imported ideas. Even though some immigrants must have found that initial experiences failed to match their high expectations, they were disposed to ignore the difference or at least play it down, thanks partly to the strength of their conditioning in the Arcadian vision, and partly because they were reluctant to admit to themselves, let alone family and friends back Home, that their sacrifices of exile had been in vain. Besides all this, the development of the colony, from which every settler benefited, depended on the confidence of British investors and emigrants in its future, and there was no surer way of undermining their confidence than to cast doubt on the existing reputation. The urge to put the colony in the best possible light was all the stronger because it had to compete for emigrants with many other New World territories while labouring under several disadvantages, of which the worst was a sea voyage longer and more costly, onerous, and hazardous than to any other. One of the few inside critics of the ideal society wrote in 1887, 'Nothing is more offensive to Colonial views than to have the dark side of things in the country fairly set forth. But should anyone write very favourably of climate, productions, commerce, institutions and the wonderful future of New Zealand, well then his future is made, he is a god out here.'[7] New Zealand's political leaders had their own professional reasons to foster the received concepts; it was easier to make plausible election promises and juggle the balls of hope in the air if New Zealand was portrayed as a blessed country than if a more pessimistic set of preconceptions prevailed. Also, events across the Tasman left the generality of New Zealand settlers with an increasing sense of their own country's separate identity and superiority. Australia had earlier been depicted in the same romantic language as New Zealand, but a succession of devastating droughts, the explorations of Charles Sturt which finally confirmed that the interior was a 'fearful desert', and a prolonged economic crisis after 1892, all forced Australian colonists to discard the Arcadian view and invent a different myth about themselves.[8] Finally, what stifled the emergence of an ideological tradition in New Zealand critical of Arcadian ideals, was that critics had no reason to stay in the country from which they were alienated, and that the ideals, like all good closed systems, were impossible to disprove. J. Adam, a former Otago Provincial Councillor, responded in 1876 to those disappointed in colonial life by saying, 'Rather than reflect upon themselves, or their want of perseverance and adaptation to the pursuits of a new life, they reflect upon the country'. Knowing that his readers would be totally familiar with the reference, he likened the grumblers to the Jews wandering the wilderness,

When the first emigrants from Goshen arrived at the confines of Palestine they were seized with a most perverse spirit of contradiction. The promised land was a failure, and the serfdom of Egypt earthly bliss. The spies indeed admitted that the land was good. The ponderous bunch of Eshcol grapes compelled them to admit that fact; yet, with one breath, they said the land flowed with milk and honey, and in the next that it was a land that starved its inhabitants.[9]

So what was the content of the visualisations? A close study of their language shows they were expressed in two modes. The first was the abbreviated mode of popular metaphors, catch-phrases, labels, colloquialisms. These were frequently used in place of larger, more detailed and explicit statements while encapsulating their meanings. The country was variously designated the 'better' or 'brighter' 'Britain of the South', the 'Land of Goshen', a 'land of plenty', 'an earthly paradise', the 'labourer's paradise', the 'workingman's paradise'. The single most common allusion to New Zealand calls it a 'land of milk and honey', a saying that persisted into the 20th century and still has currency. It is derived from the Book of Deuteronomy in the Old Testament (6:3) where Canaan, the promised Land, is pledged to the Jews, after their flight from oppression in Egypt. It is given to them on condition they serve a time of trial, that they know and practise God's laws, the myriad prescriptions and taboos communicated through Moses. The term itself is an abbreviated reference to a later statement in Deuteronomy 8:7-9. Of all the descriptions of blessed places in the Bible, colonists evidently found this the most appealing and quoted it more frequently than any other to sum up what sort of place New Zealand was.

For the Lord thy God bringeth thee into a good land, a land of brooks of water, of fountains and depths that spring out of valleys and hills; A land of wheat, and barley, and vines, and fig trees, and pomegranates; a land of oil, olive and honey; A land wherein thou shalt eat bread without scarceness, thou shalt not lack any thing in it; a land whose stones are iron, and out of whose hills thou mayest dig brass.

In turn the 'milk and honey' phrase informed yet another popular expression. This was 'God's Own Country', a catchphrase variously attributed to Thomas Bracken the poet and 'King Dick' or Richard Seddon, Premier during the Liberal era. Abstract descriptions of newly settled areas were also inclined to draw on the 'land of milk and honey' symbolism.[10]

If the metaphors are traced to their immediate sources they take us to the second mode in which New Zealand was visualised—the extended mode, detailed statements. The significance of these statements is easy to overlook. They consist essentially of clichés in various guises, that is, evocations, assertive description, incidental comment, unsystematic observation. It is their status as clichés that makes them significant. Although not the only ideas about New Zealand, they are the governing ideas. They are cited more often than other ideas and occupy more space in the sources. Through textual exegesis it can be shown that they are composed of four themes. At least one or two of the themes will be found in the same text, sometimes three, less often all four, with variations in explicitness and emphasis from source to source. Since the themes are inherently consistent with one another and were frequently strung together in different combinations, it is reasonable to assume that they were the component parts of a unitary message about New Zealand, the ingredients of a coherent vision of the society—the 'insider's view'. The themes are that New Zealand was a country of natural abundance, that it provided ample opportunities for labouring people to win an 'independency', that it was a society which naturally created a high level of order, and that its simple life guaranteed middle-class people freedom from status anxiety.

As mentioned previously, the four themes constituting the imagery of New Zealand as an ideal society were framed within an Arcadian linguistic convention. At this point it would be useful to explain the meaning of Arcadia, especially given the tendency to confuse it with other ideal society types, and since Parts II and III of the book will assess whether and how far the society actually lived up to its Arcadian self-image. The definitions employed are taken from a historical study of ideal society thought, *Utopia and the Ideal Society: a Study of English Utopian Writing 1516-1700*, by J. C. Davis. According to Davis, theories of ideal societies fall into five basic categories—the Millennial, the Arcadian, the 'Land of Cockaygne', the Utopian, the Perfect Moral Commonwealth. What they have in common is their recognition that universal human problems—moral corruption, personal unhappiness, poverty, social conflict and so on— result fundamentally from normal society's failure to harmonise human wants with economic resources. Where the five differ is in their explanations of how this fundamental human dilemma has arisen and in the prescriptions they offer for its resolution. The Millennial type assumes that economic scarcity has been caused by moral imperfection and that human wants can only be satisfied when humans become just, so proving to the Divine that they are worthy of salvation when He brings the evil world to an end. In the Perfect Moral Commonwealth type, the central idea likewise is that economic resources are deficient but that all individuals have persuaded each other through example and rhetoric to cope with the attendant problems by leading saintly lives. In the Utopian solution, it is also assumed that economic resources are in short supply, but the woeful consequences of dearth are contained by an authoritarian state establishing the institutions that strictly regulate human appetites without satisfying them. In the 'Land of Cockaygne' the problem of scarcity is wished away: natural plenty flows literally into the mouths of people who have innately gross and insatiable appetites. With the Arcadian type the problem of meagre resources is also wished away and nature provides enough to fulfill human desires. Unlike the inhabitants of the 'Land of Cockaygne', however, the people of Arcadia are innately moderate; they want and obtain only what they need.[11]

Arcadias are, then, 'natural societies' where natural abundance and the innate moderation of their inhabitants have abolished the necessity for social organisation. In normal societies an elaborate associational apparatus—composed of primary and secondary associations—organises wealth, power, and status. In Arcadias natural abundance and innate moderation take the place of government institutions, voluntary bodies, informal groupings and networks (to a large extent), and economic institutions. Natural abundance itself provides what the inhabitants need; resources are so plentiful that collective agencies are not needed for their creation, management, protection, and allocation. At the same time, the innate moderation of the inhabitants of Arcadia ensures that their wants are simple; hence the need to construct collective agencies to satisfy superfluous desires has also been eliminated. In Arcadia no contrived associations generate artificial desires, and no artificial desires generate contrived associations. From these premises follow ail the other blessings of Arcadia. It is a place of justice, prosperity, harmony, morality, social freedom, contentment, leisure, and simplicity because, by not requiring a social organisation, Arcadia has abolished the *immediate* causes of all injustice, poverty, discord, corruption. In turn, the freedom from excessive organisation is the combined effect of natural abundance and innately moderate desires. Arcadia satisfies people without burdening them with convention, obligation, collaboration, coercion, manipulation, and persuasion—all the costs of social life. This is not to say that Arcadians are hermits; on the contrary they meet and mix but only in a spontaneous, carefree, totally voluntary manner. In contrast to Utopia, the benefits of Arcadia are not imposed by the formal machinery of a strong social organisation. In contrast to Perfect Moral Commonwealth, the blessings are not derived from informal community pressures to adhere to a common moral code—the informal machinery of a strong social organisation. Unlike the converts to a Millennial solution, Arcadians do not form associations that practise certain rituals in order to prove they deserve salvation when the end of the world comes; Arcadians do not need associations of that sort, let alone religious ones, for they have already secured the land of abundance and freedom.

How then did the 'insider's view' conform to this definition of classical Arcadianism?

Colonial rhetoric did not deny that New Zealand possessed a social organisation in its governmental and judicial structures, its schools, voluntary organisations, joint stock companies, family ties, patchwork of informal groupings, and so forth. But until late in the century it largely ignored and underplayed them. The associational framework was assumed to be elementary, happily underdeveloped. Only subsequently did the 'insider's view' acknowledge the need for a strong social organisation. From about the 1890s, as will be seen towards the end of the book, the language shifted; it drew upon Perfect Moral Commonwealth and (most of all) Utopian elements to indicate how New Zealand's Arcadia was being preserved.

The aim of the next three chapters is to show that before the 1890s the blessings attributed to New Zealand—the contentment and prosperity of its working classes, its natural harmony, the freedom of its middle classes from status anxiety—were predicated upon Arcadianism and not upon any other type of ideal-society thought. The 'insider's view' claimed they were spontaneously stimulated by natural abundance. It presupposed that they were achieved within a simple associational framework and without requiring and producing a strong social organisation. It imagined that the simplicity of the social organisation together with natural abundance prevented the emergence in New Zealand of the Old World's social problems. These problems, characteristic of the universal human problems classical Arcadia said it solved, were the inverse of New Zealand's blessings. They were demeaning and inefficient paternalism, working-class poverty and disorder, and the tyrannical social pressures which forced the middle classes to live beyond their means. Assessment of how far the 'insider's view' squared with reality is deferred until Part II.

Natural abundance and the stages of material progress. The banner, 12 ft by 7 ft 6 in., of the Gisborne Chamber of Commerce, late 1890s. The banner takes as its central theme the natural abundance of Gisborne (the cornucopia in the bottom right) over which people have gained increasing control. At the top is a pioneering scene, representing the initial stages of material progress. A muddy track in the forest, the clearance of which has just begun, impedes the movement of a bullock waggon groaning under its load of wool bales. The middle shows the present and the wonderful transformation brought by the machine. A long, heavily laden train moves easily through the plain, bearing the wealth of the surrounding countryside. Another train opens up the magnificent resources of the bush. Both speed towards the modern port of Gisborne with its new breakwater and freezing works. The top righthand corner shows that life is still hard in the backblocks, in places like the Motu valley. From the cornucopia pour vegetables, fruit, and grain and inscribed on it is a list of Gisborne's other natural riches which include coal and frozen meat.
Cyclopedia of New Zealand, ii (1902)

CHAPTER I

Natural Abundance

OF the themes constituting the Arcadian conception of New Zealand, the most common was the notion of New Zealand as a land of natural abundance. The premise for the other themes running through the literature, the idea was never shaken by such upheavals as war or depression or natural disaster, and its adherents crossed all boundaries of class, religion, political persuasion, and region. The assumption had all the power of a legend. Not only was it taken for granted and extraordinarily popular, it also had its own predictable rhetoric and met with little resistance let alone reasoned scepticism.

The legend was indiscriminately applied to every part of New Zealand; it was geographically egalitarian. Rarely was any part of the country considered lacking in nature's bounty. At one remove we can see this in the rhetorical conventions used to describe the lowlands. They were variously likened to 'gardens', compared favourably to areas of the Old World celebrated for their productiveness, or depicted in absolute hyperbole as if their fecundity had burst the bounds of meaningful comparison. We can see some of these devices operating in the emigrant advice book of the widely read New Plymouth settler, Charles Hursthouse, the most sustained bucolic evocations of the colony ever written. He gushes over 'the blooming fertility' of the countryside around Christchurch; he boosts the Hutt Valley as a 'little Sicily of fruits, flowers, butter, eggs, poultry, and garden produce'; and proclaims that the south of the Auckland

Province was entitled to rank as the 'Garden of New Zealand'.[1] In his account of four years' travelling through the colonies, David Kennedy (1876) wrote of Nelson's allegedly inexhaustible resources: 'The heavens look benignly upon it—the climate is the most enjoyable in the colony', 'by universal consent, [it] is called the "Garden of New Zealand"'.[2] In 1880 the Rev. James Buller relied on the same superlatives to capture the essence of Taranaki and the whole of its hinterland through to Taupo:

From Wanganui, the traveller can penetrate to the inland lake of Taupo; or going northerly, he can visit New Plymouth, about 130 miles distant. Nothing can exceed the fertility of this part of the country: when all apprehension of native disturbances are permanently settled, it will, without doubt, justify the name that has been given to it—'the garden of New Zealand.'[3]

The stylisation of New Zealand's fertility was well represented in an article, 'Dunedin to Christchurch in 1888', published in the *New Zealand Reader* (1895). The reader, intended for children in the standards, was the first explicit attempt by the Department of Education to provide New Zealand themes in its prescribed texts. The writer describes what he calls his first impressions of New Zealand after a long visit to the Australian Colonies. No one, he says, gave him a hint of the 'sumptuous fertility of these beautiful islands', nor a word 'about the astonishing soil, so catholic in its fertility that it will grow everything worth growing, and so rich that it grows everything well'. Then in an imagined rail trip from Dunedin to Christchurch these general ideas of New Zealand's abundance are given a detailed pastoral shape, as the train moves through the landscape. Past Waitati he travels, through 'grass land spangled with marguerites just as in English meadows, and whole choirs of the Old-country song birds'. After Seacliff, to the left, stands 'fat pasturage and close strong crops of grain. The rich cocksfoot grass escaping out of the paddocks runs riot on the banks; and the clover overflowing grows along the line. Then, on a sudden, we are out on a level of tussock-land that stretches to the sea; on the other side billow after billow of meadow, with plump cattle, sheep, and horses grazing, and corn-land rolling away in hill and dale right away back, so it seems, to the very first of the distant hills.' A little later the author takes the reader past the 'splendid levels' of Maheno and Totara: 'What land! What stock! The fat, huge-framed, straight-backed cattle literally wade in sweet grass, and the horses are "pictures" both in breed and condition. Wheat and potatoes in larger fields than we see them at Home fill up the intervals between the pastures where the polled Angus and the Devon live in plenteous ease.' After going by 'rich growths of English trees' at Oamaru, the writer picks out 'exquisite pasturage, knee-deep and clovered', and 'so past Studholme, and on through the same monotony of fertility'. Then 'away again through "distressful" levels of corn and herds of fat kine to Orari'. Around Ashburton, the adjectives of luxuriance change little. The soil is rich and, as 'everywhere along the line, there are all the most obvious evidences of comfort and substance. Fat cattle, and fat, rosy, well-dressed children, are unmistakeable proofs.' And so on, and so on, the author takes us to Christchurch. Significantly, although he attempted to demonstrate how varied and interesting the landscape was, compared with the dreary 'plains' of the United States or India, the overflowing produce of the countryside encountered again and again leaves an overwhelming impression of monotony—a 'monotony of fertility'.[4]

In addition to these supposedly fertile lowlands, New Zealand possessed, usually in its interior or its mountains, a huge store of mineral wealth, or of some other riches, hidden from us for the moment, but certain to be discovered in the future. For example, Charles Hursthouse quoted a despatch from Governor FitzRoy to Lord Stanley stating that, 'Beneath the productive surface of these teeming islands are mineral stores as yet hardly known. If from merely scratching some projecting corners of the land, some twenty valuable minerals have been discovered, (coal, iron, silver, lead, copper, tin, nickel, manganese, alum, sulphur, cerium, bismuth, cobalt, and asphaltum,) what may not be anticipated after a few years of research in the interior?'[5] Sir George Grey in 1867, after securing the support of the Taupo tribes, claimed that by making the interior of the country safe again, the European population could safely spread inland, 'developing the great resources of valuable districts which are now but little known, and the advance of this Northern Island in wealth and population will consequently be very rapid'.[6] The *Evening Post* in an editorial of 3 January 1889 effused: 'Even the ground which is comparatively valueless on the surface for either pastoral or agricultural purposes is in a vast number of cases teeming with mineral wealth of one kind or another beneath.'[7]

What is significant here is the irrational character of FitzRoy's, Grey's, and the *Evening Post*'s belief. Although little was known about the resources in the interior they nonetheless supposedly exist in great quantity. The power of this illusion seems to have intrigued Samuel Butler. *Erewhon*, Butler's novel, starts off with the hero, a shepherd on a back-country station, speculating about what lies beyond the range. He acknowledges, to begin with, that no one knows. But as he dwells upon the question he becomes certain that gold must be present. It must be, he tells himself, since people deny gold is there and people always deny the presence of gold until it is found in abundant quantities. The hero's train of thought is at first glance surprising since it is the reverse of the prevailing tendency as manifested by Grey and FitzRoy, to believe in the wealth in the interior when there is little evidence for it. However, Butler was a shrewd observer of human folly and the hero's extraordinary logic is typical of Butler's use of irony to draw attention to the illogicality of wishful thinking in the colony: proof of the existence of gold depends no more on the will to believe than it does on the will to disbelieve.

What was beyond it? Ah! who could say? There was no one in the whole world who had the smallest idea, save those who were themselves on the other side of it—if, indeed, there was any one at all. Could I hope to cross it? This would be the highest triumph that I could wish for; but it was too much to think of yet. I would try the nearer range, and see how far I could go. Even if I did not find country, might I not find gold, or diamonds, or copper, or silver? I would sometimes lie flat down to drink out of a stream, and could see little yellow specks among the sand. Were these gold? People said no; but then people always said there was no gold until it was found to be abundant: there was plenty of slate and granite, which I had always understood to accompany gold; and even though it was not found in paying quantities here, it might be abundant in the main ranges. These thoughts filled my head, and I could not banish them.[8]

Even scientific writers presumed that the hinterland was filled with riches. In his *Handbook of New Zealand* (1883), James Hector had this to say about the soils of the Volcanic Plateau region: 'Towards the coast, and in some limited areas near the larger valleys, such as the Waikato and the Thames, and also where volcanic rocks of a less arid description appear at the surface, great fertility prevails, and any deficiencies in the character of the soil are amply compensated for by the magnificence of the climate'. On the eastern side of the Volcanic Plateau, there are 'occasional areas of fertile alluvium of considerable extent. It is only the latter portions of this district which can be considered as adapted for agriculture, while the remainder affords some of the finest pastoral land to be met with in any part of the colony.' On the south-eastern side of the South Island 'The alluvial soils of the lower part of the Canterbury Plains, and of Nelson, Otago, and Southland, are the most remarkable for their fertility'. The western side was somewhat more modestly endowed. Here 'the rapid fall of the rivers carries the material derived from the mountain-ranges almost to the sea-coast, so that comparatively small areas are occupied by good alluvial soil; but these, favoured by the humidity of the climate, possess a remarkable degree of fertility.'[9]

The details of natural abundance discussed up to now have features which are not entirely compatible with the pure Arcadian tradition of ideal-society thinking. Although the overall idea of natural bounty fits the classical tradition, what does not is the implication that man has changed the fertility of the lowlands and that people have yet to discover the riches of the hinterland. In the New Zealand version man has a dynamic relationship with the abundance, whereas in the classical descriptions of Arcadia it is passive. The difference reflects the incorporation into the New Zealand version of the Victorian imperative of material progress, the belief that material betterment stimulates moral growth which in its turn produces more material growth and so on in an everlasting upward spiral.

To convey the necessity of improvement, the literature implicitly arranges the details of natural plenty into three related categories. The first consists of the country's 'natural advantages', the second is what shall be called 'bush cornucopia', and the third material growth. What distinguishes them is the extent to which each was affected by human effort, the last two representing progressive transformation of the first. The connection with the classical model is not altogether lost, for material growth can only occur because natural abundance permits it. The first type of natural plenitude consisted of all the elements of nature bestowed on New Zealand which gave its potential for vast productivity. These were usually described as New Zealand's 'natural advantages', which implied that they were entirely an act of providence and had nothing to do with the human hand. The natural blessings of New Zealand, some of which have already been mentioned, included a 'salubrious' climate; a naturally productive soil; plenty of land; proximity to the major trading routes; a long coastline and naturally good harbours; luxuriant forest cover; ample fauna though not in variety; and a wide range and an ample store of minerals. Ernst Dieffenbach in his *Travels in New Zealand* (1843) commented on the fineness of the country's climate and the abundance of its vegetation cover.[10] In the 1850s an army surgeon, formerly stationed in Auckland, A. S. Thomson, wrote, 'The moisture of the New Zealand climate is evidenced by the luxuriousness of its vegetation and the heavy night-dews—but this moisture is a very different thing from the raw dampness of many countries; it produces an exquisite softness of the skin, and the inhabitants rarely suffer from that unpleasant "glazed" feeling of the skin so often experienced in dry climates.' Thomson went on to 'prove' the health-giving properties of the climate with statistics showing that the rate of mortality and infectious diseases amongst his troops in Auckland was far lower than at any other station in the Empire. Thomson's statistics were so widely used that they stimulated a sub-legend about New Zealand as a haven for the invalid and the delicate and contributed to the later idea of New Zealand as an ideal place to bring up children—plenty of fresh air and sunshine.[11]

William Swainson, Attorney-General 1841–1856, wrote in his book *New Zealand and its Colonization* (1859), that 'The salubrity of New Zealand has been established by the experience of years. For persons of delicate constitution it is probably unequalled, save by Madeira. Families have actually left Madeira to settle in New Zealand.' Swainson went on to assert that New Zealand's climate was superior to that boasted for every country in Western Europe.[12] In his *Britain of the South* Charles Hursthouse pronounced the climate as a perfect balance between excessive fineness and rigour. He accepted Governor FitzRoy's notion that the interior contained vast mineral resources. With a coastline of 3,000 miles in extent, finely divided into a multitude of bays, creeks, caves, estuaries, and anchorages, New Zealand, he thought, possessed some of the finest naval and commercial harbours in the world. Unlike nearly every other writer, Hursthouse did not consider that nature had given New Zealand an intrinsically rich soil. 'It is a virgin soil of fair average fertility, but nothing more'— and inferior to that of North America, he added. Fortunately, the climate, he said, acted as an '"elemental guano"', which more than compensated for the less than superior soil fertility, as it exercised a 'peculiarly genial, "manure-acting",' influence. That there was plenty of land available for a growing population, at least potentially, he made clear in a table of statistics on the progress of each province. One of the nine columns showed that the total area of land in cultivation or fenced was 500,000 acres. Another column, headed 'Rough estimate of area in Acres as yet required from the Natives', showed a total acreage of 47 million. He did not think New Zealand's indigenous fauna was varied or particularly useful but 'The teeming growth, perpetual verdure, and vigorous freshness of her forests, have been the admiration of every visitor since the days of Cook'.[13]

The Rev. T. H. Braim, in a survey of the Australasian colonies as a field for emigration published in 1870, claimed that Tasman gave such a glowing description of New Zealand's climate and soil that Benjamin Franklin entertained the idea of forming a colony here.[14]

Julius Vogel, in his *Handbook of New Zealand* published in 1875 by the New Zealand Government, made much of all these merits natural to New Zealand, and many historians have implied that Vogel invented them. They do not realise that Vogel was merely going through the customary rites expected of literary description of New Zealand, and that had he failed to intone the country's marvellous resources his British and New Zealand readers would have thought something was amiss.[15]

The centrality of the natural advantages theme in folk-belief is suggested by its unvarying content regardless of the variety of people who expressed it. Thus the Governor, Sir Hercules Robinson, in an after-dinner address to the Canterbury Agricultural Association in the late 1870s, said: 'Nature has, indeed, been most bountiful to New Zealand. She has given her beautiful scenery, a magnificent climate, a soil of unsurpassed fertility, an extensive sea-board, a commanding position'—and the allusions are repeated almost exactly by the Dunedin District Judge, John Bathgate, in his book *New Zealand: Its Resources and Prospects* (London, 1884). The basis of the country's remarkable prosperity, he says, is 'undoubtedly to be found in the fertility of the soil, and the delightful climate' while the long coastline, which gave most inland areas good access to the sea, and the richness of the soil, more than compensated for its distance from the British market.[16]

Similar details can be found in the accounts of New Zealand life written by representatives of the 'working class'. For example, over the 1870s New Zealand was visited by a series of organisers and publicists of English rural trade unionism. One was Alfred Simmons, Secretary of the Kent and Sussex Labourers' Union, who visited New Zealand in 1879 and described his impressions in *Old England and New Zealand*. He recounted New Zealand's Arcadian qualities and contrasted them with the Old World's natural deficiencies. The climate in New Zealand was superior and the soil, while it was variable and could be as bad as the worst in the Old Country, was also better than the best there. It would 'beat any portion of the United Kingdom you liked to name cleanly into fits. What! beat the soil of beauteous, fertile Kent, the garden of England? Beat the soil of prolific Warwick and Worcester, and the bountiful corn-lands of Lincoln? Aye, beat them all; and beat them over and over and over again.' The soil was no whit inferior to that of the United States. Land was plentiful, timber 'inexhaustibly abundant', a large variety of minerals had been unearthed, few countries were richer in raw materials; and the vegetation was of a 'grand order'.[17] Very much the same sentiments can be found in Arthur Clayden's *The England of the Pacific* (1879). Clayden, a journalist, came to New Zealand in the late 1870s too, and was the Berkshire supporter of the 'Revolt of the Fields'.[18]

Then there is the example of Christopher Holloway, Chairman of the Wootton (Oxfordshire) branch of Joseph Arch's National Agricultural Labourers' Union. A farm labourer by occupation, Holloway was invited by the New Zealand government to accompany a party of immigrant rural labourers and report on conditions in New Zealand to his union. Holloway arrived in Port Chalmers on 13 February 1874 and spent the next nine months travelling around New Zealand, covering 6,430 miles. One historian, Rollo Arnold, who has investigated Holloway's itinerary, has commented that 'Few colonists could have claimed to have seen as much of their country as he had', and that Holloway acquired an 'excellent first hand knowledge of New Zealand'.[19] Holloway himself was inordinately proud of the vast knowledge he was able to pick up in his field work: 'I mixed pretty freely with all classes of the community— from the· Hon. J. Vogel (Premier) down to the lowest settler. . . I have associated with the great landed proprietor, and with the less affluent settler, who is steadily advancing upward to a more prosperous position. I have met with the employer of labour and the employed, with the prosperous and the unsuccessful. . .'. Yet for all this intense and earnest empiricism Holloway depicted the colony in very conventional language. New Zealand possessed, he reported, a 'fine, healthy climate', 'salubrious air', 'fertile soil', a 'mild winter', 'temperate summers'; to nearly every district he visited was attributed a fine, fertile soil; his first impression that New Zealand was a working-man's paradise was repeatedly confirmed to his satisfaction.[20] The glowing accounts by Simmons, Clayden, and Holloway were echoed in the letters written by rural labourers to their people back home, whose examples demonstrate that the myth of the natural advantages was not propagated solely by business interests and suggest that working men did not have a different, opposing, conception of New Zealand.

Merging into these images of 'natural advantages' was another set of conceptions about the country's natural gifts. The abundance in this case was the material that nature almost spontaneously created, indeed could hardly stop herself from producing in prolific quantities, so happily combined were the 'natural advantages'. The material needed a human touch of the lightest kind. The allusions often hint at the 'Land of Cockaygne'. The abundance was predominantly nature's creation. The material was used after only a little preparation, yet it served man's purpose in a rough and ready fashion. Such material was of the sort associated with the primitive economic activities of gathering, hunting, and rough cultivation. When people engaged in these rude arts the wilderness supposedly became a veritable storehouse of goods that could be used for shelter, food, and other necessities.

W. K. Howitt, in his memoirs of Taranaki bush life during the 1870s, *A Pioneer Looks Back* (1945), recorded how plentiful native game was, how they shot wild pigs, wild heifers or steers which had taken to the bush, and caught dozens of eels to trade for peaches with Maoris. Hursthouse commented that at Waitara he had seen a herd of wild cattle 'browsing among the wild shrubberies', 'some of which would have done for the Smithfield Christmas-show', and predicted that once deer were introduced into the ranges they would never be exterminated. W. D. Hay attested that rock oysters were so plentiful that it was the practice in his district to burn them down into burnt lime. Salt-water fish abounded, according to Alfred Saunders. One colonist wrote from Wellington, saying, 'The books may well tell us that the harbours abound with fish; abound is a poor word—they are literally *alive* with fish. Mr. _____ and myself now almost live on them; they are delicious, and in great variety. We have one like salmon and quite as fine in flavour. On a sunny morning the surface of the harbour is a complete mass of fishy life.'[21]

Groves of wild peach trees were the most discussed symbols of 'bush cornucopia'. James Cowan, a journalist and writer on Maori and European relations, remembered above all the peaches of his childhood days on his father's farm in the Waipa Valley during the 1870s and 1880s:

The peaches of those happy dream-days on the old Orakau farm!—peaches vanished, a kind never to be tasted by the present generation. Orakau,

Kihikihi, Te Awamutu, and Rangiaowhia were then the favoured land of the most delicious fruit that ever this countryside has known. Peach-groves everywhere, the good Maori groves, trees laden with the big honey peaches that the natives called korako because of their whiteness. Tons of peaches grew in those groves, and those wanted were gathered by the simple process of driving a cart underneath and sending one of us youngsters up to shake the branches until the cart was filled with fruit. Some of the best peaches were preserved by the housewives of the frontier in a way never seen now; they were sliced and sun-dried on corrugated iron, in the strong heat of the long days, and then strung in lines and hung in the high-ceilinged kitchen, criss-crossed in fragrant festoons, until required for pies.[22]

That wild and domesticated pigs were fattened on the huge crops of wild peaches was also central to New Zealand's overseas reputation as Arcadia. It may have been the associations of honey peaches feeding waddling pigs waiting to be killed that Hursthouse had in mind when he wrote:

As to wild pigs, it is impossible even to guess at their number. They abound, however, in certain localities; and poor Hood probably had New Zealand in his eye when he wrote:

'There is a land of pure delight
Where omelets grow on trees,
And roasted pigs come crying out,
Oh! eat me if you please.'[23]

The proliferation in New Zealand of other introduced animals like horses, cattle, sheep, as well as poultry, falls into the same pattern. That they thrived in New Zealand was allegedly because of the genial climate, ample food, absence of predators. The easy naturalisation of introduced species of flora useful to people was also noted. To quote Hursthouse again, 'clover, turnip, cabbage, carrot, spinach, mint, thyme, and various stray vegetables and garden plants, spreading themselves over the country in some apparently unaccountable manner, are found in many districts mixed up with the indigenous vegetation of the country and almost threatening to oust even the vigorous natives of the soil.' James Hector in the 1883 Handbook of New Zealand commented on the facility with which exotic trees of valuable species 'flourish with a vigour scarcely ever attained in their natural habitats', and the ease with which the hop grew with 'unexampled luxuriance'. Further, he saw that all European grasses produced returns 'equal to those of the most favoured localities at Home', and that introduced fruits were abundant all over New Zealand (even in Wellington), while root and green vegetables of all kinds grew 'luxuriantly'. Alfred Simmons's vision was of 'lazy, too-well fed herds of cattle browsing upon pasture lands, the green English grass growing well-nigh up to their haunches, and upon land that has never seen the sight of a cartload of manure. Stick in a common cabbage-plant at Invercargill', he swore, 'and in the time that plant shall require to become a half-fledged child-cabbage in England it shall become a splendid tender fully-matured vegetable in New Zealand.' He was struck, too, by the yield of grain in Otago from land that did not require the supplies of manure needed at Home. One woman reminisced in the *Taranaki Herald*, 'Everybody had a good garden in the days before the Maori War. No matter what was put into the virgin soil, a good crop was obtained; and there were no blights.' There is frequent comment in the literature on the prolific crops following the bush burn. Without digging or harrowing, and with a soil clean of all weeds, seed for grass, or wheat or oats or barley, was thrown straight on the ashes, and good results obtained. The heavy crops of potatoes grown on the bush farm were also reputed to be delicious. Many writers concurred that bush country, once cleared, provided the best yields. The ease of obtaining such abundance was a source of continuing comment from 'new chums'.[24]

The pioneer family's sagging dinner table, product of this 'bush cornucopia', was the focus of another set of images. Howitt nostalgically recalled feasting on the 'good things of life', on special occasions, such as birthdays and anniversaries.

There would be fowls baked or boiled, fresh pork and smoked hams, also fish from the sea or rivers; then there were well-flavoured potatoes grown in the fresh bush clearings, kumeras and pumpkins and home-made bread cooked in the old-fashioned hanging ovens. . . . There were also peach jam tarts and Cape gooseberry 'roley-poley', and it was a poor home which did not have a 'plumduff', too. There was always plenty of milk and cream; and mead made from the wild honey found in the hollow trunks of the trees. One of the things to be remembered was the fine salt butter, which was kegged away for winter use, so often relished with the fresh bread baked so crisply in the primitive camp oven.[25]

Unlike the first stereotype, the 'natural advantages', which consist of the potential for fruitfulness, the third, material growth, is the potentiality being realised. Compared with 'bush cornucopia', people have greater influence over nature, and the plenty is correspondingly more refined, varied, and copious. To highlight how successful this improvement of nature was, those who wrote evocations of New Zealand loved to cite statistics of production, exchange, overseas trade, and population, invariably showing dramatic upward trends. The Victorian age generally was fascinated by enumeration. It has been suggested that in Britain the impulse behind the growth of statistical knowledge was the feeling that social problems were on such a vast scale that numbers not words were the only way of conveying them. Perhaps in New Zealand the avidity with which economic statistics were compiled stemmed from a conviction that not even the hyperbole in the descriptive literature could convey the perceived magnitude of its material growth. In his *The Past and Present of New Zealand*, 1868, the Rev. Richard Taylor included statistics to show how rapidly the colony had developed in such a short time, to 'make its wonderful progress most evident', to show 'what a change British industry and perseverance have effected in an antipodal wilderness, in founding a colony which has not yet attained its thirtieth year'; Charles Hursthouse said he had to make statistical projections of growth because 'a young growing colony like New Zealand sometimes exhibits as great a change, as great a progress, in five years, as an old, full-grown country like England exhibits in five and twenty'.[26]

Although the accent on economic change and energy seems to us far removed from the calm and the ease of the archetypal Arcadia, to contemporaries the conceptual distance was smaller. For one thing, although 'British industry and perseverance' were essential to progress, so was the colony's inherent prodigality. The two were well matched; even though man and nature were not integrated they were at least complementary. For another, New Zealand's progress had escaped and would continue to avoid, contemporaries were happy to report, the evil effects of industrialism and urbanisation. In an 1889 editorial the *Evening Post* doubted if it was the country's destiny to become 'a great manufacturing country . . . and it is not necessary that it should be in order to ensure prosperity and wealth'; before considering the growth of 'densely populated manufacturing centres, we should see every acre occupied and made productive, and our mineral resources fully developed'. What would predispose us that way was that 'New Zealand is essentially an agricultural and a pastoral country, and . . . no country in the world offers superior, or indeed, equal natural advantages for the successful carrying on of these pursuits', certainly not Australia with its aridity and proneness to drought.[27] Finally, although the New Zealand concept of material growth was not Arcadian, the ideal of social organisation was; it is here that the rustic simplicity and contentment essential to classical Arcadia can be found.

The domestic economy of a working man, 1880s. Williams, a railway worker and amateur photographer, made these beautiful studies of his domestic life with his Napier cottage garden as the backdrop. Most of the section seems to have been laid out in rows of vegetables and a profusion of fruit trees. Colonial working men with households used their sections as a surrogate welfare state, growing as much of their food as possible to provide against irregular employment. Williams's garden, however, was exceptionally idyllic. *Williams Collection, Alexander Turnbull Library*

CHAPTER II

The Labourer's Paradise

T HE second basic theme running through the literature is implicitly and explicitly tied to the idea of natural abundance. The male-centred theme is that natural abundance creates marvellous opportunities for working men to become materially independent, to gain what contemporaries called a 'competency' or an 'independency', equivalent to the ownership of productive capital, usually landed property. The stereotype of New Zealand is of a place where men without capital or from humble origins could become proprietors after only a few years in the colony—thus I. R. Cooper assures his readers in 1857:

Those who arrive in the colony without capital will, if they enjoy good health, are sober and economical in their personal expenses, and are able and willing to work *at any one trade*, as farm servants, boatmen, shepherds, or house servants, soon realise a sufficient capital to invest in land, cattle or sheep, and thus to render themselves and their children independent.[1]

Charles Hursthouse promises his audience in 1861:

Carpenters, cabinet-makers, painters, glaziers, masons, [etc] . . . all sorts of farm labourers, and handy jack-of-all-trade fellows, all men who minister to first wants, are certain to succeed in New Zealand. . . . It is literally true that hundreds of mechanics and labourers who landed in New Zealand a few years ago, are now substantial freeholders, cultivating their own little estates.[2]

R. B. Paul in 1861 likewise:

There is no reason why a steady working-man should not be able to purchase a twenty acre farm (£40), and stock it, within three or four years. I have known many a man who has done so, and is now a thriving farmer.[3]

T. H. Braim repeats the point in 1870:

Many a labouring man, knowing what he is about, will become a servant on a farm for a year or two. Whilst in that capacity he will keep his eye about him, spy out a bit of good land, save up his large wages, get it, and commence operations in a small way.[4]

He is echoed by Alexander Bathgate in 1874:

In Dunedin, very many working men live in their own freehold cottages, and some of the suburbs are almost exclusively filled with neat little houses, owned by working men. It may be laid down as a general principle that any man who likes to work and can use his hands will succeed. . . .[5]

Rev. James Buller repeats the refrain in 1880:

Any number of this class [farm labourers] can find employment, and it will be their own fault if, in a few years, they do not have farms of their own. . . . I know many who, by industry and thrift, have succeeded in raising themselves from the condition of labourers to that of farmers. . . .[6]

The *New Zealand Handbook* of 1888 (a more difficult year) goes over a familiar theme:

Though there is not much immediate chance of making a large fortune in New Zealand any more than anywhere else, yet a comfortable living, a house in healthy surroundings, a fair start for their children, and a reasonable provision for their own future are within the reach of emigrants if they are careful and industrious. . . . steady, careful men, willing and able to undertake farm work, who are prepared to go into the country districts, and turn their hands to anything they may find to do, are pretty safe to get on.[7]

So the certainty of property for the (morally deserving) labouring man was at the heart of the meaning of New Zealand, the 'labourer's paradise'.

There are two possible objections to this generalisation. In the first place, the goal of manual workers was often stated in terms not of material independence but of home-ownership or words to that effect (the extract from Bathgate illustrates the point). Home-ownership, it might be argued (if this be what the 'average' working-class immigrant and colonist wanted), was quite different from the desire to go farming or own some other form of enterprise generating the income (in cash or kind) to live on. On the face of it, home-ownership does not produce a livelihood and therefore does not save the incumbent from selling his labour in the wage market. In late 20th-century New Zealand, home-ownership represents consumption and residence but not the ownership of capital for the production of commodities. It was otherwise in the 19th century. Then, people talked about 'homes', the desirability of having a home-of-one's-own, the opportunity the colony gave people to acquire a home, in a very loose manner. The term often embraced productive capital, more often still land used for pastoralism or cultivation—a synonym, that is, for an 'independency', a 'competency'. Thus, for instance, Joseph Ward, defending his Advances to Settlers Bill of 1894 (which expressly excluded mortgage advances for urban residential purposes), said, 'There are at the present time in the colony a considerable number of persons now paying excessive rates of interest, who, if they had an opportunity of getting money at low rates of interest, as provided in this Bill, could apply it well, and put their shoulders to the wheel and make homes for themselves.' James Buller in his advice book for emigrants of 1880 said this in the context of a discussion about the country's land laws: 'Some portions of the country are heavily timbered: these are best for the poor, hard-working man, who by dint of his own labour will, in a few years, make a smiling homestead out of his few acres of bush. . .'. In his 1855 account of New Zealand, the Rev. Richard Taylor said the inducement to emigrate from Britain was 'To find a home; this is the desired object with many'; then in the same context, to show how well suited the country was for immigrants, he added, 'It is amusing to see how surely settlers have advanced from small means to a competency—agricultural labourers, to be substantial farmers; sailors and artizans to be merchants, and men of substance. . . .'[8]

The other problem with the extracts we quoted is that they are middle-class voices. Although they prescribe material independence as the objective of the wage-earning immigrant we cannot take it for granted that these prescriptions either coincided with wage-earners' desires or had a significant influence upon them. The wage-earners' own concept of the 'labourer's paradise' might be quite different from that projected upon them by middle-class writers. What compounds the problem is that the inarticulateness of the vast mass of working men makes it very difficult to establish their aggregate expectations and aspirations, let alone rank these in some sort of hierarchy of desires. To resolve these difficulties we need to measure how they behaved, examine what they say in their letters home, and study the statements of their leaders. The behavioural evidence will be considered in detail in the next chapter. All that will be said here is that a substantial proportion of manual workers applied for land from the Crown, and more importantly, about one quarter of all manual workers were owners of land by the early 1880s. Although neither fact in itself proves how strong the desire for landed assets was in relation to other wants, they nonetheless strongly suggest that a land-based 'independency' (of some sort) was a widely held objective. If a substantial minority owned land, it would be fair to deduce that a much larger number sought to. At first glance the evidence from letters by wage-earning immigrants opens up other possibilities. The most comprehensive examination so far has been conducted by Rollo Arnold.[9]

The correspondence Arnold has looked at was from the assisted immigrants, largely rural labourers, who poured into the colony in the 1870s. All the letters were published in the newspapers of rural and other trade unions in England. Hence it is reasonable to assume that the details they contain shaped the attitudes of those who read them, including other labourers who subsequently went to New Zealand. What is interesting about these details is that they are cited again and again, with little variation. The country is praised because its strong labour market maintains security of employment and high wages; food in the colony is cheap and plentiful (especially meat); here even labouring men can hunt game and ride horses; New Zealand is a wonderful place to work in as hours are comparatively short and the employer treats you as an equal. As we shall see later, aspects of the Old Society are, in an equally stylised fashion, set up in opposition to these marvellous features. The opportunity to own land in the colony is also mentioned. But since these references are no more frequent than those to the good material and working conditions of wage-earners, it might be argued that the image of the 'labourer's paradise' was sufficiently ambiguous to embrace two very different concepts: one focusing on improvement without a change in objective class position and the other on upward mobility out of wage-earning ranks. The argument might continue that these two concepts allude to two quite distinct categories of labouring immigrants, one seeking a more comfortable life within the wage-earning structure, the other, the more ambitious, desiring to rise out of it. On these grounds the

'labourer's paradise', if it did shape the expectations and aspirations
of manual worker colonists, would have led a great number of them
to define their satisfactions not in terms of achieving material
independence (the middle-class projection) but of attaining permanent
ease and contentment within the wage-market (which is not consistent
with the middle-class projection). A less casual reading of these letters,
however, suggests that this distinction is false, that the two concepts
are complementary parts of an overall strategy of improvement. An
idealised New Zealand allows wage-earning and petty enterprise to
be conjoined in a myriad of combinations and permutations. The
paramount theme is that the immigrant wage-earner can/will/does
over time move by degrees from being largely or wholly dependent
upon the wage market (when he first arrives in the country) to
the opposite extreme, when he largely or wholly lives off property
(during the later years of his working life). The 'labourer's paradise'
was taken by labourers themselves to mean not two distinct
alternatives but a process by which the average working man on
wages lives well and enjoys advantageous working conditions while
he naturally proceeds by small steps to become his own boss. What
was visualised was not a quick shift, from rags to riches or from
labouring to farming but a piecemeal accretion of market advantages
over time. At each stage the reliance on wages is a little less than
before, the stock of capital a little larger, and the return upon capital
and the production of commodities somewhat greater. It should be
noted that this is Arnold's own interpretation of the letters, although
he does not see them as idealising New Zealand (which this writer
does), and he says that they are specifically rural in application (which
is too narrow—we shall see that town sections were also used for
production). To illustrate the point, here is George Tapp, previously
a Kentish farm labourer, writing from Egmont village in 1874:

The Government here employed several of us at bush felling at 5s. per
day (lose no time) until we got a little experienced at the work, and then
they put small contracts to us, and men, if good hands, can earn from
10s. to 11s. per day. There are plenty of small contract jobs here that men
can take, both ground and bush work. Wages are from 6s. to 8s. per day,
day work. We have a deal of rain, being winter, so that a man cannot
always get a full week in. The people tell me such weather lasts about
two months. I have been working at bush felling, but have left that, and
am with the survey in the bush, at 6s. per day, eight hours per day, lose
no time, that being very good for a few weeks in the wet season. In summer
time a man can do much better. . . . There are no paupers here, no half-

starved homes. Everybody gets plenty to eat. . . . Any working man here can get some land and build himself a house if he likes. Nearly every man in the province is the owner of land; most working men have from 50 to 100 acres, and some more. They keep cows on it, and in a few years live entirely on their own land. . . .[10]

The statements by working-class leaders and sympathisers are broadly consistent with this perspective. Arthur Clayden characterised the prospects in New Zealand for labourers by recounting this success story about a Kentish farm labourer who had immigrated to New Zealand.

I met one of them in a road at work one day, and, as was my wont, I at once accosted him. He had been out about three years. In England his average wage was twelve shillings a week. . . .
'And what do you get per week now?' I inquired.
'Two guineas, sir, all the year round,' he replied.
'That's rather different from your old-country prospects,' I suggested.
'Why yes, sir,' he answered with a knowing turn of his head; 'instead of a big house to look forward to in my old age, I have a little one, but then he's all my own.'
'Oh, then you have already got a house of your own, have you?' I put tentatively.
'Yes, sir,' he answered, 'there he be,' pointing with his rake along the road to a pretty little verandahed cottage standing in a plot of ground by the road-side. 'I am just adding a couple of rooms to him. Step up and have a look at un, sir.'
I did so. The wife was at home and invited me to a seat in her parlour. It was a comfortably-furnished room, with a sofa and various little knick-knacks, which you rarely see in a working-man's cottage—in the English rural districts at any rate. The new rooms were a kitchen and a spare bedroom; behind, stretched out the good-sized garden, filled already with vegetables and fruit-trees. I learnt from the wife that with the exception of about fifty pounds, all was paid for. Here, then, was a further demonstration as to what New Zealand meant for the British workman! Any sober and industrious man could easily secure as the result of his toil, in an incredibly short time, a freehold house and garden.

In this Clayden represents the evolutionary process three years after the labourer had landed in New Zealand. He has his own small freehold cottage, it is almost paid off, he has begun to extend it, he has been able to furnish and decorate it comfortably, and while he is still fully dependent on wage-earning his 'good-sized' garden obviously provides him with a lot of his food and saves him money.[11]

Alfred Simmons portrayed many phases of the evolution in his *Old England and New Zealand*. He talked first of the high wages and high living standards of wage-earners—referring implicitly to what the newcomer initially experienced. He then described labouring men at about the same stage as Clayden's man and followed with a portrait of two wage-earners who had advanced to higher levels of petty enterprise and enjoyed a correspondingly larger surplus.

One man, in addition to purchasing his house and garden, had leased seventy-five acres of Government pasture land, was the owner of twenty cows, and supplied a small neighbouring town with all the milk used therein. Another man, besides having a cottage erected for himself and family, had built and rented a second cottage, had reserved a portion of his freehold land for pasture, and had already got six cows and some goats upon it.[12]

In the proceedings of the 1905 Royal Commission on Land Settlement and Tenure, we find that the same sense of the labourer's long-term objective, the same idea of the working man evolving towards material independence, has become firmly fixed in the political views of a cross-section of trade unionists. Where the visualisation is different is not about ends but means—the state should intervene to make the objective attainable. William Peake, representing the Auckland Trades and Labour Council, testified to the Commission that:

I was thinking of giving families an opportunity of keeping a cow, and an acre of good land would enable one to do so and to go in for poultry. I wish to make the workers as independent as possible. . . . there are many of the workers not in regular employment, and if they had sufficient land to do something with they would be comparatively independent. We do not wish to become independent at the expense of the community at all but I believe it would pay the country and the Government to give the workers an opportunity of acquiring a piece of decent land. There are any number who would be only too glad to occupy land and utilise it to the best advantage.

J. K. Johnston, representing the Nelson Trades and Labour Council, went further. In his eyes it was not enough for the wage-earner to be as independent as possible: he wanted to rise out of the working class altogether, which Johnston apparently thought could be achieved on sections of merely three acres:

Supposing you got 3-acre farms that you speak of for orchard, gardens, and so on, is there not sufficient for a man to do on the 3 acres?—Yes.

The object of every workman is to some day see himself out of the labour-market.

That is providing a different trade for him altogether?—They are only workmen by force of circumstances, but they are anxious to get a piece of land and cultivate it.

Robert Register, appearing for the Blenheim Labourers' Union, and W. E. Agar, president of the Lyttelton Stevedores' Union, made statements less detailed than Peake's or Johnston's but consistent with both. Albert Métin, the French visitor to New Zealand at the turn of the century, investigated workmen leasing State land of a few acres, and from his report it is plain that they valued the same sort of independence.[13]

The opportunities in New Zealand for the working classes to become materially independent were not celebrated simply because they satisfied a working-class acquisitive spirit, a lust for money. The literature presents a much more complex picture: wealth-making was not an end in itself but a means to other ends. Firstly the opportunities were valued because they freed manual workers from an old, familiar enemy—paternalism. The dependent relationships characteristic of the Old World were vilified in the literature as 'oppressive', 'bondage', 'serfdom', 'slavery'. The people of the Old World who owed obligations to the rich in return for material support were likened to the Old Testament Jews in Egypt during their captivity. Paternalism was besmirched by its association with the conflicts between landlord and tenant in Ireland. It was blamed for the vice, disorder, disease, poverty of the new British industrial cities, having done nothing to stop these evils. Most of all it was hated because of its connection with the hierarchical society of rural England whence working-class immigrants chiefly came.[14] Alfred Simmons vilified the social organisation of rural England as cruel, inefficient, tyrannous. Ruling it are the landed classes, their laws 'hang upon the land like a gigantic leech', their parliamentary power blocking enlightened legislation and protecting privilege, including their monopoly over the ownership of land. Tied to them are the tenant farmers, fettered by restrictions, sapped of initiative by tithes, game laws, crushing rents, insecure tenure, monopoly ownership, uncertain compensation for improvements, unjust and incomprehensible land laws. The tenant farmer in turn compensates for these burdens by exploiting the labourer: 'Badly paid, badly housed, badly clothed, badly fed, his education neglected, taught to be content with his semi-serfdom, sent to gaol if he takes up a rabbit to feed his hungry little ones, and sent to gaol, too, if being homeless and weary, he sleeps in a barn or wagon shed.' His pay is so low he cannot save, then when sick or jobless he has no choice but to ask for aid from the poor law guardians; often including his own employer or farm employer, they subject him to humiliating questions about how he has spent his wages, send relieving officers to pry into his hovel, and then, final indignity, lecture him on his improvidence and want of thrift, before refusing relief or granting a pittance. Simmons contrasts this appalling vision of a hierarchical society with scenes of the colonial 'labourer's paradise' where the labourer is now a fully possessed individual, the master of his own destiny. The blessings of New Zealand's fantastic resources and elementary social organisation, its 'natural' guarantees of full employment and high wages, its lack of restraining institutions, transform the character of the labourer, empowering him to win a freehold, disproving that he is innately extravagant, idle, hopeless. New Zealand has no need for oppressive philanthropy. The rare unfortunate is cared for by fraternal, spontaneous, generous giving:

[colonials] make a general subscription and place the person—a widow, for instance—in a small business, and so secure for her a maintenance. There are several charitable funds, from which persons suffering from temporary reverses are assisted; but if a travelling labouring man is necessitated and lacks food, he has but to knock at the first door he comes to and ask, and in nineteen out of twenty houses he will find that the spirit of the good Samaritan dwelleth therein.[15]

The opportunities for obtaining a competency were further revered because of their association with a cluster of other, non-pecuniary, symbolic and moral satisfactions. Attached to the whole process by which labouring men evolved towards material independence, these values fall into three categories: the requisites for success, the means by which the requisites were acquired, the place in which they were most fruitfully exercised. We will now look more closely at the details of the process and see how they conform to the Arcadian definition of the ideal society.

The Requisites

In the land of natural abundance the evolution of the labouring man towards material independence was a suitably natural one. The conditions necessary for individual success in New Zealand were imagined to operate outside a social framework. Winning a competency did not depend on collaboration, mutuality, collective arrangements—with one exception, the family, discussed a little later. It did not need the patronage of the wealthy. It did not require any of the advantages of middle-class origin, a good school (let alone formal education itself), social connections, a good family background, or inherited money. Most importantly, it did not rely upon working-class collective action or upon the mobilisation of any kind of class power—nobody, labouring men included, needed to form trade unions or other sectional interest groups to obtain a share of the 'natural advantages'. The assumption was that all such contrivances were superfluous. In Arcadia, natural abundance had largely abolished the necessity for associational props. The principal requirement instead was something internal to each man—that he discipline himself and cultivate the work ethic. The emphasis on personal qualities as opposed to socially organised ones is well illustrated in the following passage from W. D. Hay. A middle-class Englishman who had gone pioneering on the Kaipara, Hay published an account of his experiences in 1882 as a guide to potential colonists. 'In the colonies, and particularly in the younger and newer among them,' he stated,

a man must perforce be the sole architect of his own fortunes. Industry and energy, enterprise and perseverance pave the pathway to success, and yield a real and lasting benefit to him who holds such endowments. A man must prove what he *is*, not what he *was*; his antecedents go for but little, and his 'forbears' for nothing at all. In the Antipodean colonies . . . is realized, perhaps, the nearest approach to true freedom; and, in a wide social sense, the closest approximation to the ideal republic.[16]

Hay assumes that the personal qualities needed for success in the colony are the same for everyone—by implication the labourer travels the same path as the wealthiest person, who starts with no inherently greater advantages. The attributes required are in essence moral, not intellectual, with the possible exception of 'enterprise' (which, however, was not often mentioned as part of the stock of moral capital). In his social picture, individuals win material rewards only in proportion to the extent to which they have developed industry, energy, perseverance, enterprise. By definition this makes New Zealand a just society: people receive only as much as they deserve. As notable is his claim that the society is totally open—one's place in it is determined by what one's character is now. It cannot be preserved through institutional means and cannot be transferred across the generations. It is also very open in that it would be difficult to think of any other collection of personal attributes deemed essential for success that would be so accessible to so many. They are very simple virtues. To acquire industry, perseverance, energy, essentially demands self-discipline and good health, not an elaborate training or a complex process of socialisation, not talent, not imagination, not ingenuity or skill; and as facets of the personality they are not genetically derived. Hay does not acknowledge that people could nevertheless be unequally endowed with the ability to attain these attributes through variations in child rearing, training, and parental influence, that in such ways they might be socially constrained and outside the individual's own control. In addition, what is significant about Hay's imagery is that he accepts that New Zealand is a stratified society. The distribution of rewards is uneven; men do not have the same possessions because men vary in the extent to which they have acquired the simple virtues needed to get on. The stress in Hay's vision is not on equality of outcomes but on equality of opportunity—a crucial distinction which has not been understood by many historians and commentators, the radicals especially. They have assumed that intrinsic equality of wealth was part of New Zealand's ideological tradition, and have judged the society according to its actual capacity to live up to these standards. In fact it is extremely rare to find any source which praises or proclaims New Zealand on the grounds that everybody is on the same level of wealth. On the contrary, the endlessly recurring message is that New Zealand is an extremely open society in which men should command different shares of 'natural resources' to the extent that some have worked harder than others.

The Origins of the Requisites

There was nothing at all original in the idea that success depended upon hard work, perseverance, thrift, and that a man was the sole architect of his own fortunes. These imperatives were borrowed from the metropolitan society where they had been popularised by writers such as Samuel Smiles with his gospel of 'self-help'. However, they were fundamentally recast to fit the imagined advantages of the new environment. Colonial myth-makers insisted that in the new society men who possessed the personal virtues were sure to rise, whereas in the old society there was no such guarantee. On the contrary what made the Old World so unjust was that its plethora of vested interests and institutional rigidities (its monolithic social organisation) frequently prevented the virtuous from gaining a competency, while allowing the undeserving to rise in the social order or to retain wealth and position they patently had not earned. On this ground they view

New Zealand in contrast to Britain as a country of moral meaning. James Buller captured some of these sentiments in his eulogy of New Zealand published in 1880:

It must not be forgotten that the only conditions of success are precisely the same in the colonies as in England. Probity, industry, and frugality are as necessary there [in New Zealand] as they are here [in England], but with this difference,—the chances there are many, while here they are few. At home many fail in spite of requisite qualities; but in the colonies, if they fail, it is for the want of them.[17]

Central to Buller's optimism was the natural abundance myth; the reason the work ethic was rewarded in New Zealand was that the country had all the 'natural advantages'; every bit of effort spent in harnessing nature's bounty was bound, could not but help, to yield rewards. In the metropolitan society the opposite was true. In the Old World scarcity was both natural and the product of defective institutions, and the average individual stood a very great risk of being not rewarded for effort but penalised or thwarted.

These competence-winning virtues were acquired by a personal spontaneous response to natural abundance, without the intervention of society. The labourer did not become hard working as a result of peer-group pressure, the force of public opinion, the sanctions and moralising of his betters, his observation of others, the coercion of the law, or institutional training. In anticipation of modern behaviourist theory, colonial myth-makers assumed that the characters of immigrant working men were predominantly and automatically moulded by the environment. But whereas the external world of the behaviourists is a complex of value-free, multifarious stimuli, the colonial environment was seen to be dominated by the one enormously positive stimulus, the opportunity for getting on. Labourers just arrived in New Zealand would very quickly learn, by direct experience, that only by hard work could this opportunity be seized. Appropriate traits advanced the labourer towards a competency, inappropriate traits led away from it. The colony's natural advantages stimulated manual workers to be naturally virtuous. Alfred Saunders saw this when he wrote of New Zealand in 1868, 'Many persons, who have not learned to work, soon lose all their money or property in the colony, while those of steady habits, who can work, are pretty sure to rise.' In the same vein, James Buller, commenting on social mobility in New Zealand, wrote in 1880, 'Nature's aristocracy is limited to no class of society. I have often observed in New Zealand that men of the lowest social grade improve greatly in character. A man finds there a prospect before him, and this is a stimulus to exertion.' W. D. Hay in 1882 quoted the standard advice: 'Success, in a greater or lesser degree, *always* follows patient industry at the Antipodes; it can scarcely be said to be so in Britain', and Hay then added,

If he [the new immigrant] be anything of a man, before ten or a dozen years are gone he will find himself with a bit of land and a house of his own; he will be married, or able to marry, his earnings will suffice for existence, while every pound saved and invested in property will be growing. . . . There is something to work for and hope for here: independence, contentment, and competence. It is not a stern struggle from year's end to year's end, with naught at the finish but . . . the workhouse.[18]

The Setting

So far we have seen that colonial ideology had a clear sense of how certain virtues guaranteed success and how these virtues were derived. Our account, however, would be incomplete unless it is understood that the ideology also presented a particular context and course of action for the exercise of these virtues which were just as asocial and natural as the virtues themselves and their derivation. Two themes run through the mythology which justify this interpretation. The first we can piece together from the negative impressions the literature gives of the most socially developed places in the colony, its towns. The implication is that the worst place for the average individual to seek upward mobility was in the town, and the worst occupations to take up were urban occupations. The trouble in part stemmed from the simplicity and small scale of towns and the limited number of urban consumers. Hursthouse in 1861, for example, advised that clerks and 'shopmen' would not rise in New Zealand, for the country's business houses were so small they employed few assistants and most lacked a managerial hierarchy up which their employees could move.[19] The other problem was the reverse of this: the social complexity of the towns, and their advanced division of labour. Occupational specialisation created few opportunities to get on because the market for specialised goods and services was weak in Arcadia. Colonists, it was supposed, lived a simple life, they had no artificial wants or sophisticated tastes, and were able to a large extent to satisfy their moderate appetites through improvisation, by being jacks-of-all-trades. On these grounds it was widely believed that people with particular vocations, a special expertise, a formal job training were ill adapted to the colony's needs. For example, Sewell claimed in

1853 that lawyers were unwanted in New Zealand, Fitton in 1856 that all kinds of professional people were in over supply, Cooper in 1857 that clerks would not succeed, Hodder in 1862 that the clerkly had little chance of succeeding, Braim in 1870 that tradesmen and office workers were not in demand. Adam in 1876 advised clerks not to emigrate; Clayden in 1879 wrote that New Zealand was not a place for bank clerks, Hay in 1882 that the clerk and the shopman had no prospects, John Bathgate in 1884 that there were no openings for clerks, shopmen, or professional people and that the trades were full, the *New Zealand Handbook* of 1888 that all types of urban white- and blue-collar workers were not in demand.[20]

On the premise that there was little demand for artificial goods and services and that the mobility of the specialist was blocked, educational qualifications were seldom listed among prerequisites for colonial success. Conventional education was no use for getting ahead and therefore attitudes towards it were somewhat negative or indifferent. Typical was the statement in 1894 by the Liberal Minister of Lands, John McKenzie, that he could see no point in education beyond the rudiments.[21]

The limited prospects for white-collar occupations and tradesmen in the towns rebounded in turn upon urban labourers and other manual workers. As the educated could not get ahead, they tended to shift into labouring positions, at worst as billiard markers and barmen; and because the sons of labouring men had difficulty in moving out of their stratum into the trades and white-collar positions, they too helped to congest the urban labour market. In other ways, too, the towns were thought to impede the rise to a competency of the immigrant labourer. In a primary-producing country, town economies were artificial and thus prone to extreme fluctuations; while their material growth, further advanced than elsewhere, had pushed up land values, making property ownership less accessible than in the country areas. But there was a certain ambivalence towards the towns. Although they were the worst places for labourers and immigrants to advance in, the literature celebrated their solid symbols of growth and British civilisation, their churches, municipal and government buildings, railway stations, banks, harbour installations, and so forth.[22]

The second idea running through the language on upward mobility is positive, direct, and quite unambiguous. It insists that the best place for the labourer or anyone for that matter to win an independency is in a rustic setting where he alone confronts raw nature without institutions to assist him, without others to collaborate with him.

The more remote the district and the closer to its virgin state, the less it would have been converted into private property and the cheaper this land would remain. And since, at the frontier, labourers rapidly became landowners, the market for labour was inexhaustible. Jobs were always available if only one looked hard enough for them. Although men lacked the benefits of organised society in the backblocks, this was a minor disadvantage compared with the major advantage, that with nature's bounty so accessible they did not have to engage in collective enterprise to accumulate wealth.

There was, however, one key exception to the extreme individualism that permeated the rhetoric on rural mobility. Although most forms of association were thought superfluous to gaining a landed competency, the family was not. Along with the 'man alone', the family was the core unit in the simple society of Arcadia, its economic and other functions either facilitating or indispensable to the rise of the novitiate settler. For example, Adam in 1876 pointed out that if a young man marries 'a girl who knows something about dairy or household work, and is willing to assist in the house, the farmer will allow ten, fifteen, or twenty pounds more wages to the man, so that a wife is in every sense the best investment a young man can make'. Cooper in 1857 advised that 'The only men who can farm with success on a small capital, are married men, with three or four sons to assist them in fencing, ploughing, planting, etc.' John Bathgate in 1884 assumed that behind the prosperous careers of immigrants stood their children who 'were able to add materially to the family income. . . .' Saving the expense of hiring labour also helped the settler accumulate capital. Hursthouse in 1861 wrote that a wife was 'far prettier and more fruitful than patent plough, thrashing mill or thorough-bred'. The same consideration led Clayden in 1879 to admit of the settler's wives, 'How much their beneficent ministry is needed there to counteract the deteriorating circumstances of the incessant toil no one who has visited the settlers' homes requires to be told'. Some sources claimed that married men did better than bachelors because, to quote Fitton in 1856, 'the presence of females almost always carried with it an influence for good, both in external matters, and also in their far more important influence over the conduct and sobriety of the male population, amongst whom they are living'. For Richard Taylor in 1855 'a good wife' prevented the ruination of many a young man through the comforts and companionship she gave him 'in times of trial'; 'none can tell how dreary a young settler's home is without a wife, and how many temptations she saves him from.'[23] It did not strike contemporaries as ironic that the family unit they revered was based just as much on dependent relationships as the patron-client relationships they hated.

But to win a landed competency as rapidly as possible depended on more than marriage, or being in the most natural place, or learning spontaneously to cultivate the necessary personal qualities. It also depended upon following a plan of action, more implicit than expressly stated, which amounted to an informal and graduated rural apprenticeship. The assumption here was that the virtue necessary to proceed from stage to stage was automatically stimulated by the certainty of success springing from natural abundance. Richard Taylor wrote of this automatic stimulation: 'The settler finds every day something to cheer him on; he sees his farm progress, and his prospects advance; everything he does improves his place . . . he has the certain prospect of . . . a competency.'[24]

At the beginning, the newly arrived workman was supposed to move out of the town into the countryside and work at a great variety of rural jobs, picking up experience of working the land, exercising the thrift necessary to save money, keeping an eye out for a choice area in which to settle. By the next stage the budding settler has been able to buy his own small plot, usually of unimproved land since this was the cheapest, and divides his time between clearing and fencing it and working for cash on neighbouring large stations or public works so as to pay for his living and development expenses. Some time after this the maturing apprentice has reached the position of being able to produce commodities from his property and can spend less time working for others. During the final phase, the settler, although wage-working from time to time, finishes bringing all his land into production. In a few versions the settler progresses further. He sells the land and with the large capital gain earned by his improvements, he moves back to the frontier, buys a larger piece of virgin land, and repeats the whole cycle. He repeats it several times if necessary until he is entirely free of the economic necessity to earn wages. By this time he is ageing but lives in modest comfort; he employs others to tackle the more strenuous tasks he once executed all by himself, thus giving a new generation its chance of serving the rural apprenticeship and rising in the world.[25]

The beauty of the rural apprenticeship in the land of natural plenty was that it could, theoretically, elevate every successive cohort of immigrant labourers. There was no limit to the opportunities so there was no limit to the number who could be socially promoted. It was wonderful, too, in that it was a self-perpetuating mechanism of social improvement, operating almost independently of human will: the natural opportunities nurtured virtue, the virtuous provided the labour power for the successful, the virtuous inevitably rose to an independency. About the only stage where choice was required, and at which the system became prone to human frailty, was the first, when the person commencing his career had to will himself to leave the material comforts of the town and move to the country; only when he had done so was he exposed to the full force of the natural advantages; only at that point did these have their maximum power to stimulate effort. This did not mean that all men had to pursue the rural apprenticeship to get on; the ideology is quite clear that the natural abundance guaranteed the success of a variety of stratagems. But what was special about the rural apprenticeship was that it guaranteed to elevate the most humble, that it operated more rapidly than other devices, and that it was open to everyone.

In summary, the 'labourer's paradise' was designed to supply a multitude of satisfactions—economic, social, moral, psychological—and we miss the point entirely if we say that working-class immigrants were driven only by an aimless and crude materialism. The concept of the 'labourer's paradise' was a complex one, predicated upon an imagined endless stock of natural riches the overarching purpose of which was to enable the deprived and the oppressed to achieve the economic independence necessary for their social independence and individual self-reliance.

How far was the colonial notion of the liberation of the working man consistent with the principles of classical Arcadianism, particularly the twin assumptions essential to the meaning of classical Arcadia? As we saw in the Prologue one of these assumptions is natural abundance, the other is that Arcadia's inhabitants possess innately moderate appetites. Without both fundamentals, society must develop a strong social organisation, and so Arcadia by definition no longer exists, for everything in society, being organised, is the product of artifice. On the other hand, a society with natural abundance but occupied by a people with appetites that are not innately moderate is no longer Arcadia but the Land of Cockaygne (a place inhabited by people with gross, insatiable appetites). What we saw happening over the last two chapters is the injection of two Victorian imperatives—the work ethic and the belief in progress—into the concept of New Zealand as the 'labourer's paradise'. Neither conforms to the classical Arcadia whose inhabitants have a leisurely lifestyle and a passive relationship with natural abundance. Yet what the 'labourer's paradise' and classical Arcadia have in common is natural abundance; while the innately moderate inhabitants of classical Arcadia have as their equivalents the followers of the work ethic in the 'labourer's paradise'. The equivalence can be justified on the ground that, in the Victorian view, the work ethic implied moral sensibility— the avoidance of the gross, insatiable appetites characterising the people of the Land of Cockaygne. The parallel or identity between the 'labourer's paradise' and classical Arcadia does not end there. In classical Arcadia, natural abundance and innately moderate appetites are the forces that keep it free of the need for a strong social organisation and that as a consequence liberate it from the distorting and corrupting effects of culture, of artifice. In the 'labourer's paradise' the combination of natural abundance and the work ethic leads to the same result. Only the work ethic brings about success; all other means are socially contrived and therefore (in contrast to the Old World) fail to reward their possessors.

Lastly, just as classical Arcadia rejoices in the contentment of its inhabitants, so do the evocations of the 'labourer's paradise'. A stock scene in descriptions of New Zealand life was the bliss of the rising settler and his family. For example, William Satchell in his novel *The Land of the Lost* (1902) has the prophet Jess saying 'I hear the voices of the children at play among the thick-leafed trees. I hear the mothers singing at their work. Over all the land rests the peace of God.' Focusing upon the domestic felicities of the novitiate settler's life, Hochstetter imagined a 'small log-house . . . standing in the midst of the dusky bush'; the husband is felling the bush, 'the mother at home is preparing the frugal meal in the iron pot suspended by a chain over the merrily flickering chimney fire; children are playing in front of the sylvan hut, radiant with health, and with their cheeks flushed with the forest breeze; a faithful dog, chickens, and pigs are their playmates'. What the family sees before them and all round them is theirs, all theirs.[26]

Stereotypes of the middle-class dream: 'A Clearing in the Bush' from *The Imperial Album of New Zealand Scenery*, ii (1898?). To us this is a scene of desolation; to the caption-writer it represents New Zealand as a place of middle-class fulfillment. The small proprietor is certain 'in a few years' to acquire 'thousands of acres of land, and herds and flocks in proportion'.

CHAPTER III

The Middle-Class Paradise

MESHING in with the themes of natural abundance and the 'labourer's paradise' were the third and fourth themes permeating the Arcadian idealisation of New Zealand. These images appealed to the propertied, to those who arrived in the colony with capital and to those who arrived without capital but subsequently won competencies. The message of the 'insider's view' to them was that New Zealand's natural abundance and minimal social organisation prevented social conflict (notably class-driven conflict) and status anxiety.

Natural Harmony
Explicit and implicit contrasts were made in the literature between New Zealand as a naturally tranquil society and other countries where the propertied lived in constant fear of the rebellious and crime-driven masses. In 1870 Jane Maria Atkinson wrote from Nelson to Margaret Taylor that she had no wish to return to England to settle permanently. 'The dense population, the over-grown towns with their vice and misery, the ever-increasing pauperism, seem to me to present difficulties and dangers for the next generation to deal with far more perplexing and alarming than any we have to surmount in our struggle with the Maoris.'[1] Alfred Saunders likewise wrote in his panegyric on New Zealand, published in 1868,

. . . on my return to this country [England], after an absence of more than a quarter of a century, I was greatly disappointed to find that, although wages were somewhat higher, the general feeling between employer and employed had not improved; that they were systematically combining to injure each other, and that large masses of the working men of this country were so grossly misinformed and misled as not to see that proceedings which tended to ruin their employers, and drive their customers to other markets, must eventually be more injurious to themselves than to any other portion of the community.[2]

For I. R. Cooper, in his advice book to immigrants, published in 1857, the Old World's crime was one of the many symptoms of its hopelessness. 'In England,' he wrote,

men toil early and late for a small remuneration, their children half starved when young, too often are driven to crime by want; competition is carried to that extent that capital often has to be employed at a loss, and labour can claim little but its duties. The rich man frequently becomes poor, the poor man has in his old age only the workhouse to look forward to. . .[3]

Concern about crime and conflict must have weighed heavily in England because time and again the evocations of New Zealand stressed that the colony was an orderly society, in either absolute or relative terms. For example, the Registrar-General in his commentary in 1858 on the court statistics, wrote,

The view of the moral condition of the Colony presented by the Criminal Statistics, cannot but be regarded as favourable . . . . in a vast proportion, the offences [before the Resident Magistrates' Courts] were of a comparatively light character. . . .
The Returns of Convictions in the Supreme Court corroborate the conclusion that crime in the more heinous forms is not prevalent in New Zealand.[4]

F. Fuller asserted in 1859, 'The absence of crime constitutes one great charm for those living in New Zealand'. Contributing to the legend that New Zealand was a crimeless society, Hursthouse trumpeted in 1861 that 'Serious crime, too, is all but non-existent'. From the vantage point of 1868, Alfred Saunders implicitly agreed that before the gold rushes crime was very rare, and although he regretted that with the gold rushes 'the worst of crimes have become unhappily common' (for which he blamed the influx of Australian convicts), he was nonetheless optimistic about the prospects of law and order. James Adam in 1876 was impressed by how little disorder there had been during the gold rushes of the 1860s. The *Evening Post* editorialised in 1879 that crime in New Zealand was not of great magnitude—it was a worse problem in Australia. In 1880 James

Buller stated that the poorest man was induced to take a real interest in law and order in New Zealand. John Bathgate, a Dunedin District Judge, added to the tradition by commenting in 1884 on the 'almost total absence of crime':

judging from the calendar of crime, and other sources of information, the moral condition of our community will bear favourable comparison with that of older nations. Burglary is almost unknown. The most common crime is the passing of a valueless cheque by thoughtless ne'er-do-wells sent out to the colony to be got rid of.

In an official pamphlet of 1886, the Premier, Robert Stout, found that New Zealand had a far lower incidence of offending, required fewer police than her sister colonies across the Tasman, and that the frequency of all types of crime had been decreasing for 20 years. In his historical account of New Zealand, *The Long White Cloud* (1898), William Pember Reeves said of the pastoral provinces during the 1850s, 'Crime, too, was pleasantly rare in the settlements', and of New Zealand as a whole during the last half of the century, 'a more law-abiding population could hardly be imagined'.[5]

To be sure, these effusions conveniently overlooked chronic middle-class anxiety over colonial drunkenness and vagrancy, and (to a lesser degree) larrikinism. But they did represent a general smugness which was expressed in the exclusion of theft from the twenty-odd categories of offences tabulated in official court statistics from 1853 to 1872; in the lack of analysis by the Police Department of the causes of the offences described as the most serious in departmental reports from 1878; and in the virtual absence of official investigations into working conditions, strikes, and the housing, health, and income maintenance of the poor (sweating is the only exception), a marked contrast with other countries where these issues were seen as having serious implications for public order.

The image of the colony as the tranquil society had two Arcadian elements. One is the sense of bliss felt by the middle classes in response to the safety of their lives and property. The other Arcadian element is that security from working-class crime and protest is described as if it were based on a minimal social organisation. It does not depend upon the vigorous exercise of official instruments of coercion—the police, the courts, the law (even though the presence of these is not denied). It has little to do with the moralising of the church and the way youthful minds are moulded by the schools. It stems not from the press and other organs of public information and opinion.

It certainly has nothing to do with the discipline that the master exercises over the servant, the landlord over the tenant, the philanthropist over his client—for New Zealand, as the previous chapter showed, is happily spared these vertical relationships. It does not emanate from close supervision by groups over the behaviour of their members, the prevention of deviance and the enforcement of obligation and custom through the threat of group criticism, ridicule, ostracism, the loss of the advantages of reciprocity and collaboration. It is not the result of informal peacemakers resolving conflicts between friends, relations, and acquaintances.

Rather, the emphasis in the literature is on the largely natural origin of the freedom from disorder. New Zealand had achieved social harmony through the spontaneous self-interested responses by individuals to the wholly positive influences in the economic environment; to prosperity, strong labour demand, high rates of property ownership—to the wonderful opportunities of the 'labourer's paradise'. Typical of this optimistic belief in individual materialism was Robert Stout's opinion in 1886 that people born in the colony were not as criminally inclined as those born elsewhere because of their 'surroundings' and greater material comforts, and John Bathgate's comment in 1884 that the rapid economic progress of New Zealand based on its superior natural resources was creating a future where the country would have no social problems at all including crime.[6] Such statements were built on a variety of bridging assumptions. One was that the exercise of economic self-interest did not create economic conflict in the colony and thus engender class consciousness, since the bountiful natural resources of New Zealand permitted each individual to increase his supply of economic satisfactions without reducing the supply to anyone else; in other words, as nature was the source of private property, the accumulation of property was at nature's expense and not at the working classes'. Another line of reasoning was that the high wages earned by the manual workers eliminated their radical and anti-social tendencies because it was patently obvious to them that they won more money from legitimate than they could from illegitimate activity. Crime, explained F. Fuller in 1859, was absent in New Zealand 'for men able to work can make so much more by the higher rate of wages than by stealing', it is 'literally felt to be true by the labouring population that "Honesty is the best policy" ', and the 'rude abundance throughout New Zealand among the lower classes, constitutes a valid safeguard against serious disturbances'.[7] A variant upon that idea was built on the syllogism that as the poverty-stricken need to steal to stay alive, and because there was no poverty in New Zealand, it followed that there was no incentive to steal in New Zealand and thus no serious crime. In the words of an American visitor, 1904:

> Compared with some of the Old-World communities, New Zealand enjoys an immunity from crimes of a serious character. Discontent and poverty are the handmaiden of crime. But in the land of the Gold Fleece discontent finds no permanent resting-place, because poverty does not exist in this home of plenty.[8]

In addition, it was thought that the strong labour market fostered good will, giving the employer an incentive to be fair and respectful to his employees. Wrote Alfred Saunders in 1868, 'the demand that exists for labour compels every employer to see that he cannot play the tyrant or the oppressor, and that if he would be well served', he must treat those who 'serve him with kindness and with justice'.[9] A further explanation for the lack of disorder was the view, epitomised by James Buller in 1880, that working men enjoyed such opportunities to obtain property under the *status quo* that they had a stake in its preservation and saw every threat to it as a threat to their own advancement:

I have often observed in New Zealand that men of the lowest social grade improve greatly in character. A man finds there a prospect before him, and this is a stimulus to exertion. The hope of becoming in time a holder of property, induces the poorest man to take a real interest in law and order. This imparts a wonderful amount of conservatism to the working classes.[10]

Finally, it was claimed that the self-interested concern for order in the colony was engendered by the high rate of property ownership. The possession of land, William Rolleston told the House of Representatives in 1879, was 'the greatest teacher of morality', by which he meant that property-owners had something to lose, and therefore had strong inducements to act in ways which did not upset the tranquillity of society and so imperil their investments. The ownership of land, Sir George Grey suggested in a more sophisticated analysis in 1849, inevitably created an attachment to the rule of law, for landowners must exercise their minds on legal matters as these impinge vitally on the welfare of their property in the form of deeds, inheritance laws, fencing acts, impounding legislation, and the operation of the civil courts.[11]

A second, lesser, set of explanations proposed that the goodwill colonists displayed towards each other was a natural outcome of their totally open social structure. One facet of this was expressed by Alfred Saunders in 1868. 'Many persons', he wrote, 'who have not learned to work, soon lose all their money or property in the colony, while those of steady habits, who can work, are pretty sure to rise to the position of employers', with the result that the rich treated their employees with sensitivity, partly as an insurance against the day when the roles might be reversed and also because many had once been employees themselves and knew how vulnerable they had been to humiliation and how conducive that was to bad feeling. The proof was that

It is by no means an uncommon sight to see an old servant sending a valuable and acceptable present from her own ample store to a former mistress, now become poorer than herself, or to see a mistress taking a pride and pleasure in instructing her late servant to acquit herself creditably in some affluent station of life. Clever and industrious artisans, mechanics, and labourers often rise to the most important positions, and are welcomed in the highest circles of society.[12]

Another facet was described by W. D. Hay in 1882. Unlike the metropolitan society, New Zealand, he said, was free of the competition for status and the intricate social tests of fashion, taste, and etiquette which were a cause of such bitterness to those who failed. Status judgments in the colony, he went on to say, reflected the pure determination of wealth through the individual virtues. Kudos was won not by conformity to superficial and artificial criteria but because of inner qualities. This guaranteed that everyone 'is perfectly independent, and considers himself or herself on an equal footing with every one else'. No one could be cut, nobody could be wounded by social snobbery, and accordingly, he implied, relationships were never poisoned, since individuals were measured only in terms of the work ethic which the opportunity-rich environment nurtured in practically everyone.[13]

Lastly there was an unstated implication that amicability in the colony was a product of individual happiness, the assumption being that class consciousness sprang from personal discontents having no relevance to issues of class at all. If this is a reasonable inference, then there were of course, within the terms of the model, a great many sources of personal contentment helping to prevent class friction—the ecstasy of property ownership, the pleasure that came from knowing the distribution of property was absolutely fair, the joy of taking part in material growth, of knowing the country was free of the curse of paternalism, of being upwardly mobile, of the fact .that order and freedom both flourished in the colony without undermining each other, and so on.

The Natural Conferment of Status

Enhancing all these joys was yet another source of colonial felicity, the absence of status insecurities—the fourth theme in the idealisations.

To highlight this aspect of New Zealand as a 'middle-class paradise', the literature usually dwelt on the psychological stresses and strains of keeping up appearances in England. Arousing these status anxieties, was the shame and humiliation that society visited upon those who failed economically, upon people whose level of ostentatious spending was deemed inadequate, and upon those who were judged as having violated the genteel code which banned physical labour and affirmed leisure and sedentary occupations. In his eulogy of Australasia as a field of emigration, T. H. Braim (1870) played up the second of these anxieties which, he said, was responsible for greater and greater competition in wasteful expenditure:

There is a restlessness among masses of the people; a great amount of competition in every grade of society; all ranks vie with each other in expense of living, of dress, and of equipage; people dress in broad cloth who in my boyish days dressed in fustian, and silks and satins are the attire of people who used to appear in prints. And the puzzle to me continually is arising, How is all this done? How can the people, as a *whole*, make such a display? . . . I suspect from all that I see, and from what I am told, that a vast proportion of our population are given to keep up appearances. Men do not like their neighbours to outvie them in the goodness of their houses, richness of their furniture, the style of their dress, or the quality of their entertainments; and hence there is a continual and most unwholesome competition and rivalry existing. Many a man rides in his carriage who ought to be walking; and many a lady is dressed to receive visitors whose house-hold duties urgently claim her personal superintendence. But this is considered *necessary*, in order to keep up the credit of those who are in business. . . . To my mind it appears quite clear that in this great and famed land every profession and every business is *overcrowded*. The land cannot hold them, and continue to be healthy and vigorous, as of old. The remedy is *emigration*.[14]

Charles Hursthouse in his bucolic vision of New Zealand (1861) dramatised the interconnections between all three of the sources of status anxiety. First, he says, 'Brown' of Clapham Rise has the problem of trying to make money in intensely competitive conditions ('there are so many millions of people struggling to share in and divide this wealth that very many of them get very little of it, while many, trampled down in the crowd, get none at all'); then, he says, Brown's capacity to accumulate capital is eroded on the one side by tithes, poor rates and other municipal and imperial taxes, and on the other by the huge outlays on that 'showy, keep-up-appearance style of living which his family must maintain if they would not be slandered and sneered at by that ubiquitous social tyrant Mrs Grundy and her sister hags'. Such is the corruption of the English social system that people cannot retrench, 'we must often *spend* an income, in order that we may *earn* an income', social pressures compel us to spend as much on our wants as 'on the wants of *society*', such as 'gold lace, spangles, plumes, and a flunkey', in order to demonstrate credit-worthiness.

If Brown having spent £300 a year for society, for some years, refuse to do so any longer—if he retrench, sell the brougham, saddle his own horse, dig his own acre, dine at two, put Mrs B. in the kitchen for an hour or two, and Rose Ada in the dairy, what would shopkeepers, society, and the Hon. Deuceace often say and do to Brown? Say that Brown had fallen from his high estate—that Brown was no longer to be trusted—that Brown was going down hill to Coventry very fast—and they would lend him a farewell kick to accelerate his descent. . . .

   . . . did the butcher catch Mrs B. in the kitchen making a loaf, he would probably send in his bill and demand instant payment . . .[15]

Having graphically described all the torments created in England by the struggle for rank and position, the literature then drew on identifiably Arcadian ideas to show how New Zealand had solved the problems of status evaluation. In the first place the audience was assured that the colony delivered its worthy middle-class inhabitants from the indignity of economic failure. Natural abundance, it was explained, guaranteed not only the certainty of profit but also a far higher margin of profit than could be earned in the metropolitan society. Arthur Clayden, for example, highly recommended New Zealand for the man with small capital (£10,000) on £300 a year and with half a dozen boys; in New Zealand he could put out £8,000 at eight to ten per cent interest with the same security as the English three per cent; at eight per cent he would have an income of £640 and with the remaining £2,000 he could buy a good home with from ten to twenty acres of land: 'Here would be an occupation in the shape of a small farm, orchard, and garden. For £5 he could buy a milking cow, and other stock proportionately cheap. £400 would put him up a seven or eight-roomed house.'[16] Hursthouse wrote that in addition to the bigger return on capital, New Zealand offered far greater scope for the smaller investor; whereas in England business enterprises were on a large scale and out of the reach of the small capitalist, in New Zealand the same 'pursuits are conducted on a smaller, more primitive, less costly, scale, and almost every man may start as master, and find some business or occupation to suit his means'.[17] As late as 1891, the distinguished professor of agronomy at Edinburgh, Robert Wallace, after a fact-finding tour in 1889, stated, 'I believe that a hard-working young farmer with a capital of £1,000 would, under existing circumstances, vastly increase his chances of success in his own sphere if he emigrated to New Zealand. . . . Competition there is harder, and profits less, than in the early days, and such a man need not go out with the expectation of rising in a few years to be Prime Minister', but if he is cautious and learns the way of the country 'he can depend upon making for himself a competency and a home-like home.'[18] Lastly, the natural abundance meant that food and other household wants were cheap in New Zealand, and the lower cost of living took the struggle out of capital accumulation. I. R. Cooper asserted in 1857, 'It is to be presumed, from the facility with which the necessaries of life are raised in New Zealand, that it will be a cheap country, offering an easy home in which to provide for growing families, and for those . . . possessed of moderate fixed incomes.' Jane Maria Atkinson wrote to Margaret Taylor in 1857 that 'Arthur and I, with our land, house, horses and £50 a year feel I think quite as rich as we should in England with four or five hundred a year; we are quite at ease.'[19]

As for the other two causes of status anxiety in the corrupt Old World—the necessity for extravagance and gentility—these, the 'insider's view' claims, never took root in New Zealand for two reasons. The first was that New Zealand lacked the artificial associations and settings which in the Old World applied the informal sanctions penalising individuals who failed to conform. The colony supposedly contained few of Europe's public amenities, formal gatherings, and commercial amusements where displays of extravagance and genteel decorum were the norm. As proof of the lack of social pressures, it was common to highlight the informality of colonial social gatherings, their spontaneity, warmth, fun, their freedom from obligation. I. R. Cooper observed in 1857 that 'Acquaintances are more readily made, and, perhaps, sooner lost sight of than at home. Houses are freely opened for the use of friends, and travellers are welcomed with kindness without display.' E. B. Fitton in 1856 told his readers that in New Zealand there was a cheerful interchange of society, and 'from the absence of the great distinction of classes, so severely felt by persons in straitened circumstances at home, there is a freedom from formality, and a facility for becoming intimately acquainted with agreeable neighbours, which is not always to be found in longer established countries'. Charles Hursthouse in 1861 declared that the social intercourse of the colonial middle classes was marked by 'none of those scrupulous "ko-toeings", ceremonies, and distinctions which poison half our social enjoyments at home', by none of those frigid dinner-parties that made life so boring; instead it was characterised by a great deal of homely hospitality and friendly informal visiting and a quick succession of gatherings and merry-makings such as picnics and tea-parties. Edwin Hodder in 1862 added to the legend of the 'easy-going' society by commenting, 'There is less formality, fewer restraints of etiquette, and less artificial life than in England, but more genuine heartiness and friendly feeling.'[20]

The second reason that conspicuous waste allegedly never took root in New Zealand was that as a symbol of status it was totally incompatible with naturally efficient moral economy. Unlike the metropolitan society, the only means in New Zealand of winning a competency, maintaining or increasing it, were, as we saw earlier, the exercise of the moral qualities of industry, thrift, and perseverance; consequently, again in contrast to the Old World, only these attributes were (or could be) the objects of respect and prestige. What was the point of attaching kudos to anything else? Nothing else determined a competency, life's greatest prize. In England, all sorts of other, artificial, instruments determined a competency, and accordingly these affectations and conventions were its measure of reputability. In New Zealand, as W. D. Hay wrote (1882), things were stripped to simple essentials. Although 'class prejudices' had been imported they were insignificant; 'Prejudice must not be entertained against any man on account of his birth, connections, education, poverty, or manner of work', 'a man must perforce be the sole architect of his own fortunes. Industry and energy, enterprise and perseverance pave the pathway to success.'[21]

We all, wrote Charles Hursthouse in 1861, live in a more 'honest, simple, good old-fashioned, homely style'. I. R. Cooper in 1857 proudly noted that 'colonists have generally been contented to live in a frugal manner, and have not attempted to imitate the extravagance of the old country, or of the towns in the neighbouring colonies'. In a letter to a friend back home Mrs Mary-Ann Martin likewise wrote,

This would be a very dear country to live in if one had to cut a dash on Tomkins. But luckily the demon of gentility is laid for a while and so no-one is called to make that degrading struggle so common in England at meanness against show and display. Nobody thinks the less or the worse of me for riding a rough pony down the road. . . .

During a trip to Sydney in 1861, Mrs Harriet Gore Browne informed a friend back in New Zealand that people in New South Wales were far more 'gorgeously arrayed' than their counterparts in New Zealand, and 'spend £1000 instead of £100'. The consensus was that the respectable were free from status insecurity: no one was expected for form's sake to own a carriage, keep up with the fashions, buy costly furniture, engage in lavish entertainment, employ large retinues of servants, build fancy houses. In England, these things had social capital, in New Zealand, none. The irrelevance, even absurdity, of luxury spending as a token of social acceptability was epitomised by the fact that servants and labourers often dressed in finer, more expensive, clothes than their employers. According to W. D. Hay, male 'costume goes for little or nothing'. Men 'wear just what they please at all times and in all places, and without remark from others. One sees men apparelled in all sorts of ways; and it would be impossible to guess at a man's condition from his coat.' If worthy men come to a Governor's ball attired in a 'grey jumper and moleskins', they would be admitted without question. The modesty with which the successful men dressed was conveyed in stories of large estate owners who from their clothing were mistaken for swaggers. Although women were said to be more clothes-conscious, W. D. Hay summed up opinion by declaring, 'The merest Irish slut can earn her ten shillings a week as a domestic, besides being found in everything; and better-class girls get proportionately more; so it is not surprising that they can clothe themselves in fine raiment. But there is no rule to go by— the expensively dressed woman may be either mistress or maid, and the plain cotton gown may clothe either as well.'[22]

The Old World taboo on physical toil had created a double bind: if the taboo was observed and money was spent on workers and servants, one's income was diverted from capital and financial decline could set in, perhaps leading to the public humiliation of insolvency; if on the other hand the taboo was transgressed to save resources, then one was ridiculed and ostracised by polite society. New Zealand, however, abolished the double bind and its associated anxiety, for everyone alike was bound by natural economic forces to be thoroughly practical. Given that, in contrast to England, the labour market was strong and leisure had no function as social capital, it followed that there was no incentive to employ servants and workers for the provision of leisure, and every incentive to be self-sufficient or to sell one's labour. The result was, as Edwin Hodder, a former Nelson settler, informed his readers in 1862, that

hardworking men, capable of braving the burden and heat of the day, and earning their bread by the sweat of their brow, were the men who, in nine cases out of ten, rose to eminence there; while clerks, and others of the same class, who know how to pronounce an opinion on kid-gloves better than on wheat-crops, and can drive a quill with ease, but hardly know how to distinguish between a spade and a pitchfork, are considered rather as an incumbrance to an agricultural population than otherwise . . .

Colonists 'do not think it is a disgrace . . . to be seen engaged in hard manual work, as they do in London'; families were not stigmatised if they did their own chores, so wives and daughters cooked, gardened and did housework instead of hiring servants, and husbands and sons soiled their hands by labouring on their own properties.[23] In New Zealand's severely functional environment, said Charles Hursthouse, 'Mrs. Brown and Rose Ada would have to make many more loaves, pies, puddings, and beds than they ever made in Brown's establishment at Clapham Rise or Notting Hill'; but whereas this would lead to the ostracism of the Browns in England, 'no such deplorable results would ensue from the like deeds in New Zealand, where every lady makes herself useful as well as ornamental, and thus lives the longer and blooms the more'. James Buller affirmed in 1880 that no one of middle-class origins 'loses caste because he had the good sense to accept such employment as might offer itself to him, providing he does not compromise his character'. He knew men, now holding important positions, who, when they first arrived in the colony, worked as bullock-drivers, shepherds, and even navvies. This created no bar to their rising in the social scale. W. D. Hay in 1882 also insisted that the Old World's occupational distinctions had broken down in the colony; as it was plain to everyone that manual labour led to a home and a competency, gentlemanly conceptions about the inferiority of manual labour had disappeared: 'If' in England 'we attempted to work . . . as we work here, we should be scouted and cut by all our friends.'[24]

Symbolising the absolute consistency between morality, status, and material success in New Zealand was the contempt for remittance-men or 'ne'er-do-wells', described by James Buller as a 'hopeless class of young men', brought up in the Old World 'in the habits of idleness, luxury, and vanity, which mark the young "gent", but not the gentleman'. Whereas in England, their pretensions bestow on them a good income and a high social position despite their degeneracy, in the colony such qualifications are irrelevant to material success, so quite justly they slide financially and fall to the bottom of the status heap; in Buller's words, 'their money is soon melted in the public billiard-room; and, out of purse, out of credit, they are soon out at elbows also. Compelled by stern necessity, these unfortunate young men may be found as billiard-markers, boot-cleaners, or cooks' assistants, or in some still more humiliating condition.'[25]

PART TWO

The Enemies of the Ideal Society?

Slough of Despond. Deeply rutted and muddy roads and tracks aggravated the difficulties of social interaction among widely scattered settlers. Place and date unknown. *Alexander Turnbull Library*

Prologue

THE first part of the book reconstituted the comprehensive mental picture contemporaries had of their own society. We saw that in essence they visualised New Zealand as a land of natural plenty which by producing marvellous economic and social opportunities stimulated individual virtue and kept the associational framework to skeletal proportions. All these forces together yielded New Zealand its positive blessings and prevented the emergence of the enemies of a decent society. The blessings consisted of social justice, prosperity for all, harmony, contentment, a pure way of life, and individual autonomy. The enemies were demeaning and inefficient paternalism, class divisions, and oppressive status conformity, all rampant in the Old World.

The 'insider's view' has been described at some length and it is now time to assess it in its own terms so as to prepare the way for the eventual formulation of the author's own model. The assessment will be an underlying theme in the remaining two parts of the book. Part II discusses the implicit attacks modern historians have launched on it, while in Part III the author advances criticism of his own.

The implicit attacks on the 'insider's view' have been inferred from diverse orientations in the modern historiography of New Zealand. It should be emphasised that these orientations were never intended and written as conscious rejections of colonial ideology, as demonstrations of its inaccuracies and distortions. Indeed some of the historians credited with having made these implicit attacks would be surprised to know that such an entity as the 'insider's view' even existed. Nonetheless they can justifiably be regarded as implicit attacks in the sense that they are incompatible with the broad thrust of the 'insider's view' and cannot be reconciled with it except in minor areas.

The three alternative hypotheses share one fundamental attribute. They are all grounded on the assumption that New Zealand was a highly organised society and not, as the 'insider's view' would have it, a minimally organised one. Where they disagree is about the form this excessive social organisation took and the imprint it left on the culture and structure of the society. In fact they differ so markedly that they comprise three opposing concepts of the social pattern.

The first alternative, outlined in chapter IV, maintains that hierarchy—demeaning and inefficient paternalism—was a major aspect of colonial New Zealand, and that a substantial number of colonists in consequence were not independent individuals but under the authority of masters or mistresses. The second hypothesis, dealt with in chapter V, implies that the society's closeness and capacity for mutual interaction enabled the majority of the lower strata to form their own solid communities, that these associations fostered class consciousness, and that from class consciousness sprang class divisions. At the heart of the third concept, examined in chapter VI, is the idea that the colony produced extremely cohesive local communities, where the different strata were bound together by cross-cutting ties, which produced overwhelming pressures to conform, in turn creating status anxiety.

In sum the three alternatives implicitly attack the 'insider's view' from different angles. Each denies the social organisation was insubstantial. Each implies that New Zealand had a powerful structure of social ties which ensured that New Zealand would replicate the collective evils of the Old World. The unconscious intention of them all is to debunk the myth of Arcadia, to prove that New Zealand was not within its own terms an ideal society. Who, then, do we believe? The 'insider's view' or one of the three alternatives to it? How can we know which of the four competing representations of the same reality is closest to the truth, or which parts of the four are right and which are wrong?

To tackle these questions, Part II subjects the three implicit attacks to intense critical scrutiny. The objective is to determine, through a process of elimination, which of the three is the most convincing model of the social organisation and therefore is the strongest rival to the 'insider's view'. As Part II unfolds, the reader will find that particular aspects of the three stand up to critical scrutiny and pinpoint certain flaws in the 'insider's view'. By the end of Part II, however, the reader will also find that what has not survived critical examination is the fundamental assumption underlying all of the implicit attacks, namely, that New Zealand was a strongly organised society. The reader will discover that not only is this assumption demonstrably wrong but also the conflicting ideas about its specific characteristics are false as well, the notions that the society was hierarchically bonded, class-divided and afflicted by social pressures inducing status anxiety. The evidence brought forth to refute the three will show instead that the social organisation was minimal, just as the 'insider's view' claimed, though only partly for the same reasons. By the end of Part II, in short, it will be plain that the Arcadian myth of New Zealand makes more sense than the several unconscious attempts by historians to replace it. New Zealand was largely free of Old World collective problems and evils—enemies—because its mechanisms of association were not strong enough to permit their development.

Giant cabbage. A Wairarapa camp, 19th century. The cheapness of food and its
plenitude was one of the realities of colonial life. It helped to insulate working
people from dire poverty and the need to seek patronage from the wealthy.
Alexander Turnbull Library

CHAPTER IV

A Hierarchical Society?

THE hypothesis this chapter will falsify is that colonial society was hierarchical, or at least had sufficient hierarchical tendencies to make nonsense of the 'insider's view'. The discussion, it should be noted, is conducted within the terms of 'insider's view'. Hence it makes nothing of one of the outstanding realities of the colonial period—the dependence of wives and children upon husbands and fathers. Paradoxically, this area of dependence was regarded as legitimate and in no sense inconsistent with antagonism to hierarchy, even though dependence is a key feature of hierarchy.

In a mature hierarchical society the majority of the population depend on either the physical protection or the material aid of powerful individuals and reciprocate by being subservient, obedient, and loyal. The dependants are usually obliged to grant their benefactors a number of personal services, such as voting or fighting for them, working in their households or their fields free of charge or at subsistence levels, bestowing on them automatic respect and deference; and their private lives are closely supervised and regulated by the patron to ensure that the obligation is properly discharged. The patron's close management of the life of the client is usually aided by their close physical relationship—their propinquity—within the same household or the same locality; often, however, the supervision is delegated to a bailiff or some other third party tied to the patron.[1]

There are four situations in which a hierarchical society may develop. It can be imposed by an invader. It can arise when civil war, chronic social violence, banditry, or frequent invasions compel the weak to seek a measure of security through subordination to the militarily powerful (the situation that stimulated the growth of medieval feudalism). It can be caused by the arbitrariness or remoteness of official justice, which leads common people into the orbit of influential men able to exact private vengeance or bend the law (a circumstance that led to control by the Mafia over western Sicily). It can be created by a combination of over-population, economic under-development, mass poverty, blocked mobility, and extreme inequality which, in the absence of a welfare state, give the poor no choice but to become the servitors of the rich in return for material favours (a system that prevailed in western Europe before the 19th century and is still common in today's third world).

No New Zealand historian has claimed that the first three situations were present in colonial society. But some do claim the presence of the fourth, the economic precondition of a vertical bonding system, of demeaning and inefficient paternalism, as the 'insider's view' thought of it.

The historian most identified with this bleak view of colonial life is W. B. Sutch, although he stops short of saying that it engendered vertical mutuality.[2] The key to the general rigidity and dearth characteristic of 19th-century New Zealand, he maintains, was the political domination of the wealthy. They wielded their power to ensure that the Crown's landed estate ended up in their hands. The consequent land monopoly prevented the bulk of breadwinners from rising into the independent strata, a situation, he contends, reflected in every census on occupations from 1848 onwards, which shows that 'easily the biggest part of the population depended on wage labour and not on farming'.[3] As the wealthy also thwarted the development of effective state welfare institutions and of industrial protection, the wage-earning majority lived in acute insecurity: 'Just as in the British Isles, the problem was one of finding a job, keeping it, and earning sufficient to provide for all necessities and contingencies. Old age, sickness, education, destitution—for these the more fortunate minority could make some sort of provision; the majority could not.'[4] Although mass want was at its worst during the so-called 'Long Depression' of the late century, Sutch insists that it was a persistent feature of European settlement right from 1840. To prove that destitution was common at all times, Sutch draws upon a hodge-podge of evidence. It consists of undocumented statements that wife desertion 'was common', inferences from suggestions about poor or negative economic growth, inferences from high emigration numbers, two official reports (one the Auckland Committee on Pauperism of 1868, the other the Sweating Commission of 1890), the fall in nominal wages from the 1860s to the mid 1890s as indicated by official statistics, and vague, assertive description (for example, 'The records show that the pawn-shops were full of tools, the pawn-shop windows of wedding rings, and there were children sleeping under sacks split down the centre.'). His favourite evidence, however, is examples of collective protest by urban workers, which before 1888, amount to three deputations and memorials, five petitions, two street demonstrations, and after 1888, the growth of trade unions and strikes.[5]

Many other historians have likewise painted a gloomy picture of the *immobilisme* of settler society, employing the same sort of evidence as Sutch, although they tend to apply it more to the period after 1879, during the 'Long Depression'. John Martin, for example, has intimated that the average rural worker must have been permanently confined to the proletariat since the fraction of farm and pastoral labourers in the farm and pastoral sector stayed fairly constant over the whole period, 1874–1911.[6]

Some writers have gone on to claim that high unemployment and the inadequate provision by the state for the numerous poor were translated into deferential and master-servant relationships, not so much in the towns as in the rural areas, especially on the great estates of the pastoral regions.[7] So far only Stevan Eldred-Grigg, however, has postulated that hierarchy operated across a whole society, in this case the South Island, which he conceptualises as a society of 'feudalism', 'an *ancien régime*'.[8] He argues that as wool was the only profitable commodity and as wool necessitated large acreages for commercial production, the great estate owners, or the gentry, as he calls them (defined as those holding over 5,000 acres), possessed tremendous economic power which they were able to convert into a total system of clientage. The less well-off were forced to be their economic dependants. They bound shopkeepers and tradesmen in the towns to themselves by being their leading customers. They attached urban businessmen to themselves by putting up the major portion of urban investment. They drove small-holders into a sort of peonage since the gentry's monopoly over land left them insufficient to support themselves, and they needed the gentry to supply them with part-time wage work, contract work, and land for leasing. The gentry bonded wage-earners to themselves through their control over

charitable assistance and, most of all, the labour market, which they
depressed by preventing the growth of competing areas of economic
development. To reinforce the pattern of clientage, the gentry engaged
in conspicuous leisure and consumption to overawe their dependants;
they dominated the leading recreational and cultural institutions and
used these to transmit their ideology; they monopolised the formal
positions of power to prevent the lower strata from asserting
themselves politically. In implicit contrast to the general prosperity
supposedly flourishing under natural abundance, the South Island was
a land of general misery contrived by the political economy of the
landed rich. To verify claims such as that 'most of the South Island's
rural population toiled in poverty' and that 'Beggars . . . lay in
thousands under the hedgerows from Nelson to Southland', Eldred-
Grigg quotes a Dunedin clergyman who describes people 'twisted
with poverty and misery' and one large estate owner who found
'in every mail' letters begging for employment.[9] He also gives the
example of the Otago Benevolent Asylum of 1891 which supported
4,500 with outdoor relief, three per cent of the province's population;
and like Sutch he uses the high levels of emigration in the late 1880s
to indicate falling living standards and the examples of government
relief work to highlight large-scale unemployment.[10] His most
interesting evidence, however, is three indicators. One is the
widespread practice of large estates giving free food and shelter to
multitudinous itinerant labourers, which he says was the main form
of charity. Another is the high proportion of dwellings of one to
two rooms constructed of makeshift materials: 'The South Island was
based on a substratum of wretchedness. In the counties [in 1891]
24 per cent of all houses had only one or two rooms.' The last is
his extensive use of wage-rate data collected by the authorities, which
from the early 1880s to the mid 1890s register a big decline.[11]

There is no doubt that the colony displayed some of the economic
underpinnings of a hierarchical society, or of demeaning and inefficient
paternalism as the 'insider's view' saw it. The distribution of resources
was extremely unequal—the usual statistic cited is that by 1882 about
one per cent of private landowners held over 40 per cent of the
total value of landed assets in private hands. Moreover, the fact that
few welfare institutions were established by the state would imply
that the poor had no choice but seek the patronage of rich individuals.
But what about the other underpinnings—mass deprivation, blocked
mobility, under-employment, over-population? The pessimists, as we
noted, have decided that these factors also were present. Yet if they

were, what the pessimists have not explained is why they did not produce all the obvious trappings, all the cultural and institutional patterns, that typify a vertically bonded society. If the colony exhibited to a significant degree the material requisites of hierarchy, why did it not also possess a code emphasising rank and birth, more conspicuous employment of 'surplus labour' by the gentry, a bloated population of able-bodied adult male paupers, illiberal political institutions and ideology?

Starting with the cultural dimension, contemporary writers rarely perceived manual labourers in New Zealand as obsequious and menial. They are not depicted as fixed parts of a static social order, father succeeding son in the same occupation, their inferior rank signified by their speech, diet, dress, personal possessions, exclusive connection with dirt and physical toil, their absence from such aristocratic pursuits as hunting and horse ownership. Certainly we must recognise that the dominant preconception of New Zealand as the 'labourer's paradise' would have filtered non-egalitarian cultural detail out of contemporary description. But if we take the few sources that did not attempt to idealise, that stand outside the Arcadian tradition, and use them as a check on the sources from inside, we find they converge on this question. For example, in her scathing account of New Zealand life in 1887 based on her experience of Christchurch (by reputation the most status-conscious part of New Zealand), 'Hopeful' wrote that although there were '*strong class prejudices*' in New Zealand, exemplified in the way the successful snubbed former acquaintances who had 'not been so successful', 'in another way there is no respect of class'. The lower strata did not bow or 'cap' to their betters, or employ deferential titles when greeting them—'in fact, no respect' was 'shown to position, birth, or anything in that way'.[12] Similarly, Sarah Courage, a runholder's wife from Leithfield near Christchurch, whose account of her New Zealand experience dwells not on its blissfulness but on its misery, found the colonial lower strata anything but obsequious; rather their manners were 'curt', 'off-hand', strange and unpleasant at first sight—'they were not uncivil, but brusque and familiar to a degree'.[13]

It is strange as well that if hierarchical tendencies were so strong, and the labour surplus so pronounced, the rich did not take more advantage of it to surround themselves with larger numbers of retainers and servants. For example, if we work out the ratio between large estates (defined as being over 5,000 acres) and the total number of pastoral hands enumerated, we find that according to the 5 April

1891 Census, a time of the year when few casual workers were engaged, there were only 10.4 workers to every 'great estate'—a very modest average.[14] Eldred-Grigg himself is able to cite just a few examples of great estates in the South Island which had a permanent labour force of 40 or more—the largest being 60.

Similarly, a comparatively tiny number of wealthy households were able to engage more than two domestic servants; data compiled in the 1901 Census show that 97.8 per cent of all domestic servants were employed in private dwellings with only one or two servants apiece, and a mere 2.1 per cent of servants in private dwellings with three or more servants. By contrast, in 1891 about half of London's female domestic servants were employed in clusters of three or more; and in 1911 for England and Wales, 20 per cent of all domestic servants were engaged in groups of three or more.[15] Eldred-Grigg's claim that the average gentry family in the South Island employed three to four domestic servants is not an impressive measure of under-employment when in other societies aristocratic households engaged far more; three to four dozen per aristocratic household, for example, was typical in England by 1620.[16] Altogether, the proportion of households engaging servants was very small. Except for 1901, the Census never counted the actual number of servant-households. From 1874 to 1901, however, it did enumerate occupied dwellings, all of which we will assume were private households, and persons 'engaged in attendance' (about three-quarters of whom were designated 'domestic servants', many of the remainder being persons who from their designations were possibly not living-in servants of private households, but barmen, caretakers, eating-house staff, cleaners, washerwomen). With this information we can estimate the likely fraction of servant-households by making those 'engaged in attendance' a percentage of occupied dwellings (including tents). The estimate overstates the actual proportion for several reasons, the most important being that some households engaged more than one servant, and the presence of non-servants in the 'engaged in attendance' category. Comparing our calculation with the actual count in the 1901 Census, our estimate is five per cent in excess of the real proportion. Over the period 1874–1896, the estimated rate was very stable, running at about 16 to 18 per cent, before sliding to 15 per cent in 1901. The difference between the North Island and the South Island, incidentally, was minute, with the North Island having the greater proportion in most Census years—which hardly supports the theory that the South was hierarchical and the North egalitarian. To show just how low the rate of servant employment in the colony was, let us put it into an international perspective. Consulting the data in Table 4.1, it will be observed that the New Zealand figure for 1891 (18 persons 'engaged in attendance' per 100 households) is smaller than those for four of the six Australian colonies which were estimated in the same way for the same year. The greatest difference is with Western Australia which had six per cent more. Queensland and New South Wales had rates about the same as New Zealand's.

TABLE 4.1

Proportion of Households with Domestic Servants:
New Zealand compared with a variety of other societies

Society	Year	Percentage of Households with Domestic Servants
New Zealand	1891	18
Australia		
Western Australia	1891	24
Tasmania	1891	22
South Australia	1891	22
Victoria	1891	20
N.S.W.	1891	18
Queensland	1891	18
Other 19th-century societies		
Hamilton (Canada)	1851	30
Hamilton (Canada)	1861	21
York	1851	20
Preston	1851	10
England (rural sample)	1851	28
Pre-19th-century societies		
Netherlands (rural)	1749	33
England	1599	34
France	1788	20
Serbia	1733-4	30
Rhode Island	1689	30
England & Wales (100 communities)	1564-1821	29

Notes
Non-Australasian rates from P. Laslett & R. Wall (eds), *Household and*

Family in Past Time (Cambridge, 1972), pp.82, 152, 307; and M. B. Katz, *The People of Hamilton, Canada West: Family and Class in a Mid-Nineteenth-Century City* (Cambridge, Mass., 1975), p.221.

Australian percentages were calculated from T. A. Coghlan, *A Statistical Account of the Seven Colonies of Australasia, 1897–8* (Sydney, 1898), pp.68, 340; households were assumed to be occupied dwellings plus inhabited tents and dwellings with canvas roofs. The New Zealand percentage was calculated in the same way by dividing the number of total occupied dwellings (including tents) by all those persons enumerated in class 2, sub-order 2 ('engaged in attendance') in the 1891 Census.

It should be noted that the Australasian rates are not the actual ones but estimates obtained by supposing that each person 'engaged in attendance' would have been engaged in one dwelling and that each was in fact a live-in domestic servant. The non-Australasian rates, on the other hand, are actual rates. The Australasian rates thus are overstated relative to the non-Australasian.

All percentages were rounded off to the nearest whole number.

The estimated (and overstated) New Zealand rate, furthermore, is at least 10 per cent less than the true rate for a sample of rural localities in England in 1851 (28 per cent), and is less than the 20 per cent true rate for York, an English provincial town, in 1851. Likewise, it is well below the true rate for another city, Hamilton, Ontario, in Canada. The only 19th-century locality outside New Zealand which, according to present knowledge, had a lower figure was Bolton in 1861, a new factory town where women had many more alternatives to domestic work than they did in non-industrial New Zealand. What is most striking about the table, however, is the high rates of servant employment in England and other parts of Europe before the 19th century. There was a large labour surplus in these pre-modern societies, which they controlled and materially supported partly by converting it into a servile order: from an early age people were attached to others' households, performing menial tasks, owing loyalty and deference to their masters, obtaining board and some sort of training in return.[17]

It is strange, too, that if vertical bonds were common in New Zealand there were so few able-bodied male paupers. In western Europe from the 16th to the 18th centuries such was the under-employment that between 10 and 20 per cent of the population relied on charity for their survival in any one year. In late-17th-century England it was anything between one quarter and one half.[18] By contrast, in the colony the number of all persons counted as official charity cases (able-bodied and otherwise) would never have constituted more than about three or four per cent of the population and the able-bodied were a tiny fraction of these. In Canterbury from 1878 to 1880, three-quarters of the money spent on outdoor relief went to widows, deserted women, or families with sick or infirm male heads. In Otago from the 1880s to the 1890s only nine to 11 per cent of those receiving long-term assistance from the Benevolent Institution were adult males—women and children, widows particularly, comprised all the other recipients. According to the records of the Ashburton and North Canterbury United Charitable Aid Board for 1889, none of the 466 cases was an able-bodied male—most were widows and the aged and the infirm. Beatrice Webb recorded in the late 1890s that the recipients of outdoor relief from the Wellington Benevolent Trustees 'were exclusively women and (a few) very aged men . . . there was as yet no sign of the old English outdoor relief to able-bodied men'. The Department of Hospitals and Charitable Institutions in its tabulations of the causes of poverty for the years 1897–1900 indicated that for both sexes 'lack of employment' was the 'cause' of indigence in only 13 to 17 per cent of cases—the biggest single cause was old age.[19] True, we should be careful with this kind of evidence. Respectable opinion in general and the officials administering charity in particular were quite hostile to the relief of able-bodied men lest this encourage the stultifying pauperism which afflicted the Old World. Yet the stigma attached to the 'undeserving poor' was just as strong in western Europe up to the 19th century. And in New Zealand if this prejudice did deter indigent men from seeking assistance from their betters, then by the same token it must have limited the spread of vertical bonds.

Lastly, it is anomalous that if there were strong aristocratic tendencies in New Zealand, its public men should have been so swayed by politically liberal convictions. Under the 1852 constitution the colony acquired parliamentary institutions and a wide franchise; over the rest of the century democratic rights were progressively extended. A secret ballot was introduced in 1870, universal manhood franchise in 1879, plural voting in general elections was abolished in 1889, and the women's franchise came in 1893. All these measures (except the last) were granted by a parliament dominated by the economic elite without pressure from below. The point is that had this elite exercised paternalistic influence and personal discipline over the lower classes, it would have been quite irrational for them voluntarily to give the lower classes the political competence to overthrow their social power. On the contrary we would expect the elite to attempt to reverse the liberal principles of the 1852 constitution by moving towards a far more authoritarian and closed political system on the Latin American model.[20] A hierarchical social structure should have produced an appropriately illiberal and undemocratic political apparatus.

The only two possible cultural and institutional symptoms of vertical bonds the society did exhibit were political domination by the wealthy until 1890, and conspicuous consumption by great estate owners (their extravagant outlays on carriages, clothes, furniture and, especially, hospitality and housing). But there is no evidence that either functioned to create or reinforce dependent relationships. The wealthy certainly took advantage of their political power to further their own interests; but what is striking about so much of their legislation (on land matters especially) was its express purpose of encouraging labouring men to be self-reliant, socially independent. Moreover, the wealthy made up the vast bulk of candidates at elections for the very practical reason that only they had the leisure to take part in public life. Expenditure on hospitality and housing by the great estate owners was undoubtedly lavish; but its self-declared objective was to break down the barriers of geographical isolation, and in a highly transient, loose-knit society like New Zealand, such expenditure was a serviceable means of advertising success. It did, however, contradict Arcadian preconceptions about New Zealand, and it was politically imprudent, for colonists often saw it as the symbol of vertical bonding, a dreaded enemy.

The Problems of the Vertical Model Explained

The reason New Zealand failed to duplicate the more obvious institutional and cultural manifestations of vertical bonding is that its whole social environment was inimical to it. The legend of the 'labourer's paradise' was against it, as was its demography, the high rate of land-ownership, the myriad openings in other areas of petty enterprise, the resourcefulness of wage-earners, their transient propensities, the low population pressures on resources, the high and rising level of national income.

Let us now discuss these factors in detail, starting with the wide distribution of land-ownership.

The Accessibility of Land-Ownership

Sutch and other pessimists are quite in error in assuming that the sharp inequality in land-ownership, and the existence of what is often misleadingly called 'land monopoly', prohibited all but an insubstantial minority of breadwinners from acquiring land. The proper place to determine the extent of land-ownership is not in the Census data on occupations (which take inadequate account of that typical colonist, the jack-of-all-trades) but in two sets of real property statistics. One is the data tabulated in the Census from 1874 onwards on land-holdings of over one acre according to size of holdings (which historians have assumed consisted of basically rural land and therefore have treated as farms and sheep stations). The other is the data collected at varying intervals from 1882 onwards by the Property or Land Tax Commissioner which recorded private land-ownership, the fullest documentation on which was the famous 1882 Return of Freeholders, listing every private landowner by name, giving his (rarely her) occupation, address, location of land parcels, capital value of borough land, and acreage and capital value of holdings of five acres and over in counties. A brief analysis of these sources is enough to demonstrate the total fallacy of the view that land aggregation created a rigidly stratified society, permanently condemning the vast majority of breadwinners to be landless labourers. In the first instance we should note that the 71,000-odd freeholders in 1882 (exclusive of women, companies and partnerships) were equal to about half the adult males enumerated in the 1881 Census or 43 per cent of the males designated as breadwinners. These are very substantial proportions given that a good many males were members of landowners' families (youthful dependants and relations assisting without pay), or were young unmarried men not yet of an age to expect to own land. Moreover, easy access to freehold land was not the colonists' only resource. They could also lease land privately and from the Crown. Just how many leaseholders there were is impossible to determine; an unknown number of freeholders also leased land; and no research has yet counted and sorted out the different types of private leaseholders. But the Crown did keep very good records of its own land distribution activities, and from these it is plain that the population of Crownholders was substantial well before the Liberals came to power. In 1882, for example, the Crown had 9,683 tenants, equal to about 14 per cent of the freeholding population. Over the whole colonial period the Crown played a crucial role; it was, in William Pember Reeves's words, the country's largest single land-agent, landlord, and land-seller.

In the second place we should note that the unequal distribution of landed wealth did nothing to stop the 'working classes' from owning land. It has been reckoned that of the 71,000 freeholders in 1882, 33.6 per cent were manual workers by stated occupation if those with no given occupation (some of them women) and unclassified occupations ('settlers', for instance) are counted in the total; or 46 per cent if the entries without occupations and the unclassified occupations are excluded.[21] But what is of greater significance, in view of the Sutchian thesis that dependent wage-earners comprised the great bulk of the work-force, are the calculations we can make of the likely number of male manual workers who owned land in 1882. If we take the 1881 Census as our base, we find that 165,740 males were counted as breadwinners. Of these it has been estimated that between 62 per cent and 66 per cent would have been manual workers, or some 102,000 to 109,000, the lower figure being far more probable than the upper since it is grounded on more precise information. Given, as we saw, that manual workers comprised between 33.6 and 46 per cent of all the 71,000 freeholders, then in absolute numbers there must have been between 23,856 and 32,660 of them in the 1882 Freeholders Return—equal, that is, to between 23 and 32 per cent of the probable 102,000 male manuals we extrapolated from the 1881 Census.[22]

The assumptions behind these estimates do have their weaknesses; but they are broadly consistent with an 1892 Department of Labour survey on the expenditure pattern of 'working-class' households, from the published schedules for which it can be inferred that 35 per cent of the respondents owned their dwellings.[23] Although this household-based rate of home ownership is higher than the estimated range of land-ownership for male manuals in 1881/2, this is to be expected since manual household heads would, of course, have been older on average than manual males as a whole. We cannot be sure, it has to be admitted, how typical the 1892 survey returns were. Yet the 1892 figure is in line with the results of the first census on housing tenure (1916) establishing that 36.4 per cent of wage and salary households owned their houses with and without mortgages.[24] Although the 1916 census data were compiled 24 years after the 1892 survey, it is likely that the rates of 'working-class' home-ownership did not rise appreciably in the interim owing chiefly to the fact that population growth outstripped the creation of proprietors over the 1890s.

So what we can say with reasonable confidence is that by the late century about one half of all adult males owned land, about one quarter of all manual males owned land, and about one third of all households with 'working-class' male heads were home owners—proportions, it should be remembered that take no account of the additional men, 'working-class' and otherwise, occupying Crown leasehold land. Clearly the New Zealand social structure, although less open than the idealisations suggested, was not nearly as closed as Sutch and other pessimists have deduced from misleading aggregate data on occupations. Indeed, land was far more accessible in New Zealand than in many other societies for which we have comparable statistics. For example, as late as 1914 in England and Wales the proportion of *all* households with home-ownership was a mere 10 per cent;[25] and, taking another measure, the numbers of landholdings per capita, we discover that New Zealand was appreciably better off than her sister colonies of New South Wales, Victoria, South Australia, and Western Australia by the 1890s.[26] What is not so clear, however, is whether and how far these units of productive capital, especially those held by manual workers, insulated their possessors from the wage market and from the social influence of the wealthy. How was the land used? Before answering this question, it is necessary to outline why so many were able to rise into the ranks of the landed in the first place.

The Mechanisms of Real Property Mobility for the Lower Strata to the 1880s
'Natural abundance' is an inadequate description of the opportunities that propelled such a large proportion of wage-earners into land-ownership. It implies that resources were distributed in a social vacuum, which was patently not the case. The opportunities were engineered from a fortuitous conjunction of circumstances largely socially determined. One was the very low pressure of population on land supplies, the consequence of the rapid expansion of the frontier up to the 1880s and the unpopularity of New Zealand as an emigration field. Another was that wage-earners enjoyed the advantage of selling their labour in a generally buoyant labour market over an extended period from the late 1840s to the late 1870s. This advantage allowed them to make the savings necessary to purchase land. From the late 1840s the labour market was stimulated by the rise of the pastoral industry, the Australian gold-rushes of the 1850s, the large expenditure over the 1860s by the Imperial Government on its big force of troops in the North Island, the gold-rushes of the 1860s, and the Vogelite borrowing boom throughout the 1870s. The only substantial

interruption to this long period of rapid growth occurred in the late 1860s when nearly all Imperial troops were withdrawn and gold production and wool prices fell. Without doubt the pace of growth and development varied substantially from place to place, and there would have been a great deal of localised unemployment, so much work being inherently impermanent, associated as it was with extraction, construction, and the seasons. Yet the wage-earning population had strong migratory habits; people were always willing to shift residence and in demographic terms were well adjusted to a transient lifestyle. As most colonists were foreign-born (until about 1885), they had already severed their links with place, family, friends, community in the great uprooting that led them to New Zealand; there were no more ties to stop them from further and repeated moves in New Zealand. Once they were habituated to a foot-loose lifestyle, they did not stay long enough in any one place to develop those local attachments and relationships which were painful to lose. The excess of unmarried adult males in the population also facilitated mobility; these men had no children, wives, or household chattels to worry about, look after, plan for, to inject stress and effort into moving from one locality to another, to encumber their movements. Up to the 1880s, in short, the population was comparatively well adapted to the volatility of local economies and labour demand. Transience in turn acted as a safety valve: whenever job opportunities shrank or threatened to shrink in one place, people were well equipped to move to localities with apparently better prospects.

Another factor which encouraged land-ownership was that little working capital was needed to make a livelihood from the land. Conventional cultivation and land-clearance methods did not require expensive machinery or techniques; working the land was basically labour intensive, and here the small proprietor cut costs to the bone by utilising his wife and children as his unpaid labour force, something which the Census and other quantitative assessments of the 'breadwinning population' never counted. In addition, housing costs were intrinsically low; a section holder usually started off by building his own one- or two-room shack, fabricated from the nearest materials to hand—sod, raupo, slabs of wood, canvas—and added rooms in a piecemeal way as time and finances allowed. By 1892, the standard dwelling of a working man was four rooms in size—again not a large absorber of capital—and the rarity of interior bathrooms and hot and cold running water in lower-class homes, as well as of other such conveniences and luxuries as gas cookers and wallpaper, kept building expenses down. The price of proprietorship was kept low not only by elementary capital improvements but also by the small size of sections. In 1881 60 per cent of landholdings recorded by the Census were less than 100 acres in size. The combination of low cost improvements and small section size is visible in the 1882 Freeholders Return, where 47 per cent of all freeholders owned properties with an assessed value under £250. To put this in perspective, £250 was equal to 26.5 months of earnings (from all sources) available for expenditure by the average 'working man's' household in 1892.

Land-Owning by the Lower Strata over the 'Long Depression'
According to most historians (and not just the pessimists) the life chances of working men, and by implication their rate of land-ownership, deteriorated sharply during the last two decades of the century, or up to 1895 at least. Unfortunately, we cannot test these claims by analysing the data on land-owning by manual workers, for such data are scanty. However, by examining the movements in the overall level of land-ownership and the influences upon it, we can establish the likely trends of manual worker land-ownership— and what we shall establish must lead us to reject the historiographical convention.

After 1882 until the turn of the century there were four further surveys of private freeholders. These took place in 1885, 1888, 1891, and 1902. They show that the absolute number of freeholders consistently rose from 71,240 in 1882, to 80,527 in 1885, 84,547 in 1888, 91,501 in 1891, and 115,713 by 1902. True, the population also increased over the period, so we cannot determine the significance of this rise unless we allow for population growth. If we accept that adult males were the basic land-owning demographic unit, and convert the number of freeholders to a percentage of this unit, we find that the rate of ownership climbed between all but one of the survey years, 1882–91, yielding a gain of 4.59 per cent over the nine years, and then fell between the two survey years of 1891 and 1902 by 5.33 per cent leaving the position slightly worse in 1902 than it was in 1882 (see Table 4.2).

These trends by themselves do not necessarily tell us what happened to the proportion of landless men. Contemporaries appear to have regarded landless men as all those who neither owned land nor leased it from the State. The various types of Crown leasehold tenure were thought to be almost as good as the freehold. On the whole they

TABLE 4.2

Freeholders as a Proportion of Adult Males

Assessment Year	Number of Freeholders	Adult Male Population	Freeholders as a % of Adult Males
1882	71,240	141,918	50.19
1885	80,527	152,226	52.89
1888	84,547	160,201	52.77
1891	91,501	167,008	54.78
1902	115,713	233,972	49.45

Notes
1. Data on freeholders from *AJHR*, 1890, B-15; 1892, B-20A; 1903, B-20.
2. Adult male population is for non-Maoris and was estimated for intercensal periods using linear interpolation.

were cheap and secure, and although they came with rules about land use and residence, they had none of the negative connotations of 'landlordism', of subservience by the tenant to a rich and powerful landowner. In this context it is important to note that the willingness of governments to promote Crownholders fluctuated over the final 20 years of the century. The number of Crownholders jumped by two thirds from 1882 to 1888 mainly in response to the vigorous efforts of the Stout-Vogel Ministry (1884–7) to settle the unemployed. The number then slumped by a third late in the 1880s as a result of the more conservative policies of the Atkinson Ministry (1887–90) which sold Crown land to the wealthy rather than leasing it to the disadvantaged. The number jumped again during the 1890s when the Liberal Government (1891–1912) extended the state's control over land resources to an unparalleled degree so as to make land accessible once more to the disadvantaged. The Government's growing concern to devise leasehold tenures more suitable to the less well-off is reflected in the changing composition of the selectors of Crown land. In the Wellington Land District from 1853 to 1860 only 17 per cent of the selectors were manual workers; by the early and mid 1880s the proportion had risen to between 40 and 46 per cent; over the first and last three years of the Liberal Government it reached 60 per cent, about equal to the representation of manuals in the work force.[27]

As sharp as the fluctuations in the size of the Crownholding population were, however, they did not materially alter late century trends in the proportions of 'landless' men. Table 4.3 demonstrates this by combining freeholders and Crownholders together and converting the total into a percentage of adult males.

TABLE 4.3

Freeholders and Crownholders as a Proportion of Adult Males

Year	Freeholders & Crownholders Combined			Freeholders & Crownholders as a % of Adult Males	
	FH	+ CH	= Total	AM	%
1882	71,240	9,683	80,923	141,918	57.0
1885	80,527	11,610	92,221	152,226	60.6
1888	84,547	15,894	100,441	160,201	62.7
1891	91,501	10,855	102,356	167,008	61.3
1902	115,713	17,747	133,460	233,972	57.0

Notes
1. Data on freeholders came from the same sources as in Table 4.2.
2. Data on Crownholders came from *AJHR*, 1882, C-1, 9; 1886, C-1, 13 1889, C-1, 9-10; 1892, C-1, 69. Crownholders are all persons who hold land from the Lands Department; they included deferred purchase settlers, perpetual leaseholders, occupiers with right of purchase, lease in perpetuity holders, tenants of small grazing runs, tenants of pastoral runs, etc. In actuality freeholders and Crownholders were not separate categories; an unknown number of people held both types of land.
3. Adult male population is for non-Maoris and was estimated for intercensal periods using linear interpolation.

For each decade the combined rate moves in the same direction as the freeholder one: upwards from 1882 to 1891, downwards from 1891 to 1902. The gain 1882–91 is a little smaller for the combined than for the freeholder rate (4.3 as against 4.59 per cent); the loss 1891–1902 is a bit less (4.33 as opposed to 5.33 per cent).

The drop in the freeholder (and combined) rate over the 1890s cannot be linked to the so-called 'Long Depression', usually dated

1880–1895. The orthodoxy that these were depression years has become untenable, or at least highly questionable, if depression is defined as a prolonged contraction in real national income per head of European population. An estimate based on monetary data has shown that GDP per capita, if adjusted for declining wholesale prices, actually increased between 1880 and 1895 by an annual average of around one per cent despite three sets of 'bad years' (1882–3, 1888–9, 1894–5) of negative growth.[28] Even if depression is defined relatively, as a growth phase which was weaker than that which colonists were accustomed to, there is no evidence that the phase of weaker growth caused the decline in the freeholder (or combined) rate from 1891 to 1902. For one thing, the freeholder rate went up and not down during the 1880s when the economy was going through the same phase. For another, the rate hit its lowest point in 1902, seven years after the weak phase had been replaced by a strong one.

Easier to prove is a demographic explanation for the waning 1891–1902 trend. The percentage of men owning land decreased because the adult male population was growing at a faster pace. Between the survey years of 1882 and 1891 the number of men grew by an average of 1.96 per cent annually (uncompounded). From 1891 to 1902, however, it increased by an annual average of 3.64 per cent (uncompounded). That it was the more rapid rate of increase which lowered the proportion of freeholders can be demonstrated if we recalculate the percentage of male landowners supposing that the 1.96 annual average percentage increase for the 1882–91 period continued, unchanged, from 1891 to 1902. With the remodelling of the population base, the freehold rate bounces from its 54.78 per cent level in 1891 to about 57 per cent in 1902. Had the adult male population over the 1890s grown at the slower pace of the 1880s, a one per cent loss 1882–1902 would have been turned into a seven per cent gain.

An additional reason land-owning chances diminished over the 1890s was the mounting shortage of new land, especially farming land, available for settlement. The bulk of what is now New Zealand's provincial heartland was carved out in one mad rush over the 30 years from 1850 to 1880. This left a much smaller area of uncolonised and cultivable land for the expanding Pakeha population to move into during the last two decades of the century. Inevitably new rural freeholders and Crownholders in the frontier territories were far fewer during the 1880s and 1890s than in the years from 1850 to 1880.

While the gathering pressure of population on land resources did not pull down the rate of landholding until the 1890s, it had other effects which were revealed somewhat earlier. One of these was the reduction in the size of the average rural landholding (as enumerated by the Census). This first became apparent in 1881 and continued until 1906. Another manifestation was the growing disparity between the number of urban freeholders and the combined total of rural holders and Crownholders. In 1882 the two populations were about the same; for the next six years the rural total grew faster than the urban to the point where the former exceeded the latter by more than 6,000. Thereafter, however, the rural total was quickly outstripped by the urban: in 1891 the urban exceeded the rural total by about 3,000 and in 1902 the difference had reached 10,000.[29] The significance of both these manifestations of land scarcity is they show how colonial society was able to achieve (in part anyway) a growing rate of land-ownership over the 1880s. Had rural land not been subdivided more closely and had a rising proportion of new landowners not been placed on town sections (which were inherently smaller than the rural), it is probable that the relative number of landless men would have started to grow before 1891 and the colony would have been hit by a major social and political crisis.

From what has been said so far it seems unlikely that the proportion of landless working men rose significantly if at all during the 1880s and the 1890s. We can draw this conclusion from the fact that the falling trend in overall land-holding over the 1890s simply cancelled out the rising trend of the earlier decade; we can deduce it too from the broad similarity between the rate of manual-worker freeholding in the 1882 freeholder list, the proportion of working men's households with home-ownership according to the 1892 Labour Department survey, and the rate of home-ownership for wage and salary household heads as indicated by the 1916 Census. Also supporting this conclusion is the evidence that will be brought out shortly demonstrating that real wage levels and unemployment would not have worsened over the period 1880–95. It is probable, however, that the rate did slip late in the 1880s as a result of the Atkinson Ministry's conservative land policies and the sequence of two years of negative economic growth (1888–9), circumstances which may have persuaded some working men to vote Liberal in 1890. But what is just as likely is that any fall in the rate was made good during the 1890s when the Liberals successfully increased the proportion of manual workers receiving Crown land.

Land Use by 'Working-Class' Owners

At this point let us return to an earlier question: how did the mass of wage-earners who owned land use it? What Sutch and other pessimists ignore is not only the phenomenon of 'working-class' land-ownership, but also its many and varied functions in the pre-welfare-state era as a substitute welfare state, even though sections generally were small in size and low in value. Compared with rental tenure, a freehold dwelling lessened the risk of losing the home when unemployment struck; an unemployed homeowner was able to retain his dwelling for a longer period even with mortgage and rate commitments, for these commitments were paid at less frequent intervals than rent. Alternatively, during economic emergencies the owner could liquidate his landed assets, drawing upon them to eke out an existence until conditions improved or to finance the removal of his household to a more economically buoyant locality.[30] Also real property (unlike leasehold tenure) generated income from rent and speculation under certain circumstances. A rough idea of the extent of this practice can be gleaned from the Freeholders Return on the location of parcels of land owned by household heads who were manual workers by stated occupation in Wellington City. Of all these owners, a majority (66 per cent) owned only one title apiece, which in every case was sited in the city itself. But 19 per cent of the owners each had one title situated outside the city: for example, a plumber and gasfitter owned £300-worth of land in Hawera, a coach builder had a £200 property in Feilding, a labourer a £75 property in the Hutt, there was a printer with a £20 parcel in Hokitika, a tailor with real estate worth £180 in Sydenham, and so forth. At a reasonable guess, these absentee owners looked to their land as a form of savings, hoped to speculate on its rising value, and obviously were in the position to let it. Of greater interest, however, is that about 15 per cent of the owners possessed multiple titles which in every case were situated both outside and inside the city.[31] The fact of multiple ownership is a sure sign of dealing and letting activity—of petty enterprise, of 'penny capitalism', or more accurately five- and ten-shilling capitalism. Another document, the 1882 Burgess Rolls for Wellington City, illustrates the sorts of rentier activities 'working-class' multi-holders engaged in.

It was the production of food, however, that gave the vast majority of 'working-class' landholders, regardless of tenure, irrespective of whether they lived in town or country, their most important economic protection. It reduced insecurity, partly by giving them something to fall back on during spells of unemployment, partly by cutting down household costs and adding to their capacity for saving, and partly by providing a means of support during old age. Frederick Monckton, who lived near Featherston, wrote that 'Cows are kept by everyone; very few married labourers are without one'. In 1856 E. B. Fitton observed that 'By far the larger portion of the occupations of colonists in New Zealand arise, in some measure, from the productions of the soil. These may be either in the form of garden or farm tillage', and that 'there are scarce any, whether in sheep or cattle stations, or in other districts near the towns, who have not gardens and a paddock or two attached to their dwelling'. Describing the state of the labour market in 1895, the Secretary of the Labour Department characterised unskilled labourers who were permanent residents by saying that they sold their labour part-time to wealthier neighbours and for the remaining period cultivated their own holdings or gardens.[32] Literary evidence of this sort should, of course, be treated with caution—it could well be coloured by preconceptions of 'working-class' material life. But several things point to its essential accuracy.

In 1890 a public row broke out in Hastings over the borough's enforcement of a by-law against the keeping of pigs by householders, with some elements protesting that the enforcement discriminated against the poorer classes who kept chickens, pigs, cows in their own backyards.[33] Classified advertisements in the newspapers of houses for sale and to let reveal that town sections were frequently larger than the proverbial quarter acre, and contained fowlhouses, orchards, workshops, stables. The problem of wandering stock was a significant feature of borough by-laws. The town of New Plymouth in 1867 boasted 481 cattle, 2,808 sheep, 44 goats, 298 pigs, 4,297 poultry. The local Roads Board for Takapau in 1886 was requested to light up the streets 'so that unsuspecting wayfarers may avoid horses, cows, calves and pigs that roam'.[34] Before 1918 the residents of Opotiki, where there was no regular milk delivery, grazed cows in the streets to supply their own dairy produce.[35] The colony's most articulate critic observed in 1887, 'The greater number of people keep fowls, all lodging houses, boarding houses, and private families also'; in consequence, she said, eggs were in great abundance and very cheap; what made keeping fowls so popular was the great quantity of table scraps, the result of the 'extraordinary cheapness of food'. A frequent argument for shorter working hours for working men, a Saturday half-day especially, was that they needed the time to work in their gardens to raise produce to supplement wages.[36]

The sheer resourcefulness with which the 'working classes' utilised their sections is also suggested by the 1892 Department of Labour survey on 'expenditure by working-men'. The results seem heavily biased towards urban households, who were less likely to engage in 'do it yourself' than their country cousins, for the sample strongly over-represented artisans and factory workers and under-represented workers on farms and in mines.[37] Yet the summary of the findings states that some of the respondents 'have omitted entries under "fish" or "vegetables", not because they do not eat fish, but because they catch them themselves; and so, also, many get their vegetables from their own little gardens'. Close examination of each of the 106 completed schedules shows 35 respondents who must have produced all the vegetables they consumed because they failed to supply the information requested on the weekly amount they spent on this item; in addition 81 said nothing about what they spent on pickles nor 54 on jam, which likewise indicates that they made whatever they ate from the produce of their gardens. Forty-six left blank the question on the amount spent on bacon; we cannot assume that all 46 (43 per cent of the published sample) kept their own pigs and cured them; but there is good reason to believe that many would have done so, as household scraps were plentiful and slaughter-houses furnished a ready and cheap supply of fodder. Although the questionnaire did not expressly ask the respondents how they utilised their land, nine spontaneously gave details which hint at other subsistence activities and, in a few instances, market operations. Six kept their own cows (a sawmiller, three labourers, a settler/labourer, a draper's assistant) to produce milk, butter, cheese; a railway porter said he held four acres and a confectioner half an acre. A gardener whose net family earnings came to £110.5s. a year stated that £50 of this was derived from the rent of 'house-property'. The sawmiller wrote that he invested his savings in cattle, implying that he obtained a secondary income fattening and dealing in stock.[38]

In the bush areas 'working-class' small-holders had the additional resource of saving or making money out of the stands of native timber on their property. They used the timber themselves, as firewood for heating and cooking; and it furnished building materials for their houses, sheds, fences. They cut up trees for firewood, posts, rails, slabs, railway sleepers, and roofing shingles and sold them. A few would have been able to sell the timber royalties on their properties. Some also made a little cash by gathering an edible fungus that was exported to China.[39]

In sum, the colonial male wage-earner holding land was not solely reliant upon the wage market for his material well-being; he was neither fully integrated into the labour market nor an independent producer, but something in between—a hybrid peasant/worker. Subsistence production, commercial production, land-lording and dealing were all secondary occupations providing an additional income (or additional incomes if the land had more than one use). Effectively they were forms of self-employment pursued in between spasms of outside employment or job-searching and were highly dependent upon the unpaid contributions of wives and children. 'Workers' holding land, therefore, did not constitute a uniform, separate, specific, economic class in the West European sense. As a category they are generally indistinguishable from most so-called 'farmers' who likewise lived off small sections, depended on unpaid family labour, and in varying degrees alternated wage-earning with subsistence production, using their properties to make cash wherever the opportunity arose.[40]

Equipped with these economic defences, the heterogeneous male wage-earning population, although not economically independent, nonetheless had sufficient resources of their own to be masterless men. Their petty land-based activities minimised their need for charity and undercut the market power of employers. If unemployed they had the choice of not requesting material aid from the rich. They also had the choice of not working for a tyrant but withdrawing from the wage market for a period while looking for a more agreeable employer. The ability to choose, of course, would have varied substantially, the critical factor being perhaps the type of tenure— home-owners had better protection from the sanctions of the rich than private tenants, since a failure in their wages did not lead to automatic eviction.

Other Agencies Producing 'Masterless People' (1850–1880)
In addition to landholding, five other factors helped to increase the number of masterless people, though not often in ways prescribed by the mythology.

One was exclusive to single women and arose from the fact that the large surplus of adult men gave women far better marriage prospects than their counterparts back in the Old World.[41] The comparative ease with which women were able to marry lowered their participation rate in the waged work-force and reduced their competition for paid employment. This boosted their bargaining power within domestic service, source of the majority of wage-earning jobs for women up to the 1880s.

The second factor was the rapid turnover of staff at work-places. By shortening the contact between individual employers and their servants or workmen, the high turnover effectively casualised their relationship, permitting neither party to develop a sense of obligation to the other. In the case of domestic servants, their comparative youthfulness is a key sign of the brevity of their association with the households that engaged them; in 1896, for example, 70 per cent of female domestic servants were aged under 25 as against 36 per cent of all breadwinners (male and female).[42] The rapid turnover of male manual workers through the average work-place is suggested by the speed with which household heads on rental tenure disappeared from the average locality after a ten-year interval; over the last two decades of the century an 80 per cent disappearance rate was common. Although it is often asserted that the so-called permanent hands employed on large sheep-runs stuck to their employers for a lifetime and became faithful retainers, in fact an analysis of the retention rate of station-hands on a sample of three stations (Akitio, Benmore, Clayden) from the 1860s to the 1880s shows that on the average a mere 13 per cent stayed five years or more.[43]

The third factor shielding poorer people from the social influence of the rich was the excess of single adult males. In all probability, given the link between life cycle and social mobility, the imbalance would have been greatest within the ranks of the lower strata. Single men obviously had greater freedom than married men to pick and choose their jobs, to refuse to put themselves under employers who had bad reputations, paid low wages, or were too demanding. Such discretion was strengthened by the comparative youthfulness of the colonial population; up to the 1890s New Zealand had a mere handful of elderly people. As a result there were few men who, because they were old and infirm or becoming old and fearing infirmity, had no choice or felt they had no choice but to accept whatever work and wages were offered to them. The scarcity of elderly employees would also have tended to push up wages. The earning power of a young wage-force selling physical labour was intrinsically greater than an older one, and the young and fit did not have to compete for jobs with cheaper elderly workers.

Another reason for the near universality of the socially independent man was the host of openings for other kinds of petty enterprise. When, earlier, the rate of 'working-class' land-ownership in 1882 was estimated, it was assumed that male manual workers were equal to 62 per cent of all male breadwinners enumerated by the Census. From the manner in which they were referred to, the reader might have deduced that all were wage-earners. A fair proportion, however, were self-employed, particularly in frontier or extraction occupations (goldmining, gumdigging), the building trades, in transport (as carters), and in a few craft industries (shoemaking, blacksmithing, baking). By 1896, what is more, this self-employed component in the 'working class' had probably declined from a high point recorded in the mid 1860s. In 1867 goldminers alone comprised over one in five of all male breadwinners. The Census of course counted only single occupations, so a far greater number of wage-earners must have worked part of the time in all sorts of crannies of petty enterprise. Probably this sort of penny capitalism in the 'black economy' did not yield a higher income than wage-working at the same or similar tasks. But it offered a freely accessible alternative to wage-earning. No laws prevented amateurs from practising as self-employed tradesmen, and trade unions were too weak to stop them. The building trades were full of 'weatherboard hands', opportunistic handymen and other 'jumped-up ones', so the Amalgamated Society of Carpenters and Joiners complained.[44] Charles Money, a middle-class Englishman who stayed in the colony for a few years in the mid 1860s, tried his hand, both on wages and as his own boss, at an enormous range of jobs for which he possessed no experience, including goldmining, carpentry, road-making, carrying goods, cutting bush, and splitting posts.[45] It cost virtually nothing to dig gum.[46] Equally the cost of gold fossicking was negligible; and to judge from the amount of litigation by storekeepers against miners who bought goods on credit and then decamped, credit must have been readily extended to almost every stranger who entered a goldfield. Especially in rural areas it was common for all kinds of physical work—bushfelling, road-making, post-splitting, ploughing and so forth—to be undertaken under a labour contract. In a sense this was a wage payment, but under conditions which allowed men to keep their own hours, free from constant supervision, to tackle the job in their own way.[47]

Lastly, social equality was fostered by the generally strong demand for labour. Contemporary statements about 'Jack being as good as his master' (or 'Jill as good as her mistress') deserve scepticism; yet they converge with more objective sources of information: the low population pressures, the evidence of strong economic growth from the 1850s to the late 1870s, the ease with which male wage-earners could enter self-employment and land-holding (part-time or full-time), which effectively lessened the supply of labour, their willingness to follow the geographical movements in opportunity.

Do These Other Agencies Diminish over the 1880s and 1890s?
As already mentioned, the traditional view that New Zealand experienced a 'Long Depression' is now suspect, given that the estimated national income per capita in constant (wholesale) prices grew during the so-called 'Long Depression' era (1880–95). But did the 'masterless' person without land benefit from the growth? It is conceivable that the gains went to the highest and middle-income earners, leaving those on lower incomes, the majority of the work-force, in a deteriorating economic position as their static share of resources had to be divided among an ever-growing number of people. If so, then the material preconditions of vertical bonding were being put in place.

Most of the available indicators of common living standards, however, contradict or at least fail to confirm this gloomy hypothesis. Sutch and others have interpreted the fall in nominal wage rates for every category of wage-earner over the late century as representing a drastic shift of the labour market in favour of the employing classes. In the Wellington Province, to take an example, the official statistics collected by the police show that the average daily wage of a general labourer (without keep) dropped from 8s. in 1873 to 6s.6d. in 1895. Yet no account is taken of the drop in living costs over the same period, notably of foodstuffs. A price index covering 40-odd wholesale commodities declined by 43 per cent over the same period. If the general labourer's wage rate is adjusted for this fall in wholesale prices, it rose (in 1873 terms) from 8s. in 1873 to almost 11s.6d. in 1895. A more sophisticated index of trends in real wage rates, based upon official wage data for all provinces, with weightings for every category of worker, shows a rise in real wages from 1874 to 1879, followed by a much weaker growth tendency over the next two decades, but a growth tendency nonetheless, with the index going from 0.958 in 1879 to 0.996 in 1889 (1901 = 1.000) and then after some fluctuations reaching 1.035 in 1895 and 1.097 by 1900.[48]

It would be quite imprudent to take this trend alone as proof that the real incomes of the lower strata rose in aggregate. Apart from the fact that no one knows how official wage statistics were compiled and whether they were accurate, any real wage index derived from these statistics takes no account of unemployment; and it is impossible to adjust the index for unemployment because no comprehensive and systematic records were ever collected. Although there was plenty of contemporary rhetoric about joblessness, it is incapable of telling us with a reasonable degree of certainty if the problem worsened sufficiently after 1879 to increase the incidence of poverty.

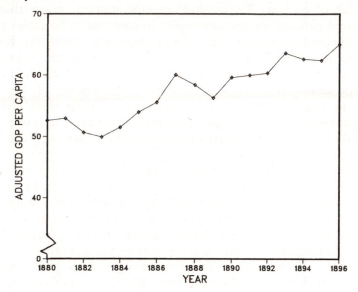

Fig. 4.1 Adjusted GDP per capita. Gross domestic product in 1880 prices.

Other objective measures, however, do not suggest that the index masks either a strong downturn in real wages or substantially higher unemployment or both from 1879 to 1895. Of these measures, the most interesting is the incidence of theft (burglary, robbery, larceny). At first sight this seems irrelevant; but a multitude of studies across a wide range of pre-20th-century societies have found that theft is a powerful predictor of trends in the living standards of the poor. Almost without exception the case-studies demonstrate that theft is highly sensitive to scarcity or need. The more rigorous of these studies show that theft climbs with either the price of foodstuffs or unemployment; if food prices and unemployment rise simultaneously, however, theft is at its worst; conversely theft tends to fall with either the price of food or joblessness; more so if both drop together.[49] In this connection it is significant that in New Zealand there was

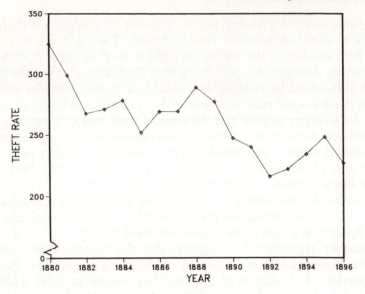

*Fig. 4.2 Theft Rate. Charges for burglary, larceny, robbery per 100,000
general population (non-Maori).*

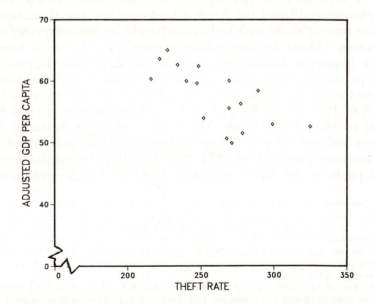

Fig. 4.3 Adjusted GDP per capita plotted against Theft Rate.

a definite overall tendency for the number of charges for theft per capita to diminish between 1880 and 1896. The incidence was about one fifth smaller in the triennium 1894–6 than in 1880–2. Although we cannot discount the possibility that fluctuations in the theft rate were influenced by changes in policing or public attitudes towards theft, there is some reason to believe that variations in living standards had the stronger impact. For the rates of theft had a strong, negative association with another more conventional measure of economic well-being, namely, estimated real gross domestic product per capita. Over the 17 data points covering the years 1880–1896, the rate of theft has a correlation with the GDP variable of -0.73 (with a level of statistical significance of 0.0008); the graphs and scatterplot in Figs. 4.1, 4.2, 4.3 bring out the relationship; the statistical test used was Spearman's rank order correlation coefficient.*

Another argument that suggests that the aggregate real income of the lower classes rose instead of declining is the fact that the proportion of dwellings of one and two rooms to total dwellings was halved between 1874 and 1901 in both the North and the South Islands. Except for 1896 in the North Island, every census year registered a fall. Eldred-Grigg's attempt to use this indicator both as an expression of poverty and to argue that growing under-employment afflicted the South Island over the last three decades of the century shows that he has fundamentally misinterpreted what it means.[50] Other housing indicators reveal that the whole housing stock improved dramatically over the so-called 'Long Depression'. The percentage of dwellings three to four rooms in size'(the standard house for the married working man) fell between every census from 1878 to 1901 in the North Island and between every census from 1881 to 1901 in the South. The fraction of larger dwellings (five rooms and over) for the whole country as well as each island rose between every census year, 1874–1901.[51] A mix of indicators compiled and published by the Government from 1877 under the heading

*The Spearman rank order correlation coefficient (Rs) measures the degree of relationship between two sets of ranked data, and is based on the sum of the square of the differences between the two ranks. If a perfect positive relationship between the two is present then an item which ranked first on one variable would also rank first on the other and so on down the line. The degree of relationship is indicated by a scale going from +1.00 (a perfect positive relationship) to -1.0 (a perfect negative one). The closer the coefficient is to zero, the weaker is the relationship.

The level of significance is a calculation of the probability that a rank order coefficient was due solely to chance. The higher the probability, the less significant in a statistical sense the coefficient is. All things being equal, most researchers would reject a Spearman correlation coefficient with a significance level of more than 0.05.

'consumption per head of population of articles in common use' shows trends that are more difficult to interpret. The indices include sugar (pounds per head of the general population), spirits and beer (gallons per head of adult males), tea and coffee (pounds per head of the general population) and tobacco (pounds per head of adult males). The sugar index tended to rise over the 1880s and 1890s. Although the alcohol indices fell, a convincing argument can be advanced that this was the result more of modifications in drinking habits and of a decline in the fraction of single men than of collapsing real incomes for the 'working class'. This leaves waning per capita consumption of tea and coffee and of tobacco from 1879 as the two remaining pieces of evidence for the pessimistic argument; but taken in conjunction with the other, divergent trends, they are hardly proof that an increasing fraction of landless wage-earners suffered from poverty and thus became susceptible to dependency.[52]

Having said that, it should also be said that the five factors which gave landless wage-earners freedom of choice during the golden age of the 'masterless person' (1850–1880) steadily diminished in power over the closing decades of the century. Unmarried female wage-earners found that their ability to escape from tyrannous employers through marriage was being closed off by the weaker marriage market, the result of the declining numerical imbalance between men and women. On top of this, a growing proportion of women were entering the enumerated work-force, which suggests that the average woman stood a greater chance of being under the thumb of such employers.

Married and single men lost some of their economic flexibility for more complex reasons. No firm evidence has been adduced that male unemployment became chronically bad, running in excess, say, of 10 per cent of the labour force over most of these years. An estimate of the number of men out of work during the 1880s suggests that in summer they amounted to about one or two per cent of the labour force, in winter about six per cent in the major towns, swelling to about 12 per cent in the worst years.[53] Indeed from what can be pieced together from the structure of occupations and fragments of information about the pattern of work, it seems that earnings were lost for the same reason as before—not through structural or cyclical but frictional unemployment, caused by illness, bad weather, and, most of all, the time wasted travelling between widely scattered work-sites.* The Department of Labour recognised the importance

---

*Structural unemployment occurs with overpopulation or when technological innovation makes workers redundant. Cyclical unemployment is caused by fluctuations in the trade cycle. With

of the latter cause by establishing in 1891 a network of job information centres around the country and providing free rail passes to job searchers.[54] But goldmining fell away as a major component of self-employment, economic growth slowed, and there was a greater frequency of 'bad years'. In these 'bad years' slumps in government loan expenditure and/or commodity prices pruned back the supply of seasonal and constructional employment, jobs involving bush clearance, land improvement, public works, house construction. With fewer such jobs, the amount of frictional unemployment would have risen as workers travelled further in search of them. General economic contraction in these years would have thrown out of work men in even intrinsically stable jobs. At the same time, the inherent capacity of men to cope with an unstable labour market declined with a relatively ageing population and a growing number of married men with children. The greater 'stickiness' of labour may partly explain why Otago and Canterbury, being more demographically mature than the North Island, were observed to have a worse unemployment problem.[55]

The shift against the 'masterless person' over the last two decades, however, was offset by several counteracting forces. New factors resistant to the formation of hierarchy arose and took the place of the older ones as they receded. Although marriage opportunities for women diminished and an increasing percentage of women entered the enumerated workforce, this did not lead a greater proportion of women to sell their labour as domestic servants—the most servile type of employment—and thus engender a surplus of cheap domestic servant labour. In fact the increasing diversification of jobs for women had the effect of lowering the proportion of women engaged as domestic servants; indeed it seems to have produced a growing shortage, for real wages of domestic servants improved quite strongly.[56]

Married men adapted to the double pressure of fewer job opportunities and the lessened personal flexibility imposed by growing family commitments and age by sending their older children out to work and obliging them to contribute to the household income. Although this did nothing for the children's freedom of choice it helped to preserve the father's independence.

Some idea of the popularity of this expedient is given by the 1892

frictional unemployment work is available but people are jobless because e.g. they are in the process of changing jobs, there is bad work organisation, inadequate information about the job market, inadequate physical access to the jobs, illness, etc.

Department of Labour survey, which asked not only for the number of dependent family members who worked and their earnings, but also the total net earnings available for family expenditure.[57] From the ages specified for dependants we can deduce who the additional family earners were. We cannot presume that all the additional earnings were at the disposal of the father, but on the other hand the survey makes no provision for remittances by children living away from home. Of the 106 households in the published sample, 96 had dependants. Of the 96, 22 (or 23 per cent) included earners in addition to the father. Only in three households was the contribution as low as one tenth of the father's earnings or less. In 12 cases there were two or more additional contributors, not surprisingly, as some families were very large indeed. One family, for example, had nine offspring, ranging from six to 23 years of age; three of them (presumably the three in their twenties including one girl), supplemented family income by £233, bringing it up to £326.12s. In six cases the total supplements were greater than the household head's own income. The survey thus suggests a high degree of interdependence and co-operation within the family. This in turn highlights the vital role played by children in supporting their parents in the era before the welfare state, before sickness benefits, unemployment benefit, the old-age pension. Such a view is difficult to reconcile with the current tendency of historians to argue that the colonial family was breaking down—but this will have to be discussed at a later point.

Despite the weaker job market, the unmarried male wage-worker was protected from dire poverty by the low cost of food and other essentials. In the 1892 working-men's expenditure survey there were five households each consisting of a solitary man. Of these a miner, earning £130 a year after being workless for a total of 44 days, owned his own hut on which rates of £1 pound a year were paid, and saved £25 yearly or one fifth of his income. A labourer on £65 a year (having lost no earnings through sickness or unemployment) paid 2s.6d. a week for a two-roomed hut, and was able to save £17 a year, or over one quarter of his earnings. A carpenter who earned over £113 after losing three months' income from unemployment, owned his own one-roomed shack on which he paid rates of 6s.8d. yearly, and although he saved nothing, he spent more on alcohol for home consumption than all but one of the 106 household heads in the published sample. A miner living in his 'own house' (a six-foot by eight-foot tent) saved one third of his £90 yearly earnings (having also lost three months' income 'from want of employment'); and a labourer who had earned £80 without loss of earning time, had no savings but rented what appears to have been a fairly large dwelling of four rooms. Single men who paid nothing for board— because they were extreme itinerants living off overnight hospitality or sleeping in the open, or because they squatted on someone's land in whares made of canvas, raupo, or other makeshift materials— also had a fair margin of fat to live on. For example, the 1893 Royal Commission on the Kauri Gum Industry reported that the cost of living of the average digger was 10s. to 12s. a week; given that the average digger earned 25s. to 27s. a week and paid nothing in board, one day's earnings sustained more than two days' expenditure. A rock-bottom wage over the 1880s and early 1890s was about 3s. to 4s. a day (without 'found'). Working for two thirds of the year, six days a week, at 3s. a day would have produced just over £31 yearly, equivalent to the living expenses of the average gumdigger. Although this would have been only a bare existence, it would have enabled survival without recourse to charity and dependency.[58]

Finally, the Liberal Government from 1891 intervened decisively in favour of the self-possessed male. The Liberals helped to break the economic power of the large estates, and in so doing established 'state socialism' under democratic control as a lasting alternative to private patronage. Old age pensions, co-operative public works schemes, Advances to Settlers, Factory Acts, the tilting of public land distribution to the small man, and so on, all preserved New Zealand from private patron–client relationships.

Conclusion
The hierarchical view has been refuted. Colonists were broadly justified in maintaining that their new land was 'abundant', and that because of this 'abundance' there was no development of a strong social organisation based on client–patron relationships. Some great estates, some parts of some regions, some formal institutions (like the police force) may have been hierarchical. But these were neither significant nor major elements in the overall social pattern and to suppose they were confuses an incidental for a central characteristic. 'Abundance' may indeed have been more culturally and less naturally determined than the 'insider's view' allowed for. Factors which had an influence included the imbalanced demography, the rapid movement of the frontier which reduced population pressures on land supplies, the flexibility of the family structure, high labour turnover and mobility,

the imported ideology which made colonists strive to secure the economic base for social independence, their resourcefulness (as exemplified by their flair for penny-capitalism), the wool and gold booms, and so on. But whether it is called a 'natural abundance' or not, it ensured that the typical colonist was a 'masterless person'. Contrary to the views of some historians, material life was not bleak, and did not engender a demeaning paternalism in which the many depended on and were beholden to the few.

Man alone. This photo of an extreme transient, travelling between jobs without
companions, is described as a 'characteristic picture' by the caption. Very few
illustrations of such men show them moving in pairs or groups. The caption also
recognises the diversity of men who became 'swaggers' and regards overnight rural
hospitality as a means of labour recruitment rather than a form of charity. *The
Imperial Album of New Zealand Scenery*, ii (1898?)

CHAPTER V

A Class-Divided Society?

IF hierarchy·did not prevail in colonial New Zealand, can the same be said of the second enemy of the ideal society, class-divisions? As the term 'class-division' is a broad one, some definition of it is required before we proceed. Theoretically there are three possible meanings. One is the uneven sharing of material resources within a society according to some objective measure (stratification). The second is the domination in a society of exclusive mixing and meeting patterns whereby people having the same economic power interact and associate mostly or only amongst themselves and so forge a common and distinct set of norms and *mores* (sub-culture or community). The third is the collective use of power by people belonging to one of these communities to win a greater portion of economic resources, at the expense of those with a different relationship to the means of production (action groups). The last two meanings seem to be more helpful than the first. With the first, it is not possible to distinguish one society from another since almost every society (except the most technologically primitive) is intrinsically unequal in its distribution of material resources. The advantage of the other two is that they allow us to place what we have called hierarchical societies (where the social organisation is vertical) in a different category from a class-divided one (where the flow of interaction and collaboration is predominantly horizontal).

The Arcadian implication of the 'insider's view' was that New Zealand was not class-divided in either the second or the third meanings. The openness of the stratification system precluded the growth of class in the second sense; there were no class-specific communities because individuals moved so frequently down or (most of all) up the proprietorial ladder that they were unable to form solid groupings coagulating around some category of wealth and income. In addition, the presence of natural abundance allegedly prevented the formation of class in the third sense; as the country was not cursed by scarcity, individuals had no reason to combine together into action groups to defend their individual interests.

The aim of this chapter will be to test the claim of colonial myth-makers that New Zealand was not class-divided in the second and third meanings. As in the last chapter, the approach will be to lay out the implicit attacks on the 'insider's view' by certain modern historians and then to falsify them. The data employed in the falsification will be used later, in Part III, to support the author's own model of the society.

The chapter does not dispute that a particular segment of the society, the great estate owners, or at least a large number of them, formed a class within the second and perhaps the third meanings above. Larger merchants and professionals of the towns, who had strong links with the great estate owners, may also have done so. To the extent it suggests the contrary, the 'insider's view' was misleading. What is disputed, however, is that the majority of the 60 to 70 per cent of the population who can broadly be called manual workers did comprise such a class. Two strands in the historiography suggest that they did. One maintains that urban manual workers were increasingly enveloped in tightly knit working-class communities; the other contends that over the whole period rural workers belonged to one large 'floating' community in the countryside. Both arguments hold that the 'labourer's paradise' was not an authentic representation of the majority 'working-class' experience; in their respective communities manual workers had their own forms of association from which evolved distinctive sub-cultures. The members of these sub-cultures spurned the goals of individual self-improvement through upward mobility, affirmed instead the values of fraternity and co-operation, and generally resisted the respectable norms and *mores* of the middle and upper classes.

1: The Olssen Thesis

The historian most associated with the argument that urban working

men were increasingly bound into class-specific communities is Erik
Olssen, in a series of pioneering and immensely stimulating publications, supported by his students, notably J. H. Angus, in unpublished
papers and theses.[1] Briefly put, Olssen's case is that the towns from
about the 1870s 'spawned' a stronger sense of class identity. The
growing size of towns and the rise of factory production led to
'residential differentiation', that is, the formation of one-class suburbs;
for example in Dunedin 'the wealthy and moderately wealthy' lived
in Anderson's Bay, Roslyn, and Maori Hill, while tradesmen and
the unskilled occupied Caversham and Dunedin South.[2] In turn, the
residents in each district formed and mixed within class-exclusive
institutions 'such as lodges, churches, and sports clubs';[3] in the
working-class districts these exclusive patterns of association nurtured
a distinct set of values that condoned drunkenness, irreligion,
'larrikinism', and Sunday sports and Sunday work as well as rough
pastimes such as boxing and cock fighting—'much to the horror of
the respectable and pious' residents of the wealthier suburbs.[4] Then
in the late 1880s and early 1890s, he says, the people in these working-
class districts were radicalised. Triggering this was the example of
the New Unionism sweeping parts of the world (dramatised by the
1889 London Dock Strike), the 'depression' (which brought
unemployment, 'the loss of certain customary rights, such as the eight-
hour day for most skilled men', and blocked upward mobility for
many), and a spurt in the more capital intensive forms of factory
production which reduced 'in large part, the artisan's hope of achieving
independence' as well as his status.[5] The working-class community
acted as the recruiting ground for a host of new trade union
organisations, and provided a ready market for radical and socialist
journals and pamphlets and for 'local papers such as the *Otago
Workman*' which 'reflected a working-class cultural identity and
articulated working-class demands'.[6] With the Maritime Strike of 1890
class consciousness reached its peak; and although the strike was
lost, it induced union leaders to form their own Labour Parties and
nominate, finance, and campaign for their own working-class
candidates at the 1890 General Election: in Dunedin on election day
the mass mobilisation ensured that the 'working-class suburbs voted
overwhelmingly for Labour Party candidates' which in turn
underpinned the victory of the Liberals.[7]

In determining how far Olssen's model should be preferred to
the 'insider's view' the crucial issue is the proportion of manual workers
who belonged to what we can call the working-class social organisation

or, in Olssen's language, working-class communities. Did all do so
or only relatively few? This is the crucial issue since Olssen stresses
that urban manual workers socialised in exclusive and powerful
associations that engineered their separate culture and acted as a
necessary condition for their political mobilisation; in the 'labourer's
paradise' in complete contrast, all manual workers were absorbed
into a minimally organised society where everyone shared an
individualistic culture and the mechanism of political mobilisation
had been abolished. Although Olssen never explicitly says that most,
or all, manual workers were enveloped in their own 'communities',
the capacity of his model to erode the 'insider's view' is a function
of the proportion of manual workers it can demonstrate as belonging
to these 'communities'. The greater the proportion, the greater the
erosion; if a majority belonged, then certainly his model deserves
to take precedence; the smaller the minority, the more tangential
is the feature he is describing to the total social pattern. We will
now examine his evidence closely, asking three questions of it. Does
it prove that residential differentiation existed to a significant degree?
Does it establish that a working-class sub-culture was widespread
amongst manual workers? Does it show that a significant proportion
were politically mobilised and recruited within trade unions? As Olssen
regards the Dunedin working-class community as the strongest in
the colony, much of the discussion will centre upon it; if his model
has precedence, Dunedin should be the first place to show it.

Residential Differentiation
To demonstrate that Dunedin by 1890 was residentially differentiated
to a significant degree, Olssen uses impressionistic observations about
where the various strata lived and appears to rely on a quantitative
analysis by J. H. Angus which is part of an influential and most
impressive doctoral thesis on the politics of Otago in the late 19th
century.[8] As impressionistic evidence by its very nature is inadequate,
this leaves the quantitative data. Angus firstly took all the occupations
listed in two aggregate sources (Stone's Street Directory of 1884 and
the Electoral Rolls of 1881) and from each source ascertained the
proportion of persons, classified under seven occupational categories,
who lived in five districts of the city according to one source and
six districts according to the other.[9] Why both sources were used
is not clear, since with the exception of one district, Roslyn, it is
apparent from place names that they do not share the same boundaries.
In the case of Roslyn it is somewhat disturbing to note that the

Directory gives a combined percentage for tradesmen and labourers, about 13 per cent lower than given in the Rolls, which raises the whole question of the reliability of both sources. It is even more disturbing that at the outset no definition of 'differentiation' is offered; so that we end up not knowing how much variation from one district to another proves its existence. It certainly is not self-evident that there is much variation in the percentages he adduces; for example, assuming that tradesmen and labourers equal the 'working class', we find that in the Roll their combined percentage only ranges between 44.3 for the lowest district and 58.5 for the highest. (The Directory, to be sure, yields a wider range, of between 45.8 and 84.8 per cent; but which source do we take as the best measure of differentiation? Angus does not say.) Even if it could be agreed that these differences are considerable, they still do not prove the absence of interclass propinquity; for what his method fails to exclude is the possibility that within each district, middle-class and manual-worker residences were sited cheek by jowl. In fact it is the prominence of internal mixing that has been highlighted by 15 case-studies of a selection of town and suburban electorates during the mid 1920s (Wellington East, Wellington Central, Wellington South, Christchurch South, a portion of Eden, Hamilton, Palmerston North, Rotorua, Gisborne, Napier, Wanganui, Nelson, Timaru, Invercargill, New Plymouth).[10]

Secondly, as additional measures of differentiation, Angus constructed two housing indices from Census tabulations on dwellings by boroughs.[11] They embrace a selection of nine boroughs in Otago/ Southland, including six in Dunedin. One is an index of overcrowding (the ratio between the general population of a borough and the total number of rooms of all its dwellings); the other measures the density of smaller and by implication less valuable houses in the housing stock of a borough (the ratio between dwellings with four rooms and those with six). The reason, it seems, for the construction of these indices of differentiation is that unlike the occupational data taken from the street directories and electoral rolls they have the same geographical boundaries as polling-booth data Angus collected on the Dunedin Labour Party's share of the vote in the 1890 General Election. Hence the tabulations of housing across the six Dunedin boroughs are supposed to provide the explanatory variables for the geography of working-class consciousness in Dunedin. The match between the spatial distribution of the Labour vote in 1890 and the spatial variations in housing conditions is offered as the critical proof that class segregation was fundamental to the development of a distinct working-class culture. Angus does not spell out how the voting pattern matches the differences in housing. But if we test the relationship ourselves employing a simple statistical technique (Spearman's rank order correlation coefficient), it is clear that the fit is not a close one for the six Dunedin boroughs. The correlation between the percentage of votes cast for the Labour Party and the ratio of dwellings of four to those of six rooms is only $Rs = +0.21$ (to be significant at the 0.05 level the value needed to be 0.829). The correlation between Labour's share of the vote and the average number of persons per room is negligible ($Rs = -0.01$).[12]

None of these criticisms of Angus's methodology disproves the existence of a high degree of differentiation in Dunedin in the last quarter or so of the 19th century; they reveal, however, that a sufficient *prima facie* case has not been advanced by Olssen. The implication of this is that if differentiation, the engine of working-class community development, has not been established, then we can reasonably doubt whether the working-class community itself was a reality.

The Working-Class Sub-Culture

Olssen also claims that a defining characteristic of the working-class community was the existence amongst manual workers of a sub-culture. One symptom of this, he says, was that they interacted within the confines of their own local institutions—sporting clubs, lodges, churches. It is impossible, however, for us to evaluate his argument here because he tells us nothing about the voluntary organisations of Dunedin; nowhere is it apparent that either he or 'anyone else has attempted to identify and count them, map them, enumerate the memberships of each, estimate what proportion of the population in each district belonged to them, demonstrate that the personnel and activities of the bodies in the 'working-class communities' were different from those in the well-to-do suburbs. The second manifestation, he suggests, was that the residents of 'working-class communities' exhibited distinctive traits—which of course they should do if they mixed exclusively and intimately amongst themselves. He does offer some evidence on this point,[13] but it is thin and unsystematic and it is impossible to deduce from it just how many manual workers in 'working-class' areas had the same pastimes, drinking habits, the same attitudes to work, to criminal deviance, to religion and so forth— whether in fact the mass of manual workers were separated from the wider society by their adherence to their own particular values, social imagery, *mores*.

His best and most illuminating documentation of a possible working-class sensibility are the views expressed in a radical Dunedin weekly, the *Otago Workman* (1887–1907). Olssen rightly says that the paper with wit and bite attacked the royal family, capitalism, respectable public figures, the foibles of the well-to-do, and constituted authority, and vigorously championed working men and the Labour cause. But given the scantiness of his other evidence for the 'subculture', we have no reason to agree with him that its sentiments encapsulated the *'mentalité'* of the 'working-class community' of Caversham and South Dunedin. For that matter he fails to show that the paper was ever read by a majority of the city's manual workers or that its readership was drawn mostly from this category, for his only support for these claims is the internal textual evidence of its opinions and its unsubstantiated assertions that it sold 5,000 copies an issue.

Union Membership and Class Mobilisation in 1890

How many manual workers were in fact radicalised in 1890, the climax of 19th-century working-class consciousness in urban New Zealand? It is not possible to measure this by examining the share of the vote received by Labour or radical Liberal candidates in the 1890 General Election; the fraction of the Labour/radical Liberal vote that came from the middle classes is beyond determination; and polling-booth analysis of working-class districts depends upon the matching of polling-booth areas with these districts, the existence of which no one has yet precisely established. (Some historians have employed the geographical distribution of the Labour/radical Liberal vote, but this is a tautologous method since the distribution of the vote is used to prove that working-class districts existed and these in turn are used to prove that the majority of manual workers voted for Labour/radical Liberal candidates.) This leaves trade union membership, estimates for the size of which, at its peak in mid 1890, vary enormously.[14] The most likely figure (which Olssen himself cites)[15] is 35,000 men and women, equal to 23.5 per cent of all wage and salary earners enumerated in the April 1891 census. Certainly the wage and salary population includes many categories of manuals who theoretically should be excluded from the base since the point at issue is the rate of unionisation by urban workers. On the other side of the equation, however, the estimated total of unionists includes a host of 'rural' unionists (such as shearers, gumdiggers, flax workers) as well as an unknown number of men who operated in the casual labour force and floated between urban and rural jobs. But if we keep them all in the unionist total of 35,000 and at the same time omit the more likely 'rural' workers (20,176 farm labourers and station hands) from the 1891 base, we still come up with a rate of unionisation which is small, 27 per cent. In the four main centres the rate was possibly higher, but how much is impossible to say since data on trade union membership and the occupational structure of the centres are not sufficiently precise, and the problem of defining an urban 'unionist' insurmountable (the figure for union membership claimed by some contemporaries for Dunedin in 1890, for example, almost exceeds the probable number of male and female manual workers in the city).[16]

It is true that the 23.5 per cent colony-wide rate is comparable with that for the eastern colonies of Australia, which have a reputation for being highly class-conscious.[17] Yet if the Australian comparison is pushed further the result is instructive. In the early 1890s Labour parties sprang up in the eastern colonies using the trade union movement as a power base (the New South Wales Labour Party in its first electoral contest in 1891 won nearly one third of the seats in the Legislative Assembly); by 1899 they had galvanised enough electoral support to hold the balance of power in three of the legislatures and act as the Opposition in another; they continued to mobilise support to the point where the ALP was able to form a minority government at the Federal level in 1904, and again in 1908-9, and two majority governments in 1910-13 and 1914-16.[18] In New Zealand, however, the union movement practically disappeared in the aftermath of the 1890 Maritime Strike; it was incapable of sustaining the development of an independent, colony-wide, Labour party until 1904. Although in the 1890s a considerable number of self-styled Labour candidates won parliamentary seats with the backing of *ad hoc* trade union electoral organisations, only about six of these 'Labour' parliamentarians were manual workers (four from Dunedin, two from Christchurch, and one each from Invercargill and Wairau);[19] none of the 'Labour' parliamentarians acted as independents in the House— all were assimilated into the Liberal caucus. Moreover, six is a negligible figure considering that the payment of M.H.R.s commenced in 1884, and given, too, that over the 1890s there were roughly 15 wholly and mainly urban constituencies, each with about 60 to 70 per cent of manual workers on their electoral rolls.[20] If they existed at all, 'working-class communities' either had a poor sense of their cultural autonomy and identity, or else embraced a miniscule proportion of the manual workers dwelling in urban electorates.

The 27 per cent rate of 'urban' unionisation achieved in 1890 has three noteworthy features. One is that it was nothing like a majority. The second is that it represented the *peak* of trade union membership over the 19th century. The third is that it endured for no more than about four months. Unionisation from 1889 to 1890 was a flash in the pan, given that the estimated number of unionists exploded from 3,000 in 1888 (equal to, say, six per cent of all wage and salary earners), to the 35,000 peak in mid 1890, before collapsing to 8,000 by 1894; thereafter membership only rose when unions were granted legal protection under the Industrial Conciliation and Arbitration Act. Working-class mobilisation in 1889–90, in other words, was an aberration in the history of the colony, characterised by the fleeting appearance of working-class action groups representing a minority of urban manual workers. These characteristics, it should be added, had always defined the colonial labour movement; in 1864, 1875, 1881, 1885, trade unions (with even smaller proportions of members) had suddenly grown and just as suddenly died.[21]

A pattern of such fitfulness does not suggest that the towns contained close-knit working-class communities embracing the vast bulk of manual workers. It suggests instead that the rudiments of such an organisation existed, were sufficient to transmit radical messages and give rise to instant action groups that shaped discontent, but were not sufficient to bring together the radicalised and the discontented into a permanent and independent labour movement let alone a majority one. What made 1889–90 exceptional may have been the growth of stronger associative capacities in the late 1880s. More important, however, was the sheer coincidence of two highly inflammable circumstances: the sudden appearance of a particularly powerful radical ideology (New Unionism) at the same time as the colony experienced two of its worst years of negative economic growth (1888–9). The pattern, of course, does suggest that the 'insider's view' was wrong in implying that New Zealand was totally free of class-division. But bonds between manual workers were so insubstantial and loose that it can hardly be said that a model of class-division deserves to replace the 'insider's view'. The latter still stands, fundamentally intact, if the absolute element is qualified. Olssen has asked the wrong question; the question is not why collective class protest arises but why so little of it even occurred and why its scale was so small.

What Blocked Close Association Between Manual Workers?

The central feature of Pakeha New Zealand—the political tranquillity of wage workers—which Olssen has failed to explain, originated from five interrelated factors. The first was the extension of the franchise which in the 1890s helped to divert grievances away from direct action into the ballot box. The second was the colony's material success. As shown in the previous chapter, the colony did in fact grant ample opportunities for petty competencies and positions of social independence, and the consequent satisfaction of material and social expectations helped to legitimate the *status quo* as well as the 'insider's view' itself. A third is that the colony (unlike its counterparts across the Tasman) never developed the large conurbations that maximise the chances for the discontented to mix exclusively with one another and reinforce one another's opinions without coming into contact with the moderating ideas of the contented. The fourth is that manual workers enjoyed comparatively little propinquity; as the next chapter will demonstrate, they played a minimal part in the colony's informal and formal groupings. The fifth reason is related to their extraordinarily transient lifestyles, the remaining theme of the chapter. All five factors explain why the membership of trade unions and other action groups was so minute and why collective protest was so rare. The fifth, however, additionally explains why action groups were so short-lived and why strikes (like the 1890 Maritime Strike) were so easily broken by employers without assistance from the state.

By transience is meant the migration of households or of members of a household from one locality to another at some distance. That the colony's high rate of transience undermined associative capacities is based on two assumptions. The first is that it reduced the chances for individuals living (or working) in the same locality to become intimately acquainted and evolve patterns of reciprocity. As small as the average locality was, its high turnover of residents deprived them of the prolonged contact necessary to forge relationships that went beyond the superficial. Habitual transience, to which manual workers were especially prone, was even more destructive to social ties, including those depending on a sense of class solidarity. As it was a general expectation of the habitually transient that they would never sink roots in any one place, they felt little incentive to identify with the lives, problems, and careers of the people they encountered, or to gain their approval by adhering to their normative code. The second assumption is that transience weakened associative capacities because it was a strategy for material betterment which acted as an alternative to collaboration and collective action. Transience, that is, was an individualistic and conservative mechanism of self-improvement. Transients sought to improve their prospects by moving from place to place instead of staying in one place and helping one another out by collaborating in an informal fashion or by banding together formally to struggle for a larger share of the local cake (through, for example, the establishment of trade unions).

The theoretical questions begged by these assumptions will be discussed a little later. For the moment let us note the things that give them a measure of plausibility. One is the coincidence between the high transience and the rarity of organised working-class protest over the century. Another is that several case-studies from other societies came to parallel conclusions. For example, J. W. Scott's investigation of the glass workers of Carmaux in 19th-century France found that unionisation and militancy arose only late in the century when the workers led more settled lives.[22] Likewise Stephan Thernstrom in a massive study of social mobility in 19th- and 20th-century Boston concluded that the rootlessness of urban workers hampered the rise of a powerful socialist movement in America by choking the growth of strong working-class communities from which such a movement could recruit a mass following.[23] Corroboration is also given by the fact that the victory of New Zealand's Labour Party was catalysed during the 1930s Depression, when households experienced an unprecedented degree of residential stability.[24] Linguistic usages give further weight to the assumptions. As will be demonstrated later, contemporaries used as labels of social description the terms 'settler' and 'drifter' (often as explicit antithesis) more than 'working class' or 'labouring classes' or 'middle class', and frequently used them in place of occupational designations. Also suggestive is the usage of the more neutral and critical observers. They refer often to the pronounced geographical mobility of the population but say little or nothing about its 'working-class communities'. For instance, the Fabian socialist William Pember Reeves in his classic, *State Experiments in Australia and New Zealand* (1902), writes on three occasions about the foot-loose character of the labour force but rarely mentions the social organisation of the men and women within it. By implication their itinerancy and not their group life is what strikes him as significant:

The country people in the colonies move about; most of the workmen are real nomads. I do not mean only the classes whose work keeps them always moving—the drovers, mail-carriers, hawkers, waggoners—who seldom pass two consecutive nights on the same spot. There is a class of gold-seekers who, though far fewer now than when the alluvial fields were richer, still roam about 'prospecting'. . . . The harvesters, too, in most farming districts are not resident labourers, but come along at harvest-time as Irishmen cross to England. . . . The axemen employed in bush-felling usually go in small parties, take contracts to clear patches of forest, and when their work is done pass on. . . . The shearers . . . are the most persistent wanderers of all. . . . Artisans and general labourers seem to share in the readiness to shift their ground. Even farmers sometimes display it, and are prompt to sell out, either because they are not successful or because they are.[25]

The same sense of transience and want of associations is conveyed in Thomas Arnold's letter home in 1849:

a very short experience of colonial life teaches one what a roving changeable set we colonists are, how easily moved to shift our quarters by any slight inducement, in the absence of the *fixing* power which old local and family associations possess at home.[26]

In 1887, 'Hopeful', that caustic reporter on Christchurch society, was aware not of its 'residential differentiation' and the attendant close-knit neighbourhoods, but of the 'roving disposition' of its people, expressed in the frequency of wife desertion, the high concentration of lodging houses, the disproportionate number of unsettled single men, and the absence (in contrast to England) of sentimental attachments 'to place, locality, or friends'.[27] True, such linguistic and literary documentation must be treated with caution since its typicality is difficult to prove and it could be unconsciously tainted by preconception. Even so, the implication that transience stunted class-consciousness deserves to be taken seriously because other evidence for the extraordinary restlessness of the population is so over-whelming. The next two sections discuss this evidence and advance explanations for transience itself.

Dimensions of Transience

Of all colonial behaviour, transience has perhaps been the subject of the greatest misunderstanding.[28] The prevailing historical interpretation is that most of the population was settled except during the gold-rushes, the Anglo-Maori wars, and the late 1880s (when the 'Great Exodus' to Australia took place), and with the exceptions of two particular social categories: those who 'drifted' from the South to the North Island late in the century, and 'swaggers'.[29]

Quantitative studies, using street directories, of the movements of household heads, however, show clearly that the phenomenon was to varying degrees normal to all strata everywhere over the whole period. The listings of household heads in this source are surprisingly complete. The total number of heads recorded for separate cities and towns deviates by no more than two per cent from the tabulations by the Census of occupied dwellings where the boundaries are the same. (The discrepancy is greater, however, for counties, where the directories missed out appreciable numbers of households.)[30] Street directories were published and compiled annually by private firms to give purchasers access to the names, addresses, occupations of possible clients. To determine the rate of transience the analysis follows the technique pioneered by North American historians.[31] In any one year all individual households in any given locality are noted and then systematically compared with the list of households for the same locality ten years later—the proportion who have disappeared constituting the transiency rate. So far 15 rural and urban localities have been examined using this method, most of them in the North Island over the last two decades of the century : Wellington, Hutt County, Johnsonville, Nelson, Greymouth, Oxford (West Canterbury), Marton, Masterton, Wanganui, Turakina (rural Wanganui), Levin, New Plymouth, Normanby, Patea, Blenheim (see Table 5.1). To be sure, a few households disappeared not because of shifting but because of the death of their sole member. As against that, our procedure understates the actual amount of migration. Firstly, it takes no account of households which moved in and out within the 10-year period. Secondly, the research has focused on the last three decades of the century and the most residentially unstable decades, the 1850s and 1860s, have thus been excluded. Thirdly, household heads were inherently far more stable then the occupants of hotels, and boarding and lodging houses, or servants and labourers who lived in, or young adult males who were family members. Finally, it takes no account of the many male household heads who left their families for long periods of the year in order to engage in casual work.

The median transience rate for the 15 localities is 57.5 per cent—

TABLE 5.1

Transience Rates for Households in Fifteen New Zealand Localities over the 19th Century

Place	Base Year	End Year	Proportion of Households disappearing between Base Year and End Year, or Rate of Transience (%)
Blenheim	1875/6	1885/6	58
Greymouth	1875/6	1885/6	76
Hutt County & West Coast (Wgtn)	1868	1878	58
Johnsonville	1875	1885	71
Johnsonville	1885	1900	70
Masterton	1872	1882	33
Masterton	1882	1892	42
Masterton	1892	1902	45
Marton	1881	1891	52
Marton	1891	1901	43
Nelson	1875/6	1885/6	57
New Plymouth	1878	1889	49
Normanby	1878	1889	74
Ohau (Levin)	1878	1888	50
Ohau (Levin)	1888	1898	66
Oxford	1878	1888	65
Oxford	1888	1898/99	48
Patea (& district)	1878	1889	63
Turakina (rural Wanganui)	1866	1876	51
Wanganui (town)	1866	1876	62
Wellington (city)	1868	1878	64
Wellington	1870	1880	59
Wellington	1880	1890	57
Wellington	1890	1900	53

Notes
1. *Sources*: D. Beaglehole, 'Geographical Mobility: Wellington 1880–1890', B.A. (Hons) History research paper, VUW, 1982; D. Beaglehole, 'Geographical Mobility, Wanganui and Turakina 1866–76', Hist. 316 research paper, VUW, 1980; P. M. Shone, 'Marton: New Zealand Geographical Mobility . . .', Hist. 316 research paper, VUW, 1981; M.

Harkness, 'Geographical Mobility in Wellington, 1868-78', Hist. 316
research paper, VUW, 1980; J. Pegden, 'Geographical Mobility of the
Levin Area from 1878 to 1929', Hist. 316 research paper, VUW, 1983;
F. McGrath, 'An Investigation into the Population Mobility of the Town
of Oxford between 1878 and 1949', Hist. 316 research paper, VUW,
1983; D. Robertson, 'Geographical Mobility: Rates of Persistence and
Transiency in Masterton 1872–1902', Hist. 316 research paper, VUW,
1984; R. B. MacBeth, 'Geographical Mobility in Taranaki, New Zealand
1878–1889', Hist. 316 research paper, VUW, 1983; A. Foster, 'A Survey
of Geographical Mobility in New Zealand: Blenheim, Nelson and
Greymouth 1875/6–1885/6, Hist. 316 research essay, VUW, 1983; D.
Pearson, *Johnsonville: Continuity and Change in a New Zealand Township*
(Sydney, 1980), p. 102.
2. Percentages are rounded off.

that is, there was about a six in 10 chance that any given household
would disappear from any given locality after a 10-year interval. To
assess the significance of this figure, we can compare it with the
rates adduced for different cities, towns, and counties in North America
for the 19th century, which generally range between 40 and 60 per
cent.[32] The comparison is revealing. American historians have
interpreted their rates as suggesting that North America was highly
unsettled. Their 40 to 60 per cent normal range, furthermore, is
partly composed from studies of adult males, who are more prone
to transience than households. Thus the New Zealand average rate
must be high, being towards the top end of the North American
scale.

Analysis of households by their land-owning makes it quite clear
that the lowest strata in colonial society (as in North America) had
the strongest migratory dispositions. Generally speaking, households
owning no land were two to three times more likely to disappear
from a locality than land-owning households. Taking the analysis
further, Table 5.2 gives the transience rates for four categories of
household heads according to the value of the land they owned in
a sample of localities. In every case the percentage of household heads
in the £1000 and over category who disappeared after 10 years is
far lower than the percentage for the household heads who owned
no land at all. In New Plymouth, for example, 35 per cent were
transient in the £1000 class, as against 66 per cent from the non-
owners class; in Marton only about five per cent of the £1000 category
were transient, whereas about 78 per cent of those without land
were transient; in Wellington City the rate of transience was about

16 per cent for the highest group, and 67 per cent for the non-owners; for Oxford the respective figures were about 33 per cent and 85 per cent.

TABLE 5.2

Transience Rates for Different Categories of Householders in Four
Localities
(% who disappeared after 10 years)

Place	Non-freeholder	Freeholders according to assessed value of their land in 1882		
		£1 to £499	£500 to £999	£1000 & over
New Plymouth	66	43	37	35
Marton	78	70	50	5
	(N=150)	(N=50)	(N=36)	(N=77)
Wellington	67	26	22	16
	(N=192)	(N=65)	(N=25)	(N=44)
Oxford	85	48	45	33
	(N=104)	(N=61)	(N=20)	N=27)

(N = number of transients and persisters combined)

Notes
1. Raw figures for New Plymouth are not available. The Wellington data have been derived from a systematic sampling of a total of 3460 household heads.
2. *Sources:* MacBeth, 'Geographical Mobility in Taranaki'; Shone, 'Marton: Geographical Mobility'; Beaglehole, 'Geographical Mobility: Wellington 1880-1890', Table 4:1, p. 41; McGrath, 'Population Mobility of Oxford'.
3. Percentages are rounded off.

The culture of a people in motion expressed itself in colonial architecture. The towns were full of boarding houses, lodging houses, houses advertising rooms to let and so forth. 'Hopeful' reported in 1887,

. . . I must tell you that in the chief towns of New Zealand a very considerable part of the town and its suburbs is entirely composed of lodging houses. There are many who endeavour to get their living solely by this means. . . . You may see in Christ Church, and other towns in the Colony, an incessant reminder that accommodation for the traveller or 'new chum' may be found here or there, the announcement written in large letters over the house or on a card, 'Board and Residence for Single Men,' 'Board and Residence,' 'Apartments to Let,' 'Furnished Apartments to Let,' 'Unfurnished Apartments;' then the daily papers have any amount of advertisements to the same effect, some of which strike a new comer as very remarkable.[33]

In 1879 Alfred Simmons uttered only one criticism of New Zealand, its failure to enfranchise its teeming population of lodgers: 'Hundreds, nay thousands of educated and more than averagely intelligent men, many of them holding substantial positions, permanently reside at spacious hotels, which are consequently very numerous, and are to be met with from one end of the colony to the other.'[34] The counterpart of the lodging house in rural and new areas was the one- or two-roomed shack. That these dwellings housed an impermanent population can be deduced from their small size, their construction from temporary, makeshift, materials—including timber slabs, sod, canvas, raupo—and from contemporary diaries and journals. When, for example, the 25-year-old bachelor, Thomas Arnold, arrived in Wellington in late May 1848, with the intention of going farming, he took up a section on Porirua Road in June where he built his 'own little warè' in August. He must have lived in it for a little over seven weeks in total, since he travelled through the top half of the South Island from early October to December, and although residing in Wellington in January and February the following year, he moved to Nelson in March where he became a teacher until leaving the colony in late 1849 after a brief visit to Wellington.[35] From Lady Barker's observations in 1867, it is apparent that single men were not the only temporary inhabitants of such dwellings in new areas:

> When a shepherd has saved a hundred pounds, or the better class of immigrant arrives with a little capital, the favourite investment is in freehold land, which they can purchase, in sections of twenty acres and upwards, at 2 *l* the acre. The next step is to build a sod hut with two rooms on their property, thatching it with Tohi, or swamp grass; a door and a couple of window-frames all ready glazed are brought from Christchurch in the dray with the family and the household goods. After this rough and ready shelter is provided, the father and sons begin fencing their land, and gradually it all assumes a cultivated appearance. . . . But the real fact is, that the poor farmer perhaps finds his section is too far from a market, so he is forced to abandon it and move nearer a town. . . .[36]

In addition to the quantitative and architectural evidence, the large size and composite nature of the floating population imprinted itself on a wide range of state activity. This is reflected in official preoccupations with vagrancy, one of the four most common offences, and the focus of attention by the newly formed Labour Department in 1891.[37] It is visible, too, in the legislature's convoluted attempts to discriminate between respectable and unrespectable transients whenever it extended the franchise. The 1875 Lodgers' Franchise Act enfranchised the sole lodgers of private homes, as long as they had resided in the same electorate for 12 months, but not men living in large boarding houses. Subsequently, in 1879, when all adult men were given the vote, those with less than six months' continuous residence in the electorate were excluded, a term which was reduced to three months in 1893.[38] The taxation policies of successive governments were likewise constrained by the volatility of the population. Before 1891 there was no system of personal income tax; most government revenue came from customs duties and the receipts of land sales. The Grey Government in 1878 introduced a land tax, but this was abolished in favour of a wider-ranging tax on property in 1879, which in turn was replaced by a graduated land tax (with a partial income tax component) in 1891. The ostensible reason for the 1878 measure was to lighten the burden of individual taxation on the 'labouring classes'. John Ballance, the Colonial Treasurer, stated quite explicitly that he thought an income tax would be far less suitable for this purpose, even though it had been introduced in England, because in England 'the settled nature of society and of commerce renders it much more easy to impose such a tax than in a young country, where there is a shifting population, and where commerce is much more variable in its nature'.[39] Similarly, concern about itinerancy was the driving force behind the closer land settlement schemes pursued by most governments from the early 1880s. As one parliamentarian acknowledged in 1895: 'With reference to the remark made as to the population of New Zealand being a very migratory one, that is perfectly true; but all the legislation we are indulging in in reference to land is in the direction of endeavouring to attach the people to the land, and to settle them there.'[40]

In regions where transience was most common, furthermore, it had a devastating impact on civic virtue. The administration of Westland County (1868–73) and Province (1873–76), for example, was characterised by gross dishonesty and ineptitude, unchecked by the voting population of goldminers who did not stay long enough in the region to feel disadvantaged by the chaos.[41]

The incessant swirl of people through each locality also flattened regional variation in dress, speech, diet, leisure pursuits, work habits, aspirations, and so forth. Historians have correctly stressed that structurally some areas differed from others—especially in demography up to the 1880s, in the distribution of land, transport facilities, education services, in the degree of industrial development, in economic growth. But what they have overlooked is that with some exceptions cultural uniformity was superimposed upon these structural dissimilarities. Geographical mobility was so strong everywhere that it homogenised the lifestyles of colonists, and prevented almost every locality from insulating itself from the wider society to the point where it could evolve its own sub-culture.

Explanations for Transience
The emerging consensus in the literature on geographical mobility in 19th-century North America and Australia is that there were strong connections between transience, age, and vertical mobility. Up to about the age of 30 men tended to be the most migratory, as they searched avidly for opportunities to 'get on' (usually equated with the acquisition of landed capital), marry, form households, become pillars of the local community. Thereafter transient proclivities diminished sharply, with the big exception of men who failed to 'get on' and ended their lives unmarried, unpropertied, and permanent members of the casual labour force. In short, transients can be divided into two categories, the 'strivers', the younger men who still had a chance of succeeding in life, and the 'derelicts' who had lost the chance.[42] How, then, does New Zealand relate to this pattern? Unfortunately our archival data are so limited that it is impossible to say. We cannot determine with a reasonable degree of rigour why some men ·eventually settled down while others became derelicts, nor the likely strength of the derelict element in the total population of colonial flotsam and jetsam. Our explanations for transience, therefore, unavoidably compound the two categories and to that extent are unsatisfactory.

    Fundamental to the domination of transience in colonial life were four mutually reinforcing factors. The first was the Arcadian myth of New Zealand as a land of natural abundance with boundless opportunities to achieve competencies. Instead of generating aspirations for a static life of patient industry, of ease and tranquillity, taking things as they came, the myth of abundance inflamed desire and hope until they were converted into a mentality of ceaseless striving. A working man and new immigrant, W. M. Burton, was thus affected when, in a letter from Taranaki in 1875, he wrote, 'The desire to find a cheap and pleasant home has made me a wanderer for some time'.[43] Specific themes in the mythology, furthermore, actually taught colonists that itinerancy was essential to 'getting on'. The 'Erewhon syndrome', the conviction that better, as-yet-undiscovered resources and opportunities lay waiting 'over the range', was widespread. In addition the idea of the 'rural apprenticeship' expressly commanded the property seeker to gain 'character' and experience by shifting from job to job in the backblocks.

The second factor was demographic: as noted in the previous chapter, the population included a disproportionately large number of single adult males and immigrants who were more able to move about than men encumbered by family responsibilities and local attachments. The demographic structure, it might be added, strongly implies that up to the late 1880s the number of 'derelicts' would have been very small.

The third unsettling condition in the colonial environment was the spectrum of jobs which were inherently itinerant or were highly conducive to restless urges. The police authorities, for example, shifted constables often from place to place to prevent them from integrating with local people; employees in bureaucracies with many branches around the country—bank officers and civil servants, for example—moved frequently as a means of promotion; atrocious accommodation in new areas caused a high turnover of discontented primary schoolteachers; the reluctance of sheep station owners to accommodate family men forced single hands wanting to marry to change domicile; a combination of loneliness and a favourable marriage market was the cause of the residential mobility of domestic servants in rural areas; 53 per cent of Presbyterian clergymen spent five years or less in their pastorates over the period 1840 to 1901.[44] Most job-related migration, however, was built into three types of blue-collar employment. One was goldmining, gumdigging, timber-milling and other kinds of extractional work. What made these jobs short-lived was that their raw material was both limited and highly unpredictable. For example, E. B. Fitton in 1856 wrote of sawyers, 'This employment . . . is generally followed by a roving class of men, who, when the timber is cleared away in one locality, go off and take up a new abode, wherever they can find employment, either in the same settlement or elsewhere.'[45] The second type, seasonal work, was by definition of limited duration. When the yearly task on one property was over the men were forced to find work elsewhere—bush-felling in the North Island from June to December; shearing in the North Island in November and December and in the south in January and February; haymaking in January; harvesting grass seed in the East

Coast, Wellington, and Christchurch areas in late summer; harvesting grain in the South Island and potatoes in Oamaru from March to April; grass-seeding and fencing in late autumn; ploughing in August and September; rabbit-poisoning in June and July.[46] The third, construction work, was also inherently short-lived, for once the project—the road, railway, building, telegraphic line—was completed, the men were compelled to search for work elsewhere. Had settlement and economic activity been spatially concentrated, as in Australia, the men in these impermanent jobs need not have changed domicile to find new ones; which is a good reason for believing that the New Zealand population was more itinerant than the Australian.

TABLE 5.3

Occupations Most Prone to Transience

	1874 Number	1874 % of total workforce	1896 Number	1896 % of total workforce
Primary				
Kauri gumdiggers	227	0.17	3,343	1.14
Gold miners	15,438	12.16	13,055	4.45
Sawyers	1,926	1.51	3,436	1.17
Other Primary (excluding employers)	27,539	21.69	74,681	25.49
Construction				
Houses etc.	5,694	4.48	3,345	1.14
Roading etc.	2,158	1.70	3,530	1.20
Labourers (undefined)	7,880	6.20	16,299	5.56
Stevedores	71	0.05	823	0.28
Flaxmill employees	507	0.39	418	0.14
Freezing workers	NA	NA	1,334	0.45
Other Labourers	NA	NA	3,160	1.07
Total	61,440	48.3	123,424	42.1

Note
Data taken from 1874 and 1896 Censuses.

Conjectures about the number of people engaged in short-lived manual jobs vary from the Department of Labour's assertion in 1893 that 'the bulk of the manual work is only suited to a nomadic population', to Bradshaw's impression in 1883 that 'A large percentage of the working people are migratory', to a modern historian's estimate of one fifth of male breadwinners in 1891.[47] Directory listings of household heads understate its extent by taking no account of the side occupations of 'farmers' as casual labourers, and by omitting single men who were far more foot-loose than household heads. A better idea can be gleaned from the occupational data in the census. Table 5.3 enumerates all the manual occupations whose holders, from what we can tell from contemporary job descriptions, were likely to be migratory, either full-time or part-time. Non-employing farmers and pastoralists have been included on the grounds that so many were part-time casuals. The total is substantial, representing just under half of all 'breadwinners' (male and female) in 1874 and not much less than that in 1896.

The fourth fundamental destabiliser of the colonial population was the presence of sharp but fluctuating differences in economic growth and prosperity from region to region or even within regions (which takes no account of the disparities between New Zealand and the Australian colonies). The Registrar-General noted in 1921, when matching the place of birth given in birth certificates of the New Zealand-born with the residences on the Census schedules for an age-representative sample of the population: 'Thirty or forty years ago the rate of progress and development of the various districts exhibited more divergence than is now the case, and probably conduced to greater internal movement of the population.' He was surprised at how many people aged 65 and over lived at a distance from their places of birth in New Zealand.[48] 'Hopeful' commented in 1887 that 'a Colonist rarely attaches himself to any particular town or place, he is always ready to move elsewhere should things appear brighter or more lucrative in another part'.[49] William Orchard revealed an acute knowledge of variations in the living costs and remuneration between different parts of New Zealand, which drove him hither and thither to maximise his advantages. A Cornishman, Orchard emigrated to South Australia in the late 1840s, tried his luck on the Victorian diggings in the 1850s, shifted to the New Zealand goldfields in the 1860s, then returned to Melbourne in the late 1870s. He recalled in his journal:

In N.Z., if things got bad in one place we sought another. We have travelled all over N.Z. by coach, waggon and steamer and never made any mistakes. When things got dull at Christchurch or the E. Coast we crossed the Dividing range (perpetually covered with snow) with a 6 horse waggon to the West Coast where we made more money. One side of the range eggs were 3/- per dozen and butter 3/- per pound while on the Christchurch side (Canterbury Plain) we could buy these eggs for 6^d per dozen and the butter for 5^d per lb, but that showed it was a poor place. In one place I could earn 10/- per day and in the other 30/- (a rolling stone gathers no moss they say). That old adage might hold good in England where things are much about the same in all parts of it, but it does not do out here where things are so fluctuating. . . .

My idea is to get as far away from old settled places as possible, follow up the new places where labour is well paid.[50]

Similar temptations to change domicile in pursuit of real or illusory better prospects are implicit in a host of biographies. Richmond Hursthouse, born in New Plymouth in 1845 to John and Helen Hursthouse, shifted with his parents to Nelson in 1860 (as part of the great exodus of the European population upon the outbreak of the land wars), returned to serve two years with Atkinson's bushrangers; in 1868 he went to the Thames gold-rush; soon after he moved to Melbourne where he worked as an engineer (1868–71); then in 1871 he travelled to the Gulgong rush, subsequently crossed the Tasman again to the Coromandel diggings; then moved to Nelson in 1875 where he tried farming and was member for Motueka until 1884; from there he shifted to Wanganui before dying in New Plymouth in 1902. Another case is that of John Wain. Emigrating as a boy from London in 1850 accompanying his employer, he stayed initially in Port Chalmers working as a handyman, went in the early 1850s with his father to the Victoria diggings where they lived for two years, returned to Dunedin and worked there for a few days, moved to Half-Way Bush for one year, shifted to West Taieri where for six months he handsawed timber, returned to Dunedin and after a series of odd jobs became a transport contractor and part-owner of livery stables; with the discovery of gold at Gabriel's Gully he tried his luck there for six weeks, went back to Dunedin, sold his share in the livery business and bought a hotel, which he operated in conjunction with a coaching business; then leasing the hotel, he became a contract railroad builder, living all over Otago, before settling in the vicinity of Dunedin. The gold-rushes and the urge 'to get on' are associated with the foot-loose career of another man, George Pain. After landing in Petone with his parents in 1840, he went to Johnsonville in 1855 where he worked on a farm for

10 years; subsequently he walked to the Wairarapa and worked on a sheep station for a year, shifted to another sheep station where 'I began to chafe at the slowness of life, and like all young fellows, I was looking forward to getting a wife, and I felt that if I were to make money faster, I must try something else'; he therefore saved £100 from buying and selling horses as a side occupation, and resigning his job, travelled to Wellington, bought a stock of clothes with his savings and became an itinerant seller in the Wairarapa; with the discovery of gold at Thames, he travelled there to try his luck and within three months lost everything; returning to Wellington, he went back to his hawking job; after three years of this he saved enough to buy a 100-acre property; he then bought a general store and ended up settling in the Martinborough district as an owner of several large sheep stations and a brick works.[51]

Lastly, much of the volatility of colonials stemmed from the fact that although entering the ranks of minor proprietors was relatively easy, progress from there into the middling strata was exceptionally difficult. As this reality was obscured by the optimism of the ideology, most small proprietors were doomed to prolonged wandering, frustrated with their existing achievements, always expecting to do better at the next destination. It was the potency of these unrealistic hopes that accounts for the surprisingly high rates of transience of most landowners, since the small were by far the majority. It explains, also, the inverse relationship, indicated by Table 5.2, between the value of land-ownerships and migratory proclivities. The tiny number of household heads with the largest land values had least incentive to quit the locality, which had more or less satisfied the desire for complete and comfortable independence. The large quantity of household heads in the lowest land-owning category, by contrast, had far less reason to settle in the district because their competencies were incomplete. The medium owners were more transient than the largest and less than the smallest, since their landed capital was neither sufficient nor inadequate for a 'competency' but somewhere in between.

The obstructions to the rise of the smallest owners contradict the colony's view of itself as a place of unlimited wealth-making. In part they seem to be attributable to the land aggregation activities of the large estate owners. If the landholdings enumerated in the 1896 Census for the nine provinces are divided into three categories— the small (one acre to 100), medium (101 acres to 5,000) and large (over 5,000 acres)—there is a very strong tendency for the provinces with the biggest percentages of large holdings to have the lowest percentage of medium holdings (Rs = –0.90, significant at the .01 level). But much more analysis is needed before we can conclude that the large estates restricted the growth in numbers of medium holdings by creating a shortage of land for settlement, thus trapping the 'strivers' in the small category. The obstructions also seem to have resulted from the limited opportunity for small capitalists to produce for the market. Their general inability to raise export staples, as well as the fragmentation of the economy into a multitude of dwarf markets, severely reduced the demand for goods and services produced locally and thus circumscribed the capacity to accumulate capital from profits. These market restraints expressed themselves not only in the relatively high transience of small proprietors, but also in the high proportion of production consumed within the home, in the unspecialised nature of local production, in the clamour for more local amenities which would attract migration from outside and push up the number of potential clients and customers, in 'do-it-yourself' as a means of conserving scarce cash, and in the high frequency of second occupations.[52] Small owners were also greatly addicted to land speculation as a way of compensating for the meagre incomes they earned from the land. The possibility that they deliberately shifted about in search for the places with the best openings for land speculation is suggested by their inclination to possess multiple-holdings and its corollary : that rates of transience were many times higher among multiple-title than single-title holders.[53]

To escape the small-owner trap without migrating essentially required inherited wealth or appropriate political connections, which of course negated the whole idea of New Zealand as a place of equal opportunity. The alternative was extreme occupational versatility, to be the supplier of as many goods and services to a locality as possible. James Bodell, for example, once an imperial soldier and then a hotelier in Tasmania and Victoria, where he lost his capital, came to New Zealand as a sergeant in the Waikato Militia, was demoted to private, and in 1864 went to Tauranga as a military settler, remaining there from the completion of his service in 1866 until he died in 1892. The key to his ability to sink roots in that tiny and unpromising town was that after a brief and unsuccessful stint at gold prospecting, he, in his own words, 'undertook the duties of Town Barber, Undertaker and Builder, Cordial and Ginger beer, Hop beer & Cider Maker', to which he progressively added the occupations of photographer, auctioneer and commission agent, insurance agent, grocer, estate agent, land speculator, rentier, general merchant, collector of rents and debts, agent for Auckland lawyers, sawmill owner, shipping proprietor.[54] The weaker economic growth and the greater frequency of 'bad years' after 1880, however, would have diminished the returns from occupational versatility. For this reason many small proprietors were finally pushed into adopting a radical option, to support the breakup of nearby large estates, so as to give the smallest owners access to larger plots of land, and to increase the size of the local population so that the demand for goods and services in the immediate area would expand. The Liberals won votes in and around the small towns (the backbone of their power) in 1890 and after by offering precisely this redistributionist alternative to transience.

The Transience Model Questioned

The assumption that high transience stunted the class-consciousness and propensity to associate of the lower strata, may be questioned on various grounds. One is Tamara Hareven's research on French-Canadian factory workers of Amoskeag in New Hampshire over the late 19th and early 20th centuries, which shows that their itinerancy operated within an effective framework of kinship-based mutual aid, implying, in turn, that itinerancy does not necessarily keep people apart.[55] In fact, however, these kinship ties were integrated with factory paternalism and did not create class solidarity; and, besides, the Amoskeag case-study is irrelevant to New Zealand. As the next chapter will demonstrate, colonial workers, unlike their French-Canadian counterparts, just did not have the capacity for kinship formation.

Another claim is that migratory manual workers compensated for frequently ruptured primary relationships (with, say, neighbours and workmates) by being avid joiners of organisations, of churches and sporting clubs, and thus maintained their social affiliations at the institutional though not at the personal level.[56] But, as we shall again see in the following chapter, the lower strata, for the most part, did not have the leisure and other requisites for membership of formal groupings, so this objection to our model is inapplicable as well.

The other possible criticism might be based on Eric Hobsbawm's classic essay on the 19th-century tramping artisan in England.[57] Hobsbawm implies that transience was perfectly compatible with trade unionism. In fact it boosted it, for unions encouraged some of their members to move out of the district and tramp for a period between branches of the union looking for work, receiving a sustenance allowance at each one; a strategy intended, by reducing the labour supply, to lessen the chance of black-legging during strikes and to maintain union bargaining power during slack periods of employment. But this counter-example also fails to throw doubt on our assumptions, for there is no evidence that New Zealand trade unions operated tramping systems, and it is quite unlikely, given their general precariousness, that they had the capacity to do so.

2: Mateship

The second implicit attack on the 'insider's view' that New Zealand was not class-divided comes from J. O. C. Phillips in his interpretation of 'mateship' in colonial rural society. It should be noted that Phillips relates 'mateship' to gender-division and not expressly to class-division, as the 'insider's view' understands it. Nonetheless, his notion has strong parallels with the concept used by some left-wing historians of 'primitive rebels', peasants, and workers (invariably men, usually in a rural setting) who are alienated from society and consciously opt for a rough lifestyle which they know the dominant classes find offensive, disorderly and threatening, but whose conduct is 'pre-political', not inspired by a radical political ideology.[58]

Phillips agrees that males in the colonial lower strata were phenomenally unsettled and lived outside voluntary organisations as well as the family unit, but claims that they formed 'mateship' ties instead, intimate bonds with other men, and that these relationships were part of a wider floating male 'community' fostering the values of sharing, egalitarianism, and 'machoism'. It was, he says, 'in the rural and frontier regions that exclusively male communities developed and where a male culture was most likely to develop' amongst men like goldminers, gumdiggers and the labourers of backblock stations. Extreme transience, he implies, did not engender atomisation at all:

> It was natural that in sharing the physical burdens of work and the delirious joys of leisure, men should develop close personal relationships. As in Australia, a tradition of mateship quickly emerged. Usually for functional reasons of safety and cooperation on the job, a close relationship between two men would be established. The trusting, if unemotional, nature of this relationship would flow into the wider mateship of the male community. This was an informal and highly egalitarian community where nicknames were quickly substituted for surnames.[59]

Although little hard evidence has been adduced for these claims they will be taken seriously, partly because they are derived from a much more substantial work on 'mateship' in Australia by Russel Ward, which does invite comparisons with New Zealand,[60] and partly because the migratory flow of casual labour between town and country suggests that, if the argument is correct, 'mateship' would have been common amongst the urban lower strata as well.

If 'mateship' were a powerful and common agency of association then its existence should have been displayed in three forms : a high frequency of male peer relationships, an enduring and distinctive collection of norms characteristic of an 'out-group', and an environment highly conducive to stable and intense interaction between foot-loose men.

A High Frequency of Male Relationships?

As with the other requisites of the mateship model, this element is exceedingly difficult to test, the men having left so few traces of their behaviour in contemporary records. The available scraps of systematic data, however, do not support the hypothesis that pair-bonding was a major feature. They point instead to the prevalence of the 'man alone', the loner.

One setting showing this is the criminal courts, the cases before which yield rich insights into the world of the male drifter, the chief category of offender. If it is agreed that boon companions in legitimate activity would also have recruited one another for the illegitimate, and that in a mateship society group and joint offenders would comprise most of the offenders, then 'close male relationships' must have been unusual. Joint and group offenders feature in only eight of the 81 cases of petty violence before the Wellington Magistrate's Court in 1866; 10 of the 106 cases of theft in the same court for the three years 1865-7; 20 of the 182 cases of vagrancy before the Wellington Magistrate's Court during the two years 1875-6; seven of the 35 cases of vagrancy before the Kaiapoi, Christchurch, and Lyttelton Magistrates' Courts from June 1866 to June 1868; and 21 of the 192 violence cases appearing in the Wellington Magistrate's Court for the three years from 1870 to 1872.[61] Past societies with bonding systems known to be strong produced much greater proportions of criminals who operated in associations. One example is early 14th-century England where 55 per cent of felons before the courts had accomplices; another example is England from 1560 to 1640 where a median of just over 60 per cent of the vagrancy cases involved groups of two or more persons.[62]

Death was another context in which the 'man alone' rather than 'mateship' was prominent. Amongst the evidence here is the missing details on the death certificates of 378 adult bachelors, all with manual occupations, who died in Wellington City over selected years between 1876 and 1890. The officiating doctor or coroner was required to fill in a standard form supplying biographical details on 14 items, including cause of death, name of the deceased, address, age, occupation, place of birth, length of time spent in New Zealand, father's name, father's occupation, mother's christian and maiden names, and so forth. The doctor or coroner would have had little trouble in obtaining these data if among the bedside mourners or grief-stricken at the inquest were a faithful friend or group of 'mates' familiar with the past life and background of the deceased. Yet in 43 per cent of the documents the certificating officer failed to specify place of birth, the length of time spent in New Zealand, the father's name, father's occupation, and mother's christian and maiden names. In a further 15 per cent, father's name, father's occupation, and mother's maiden and christian names were left blank, and in seven per cent the father's name, father's occupation, mother's maiden and married names, and years spent in the colony. In total, 65 per cent of the certificates were left incomplete. The dead were sufficiently anonymous, alone in the world, for no one to be aware of key aspects of their biographies.[63]

Indicating that this situation was not unique to Wellington, was the failure of coroners all over New Zealand to put names to a considerable number of Europeans who died from drowning in inland waterways.[64] For the years 1851–1887, 2,235 persons were officially recorded as having drowned in inland waterways; of these 127 could not be named, about six per cent of the total. To be consistent with 'mateship' theory the rate should have been lowest in those periods and provinces where the 'male community' had reached its fullest development and 'close relationships' between men were at their most prolific. The facts speak otherwise. The rate of unidentified corpses was highest in Otago/Southland at the height of the gold-rushes, 1861–5, with an incidence of 19 per cent; followed by Westland in the same period, 16 per cent; and Nelson Province, likewise in a gold-rush period, 1866–70, of nine per cent. Significantly, extreme transients themselves believed that their own kind died alone. One reminisced, 'To crawl into the scrub or bush or tall tussock, or to fall into some ditch along the road or rail to die, was not an unusual ending for men of that old and vanished brigade.' People close to extreme transients had the same impression. A former West Coast surveyor wrote that 'right along the West Coast you will find graves. . . . Some wandered into the bush, some died by the riverside. They had no further use for life and no friends. They cashed their last cheques at death's counter and passed silently into the forgotten.' Gilkison's anecdotal history of Otago published in 1930 claims that 'The number of men who disappeared and were never heard of again was very large.'[65]

Symptomatic, too, of the insubstantiality of pair-bonding and the 'male community' is the low rates of membership and survival of rural trade unions. In Australia 'mateship' provided the building blocks for the growth of a powerful pastoral union from 1886, the Amalgamated Shearers' Union, which in turn produced the organisational base for the penetration of the Labour Party into the rural electorates of New South Wales.[66] In New Zealand, by contrast, there was no rural Labour Party and the various attempts to unionise the shearers collapsed very quickly: a handful of localised bodies emerged in the South Island over the 1870s and lasted for a season; from 1886 the Amalgamated Shearers' Union tried to set up branches in New Zealand but none survived the year 1888; finally a Shearers' and Labourers' Union operated between 1896 and 1898 before collapsing.[67]

The extreme individualism of the single male is also attested by the published schedules for the 1892 Department of Labour survey on the expenditure of working men. Five of the 106 respondents were single men occupying their own households; from the internal evidence there is no indication that any shared their dwellings. This pattern is quite consistent with the growing provision by the state from the 1880s for the welfare of elderly men: the number of inmates aged 65 and over in old men's homes expanded from 247 in 1885 to 658 by 1900, old age pensions were introduced in 1898, and by 1901 40 per cent of Europeans over 65 were receiving the pension despite the strict eligibility criteria. These measures to some extent reflected the upsurge in the absolute and relative size of the elderly population and their comparative poverty; but they also signify the obvious limits of informal mutual aid and thus the ties between transient men.[68]

An Enduring and Distinctive Normative Code?
True, there are plenty of examples of reciprocity between strangers, including the 'shouting' of drinks, making contributions to

subscriptions for the sick and injured, miners offering shelter and food to wayfarers, and so on. Many extreme transients praised the generosity of their fellows. Theophilus Cooper wrote in his diary at the Thames goldfield on 28 November 1867 that diggers were on the whole 'ready to do a good turn, ready to render a helping hand, ready to sympathise, to give good advice to all who are in need of it'. But these examples cannot be taken to signify the existence of 'the male community' because a wealth of counter-examples reveal extreme transients as having no sense of obligation and collective morality at all. Theophilus Cooper added to the statement above, 'Yet there are many very indifferent characters among them [the diggers], ready to take every mean advantage of ignorance, simplicity, or helplessness.'[69] Gilkison's *Early Days in Central Otago* relates many nasty incidents on newly discovered goldfields before they obtained Warden's Courts, the official institutions responsible for registering claims and arbitrating disputed claims. One of Henry Scott's main tasks when he took charge of the shearing shed at Rocklands Station for the season was to settle disputes between shearers over tallies. In his memoirs Thorne Seccombe recorded at length the mean deceit, which no one stopped, of drovers who sold a worthless horse to an innocent stable-man in Rotorua. The word 'mate' was used by a Wairarapa casual labourer, W. J. Cox, not as a term of affection and attachment but in a neutral and detached sense to describe anyone he happened to work or travel with and including not only men he liked but also those he detested or was indifferent to. Frequent in Cox's remarkable diary are the references to 'workmates' whose laziness and incompetence upset Cox's working rhythms, slowed him down, forced him to shoulder an unfair burden of the work, and caused breakages of machinery and equipment which led the whole team to lose earning-time. To these examples can be added the quantitative evidence showing that frontier areas suffered from a great deal of interpersonal conflict.[70]

This leaves 'machoism' as a possible indicator of an alternative male social organisation. On the face of it extreme transients belonged to what Wolfgang and Ferracuti call a 'subculture of violence'.[71] Men unlisted in the street directories and electoral rolls (a sure sign of absence of domicile) were over-represented amongst the violent offenders appearing before the courts. The number per capita of convictions for violence, furthermore, peaked during the least settled phase of the 19th century (from the 1850s to the 1870s), and historically, from 1853 to 1931, it had a strong statistical relationship with the distribution across the nine provinces of adult males, of (in a negative direction) adult females, and of proxy measures of transience and new areas of settlement.*

Examined more closely, however, the sub-culture explanation for violence carries little weight. Several factors strongly suggest that violence was not the result of social pressures exerted within lower strata male groups. To start with, the number of convictions for petty violence per 100,000 males aged 21–40, the category most 'at risk', which rarely fell below 1,200 cases a year between 1853 and 1880, fell sharply over the last two decades of the century, reaching 628 by 1900. The sheer magnitude of this decline over a 20-year period suggests that violence was not an esteemed value cultivated by male peer groups. The traits and norms of groups are not so easily changed; only the behaviour of isolated individuals could have been tamed so radically. The drop, furthermore, could not have been induced by shifts in the mode of policing, court procedures, public reporting habits (see the section on 'Interpersonal Violence' in Chapter VII). In addition, as will be seen in a later chapter, civil litigation had a strong connection with violence; as civil litigation, the taking of legal remedies to resolve a dispute, is not assumed to be a 'macho' characteristic, the connection between the two suggests that violence was not, either. Lastly, what discounts the sub-culture model is that the colony threw up only three robber gangs of three or more members apiece, all three confined to the 1860s decade. One gang of four in September 1863 held up a bank official on the Tuapeka–Waipori Road, and was never heard of again; another was the 'Garrett Gang', with approximately seven members (witnesses were not agreed as to how many exactly); and the 'Maungatapu Murderers', a foursome— making a total of about 15, a tiny number when it is remembered that New Zealand's six sister colonies, especially New South Wales and Victoria, bred perhaps 300 bushrangers between 1861 and 1880, the Ned Kelly gang being the most famous example.[72] The three gangs, what is more, must have been exceptionally loose-knit, for they enjoyed but a fleeting existence. The 'Garrett Gang's' thieving was restricted to a series of hold-ups over one *day* on 18 October 1861, at Maungatua in Otago. The most notorious deed of the 'Maungatapu Murderers' was the robbery and cold-blooded killing of five travellers on 12–13 June 1866 in Nelson; by the time the

---

*In statistical analysis, a proxy measure is one that is used in place of a variable which cannot be employed in the analysis because of insufficient data. The proxy, to be valid, should be symptomatic of the same condition.

'murderers' were arrested six days later they had been together for less than three weeks; and although two of the members had been 'mates' since 1862, it is significant that it took an abnormal institutional context (their confinement in the Dunedin gaol, 1862–5), to cement their relationship. To put the ephemeral nature of both groups into perspective, it should be noted that the Ned Kelly gang in Victoria, Australia, lasted for two years (1878–1880) and that the average life span of a bandit-group in a peasant society is from two to three years, according to Eric Hobsbawm in his *Bandits* (1969). Moreover, whereas the 'Murderers' were the targets of popular hatred, the Kelly Gang was then and later the source of popular romance and received enough regional and local sympathy and support (especially from kin) to prolong its life, factors which Hobsbawm says are essential to the longevity of bandit-groups.[73]

Mechanisms of Stable and Intense Interaction?
Without doubt the colony contained a multitude of settings in which foot-loose males met and mixed. At the same time, however, little of the contact within these settings was sufficiently sustained and intense to yield pair-bonds and an alternative value system.

   In the first place, a large but unquantifiable segment of the floating labour force was not permanent but consisted of 'temporaries' and 'intermittents', men whose short or disrupted working careers did not allow them to forge links with other floaters. Among the temporaries were newly arrived immigrants like Henry Scott, who came to New Zealand in 1873 aged 22 and spent the next three or so years drifting around the south of the South Island working in turn as a farm-labourer, policeman, cutting a track on contract, shooting pigs on contract, labouring on a sheep station, foreman of a shearing shed, operating a horse team, gold-prospecting, as a bushman, and a collector of newspaper subscriptions, until he finally settled down as a journalist for the *Licensed Victualler's Gazette*. When the creditors took over his Epping brickworks, J. W. Reed, whose son was co-founder of the well-known publishing firm, emigrated to Auckland in 1887 with his wife and four children. Unable to find employment in Auckland, and leaving his family behind, he went to Otorohanga where he tried working in a navvy gang. Not accustomed to physical toil, he was sacked, and travelled to North Auckland where he made a living from gumdigging, and within about a year had saved enough money to buy 29 acres near Whangarei, which he farmed over the next 20-odd years, supplementing his income with gumdigging and contracting.[74] A further class of temporaries were normally settled labourers and artisans who, as the Department of Labour reported in 1895, were shaken out of their niches in the bad years and returned to them when prosperity returned. Some of these men ended up in navvy gangs under the co-operative system instituted by the Department of Public Works in 1891: 'Without discrimination, the saw-sharpener, and the boot-polisher, and the best Irish navvies were all put on together'.[75] Temporaries also included short-stay immigrants, especially during the gold-rush decade of the 1860s when 195,000 persons came to New Zealand and 81,000 poured out again.[76] In addition to the temporaries, intermittents bulked large in the itinerant labour force. Farmers and farmers' sons must have been well-represented here for many sources refer to their dependence on secondary employment in a wide range of extractional and seasonal jobs. For example, some of the navvies in Otago during the 1870s were small farmers looking for cash; Mrs Hamlin of Northern Wairoa had practically to manage the farm and house by herself, as her husband was away contracting most of the time, and came home only once a month; a settler's wife in the Rangitikei, Mrs McKenzie, and her daughters milked 80 cows and kept the farm going while the husband and sons were away at work; the settlers in the Forty-Mile and Seventy-Mile Bush areas migrated for months at a time to the Manawatu for bush-felling contracts; small farmers from the Nelson region made an annual trek to Marlborough and Canterbury during the shearing season, and so on.[77]

Working and travelling patterns reinforced the atomising effects of the high turnover within the ranks of extreme transients. To a large extent, the organisation of seasonal, extractional, and construction work was not based on permanent work-teams with a regular personnel and fixed division of labour, each gang travelling as a complete unit from work site to work site, undertaking the same functions at each place; instead the groupings were temporary and on-the-spot formations; each recruited from a (predominantly) random collection of wayfarers for a specific job and disbanded after the task had been completed, the men then going their separate ways.

The characteristic work-team of the 1860s, except at the highly capitalised and mechanised work-places, was made up of partnerships between self-employed men, usually two in number, rarely more than five, entering into highly informal arrangements for operating a mining claim, or some other 'get rich quick' scheme. From all accounts the partnerships were frequently the spontaneous creations of total strangers who met by chance in a pub, on the road, in a store, and so forth. The same looseness and informality predisposed these groupings to a brief existence. Partly this was a response to the speculative nature of mining and other ventures during the 1860s, as well as to the intrinsic impermanence of most successful claims and localised booms in the same decade. When Edwin Hodder, for example, spent six weeks on the goldfields in Aorere in the late 1850s, he belonged to two quite different work groups.[78] Often, too, partnerships were dissolved almost as soon as they were formed because of the feverish sense of one or another of the partners that better opportunities lay elsewhere. W. J. Barry recorded in his memoirs that when he arrived in Dunedin from Melbourne in early 1862, he first sold the horses, carts, and harnesses he brought with him, then over the next year led a wandering life, engaging in a quick succession of operations. He hawked five van loads of fish on the road with a former Ballarat acquaintance who happened to come along and then split with him, for Barry wanted 'to have a look around awhile', whereas the other wanted to go butchering or prospecting. Then Barry became a dealer in flour by himself, and while travelling in search of animals to purchase for a butcher's shop at Dunstan, he fell in with two men he knew, with one of whom he went prospecting for a day before they parted, Barry going off by himself in search of livestock, the acquaintance staying to pan for gold—Barry never mentioning him again. During this search Barry teamed up with another man, Grindley, to butcher sheep on the roadside to sell to diggers, before this equally brief partnership was terminated by an unspecified misunderstanding. Five months later Barry returned to Dunstan, and subsequently in 1863 moved to Cromwell where he more or less settled.[79]

Another example of the discontinuity of relationships between wandering men in the 1860s is given by Charles Money, an Englishman and bachelor of middle-class parentage who arrived in New Zealand in 1861, practically penniless (although he appears to have received occasional remittances from Home), and returned to England in 1868, staying, that is, a mere seven years. Over this period Money changed jobs 41 times, taking on approximately 14 different occupations, sometimes self-employed, sometimes on wages. Most of his jobs were prospecting (nine times), back-packing goods (six or seven times), road-making/bush-clearing/surveyor's chainman (six times). Three times he held commissions in the Colonial Defence Force; once or twice he worked as a cadet on a sheep station, also as a station-hand, contract fencer, canoe/boat hand, firewood contractor, post-and-rail splitter, puddle-machine operator, clerk, baker's assistant, carpenter, operator of a circulating library. A restless urge to try his hand at anything going, as well as the inherent instability of the work he took on, led Money to roam at one time or another through all New Zealand's provinces bar Hawke's Bay, Southland, and Marlborough. He was a member of 13 different work-teams, only some of them for goldmining, lasting an average of about five weeks. When a job finished, the partnership was dissolved, and its members usually dispersed; although he parted amicably from his work-friends, his relationship with them apparently meant so little to him that he seldom travelled with any of them. Rarely did he see them again, or try to. Only with one man, Rowley, did he re-form a partnership. His first partnership was with Fitzgerald and another for three months on the Otago diggings, mining a claim. The next was with Rowley for an unstated period; they tried their luck on another part of the Otago diggings, jointly sold their services as guides across the Southern Alps, and went prospecting at Westport and built a store. Rowley and Money then teamed up with two others to engage in gold prospecting at Waimangaroa, which lasted a month. The fourth partnership saw Rowley and Money as a twosome again, for an unknown period, back-packing supplies on contract and bush-clearing, also it seems at Waimangaroa. He subsequently parted from Rowley, and his fifth partnership was with three unnamed men who prospected for gold at Waimangaroa, this team lasting seven to eight months. The sixth was with a former Lancashire coalminer, 'Lanky'; the two of them went prospecting for a month at Waimangaroa. With the seventh, Money teamed up with two unnamed sawyers for a few weeks, prospecting somewhere on the West Coast. Next, he collaborated with an unnamed man formerly employed by a party of surveyors; the two prospected together somewhere on the West Coast for about a month. With 'an old mate' (probably from the Colonial Defence Force) he tried prospecting for what seems to have been a very brief period at Arnold, near Greymouth. His tenth (and apparently fractious) partnership was with 'a young fellow' over a period of six weeks, when they were both engaged on contract to clear a track over the ranges. The eleventh was in South Taranaki where with 'three good fellows' he cut firewood for a month on contract. Partnership number twelve was with 'an old troop mate' in south Taranaki somewhere; it was for a week, splitting rails and posts. The last which endured for two months, was with a 'hard-working chap', fencing somewhere in the Manawatu.[80]

With the continued expansion of pastoralism, the rise of wheat farming, the clearance of the Great Bush in the North Island, the steady improvement of pasture from the 1880s, transitory combinations of shearers, musterers, grain-harvesters, bush-fellers, fencers, etc., usually comprising wage-earners and controlled by employers, took over from the partnership as the main work-unit of the floating labour force. Perhaps the most organised form of seasonal work was shearing. After the 1860s the practice in the larger sheds was for a shearer to have a permanent place booked for him which he would return to season after season. But until the 20th century shearers as a rule did not go about in permanent contract gangs; instead they moved on their own accord from shed to shed.[81] The recruitment of most other kinds of casual labourers was generally more haphazard; each individual simply wandered from door to door at the most likely place and time of the year hoping that something would turn up, sustained between jobs by overnight hospitality provided by rural householders. When a job was found, he would be combined with other itinerants by the farmer or station-owner or their deputies into an instant work team, which might also contain permanent hands and perhaps members of the owner's family.[82] In some districts it was the custom for a farmer or pastoralist to share his instant work-gang with his immediate neighbours; but this less primitive method of organising seasonal labour appears to have been a minority practice. J. C. Andersen in 1916 accounted for the infrequency of permanent gangs in the grain-growing area of South Canterbury by observing that their formation required a large and settled population of agricultural labourers which the region did not possess.[83] In addition what probably discouraged the rise of the contract-labour entrepreneur was the large scale of grain production, which made it worthwhile for each producer to acquire his own machinery. Also the wide dispersion of sheep stations and grain-producers, again a consequence of the large scale of production, plus poor transport and communication, impaired the ability of would-be contractors to move a labour-gang from property to property in synchronisation with the varying seasonal demands of a diversity of clients.

From a range of sources it is clear that the men leaving one casual job in search of another dispersed in all directions and travelled alone far more often than they wandered in pairs, threes, or larger parties. D. McKee Wright, an Otago station-labourer who later became a Baptist minister, recognised this in his poem, 'While the Billy Boils'. W. J. Cox, an intermittent transient (he spent most of his colonial career in Carterton working as a casual labourer), was forced by a flat job market over the years 1891–3 to take up the swag. For a total of 152 days Cox blindly meandered around the Manawatu, Wairarapa, and Hawke's Bay, fruitlessly looking for work and living off charity. On approximately 100 of these days (or two thirds of the total) he journeyed by himself. His most stable association (he went through about 12 altogether) lasted 32 days (and it was with a man he never saw again). With a single exception he had met none of his companions previously, nor did feel close to them or express regret when parting from them. Certainly one fellow crossed Cox's path again later in life (several times in fact) but these were brief encounters for the sole purpose of borrowing money; although Cox obliged, he thought the man a nuisance, being glad when he left. During his few years on the road, Henry Scott teamed up with a former shipboard acquaintance for his first job as farm-labourer and his fourth and fifth jobs as track cutter and pig-shooter; but the 'mateship' only lasted several months in total and they never met again. Otherwise he appears to have travelled alone and the only workmate he mentions was a man with whom he briefly went prospecting. Although he had a regular group of drinking companions at the Shamrock Hotel in Dunedin, he appears to have visited Dunedin on just three occasions for a few weeks each time. When at the turn of the century, a young English adventurer, E. W. Elkington, went 'on the Wallaby' for five weeks in Hawke's Bay, he fell into the company on his first day out of 'Happy Jack', a professional tramp, and together they obtained food and bed at the same station; but the next morning when all the swagmen were turned out, 'each man went off in a different direction, as it is considered bad policy to travel in a crowd', and thereafter Elkington walked by himself. At the first station, he noted that of the hospitality-seekers like himself, 'Many of them knew each other, but others were evidently strangers— new men on the look-out for work'. Of eight persons born at the turn of the century in the south of the South Island and interviewed about swaggers for an oral history project, only one distinctly remembered that swaggers travelled in pairs. The other respondents remembered that swaggers mostly 'travelled alone', 'normally only one' would turn up at the door, 'Normally they arrived in ones and twos', 'they arrived separately', 'I can never remember any more than one calling at once', 'they invariably travelled alone'.[84]

One reason transient labourers travelled alone was that the labour forces of most rural establishments were so tiny and the resources of rural households so small that a man by himself stood a better chance of getting a job or 'shakedown' than two men, let alone a bunch, tramping together. Wayfarers also walked alone to lessen the sense of threat small, geographically isolated households—especially children and women—felt when strange men knocked on the door requesting food or work.[85] It is likely, too, that the police paid solitary transients less attention than bands of transients. Moreover, a hard core of mobile labourers were notorious loafers who ruined the job prospects of any genuine work-seeker accompanying them.[86] Another reason was that the material well-being of itinerant workers did not depend upon peer support. Work and overnight hospitality, the two essentials for their survival, were not derived from reciprocal arrangements amongst themselves but with other social categories, namely, rural householders and employers. Life and death did not hang on the resources Elkington noticed that wayfarers did pool— books, conversation, tobacco—with the result that they had little material pressure to extend their associations beyond brief and casual encounters, to stay together on the road for a protracted period until sufficient trust and mutual knowledge had grown to allow the sharing of more valuable goods and services. Besides, the cheapness of a subsistence lifestyle in New Zealand, coupled with the fact that many of the foot-loose were so deprived of property they had little to exchange, undermined the incentive of men to tramp together for the sake of building up ties based on economic interdependence and obligation. Perhaps, too, the lower frequency of natural hazards and the shorter distances between back-country stations made road companions less necessary than was the case in Australia.[87]

Lastly, it seems that racism sometimes divided the floating work-force, extractional and pastoral, and did its bit to prohibit mateship and the manual male community. Animosity towards Dalmatians contributed to the fragmentation of gumdiggers. Anti-semitism helped to destroy the 'Maungatapu Murderers' : one of the gang, Sullivan, who was anti-semitic, loathed another member, Levy, a Jew. So obsessive did his prejudice become that when taken into custody he convinced himself that Levy would act the Judas. It was fear of this probability that triggered Sullivan to engage in his pre-emptive strike—he turned Queen's evidence in return for a pardon, converting the tenuous charge of suspicion of murder into the solid one of actual murder.[88]

Conclusion

In this chapter the 'insider's view' on class has been defended from two implicit attacks. One comes from those historians who maintain that urban workers from 1870 were increasingly drawn into working-class residential communities which became radicalised on a mass scale after 1888. The conclusion, instead, was that the residential differentiation necessary for the development of a working-class community does not seem to have occurred in the most likely place (Dunedin); and that without this community as a base, only a small and highly unstable minority of urban workers were capable of being mobilised into working-class action groups from 1889 onwards. Where the 'insider's view' went wrong was that it claimed no class-divisions at all existed or could arise in New Zealand, and it overestimated the effect that New Zealand's opportunity for advancement had in preventing them. What was more important in blocking the development of both communities and action groups was a cluster of forces of social isolation, including heavy transience, which had the effect of keeping inter-personal relationships to a superficial level and of providing an alternative to collective action as a means of advancing individual self-interests. The colony's high rate of transience, to which all strata were prone, had a much stronger impact on colonial life than class organisation, and was basically caused by the excess of young, single male adults and immigrants in the population, the large proportion of inherently impermanent jobs, the geographical disparities in economic conditions, and the limited opportunities for social promotion out of petty proprietor ranks.

The other tacit attack on the 'insider's view' on class maintains that in the rural areas lower-strata males formed strong groupings supportive of a 'macho' culture. This was rejected on the ground that New Zealand offered few settings in which groupings of this sort could flourish. Contact between extreme transients was minimised by the brevity of their work-teams, by their habits of solitary travel, and by the high turnover of men in the casual labour force (as well as in New Zealand as a whole). All the available evidence points to the fact that the companionless nomad was far more typical than the man with mates. For these reasons it is difficult to see how lower-strata males on the frontier produced let alone reproduced a culture of roughness and solidarity; what they lacked were the group pressures, the power, to induce one another to live up to this rebel code. There is certainly little sign that such a code was expressed (as it has been in real 'macho' societies) in widespread banditry and gang activity, in honour and the feud, in enduring traditions of massive rates of drunkenness and assaultive behaviour, receptiveness to an ideology of union militancy and political radicalism, and well-defined customs of mutual aid extending throughout life.

Geographic isolation. A slab-timber shack, without nearby dwellings, Mauriceville in the 1890s. The original survey plan of 1875 was for what was called a 'Township', each section being about 40 acres in size. *Alexander Turnbull Library*

CHAPTER VI

A Society of Cohesive Local Communities?

OF the two implicit attacks on the 'insider's view' refuted so far, one assumed that New Zealand's powerful patterns of interaction and collaboration flowed in a vertical direction, creating an enemy in inefficient and demeaning paternalism, while the second believed that the flow was horizontal and the enemy was class-division. The third implicit attack likewise presupposes New Zealand had a strong social organisation. It differs by intimating that the flow criss-crossed, producing far more localised cohesion on the one hand, but at the price of status anxiety, the third enemy, on the other.

The historical writings from which this third concept has been extrapolated see New Zealand as a vast collection of local communities, to one or another of which the vast majority of colonists belonged. The intense cohesion of each one is usually put down to its small population and to the geography of New Zealand, which isolated one settlement from another, giving individuals no choice but to socialise incessantly within the same tiny circle of local people, so breaking down barriers of religion, ethnicity, occupational background. Local integration was enhanced, apparently, by the fact that social elements from the extreme ends of the spectrum—swaggers and large estate owners—did not usually belong to the local community but had associations of their own.[1] One historian has maintained that in addition to geography, the past experience of village life in the Old World drew local people together: 'As settlement continued its advance across the uneven, cross-grained, craggy scramble of landscapes, it was forced into localised pockets, a circumstance which served to nurture the village outlook which so many of the immigrant stock brought with them.'[2] For another historian the impetus behind local cohesion came from the homogenising influences of the frontier—which gave local people similar occupational experiences, compelled them to co-operate to overcome the rigours of pioneering, and presented them with a common Maori foe—and the speed with which institutions were established at the inception of each settlement: churches, lodges, military groups, cricket clubs, and race meetings.[3]

The exact nature of the criss-crossing ties within each community has been spelt out by a historian with these words:

in rural areas. . . . kin, age, sex, and religion provided the bonds within communities. In general, country people shared the same aspirations, the same values, belonged to the same clubs, sent their children to the same schools, played the same games, and belonged to a church. . . .

. . . Often intensely suspicious of strangers and of cities, these communities tended to be inward-looking, self-reliant, and church-centred. . . . Communication was informal, by networks of neighbours or kin. . . .

By 1890 people in urban areas already thought of themselves as members of groups and took action through their group institutions. Voluntary organizations proliferated.[4]

Although none of these historians says so explicitly, the implication of their view is that the tightly knit local community was a virulent breeder of oppressive status conformity. What must be made clear is that the operation of this enemy in the New World did not create status anxiety in the same way as it did (according to the 'insider's view') in the Old, where it stemmed from the social pressure to spend in excess of a limited income. It afflicted a much broader spectrum of people (including the local community's heterogeneous collection of 'masterless people', its manual workers and petty proprietors) and it did not lead to conspicuous leisure and consumption. The colonial version of the enemy (the historians imply) was an inevitable by-product of the local community's cohesion. In the hierarchical and class-divided models social differences express economic differences. But in the 'local community' model, even though individuals and strata vary in their economic power, everyone must appear to be the same as everyone else; the cultural expression of differences of any sort is suppressed. This prohibition flows from the tight interlocking web of propinquity and mutuality. The intense mixing and meeting of people across the (not extreme) boundaries of wealth and income necessarily produces uniform opinions and values and habits. The sheer frequency of the interactions places every person under the observation of at least some other local person all or most of the time. As a consequence any deviation by the individual from the community's narrow, uniform, normative code is immediately known by the rest of the community, and invariably leads to communal punishment, to adverse gossip, ridicule, criticism, ostracism—the loss of the benefits of community life, of mutual aid and fellowship. As there is no other source of these benefits but the community itself, everyone accordingly is afraid of everyone else in case his or her behaviour is thought to be deviant.

In the other two models, individuals are also punished for their deviations and the fear of this likewise induces conformity to their respective normative codes. But in the 'local community' anxiety about not conforming is more intense. Although everyone is culturally or consciously equal, in terms of economic power everyone is not objectively equal. Thus in the local community individuals must spend time and effort in appearing to be the same, in living up to the normative code, trying to maintain the approval of everybody, to disguise the fact that objectively, in terms of economic power, they are different. Status anxiety of this magnitude rarely occurs in hierarchies because everyone is born to a station in life and inherits different shares of economic power; no one is anxious about inequality because everyone knows it is intrinsic to the system. Nor does it occur in a rigidly horizontal (class-divided) society, since people in each class know they have the same economic power; they do not have to worry about being unequal because objectively they are equals. A fluid horizontal society, however, may engender heightened status anxiety because frequent mobility causes uncertainty amongst individuals within the same class as to whether each will always have the same economic power as the other; the status insecurity of middle-class England (which the 'insider's view' complains about) was the outcome of this fluidity. So in contrast to the 'insider's view', which asserts that the colony was free of the artificial and elaborate settings producing status anxiety in the Old World, the alternative view implied by some historians is that status anxiety of a different kind was engendered by the culturally egalitarian but objectively unequal local community.

If the 'insider's view' on the organisation of the society is wrong and the alternative construct is right, we would expect the tremendous strength and inclusiveness of the 'local community' to have been derived from and expressed in any or a combination of four associational frameworks: communal festivals, kinship, the neighbourhood, voluntary institutions. Each of these possibilities will now be examined in detail and refuted.

Bonding through Community Festivals?
We can safely discount the social significance of communal festivals, the day or so of jollities variously featuring regattas, sports, A. and P. shows and horse races held annually, sometimes twice a year, in the smaller districts, more often in the larger, sometimes of longer duration as in Carnival Week in Christchurch every November. They were too diffuse, fleeting, and infrequent to be effective instruments of social interaction. Also their popularity and unitary function could wane. For instance, the Wellington Anniversary Day celebrations, arranged by a single *ad hoc* Festival committee at the end of every January, took the shape of a regatta, followed by 'rural sports' on Te Aro Flat and then an evening ball for the well-to-do, and attracted comparatively huge crowds up to the early 1850s. For the rest of the century attendance tended to slump, as the holidaying populace were drawn away to a multitude of competing attractions organised each regatta day by a variety of segmented groupings: the shipping companies ran harbour excursions of their own accord; the Wellington Jockey Club held its own races; the Burnham Water Races took place independently on the Miramar Peninsula; the Lower Hutt Parish Committee established an independent fête; a Caledonian Games Committee conducted a separate set of festivities; the railways off their own bat ran excursion trains to Paekakariki and the Wairarapa, and special services to the race meetings in the Hutt, Masterton, and Carterton; and the Druids went their separate way with a fête as well. The fading popularity of the regatta was recorded by the press in such doleful comments as 'the day was not observed with the same spirit which has been manifested on former occasions'(1856); 'Fears were at one time entertained that the aquatic sports would not take place at all' (1857); 'the large assemblage of persons . . . [was] nothing to be compared with the meetings that took place in the earlier years' (1862); 'the regatta did not come off on the proper day; the excursion trips took away a large number of those who would have attended it' (1870); 'there is every possibility of the 35th anniversary of the founding of the province and colony being celebrated only by the adjourned Caledonian sports' (1875); in past years the regatta had been 'hardly a success, and poorly

patronised' (1880); 'attendance of the public was not so great as had been expected' (1883); the regatta seemed to interest only the 'aquatic section of the community' (1890). Symbolic of the decline of the regatta as a communal rite was the disappearance in 1880 of the *ad hoc* committee of citizens who organised it and the appropriation of the event by a voluntary organisation, the Port Nicholson Yacht Club.[5]

Local Bonding Through Kinship?
At first sight, kinship seems to be a more promising explanation for local cohesion. There are some outstanding examples of the interconnections between local families. In 1842 Helen Hursthouse, her husband John, and his brother Charles immigrated to New Plymouth. In 1850 they were followed by J. C. Richmond, the nephew of Helen Hursthouse, and his brother H. R. Richmond. In 1853 they, in turn, were joined in New Plymouth by another family grouping. This included two Atkinson brothers, Harry and Arthur, who were friends of the Richmonds, their sister Emily, who came with her husband C. W. Richmond (brother of H. R. and J. C.), Jane Maria Richmond (sister of C. W., H. R. and J. C.), and two cousins of the Richmonds (Charles and Calvert Wilson). Soon after arriving in New Plymouth, Jane Maria Richmond married Arthur Atkinson, Harry and Arthur farmed 200 acres together, and subsequently the members of the several families and their offshoots engaged in an extensive pattern of mutual aid, notably in public life. A further illustration of clannishness is that of John Andrew who immigrated to Lyttelton in 1856 with a group consisting of his wife (Emma Fendall), their daughter, his brother-in-law Charles Fendall and a friend Phillip Luxmoore; already living in Christchurch were Emma's three brothers, and her widowed father. John Andrew, Luxmoore and Charles Fendall explored the back country together looking for pastoral land; then Luxmoore worked for John Andrew as a cadet on his run; and when Luxmoore obtained his own run he married Emma's sister.[6] There are many other cases of adult brothers and sisters and interrelated families migrating together, of these groupings settling (at least initially) in the same place, forming partnerships (pairs of brothers particularly) to own and lease pastoral land, and engaging in other forms of joint enterprise.

But it would be crass to assume these examples are typical and that the organisation of any local area was based on the interweaving of its households through marriage and blood, as Arensberg and

Kimball, for example, found in their classic study of rural Ireland, or on the close collaborations between mothers and married daughters that Young and Willmott discovered in their equally well-known case-study of Bethnal Green in the early 1950s.[7] In fact, the probability of any given individual having aunts, uncles, in-laws, cousins, nephews, nieces, grandparents, grandchildren living in the same locality would have been very small, although it would have risen from the 1880s onwards.

Some insight into the dearth of kin outside the immediate family is provided by the 1892 Department of Labour survey on 'working-men's' expenditure. Of the 106 households which furnished returns only two possibly included persons born outside the immediate family. One was a boot-finisher—who gave the number and ages of his 'family' as 'Males, 13 and 5 years; female, 27 years'—where the female is too old to be a daughter, and too young to be a wife with a child aged 13, and thus could either be an outside relative, a boarder, or a second wife. The other was a miner who gave the number and ages of his 'family' as 'Males, 3 years; females, 22 and 11 years'— where the same possibilities hold. Of the remaining households, five were single men living alone, five consisted of a husband and wife living by themselves, 19 provided no data at all about number and age of 'family' (i.e. other household members), while for each of the remaining 75 the ages of the 'family' are youthful and close enough to indicate that they were the offspring of the parents.[8] The failure of kinship to manifest itself in a large number of 'extended families' each occupying the same household is perhaps unsurprising since this set-up was not customary in the Old World either. However, New Zealand's conditions were different. The reason why, on the whole, relations did not share their accommodation in England was that they were relieved of the obligation to do so by a comprehensive system of poor relief, up to the mid 19th century at least.[9] As statutory welfare for the indigent was far less developed and generous in New Zealand, the sense of responsibility to the kindred should have been proportionately stronger. Theoretically, therefore, 'working-men's' households in New Zealand had greater pressures to take in ageing, frail, or lonely relatives than they did in the country of origin. That none definitely did so cannot be attributed to an imperfect sense of obligation; weighing against this possibility is the other pattern in the survey returns, the fact that of the 96 with dependants, 22 included persons (adult children in at least eight cases) who 'made their earnings available for the expenditure' by the family. Nor can a complete explanation be that though they had kin in plenty, these, because of the high standard of living, did not need looking after. There is a good deal of oral evidence that during the inter-war period when living standards were just as high, probably higher, many families accommodated an unmarried, usually elderly, relation, though not necessarily on a permanent basis. Rather, the main reason such mutual aid was less widespread amongst colonial families was quite simply that they had so few relations—needy or otherwise—living in the colony.

What is consistent with this interpretation is that various state agencies were forced to care for an abnormally large number of needy people who had no one (relations included) to look after them. Officials in charge of the Lunatic Asylums often complained that their institutions were the dumping ground for persons with 'transient and comparatively trifling affections of the mind' who in other societies would have been in some form of community care. Put into this class were the aged, drunks, and imbeciles. Dr Grace, of the Karori Asylum, reported in 1871 that 'dozens' of his charges would in England have been minded at home. Dr Hacon of Sunnyside claimed in 1882 that many of his patients could not be released because they had no one to see to them during their convalescence.[10]

According to the authorities, however, the gaps in kinship aid were most evident in the case of the elderly. The Inspector-General of Hospitals and Lunatic Asylums, Dr Duncan MacGregor, referred to the 'disproportionate numbers of our population who at this stage of our history have grown old without contracting family ties' and were finding their way into hospitals or mental asylums because they had no one to tend to them; all that was wrong with them was that they were 'merely friendless'. The introduction of Old Age Pensions in 1898 and the spread of old men's homes and refuges were mute testimony to the considerable number of kinless ('merely friendless') men which the ageing of the population brought into relief late in the century.[11]

Although official pronouncements on the composition of the institutionalised population need to be treated with due caution, they do make sense in this context. They fit what may be termed the causative evidence of kinlessness: the operation of three factors in particular. The first was the status of colonists as an immigrant people. Apart from the first decade of colonisation (the 1840s), the annual rate of population inflow from 1853 to 1874 was the highest Pakeha society has ever experienced. The aggregate number of immigrants from 1861 to 1880 was equal to 396 per cent of the 1861 non-Maori population.[12] Even a migrant society like the United States from 1820 to 1900 experienced nothing like New Zealand's rate of inflow measured on a decennial basis.[13] Before about 1885 over half the colonists were overseas born; although the proportion slid to 42 per cent in 1891 and 33 per cent in 1901, it was much higher in the older age groups—as late as 1906, 51 per cent of those aged 21 and over had been born outside the country. Just how sizeable this overseas-born bulge was, is frequently overlooked when the colony is lumped with other 'new' or 'settler' societies as if it were indistinguishable from them. In 1891 the colony's percentage of foreign born was higher than that for New South Wales, Victoria, Tasmania, and South Australia; and much higher than for the United States as a whole (14.3 per cent in 1890).[14]

Continuity between Old and New World kindred ties would have been maintained had the newcomers brought all or most of these with them. But several things suggest that most newcomers came alone or as members of their immediate families and thus left most of their blood and affinal relationships behind. One is that the emigrant population rarely contained a whole village or a segment of a whole village which journeyed together and settled in one place together—a 'colonised community' in the words of the American historian, Page Smith.[15] From 1850 to 1900 only about a dozen such communities appear to have existed and the population of each was minute: they included the Bohemian settlers at Puhoi (1863), the Northern Irish of Katikati (1875–8), the Scottish Highlander settlement at Waipu who came via Nova Scotia (1854), another Bohemian colony at Ahuroa (1866), a group of Lincolnshire families at Mangonui (1850s), a group from the Isle of Man (1850s), another Nova Scotia group (originally Highland Scots) at Whangarei (1850s).[16] As one parliamentarian stated in 1880 when ruminating on the characteristics of New Zealand's colonisation: 'There was a fortuitous concourse of immigrant atoms, and they found themselves in New Zealand.'[17] Another pointer is the acute shortage of adult females in the population. The peak excess of adult males over adult females was in 1867 when the ratio was about 2.27:1; although the disparity had shrunk considerably by 1891, it was still marked with 1.21 men to every one adult female.[18] At the very least this imbalance can be interpreted as meaning that most adult males arrived without female kinsfolk—wives, mothers, daughters, sisters, grandmothers, aunts, nieces, in-laws in various degrees—and that for years after their arrival many men had difficulty in finding a wife and acquiring a network of kinsfolk. The imbalance does not preclude the possibility that men emigrated with their male relatives; but the enfeebled state of 'mateship' bonding is good evidence that this arrangement was not common or if it were, it soon broke down. Another demographic distortion that tells us kin bonds were thinly represented in the immigrant population is the dearth of elderly people enumerated in successive colonial censuses over the 19th century. Table 6.1 compares the fraction of persons aged 65 and over in New Zealand and in England and Wales; it shows that, whereas the elderly always comprised about five per cent of the British population from the 1860s onwards, it was not until the end of the century that anything like that percentage was reached in New Zealand. In the 1860s England and Wales had about six times the proportion of aged persons as New Zealand, and in 1881 over three times the proportion. Colonial families were thus more likely to be isolated from the influences of older kindred, which not only deprived colonial children of grandparents but also parents of the persons who conventionally helped them raise their offspring. The isolation helps to account for the rapid growth of the Plunket Society after its foundation in 1907. The scarcity of grandmothers up to the 1890s weakened informal traditions or folklore about child-care and child-raising which are usually passed from mother to married daughter. With its body of alternative dogma and enthusiastic precept, the 'Plunket system' filled an intellectual vacuum and was readily accepted.

TABLE 6.1

Percentage of Persons Aged 65 and Over

	England and Wales	New Zealand
1861	4.64	0.71
1867	-	0.85
1881	4.57	1.42
1896	-	2.95
1901	4.66	4.05

Notes
1. New Zealand data are for non-Maoris and were compiled from *Census of New Zealand*.
2. England and Wales data are calculated from B. R. Mitchell & P. Deane (eds), *Abstract of British Historical Statistics* (Cambridge, 1962), p.12.

The pronounced imbalances in the demographic structure also suggest that the relative scale of chain migration was too small to reconnect many with a large coterie of relations. (Chain migration is the process by which newcomers facilitate the migration of those left behind.) Confirming this indirectly is the makeup of the inflow during the 1871–91 period, some 361,000 persons. Although we cannot tell exactly how many were relations joining relations, we can obtain a fair idea from the fact that of this total, one third, or 115,000, were government-sponsored immigrants, that is they received some government grant or other to encourage them to come. Of the 115,000, 28 per cent were nominated by residents in New Zealand; who precisely did the nominating is unknown, but obviously it was a mix of relations, prospective employers, friends—it is highly unlikely, in short, that all the nominated were relations joining relations. The 28 per cent figure in turn can be used as a rough guide to the absolute maximum proportion of all immigrants who were kin joining kin.[19] Consistent with this argument is the fact that chain migration rarely features in the myriad of advice books to immigrants; and the two major studies of the Vogelite assisted immigrants of the 1870s have not uncovered material showing its importance.[20]

The second circumstance restricting blood and affinal relationships was the short biological history of the colonial population. At any point before 1900 there had been too little time for settlers through natural reproduction to fill the kinship gaps left by the selectivity of immigration. A good illustration of this is that in 1901 only four per cent of women aged 50 and over (roughly equal to the grandparent generation) were New Zealand born.

The third circumstance was heavy internal migration. Even if the individual emigrated with a large group of relatives or was subsequently joined by a stream of them or was a member of a large established family, the restless dispositions of most of the households would soon have dispersed them, placing them outside the range needed for effective association and collaboration.[21] As noted in the previous chapter, a household had about a 60 per cent chance of disappearing from a town, city, county, after a decade from the late 1870s onwards (and a greater chance before then). With the appalling state of transport and communications, especially in inland areas, kindred households once dispersed obviously were incapable of sustaining as much visiting and reciprocity as when they were close neighbours. Logistical restraints thus would have reduced the physical display and discharge of obligation to peripheral matters—attendance at occasional family rituals such as weddings, funerals, christenings, and Christmas gatherings.

Community Through Neighbourly Bonding?

Our inability to locate the powerful organisation of the undifferentiated community in festivals and the kinship structure leads us to yet another option: informal ties between neighbours. Yet despite the temptation to believe that in a small-scale—'face-to-face'—society neighbours must have visited and helped one another practically every day, in fact contemporary references point in the other direction, suggesting that visiting and helping were infrequent, that the neighbourhood was more a geographical expression than an association.

During a visit to Akaroa in the mid 1850s, Henry Sewell noted how physically isolated each householder was, 'At present life in these places must be a mere solitude'. In a letter from Taranaki in 1851, H. R. Richmond informed his brother in England that 'one thing is certain that people visit very little here, so we must not reckon on seeing much of anyone but Aunt & her family'. Mrs Rhoda Coote wrote in her diary soon after she and her husband moved to their sheep station west of Masterton in 1864, that she was 'so far removed from everything and the road through the bush of nearly a mile so bad as to be almost worse than none'. Reminiscing about her childhood during the 1850s on a sheep station near Kaiapoi, five or six miles from the nearest post office, Mrs Withers drew attention to the remoteness of neighbours. She distinctly remembered what an event the coming of visitors was: 'I would look up the road, and perhaps notice dust in the far distance and call out to Mother, "I can see people on the track," the announcement causing the greatest excitement to all in the house'. Lady Barker in 1866 commented on the superficiality of neighbourly interaction in Christchurch: 'Visiting appears to be the business of some people's lives, but the acquaintance does not seem to progress beyond incessant afternoon calls; we are never asked inside a house, nor, as far as I can make out, is there any private society whatever . . .' William Pember Reeves spent part of his youth as a cadet on a sheep run near Ashburton, 1876–7. The two nearest homesteads were each five miles distant which, he says, was so far away that during his 16 months' cadetship he managed to visit one place only twice and the other 15 or 16 times; the resulting want of social stimulation contributed to his overwhelming sense of boredom and futility, described in some of the most haunting prose in colonial literature. Robert Petch, a

Marlborough runholder, noted in 1880 that it would be imprudent for him to bring a girl out from England to be his wife, 'for an English girl accustomed to society and flying round to parties, towns etc, to come and settle as a squatter's wife out here I think it is rather out of the question.' The anonymous lady immigrant, 'Hopeful', describing Christchurch in the 1880s, found that 'There is not the same amount of social intercourse in the Colonies as at home, where different families from the same locality visit each other'; this was particularly true, she felt, of respectable tradesmen in the towns: 'they live very much to themselves, are suspicious of each other, and the one thought and aim is to *make money*'. Sarah Courage summarised her impressions of 26 years as a runholder's wife in Leithfield, some 25 miles north of Christchurch, by saying 'The homesteads are too few and far between to allow of much visiting. We may have neighbours—half a dozen families within a radius of a dozen miles, or, what is much more likely, half the number at double the distance.' It was difficult for people in England to realise the extreme isolation of an up-country life: 'Month in and month out there is nothing whatever to vary the daily current of one's life. The sameness is terrible'; she herself found that six months at a stretch could go by without visitors.[22]

Even under abnormally favourable circumstances rural dwellers called upon their neighbours with surprising infrequency. D. MacRae, an Otago farmer, near Hokonui, lived within an hour's ride from his uncle's station; yet, according to his diary, he (sometimes accompanied by his wife) called upon his neighbours a mere 15 times in 1898 and was visited by them eight times, while in 1900 he called on 21 occasions and received seven calls in return. W. B. Matheson of Eketahuna was more sociable but not as much as we would expect of a man who was Chairman of the Roads Board, had strong political ambitions, and a coach route with a service three times a week running through his farm. The systematic record he kept in his diary indicates he had contact with his neighbours 108 times over a sample period of 600 days (in 1890, 1892, 1894, 1896, 1898) or an average of just one contact for every five and a half days.[23]

Analyses of the few references to neighbourly calling give some clue to why the practice may have been uncommon. Generally it had a purely social or diversionary objective—gossiping, swapping of news, such at-home entertainment as dances, party games, music-making. Occasionally business was transacted and, in back-country areas, church services were held. Seldom, however, were goods and services exchanged, which suggests that there was insufficient co-operation between neighbours to warrant much visiting. Neighbourly help was largely confined to emergencies—birth, fire, illness, death, accident, flood, a lost child—by definition, exceptional circumstances. Although W. K. Howitt wrote ecstatically about the goodwill and good fellowship between neighbours during his childhood at Okato, Taranaki, he could only illustrate this in an otherwise vivid and detailed portrait of pioneering life by alluding vaguely to the 20 miles neighbours were prepared to ride in order to buy a bottle of pain-killer 'just to soothe a sufferer's rheumatic shoulder'.[24] Examples of reciprocity during the busy times of the year—harvesting, mustering, shearing, haymaking—are certainly plentiful after about 1900; but a mere handful of such instances can be found before the 1890s, and most of these are restricted to the grain-growing regions.[25] As for more sustained or continuous economic co-operation, there are no known examples remotely resembling the situation cited by W. J. Gardner in his history of the Amuri where, during the early part of the 20th century, 10 or so adjoining farmers, on a newly divided large estate, pooled their labour and implements for ploughing, harrowing, sowing, harvesting, carting, stacking, fencing, digging, mustering.[26] Nor, for that matter, have any cases been discovered so far of neighbours in town or country who routinely helped each other out by lending money, in house building, minding children, shopping, finding employment. Of course it is possible that contemporaries may not have thought it worthwhile to record these arrangements; possibly, too, they were customary in streets dominated by manual workers and are not visible because so few of the submerged wrote memoirs and diaries. But counting against the first possibility is the low turnout at elections before the 1880s, especially in rural districts, in an era when candidates supposedly relied on support from 'friends and neighbours';[27] and if there were a great deal of informal economic reciprocity it is legitimate to ask why it was not formalised and did not lead to stronger organs of local self-government or something akin to the system of parish self-help along the traditional English model. Difficult to reconcile with the second possibility is that such a small proportion of the mainly lower class offenders before the courts had neighbours (or anyone else for that matter) as their accomplices.

Nothing in colonial ideology directly or indirectly put a high value on neighbourly collaboration. The idealisations of New Zealand did not tell immigrants that the country was a good place in which to reproduce the closeness and interdependence of the English village. Accordingly it seems improbable that the forging of neighbourly bonds was a strong, let alone a paramount, expectation and aspiration. Instead the primary theme in colonial imagery, as we noted, was individual self-reliance, its ways and means and satisfactions, and this hardly encouraged a spirit of collectivism among households in the same street or road.

In addition, it makes little sense to believe that neighbourly ties were widespread and powerful, since for a long period most localities were deficient in much that initiates, stimulates, strengthens these ties. Few people would have had kinsfolk living in the same street or road, conventionally the most fertile source of neighbourly mutual exchanges.[28] Not until the end of the century did farmers take whole milk or cream to the local dairy factory each day and exchange gossip while waiting in the queue. The chances that a large proportion of adjoining households were introduced and acquired familiarity through membership of the same voluntary organisations were depressed by the low rates of affiliation to churches, clubs, lodges, and so on, a point discussed in the next section. Belying the claim of some historians that the school was a key activator of local relationships (including by implication, the neighbourly) is the fact that before the 1870s the majority of children of school age failed to receive any formal education at all. Even when primary schooling became nominally compulsory with the 1877 Education Act, the marginality of perhaps most families to the local school is evident from the high rates of truancy, it being not uncommon for a quarter of children in a school to be absent for three-quarters of the time and another quarter for half.[29]

It is true that from the 1880s the proportion of colonists linked to these kinds of neighbour-creating associations would have grown. Over the whole period the colony also appears to have offered an abundance of casual settings—pubs, the general store, common work-places in the towns, and so on—that should have allowed people from adjoining or close-by houses to meet and mix, and thus in theory prompted them to call on one another in their homes. The companionships formed between emigrants during the voyage out likewise should have provided a base for neighbourly relationships. Two atomising agencies, however, would largely have undermined the bonding power of these settings.

In the first place, regardless of how many people lived in a locality, most of their contact would have been disrupted and dissolved by their phenomenal transience. As birds of passage colonists rarely stayed in one place long enough to acquire solid attachments and obligations to others living there. Acquaintanceships and friendships were usually snapped before they had much chance of developing beyond the superficial, which in itself goes a long way in explaining why most instances of neighbourly mutual aid were confined to the occasional crisis.

The second and overlapping atomising agency contradicts twin assumptions in much of the historical literature. These hold that physical remoteness and poor transport and communication in colonial New Zealand forced settlers in the same locale in some unspecified fashion to live in each other's company; and that the four main centres plus a rash of small towns and villages constituted the total settlement pattern.[30] Missing from this schema is the reality that the population was so small and scattered and transport and communication so primitive that a large minority of households were isolated, buried in space, had such poor access to the nearest habitation that in no meaningful sense did each belong to a neighbourhood, let alone a 'local community'.

The likely proportion of the population dwelling in geographically isolated households can be estimated from successive censuses, which from 1874 enumerated the residents in varying sizes of settlements ranging from the four main centres to the smallest hamlet. All these we shall term the 'clustered segment'. So small were the smallest of these settlements that it is reasonable to suppose that the residuum—the difference between the total population and those dwelling in the clustered segment—must have lived in isolated households (apart from the less than one per cent enumerated as the shipboard population). We will assume that the clustered segment should include all borough-dwellers. This, it should be noted, overstates the number of people with near neighbours, as the population of boroughs tended to be thin and well scattered, a consequence of the ribbon as opposed to nucleated pattern of their development, their small populations, the comparatively large size of sections, the excessive ambition of subdividers who laid out towns on a scale greater than was warranted by the actual demand, and the consequent separation of residents by appreciable areas of unsold and unoccupied land.[31] We will also assume that the clustered segment should include all the persons inhabiting counties and rural districts adjacent to the boroughs of the four main centres, the probable suburban population;

their inclusion likewise exaggerates the number of people living in close proximity, for unlike modern suburban dwellers who live squeezed together on sections of one quarter and one fifth of an acre in size, the colonial suburban sections were anything between three and 20 acres in area and were interspersed with extensive tracts of farm land.[32] On top of this our calculation of the clustered segment will take in the total number of people living in town districts. These arose under an Act of 1881 and were semi-autonomous legal units without the power of boroughs; again they were highly rural in character, for their populations were small (mostly between 200 and 500) but they were legally entitled to embrace an area of up to two square miles.[33] Lastly, we will assume that the clustered segment should include places deemed by the Registrar-General to be 'of the nature of townships, villages, or small centres without boundaries'. He admitted that it was 'impossible to say that the populations of these small centres are all strictly accurate. . . . In different cases more or less of surrounding country may have been considered as belonging to the centre, but there is at least at each place mentioned some sort of nucleus of population, if not a well-defined village or township.'[34] In other words, a considerable number of people were counted as living in very generously defined villages and hamlets when in actual fact they lived considerable distances from them. If now we sum the populations given for all the four categories, (boroughs, suburbs, town districts, and 'some sort of nucleus of population'), we can work out what fraction they amounted to of the colony's total European inhabitants. The results are given in Table 6.2. From these we can infer that the remainder of the population before 1901 (between roughly 36 and 47 per cent of the total) dwelt in households that were physically remote from other households— an understatement, it should be remembered, since the definitions of a population cluster were excessively broad.

What helped to deposit at least 36 to 47 per cent of the population in the 'boo-ay' was the same thing that made the colony materially successful, its low population pressures on land supplies. When in 1882 half of adult males owned land and 43 per cent of the freeholders occupied sections of five acres or more in counties (although not all were resident), there was an inevitable tendency for settlement to be extremely dispersed. From the early 1880s the vigorous and successful prosecution by almost all governments of settlement in the backblocks worked in the same direction; in fact it was deliberately

TABLE 6.2

The Clustered Segment of the Population at Successive Censuses, 1874-1901

Total Persons Occupying:

Year	Formal Clusters (i) Boroughs	(ii) Town Districts	Informal Clusters (iii) Suburbs of Four Main Centres	(iv) Townships, Villages, Small Centres	Aggregate (i+ii+iii+iv)	Aggregate as a % of Total Population
1874	117818	none	23883	not specified	141701	62
1878	163028	none	18069	37229	218326	53
1881	194981	none	17801	55206	267988	55
1886	245612	29026	31986	38010	344634	60
1891	270343	28077	23317	76995	398732	64
1896	307294	21184	22811	100862	452151	64
1901	350202	17217	28612	131793	527824	68

Notes
1. The data are for non-Maoris as enumerated by each Census. Percentages rounded off to nearest whole number.
2. Borough population is that enumerated by the Census except in 1874 where it is designated as 'Cities and Towns'.
3. Town districts. Populations as specified by the Census. For 1886 Devonport has been taken out of this category and placed in the suburban.
4. Suburban population is that residing outside boroughs where the Census indicates a suburb exists. In 1874 it takes in the electoral districts of Parnell and Newton, the portions of Christchurch East and West outside the town belt, and portions of the suburbs of Nelson electoral district; the Dunedin component has been defined by the author as the road districts of N.E. Valley, Roslyn, Mornington, Caversham, Green Island, Waikari, Kaikorai, Half-way Bush. For 1878 the area takes in the road districts for Auckland and Christchurch specified by the Census (p.13) as suburban; and the ridings of N.E. Valley, Waikari, Kaikorai for Dunedin. For 1881 and subsequent Censuses the suburban component is the non-borough and non-town district population specified by the Registrar-General.

5. Townships, villages, small centres, etc. The Censuses of 1878 and 1881 define these as towns situated in road districts; that of 1886 as 'villages, the population being classed rather as rural than urban. The majority . . . have been laid off for future occupation by a more truly town population'; that of 1891 'as small centres of population and settlement, but, having no recognised boundaries, more or less of the country has been included by Sub-Enumerators according to their judgement and without check'; that of 1896 and 1901 as 'places of the nature of townships, villages, or small centres without boundaries . . . more or less of surrounding country may have been considered as belonging to the centre, but there is at least at each place mentioned some sort of nucleus of population. . .'. It is likely that there has been some double counting of this and the informal suburban category.

undertaken to rusticate as many people as possible. Typical was the statement by William Rolleston, the Minister of Lands, in defence of his perpetual lease proposal of 1882,

What I believe this Bill will do is to diffuse population over the country and also promote the distribution of land among a much larger number of the population than has hitherto been the case. It will prevent the aggregation of large estates. It will prevent, as I believe, in the future, those extremes of poverty and wealth which are the curses of older countries. It will provide for the relief of local taxation. It will further induce people to come from the Home country to settle with their families here, and generally I believe if this Bill has fair play, it will, in the future, be a thorough blessing to the country.[35]

Colonial ideology also facilitated the scattering of households across the countryside. As we noted previously, towns were not imagined as the seat of satisfied ambition and rural life was not treated with contempt or opprobrium. Rather, serving a rural apprenticeship was perceived as the best means of obtaining a competency for the sake of which individuals and families were urged to avoid the long-settled areas and seek opportunities in the hinterland where greater 'natural abundance' lay, undiscovered.

It might be argued that even if not concentrated in villages, then country households were sited close together in twos or threes. But land speculation and absentee ownership were so rampant that it is unlikely such bunching was common. Whenever land was subdivided speculators usually acquired many sections in the block and failed to settle there, waiting for an opportune time to sell on a rising market, thus keeping those who did reside on the block separated by large, unoccupied portions of land. Bunching was minimised too by the practice in bush areas, where unimproved land took a long time to bring into production, for genuine settlers to defer residence, living with their families in a nearby town, wage-earning at intervals, commuting to their sections every so often to clear them. Besides this, it was rare for all sections in a subdivision to be bought and settled immediately; sale and occupation proceeded in a piecemeal fashion over a considerable period. Absentee ownership was common, and by no means confined to large estate owners. We have already seen that in 1882 over half of Wellington householders owning land held their plots outside the city, scattered all over the southern half of the North Island; three-quarters of all the colony's freeholders in 1882 resided in towns but only 43 per cent owned land there.[36]

Widely scattered householders were kept isolated by primitive communications and transport. In inland areas the movement of goods, people, messages, chiefly depended on horses and walking. Yet the condition of roads and tracks was generally atrocious. To demonstrate this we only have to consider the attention the subject received at the hustings in general elections—colonial politics, the saying goes, ran along roads and bridges. Accounts and reminiscences of the pioneer period dwell at length on the shocking state of local roading. Charles Hursthouse in 1861 wrote that the main roads within a radius of six to 10 miles of the chief towns were tolerably good, 'but the common bush-roads of the country are little better than rough cart tracks, thickly studded in wet weather with many a mud pit and "slough of despond"'. In October 1875 an Inglewood settler described his problems of access this way, 'We are about 10 miles in the forest, and it took us 10 hours to go 17 miles, and we had 2 horses to each cart, and we had to follow the cart and hang at it to keep it from tipping over very often; at other times we lift them up a hill.' Highlighting the terrors of the Alfredton road in the 1880s is the legend that a passing horseman rescued a man lost up to his armpits in the mud for nearly a day. A former section holder on the Feilding Small Farm Settlement, near Apiti, recalled that in the 1880s it took from daylight to dusk in mid winter to travel the 20 miles from the block to the nearest store; on one of the two tracks 42 fords had to be crossed, while the other gained for itself the common name of 'Suicide Track' because it claimed the lives of so many horses. A less impressionistic idea of how bad roads were can be deduced from the first official survey of roading in 1921.

It showed that of 64,000 miles of roads, 23 per cent were unformed legal roads, eight per cent were bridle tracks, and 26 per cent were unmetalled roads the width of a dray; only 43 per cent had metalled surfaces and were a dray's width or more.[37]

Roads were poor for various reasons. Road engineering, for one thing, was inherently difficult in a country with a heavily folded terrain, a high rainfall, broad and swift rivers, dense bush cover. The papa sub-soil in many areas guaranteed that for eight or so months of the year roads were like porridge. For another, as many districts were poorly endowed with suitable road metal, and as it did not pay to cart metal more than five and a half miles, the cost of providing all-weather surfaces was high. Bad roads also were the creation of the society's own culture and institutions. The intense desire for competencies and the success in satisfying it, helped the frontier to expand rapidly and to produce a low-density population. In turn, the rapid extension of settlement created a lag between the arrival of population in any one place and the establishment of transport and communication services there; and the wide dispersal of households raised the cost of linking them by all-weather roads to almost prohibitive levels. In addition, as most settlers were small and dependent upon subsistence production, they could not afford to pay more than nominal rates, which deprived the local bodies responsible for road construction and maintenance of adequate funds. Finally, it barely needs to be said that scattered householders had no motor-cars or telephones to break down space between them.[38]

Local Community Through Voluntary Organisations?
The preconception that the residents of the 'local community' were sewn together tightly by near-universal and frequent participation in a mass of voluntary organisations has been influenced by a remarkable sociological investigation of a west Canterbury rural district during the inter-war period, a study of Oxford by H. C. D. Somerset published in a small book entitled *Littledene*.[39] It is quite clear, however, that voluntary organisations during the colonial period excluded the bulk of the population in any given locality, and that projecting the *Littledene* model back into the colonial past is quite invalid and unhistorical.

The situation is exemplified by attendance at church services. The Registrar-General in every census from 1874 onwards collected data on the number of those 'usually attending' at every place of worship (which included purpose-built churches and chapels as well as makeshift accommodation), and the accuracy of the figures has been independently verified. If we assume that the total non-Maori population was eligible to be 'usual attenders' and convert the latter into a per capita rate, we find that an average of only about quarter of the population belonged to a church from 1874 to 1896, within a consistently rising trend going from 20.2 per cent in 1874 to 29.4 per cent in 1896. By international standards, these proportions are not high. They are appreciably lower than those in older societies where the church was the 'centre of the community'—England and Wales (where the rates were roughly 12 per cent higher) and Scotland. They were also lower than those for the frontier societies across the Tasman—New South Wales, Victoria, South Australia—and, it should be noted, are apparently inferior to those for 'Littledene' during the 1930s where, Somerset says, three quarters of all households were represented at church every Sunday.[40]

It cannot be argued that colonial church membership was reduced by peculiar factors not affecting other so-called 'community institutions'—lack of piety, for example, or an exceptionally large number of believers whose faith placed comparatively little value on church attendance. Membership of other formal groupings was even lower. From the data compiled by the Registrar of Friendly Societies it can be calculated that their financial members expressed as a proportion of European males in the enumerated work-force averaged about 14 per cent between 1876 and 1900, within (like church attendance) a steadily rising trend from eight to nine per cent in the mid 1870s to double that by 1900, rates which are overstated as men often belonged to more than one body. Again, in international terms, these proportions are not high. Friendly society membership in England and Wales was equal to about half the population of males in the work-force in the early 1870s. The earliest available data for the six colonies across the Tasman are for 1891–2. They reveal that the New Zealand percentage (12.6) was about the same as Queensland's (12.1) and more than twice the rate for Western Australia (4.9); but well below that for the other three colonies, New South Wales (20.5), Tasmania (23.2), and Victoria (24.4). It is also minute compared to the 75 per cent at 'Littledene'.[41]

On top of this, the Volunteers embraced an average of only about five per cent of all European males aged 15 and over between 1874 and 1896, with a high of 6.2 per cent in 1881 and a low of 2.9 per cent in 1896. Paid-up members of one of the few women's organisations, the Women's Christian Temperance Union, amounted to about 600 in 1893 (less than one per cent of the adult female population). From the returns furnished to the Registrar-General on the combined membership of public libraries, mechanics' institutes, and all other literary and scientific institutions, we can work out that these incorporated a static nine per cent or so of adult males between 1874 and 1896; although the returns were incomplete, they do include libraries which are very loose associations.[42]

Then there is the example of sports clubs and teams. To ascertain popular involvement in these, four local case-studies have so far been conducted using as their source material newspaper reports of sporting events. The researcher itemised all the games played over a week in each of the winter or summer peak months, counted or estimated the number of players involved in each (excluding visiting players), and then aggregated the players from the winter and summer peaks respectively. For each locality, it has been assumed that males and females eligible to play were confined to the 15-to-40 age bracket. Where actual age-specific figures were not available, the number of persons in this bracket in each likely catchment area has been put at 39 per cent of the Census-enumerated total population in that area. This is the proportion of persons aged 15 to 40 in the New Zealand-wide population for 1891. The results are given in Table 6.3. The table shows that in the Greater Wellington area in 1895, four types of sports were reported for 7–14 January, involving approximately 311 players, equal to about two per cent of the estimated population aged 15 to 40 in 1896; for 4–11 July one organised sport (rugby) was reported with roughly 465 players, or almost two and a half per cent of the estimated population aged 15 to 40. According to the coverage of the *Taranaki Herald* in the week beginning 1 June 1894, only rugby was played in all Taranaki with about 153 players, representing almost two per cent of the province's 1891 population aged 15 to 40. Using the reports in the *Wanganui Chronicle* and *Wanganui Herald* for the 5–25 July 1896, it was found that just one team sport, rugby, was played with approximately 112 team members, equal to about two per cent of the estimated population (including Maoris) of Wanganui borough and Waitotara and Wanganui counties, aged 15 to 40. The last case-study, of the Greater Auckland area, ascertained from the *New Zealand Herald* that eight different types of games were played during the week 14–19 January 1895, involving about 336 participants, roughly one to two per cent of the estimated persons aged 15 to 40 in the likely catchment area; and over the winter week, 15–20 July 1895, at least 458 players in

10 organised sports, two per cent of estimated population in the eligible age-bracket.

TABLE 6.3

Estimated Number of Players of Organised Sports in Selected Localities, 1890s

Place	Date	Total Players		Estimated Population Aged 15-40 in Catchment Area	Players as a % of Estimated Population in Catchment Area	
		Summer	Winter		Summer	Winter
Auckland	1895	336	458	22,470 (1896)	1.49	2.03
Wellington	1895	311	465	20,168 (1896)	1.54	2.30
Taranaki	1893	not studied	153	8,338 (1891 actual)	-	1.83
Wanganui	1896	not studied	112	5,031 (1896)	-	2.22

Notes
1. *Sources:* G. B. Cumming, 'A Comparative Study of the Popularity of Sport in Auckland, in 1895 and 1926', Hist. 316 research essay, VUW, 1983; B. O'Riley, 'A Comparative Study . . . into Participation in Winter Sport in the Taranaki Province in 1893, 1913, and 1933', Hist. 316 research essay, VUW, 1983; C. R. Turney, 'A Comparative Study of the Rate of Participation in Rugby, Hockey and Soccer in Wanganui . . . in 1896 and 1926', Hist. 316 research essay, VUW, 1984; I. Young, 'A Comparative Study of the Organised Groups and Clubs of Wellington in 1895 & 1926', Hist. 316 research essay, VUW, 1982, pt. II.
2. Catchment area population. Auckland — Boroughs of Birkenhead, Devonport, Newmarket, Newton, Parnell; Road Districts of Arch Hill, Eden Terrace, Epsom, Mt Albert, Mt Eden, Mt Roskill, One Tree Hill, Pt Chevalier, Remuera; Riding of Northcote. Wellington — Boroughs of Lower Hutt, Petone, Onslow, Wellington, Karori, Melrose, and Hutt County. Taranaki — whole province. Wanganui — Wanganui Borough, Counties of Waitotara and Wanganui. Wanganui base population includes Maoris; those for the other three areas are for non-Maoris.

It is possible that newspaper reporters failed to cover many fixtures; the aggregates also fail to pick up sports for which no teams and no lists of competitors existed (notably horse racing); and possibly in the weeks chosen bad weather or some other contingency may have cancelled many of the games. Nonetheless there is sufficient similarity in the rates of participation across the four case-studies to suggest that the under-recording was not substantial in any one instance. The significance of the figures is that such a tiny component of the eligible local population were players—the upper limit being about three per cent. Unfortunately, it is not possible to compare these rates with those of other societies, the data not being available. It is possible, however, to compare them with the New Zealand-wide rates in 1926 using the returns submitted by all sporting organisations to the Registrar-General in a one-off census of their activities.[43] These reveal that approximately 58,213 people were affiliated to clubs engaged in winter sport (rugby, hockey, league, rowing, soccer) or 11 per cent of the population aged 16 and under 40; and 74,791 affiliated to clubs engaged in summer sports (tennis, bowls, cricket, golf, athletics, swimming, croquet, boxing), 15 per cent of those 16 and under 40. New Zealand-wide participation in 1926 was roughly three to five times higher than the upper range in the four places during the early and mid 1890s. Although it might be contended that the comparison is inapt because the range of sports had broadened immensely by 1926, this misses the point that late-19th-century New Zealand was capable of sustaining only a very limited choice of organised sporting pastimes.

Moreover, contrary to what Somerset discovered in 'Littledene' during the inter-war period, the voluntary organisations of the colonial era were so precarious that it would be legitimate to infer they were too weak to exert much influence on their adherents. For example, of the 10 lodges operating in Wellington in 1858 only four remained by 1868; of the 24 that were founded over the whole colony between 1865 and 1868, half had dissolved by 1885; and of the six founded in Auckland Province over the 1870s, just two lasted the century. Literary institutes, mechanics' institutes, athenaeums—adult education institutions for working men, imported from England—were even more death-prone. A host of them were established from the 1840s to the 1870s in the main settlements, equipped with reading-rooms, libraries, classes, lectures. Yet most did not survive the 1880s, let alone the turn of the century. By 1900 some 80 remained (10.4 for every 100,000 population); and of these most had been assimilated by municipal libraries or consisted merely of a room in which a handful of members played draughts or chess. In Australia, by contrast, they multiplied and assumed a far more vital role in local intellectual and community life. By 1900 Australia had about 1,000 of these bodies (27 per 100,000 people); and so vigorous was their role that they retarded the emergence of municipal libraries.[44] Sports clubs were equally frail. For example, over the period 1871–99 65 rugby clubs were formed in Wellington and of these 54 collapsed; of the 11 cricket clubs founded between 1883 and 1900 in Wellington, six crashed before the end of the century—and so weak were these clubs that the Wellington representative side sometimes had to field 22 players to make games against overseas teams worthwhile. Likewise, the majority of Manawatu's rugby clubs virtually or completely folded up over the years 1896 to 1902.[45] The same transitoriness afflicted farmers' pressure groups. Eight sprang out of local Farmers' Clubs and A. and P. Associations, mainly around the Otago/Southland region, between the late 1880s and late 1890s: all soon expired. The first was the New Zealand Farmers' League, 1886–7, which was formed to persuade farmers to vote in the 1887 general election for candidates supporting League policies, but aroused little interest. Another was the New Zealand Farmers' Union, operating between 1889 and 1891; it lobbied members of parliament and held two conferences yet had no discernible impact on voting patterns. Just as short-lived were bodies started up in Wanganui and Papatoetoe in 1890; the Farmers' and Country Settlers' League of 1892; the Southland Farmers' Union of 1893; a Taranaki organisation in 1897; the Waikato Farmers' Trust of 1899. Only with the establishment of the Farmers' Union in 1899 was a farmers' lobby group put on a permanent footing.[46]

Three overlapping sets of circumstances kept down the membership and hastened the demise of voluntary organisations. One was the inevitable time-lag between initial colonisation of an area and growth to the point of being able to sprout formal leisure groupings. Resources were scarce among the earliest waves of settlers, who had to give priority to the provision of shelter and making a living, and their numbers were initially too low to support communal institutions. For these reasons, it took one year after Timaru's first immigrant ship landed in 1859 for the foundation stone of the Anglican church to be laid, one year before the Jockey Club was founded, four years for the first cricket club, seven years for the Presbyterian church. Although Hawera's sections were laid out in 1870, the first church (the Roman Catholic) was not established until 1875, the first rugby club and Presbyterian church in 1876, the cricket club in 1877, the first lodge in 1880, and the Anglican church in 1881. With Hamilton, first settled as a military township in 1864, the formation of the earliest lodge and cricket club had to wait two years, the Presbyterian church two to three years, and seven years elapsed before the town

obtained its resident Anglican minister. The sections of the future
Hastings township were laid out in 1873; yet the Anglican church
was not built for four years, the first lodge for four years, the cricket
club took five years, the permanent race course six years, the Roman
Catholic church nine years, the Presbyterian 10 years. The township
sections for Havelock North began to sell in 1860 and all were sold
by 1862; but the earliest church (the Presbyterian) did not arrive
until 1871, the cricket club until 1874, the Anglican church until
1876, the mechanics' institute until 1870–3. The lag was most
noticeable in pastoral districts. For example, although the sheep runs
of the Amuri were established in the 1850s, it was not until 1874,
at the end of a generation of settlement, that the district had its
first regular clergyman (a Presbyterian), followed by the earliest cricket
club in 1875, a permanent race course in 1883, and a rugby club
in 1902.[47]

The second circumstance was the rapid extension of the frontier
in the 30-year period from the 1850s to the 1880s. By sucking into
new areas such a large component of the total colonial population,
the rapidly moving frontier exposed a maximum number of people
and settlements to the lag effect. The speed with which fledgling
settlements proliferated can be measured by the growing number
of post offices from less than 24 in 1854 to 856 in 1880.[48] It can
be traced, too, in the mushrooming of tents and one- or two-roomed
shacks, the extemporised shelter constructed by the initial inhabitants
of a virgin territory: they shot up from 10,500 in 1861 to 26,500
in 1864, fell to 19,500 during the early 1870s, rose again to 25,000
in 1881, before ebbing gently from that point onwards.[49] As a
consequence of the massive movement of people into new areas,
drawn by the lure of gold, free land for military settlers, pastoralism
and public works, by 1881 very roughly 57 per cent of the non-
Maori population resided in places which had not been settled in
1850.[50] The slower expansion of the frontier from the earlier 1880s
onwards (discussed in a later chapter) goes a long way in explaining
the rising membership rates of many types of voluntary organisations,
for it meant that an increasing fraction of the total population occupied
older settlements where the lag effect had passed or was waning.

The third circumstance was what may be termed the lack of 'critical
mass'. To be able, without a demoralising struggle, to recruit enough
members to staff its management committee properly, obtain a
competent leadership, keep its finances healthy, supply the actors
for its collective rituals, a voluntary organisation needs a minimum

population of potential joiners. This is the critical mass. The thin
spread of population across microscopic settlements and isolated
households was an obstacle to the development of the critical mass;
but it was not the only one. As Somerset's research of inland
Canterbury in the late 1930s demonstrated, a great number and variety
of formal groupings can flourish in country areas with populations
both minute and scattered.[51] There were, however, in the colonial
era, several factors which no longer operated or were less potent
by the time Somerset investigated 'Littledene'. Primitive transport
meant that only those living closest to a town found it worthwhile
to join a club or society. Unless more remote settlers were wealthy
enough to take time off and pay for overnight accommodation, they
stayed home. Lack of kinship, and other relationships, already explored,
meant that organisations were less able to rely on friends to enlist
friends. Transience constantly robbed them of active members—as
the churches observed. In 1894 the Presbyterian General Assembly
found that mobility had eroded the loyalty of the members of its
congregations so much that it resolved that 'In the case of families
leaving one district for another, the Minister of the district left should
immediately acquaint the Minister into whose district the removal
has taken place with the fact. In our colony where the population
is so migratory that course of action ought to be insisted on.'[52] All
this attenuated the 'critical mass', and it was further clipped by
circumstances specific to particular activities. For example, young,
unattached, adult males (who were an abnormally large segment of
the population) had less incentive to secure the benefits of lodge
and friendly societies than the higher concentration of family men
had by the 1920s; the recent origins of most sports in the 19th
century meant that sports clubs and teams did not have access to
the ready-made body of adherents which their successors were to
enjoy in a later age; the sharper sectarianism of the 19th century
discouraged the denominations from pooling their scanty resources
to build a single place of worship. In addition, whereas by the 1920s
a self-conscious passion for joining permeated New Zealand culture
and was at least as important as 'getting on', colonial ideology,
preoccupied with the latter and saying little about the former, gave
its people a different set of priorities.

   On top of all this, the typical locality in the 19th century had
a far tinier pool of potential joiners than its 20th century equivalent
because its 'leisured class' represented a much smaller element in
its population. For practical and cultural reasons women and children

were barred from forming or joining most types of formal groupings, the outstanding exceptions being the church (where women were probably over-represented) and the Sunday School (which claimed a membership rate of just over 52 per cent at its lowest point in 1871 and 70 per cent at its highest, 1901, in relation to the number of children [non-Maori] aged 5–15).[53] The mass influx of women and children into secular clubs and societies—especially those related to sport—did not start to take off until about the decade preceding the First World War in the case of children and after the war in the case of women. By 1900 there was little evidence of this future trend; in Wellington, for example, of the 67 sports clubs, only 12 catered for women (two for ladies' hockey, five mixed tennis clubs and five mixed bowls clubs), and none specifically for children with the exception of a handful of secondary school teams.[54]

It would be over-simplifying to say that voluntary organisations were the exclusive preserves of adult men. Manual workers, too, were largely disqualified from joining, but for different reasons. The middle-class-dominated committees of most clubs and societies could not afford to exclude them, as their equivalents in England did, through high membership dues and discriminatory rules; to do so would have exacerbated the struggle to establish institutions and keep them alive. Nonetheless, working men were grossly under-represented in most bodies, even the most socially open. Wellington cricket clubs in the 10 years 1878–88 drew only 28 per cent of their players from manual ranks—well below their overall rate of representation in the male work-force, about 60 to 70 per cent. The inequality was not as pronounced for Wellington's rugby teams but it was still substantial, being 41 per cent over the 1879–89 period. In rugby teams in the Manawatu region, manuals represented only 27 per cent of total players in the 1878–88 block of years. Ironically even a body like the Wellington Working Men's Club formed in 1877 had difficulty recruiting 'working men'; just 46 per cent of its new members were manuals over the years 1887-1896.[55] Lodges and friendly societies had rules demanding regular and frequent payment of subscriptions, hence it was principally the irregularity of earnings that kept manual workers out (itinerant workers especially) and that forced one third of all members over the late century to relinquish their membership.[56]

The over-riding factor, however, stripping the generality of working men of opportunities for organised leisure was the nature of colonial working-time. What suggests this is that the proportion of workers in Wellington organisations rose dramatically from the mid 1890s to the 1930s, at the same time that legislation and trade union action were standardising work-time, and shortening it by an average of almost six per cent between 1909–13 and 1934 for male employees, excluding pastoral and agricultural workers.[57] By contrast, over the 19th century only a minority of workers enjoyed the set working-day of eight hours or less that would have left enough energy, free time, and predictable time for Saturday afternoon sport, evening meetings, or even Sunday church services. The lucky few included employees in the building trades, and on the Thames goldfields, some day-labourers and navvies in the towns, 'mechanics' (except those in the government workshops, who worked 12 to 14 hours a day), and some factory operatives. No legislation regulated men's working-hours until 1891 (for coal miners), 1894 (a half-day holiday for shop-assistants), and 1901 (a 48-hour week for factory workers); trade unions had little power to negotiate for civilised working time.[58] It is inconceivable that Auckland timber-mill hands (reported to be working 10 hours a day and by implication 60 hours a week in 1887 and 1889), Colonial Sugar Refinery employees (a 12-hour day in 1897), paper-mill workers (a 12-hour day in 1901), and woollen-mill workers (a nine-hour day in 1887), found joining a leisure grouping worthwhile. In these cases employers probably maximised hours of work to make their products internationally competitive.[59] Railway employees, on a 10-hour day in the 1880s, were deprived of a Saturday half-holiday as traffic volumes for the whole country were heaviest on that day. The daily hours of engine-drivers fluctuated wildly from day to day to constitute their 60-hour week, to which must be added the time they had to spend getting up steam.[60] Preference for contract jobs impelled navvies and day-labourers to deny themselves free time; they exerted themselves for as long as possible on the days of fine weather to recoup the money not earned on bad days, a pressure that increased if they lived away from home, camping.[61] Not until 1891 were postal officials granted a Saturday half-holiday; over the whole century they were expected to work into the night if mail had to be cleared, often the case at the ports when a steamer brought a flood of overseas mail, or in country towns when the post had to be loaded on to the trains or off-loaded and sorted at any hour.[62] It is doubtful if wharf labourers were able to match their spare time to the fixed schedules of sports and other meetings, since, to match erratic shipping movements and cargo flows, they were engaged by the hour at any time over the day and week.[63] The eight-hour day of city waggoners and draymen did not include the time spent feeding and harnessing animals (one and a half to two hours in the morning); during the wool season those in rural service centres operated 18 hours a day including Sundays.[64] Country blacksmiths had to be prepared to work around the clock during the harvest season; flour-mill hands during the busy time of the year worked a 12-hour day in two shifts; harvest hands worked all hours, day and night, depending on the weather; shearers likewise had no fixed timetable and would labour 16 hours daily when dry weather followed wet; domestic servants, hotel workers, boarding-house staff were the first to rise in the morning and the last to retire; the working day of permanent hands on stations and farms was prolonged even during less busy periods by the need to tend to working animals.[65] In all these instances, the domination of nature over productive processes or the lack of labour-saving machinery, or both, meant that working by the clock was not feasible. Opportunities for organised leisure were also denied to shop assistants and men in shop trades (bakers, butchers, tailors), who commonly toiled 60 to 72 hours a week, as well as tramwaymen, on a 70- to 80-hour week; their leisure was sacrificed to serve the majority of people with barbaric hours.[66] Employers may on occasion have given their workers time off to attend meetings and gatherings, but there is no evidence of this. Furthermore, no account has been taken of time workers would have needed to spend in their gardens and plots with subsistence and quasi-commercial production.

So, this was another hindrance to the development of the 'critical mass', the absence in most localities of standardised work-time across most occupations, with which voluntary institutions could synchronise their activities.[67]

Conclusion
This chapter has largely vindicated another aspect of the 'insider's view', its claim that New Zealand lacked the social mechanisms to ensure conformity and status anxiety. The means of association at the local level were so thin, and such a large proportion of individuals had little or nothing to do with them, that social pressure to 'keep up with the Joneses' must have been exceedingly weak. The typical colonist did not have to worry about keeping up appearances in order to win community approval and avoid community sanctions.

PART THREE

The Real Enemies of the Ideal Society

Social isolation produces family solidarity? A debatable consequence of atomisation was that it strengthened the immediate family. Generally, family members could not look to kin, neighbours, work-mates, or other associates for mutual aid. The function of the home as a provider of recreation, companionship, labour, childcare, and other goods and services was accordingly enhanced. *Alexander Turnbull Library*

Prologue

HAVING rejected the idea that colonial New Zealand possessed a strong social organisation supportive of hierarchy, class-divisions, oppressive status anxiety, it is now necessary to demonstrate what the real enemies of the ideal society were. The overarching hypothesis is that the 'insider's view' is basically correct: New Zealand in fact was a minimally organised society. Although some people lived close to others and interacted with them, social isolation was the prevailing tendency; much more so before 1880, however, than after. Support for the argument comes from the knowledge accumulated in a piecemeal manner over Part II. If that knowledge is summarised in a more systematic fashion it yields the following hypothesis, focusing on the primary and the secondary causes of social isolation.

The primary cause arose during the period between the 1850s and the 1880s, when the population was swamped by a tide of immigrants, by people who had been severed from their associations in the metropolitan society and had not dwelt long enough in the colony to replace those that had been lost. It is possible (and the issue will not be probed) that the atomising effect of immigration was greater in New Zealand than in early Australia and in British North America. A larger proportion may have immigrated as bondless individuals: the New England colonies were transplanted religious associations and their off-shoots; a big contingent of the immigrants to the mid Atlantic colonies of British North America arrived vertically bonded as indentured servants; while the penal settlement, chain gang, and (most important of all) the assignment system may have endowed the initial wave of immigrants to Australia with an organisation in embryo.[1] Although Wakefield's schemes were designed to prevent atomisation, it is not known whether and to what extent the Wakefield immigrants in fact came from the same village or were related kin. The Wakefield settlements, anyway, were sooner or later overwhelmed by the influx from the 1850s onwards.

The secondary cause was the host of indigenous factors that long retarded and disrupted the replacement of the former bonds. The lightning expansion of the frontier up to the 1880s pushed most colonists into new areas where they were strangers to one another, and where for an initial period no institutions existed to facilitate mixing and meeting. The scantiness of kinship ties deprived colonists of a natural base for the development of community ties. A scattered population, little leisure for organised recreation, and the difficulty of recruiting and retaining members undermined the capacity of voluntary organisations to arise and flourish. Foot-loose colonists formed only fleeting relationships. The brief engagement of itinerant workers and their solitary travelling habits prevented them from developing 'mateship' ties. If that was not enough, a large minority of settled households were geographically isolated, physically remote from other households and the formal groupings of the towns. In addition, the colony's ruling ideology of extreme individualism inhibited the growth of institutions below the state level. The generally strong labour market, the remarkable resourcefulness of manual workers, and the multitudinous opportunities for petty enterprise converted practically every male and female breadwinner into a masterless man or woman.

But if New Zealand lived up to the idea of itself as a minimally organised society, this did not mean that the society was in fact ideal in its own terms. One of the two aims of Part III is to demonstrate that it was far from ideal, indeed it was badly flawed. It certainly was a materially abundant society—even though advancement from the petty proprietor and penny capitalism level was not nearly as dependent upon individual virtue as the 'insider's view' maintained. Without doubt, too, it generally fulfilled expectations that it was a 'labourer's paradise' and able to foster personal autonomy—though not always for the reasons claimed by the 'insider's view'. And yet these blessings should have been accompanied by others—felicity and natural order and harmony—and there is overwhelming evidence that such blessings were in short supply. The root cause of this was the minimal organisation itself. What it created was a great deal of loneliness, a source of misery not felicity; a severe drinking problem, a symptom of individual licence not order; a massive amount of disharmony—not the organised disharmony that the class-division model refers to but an altogether different kind: interpersonal conflict expressed in violence and civil litigation.

This leads to the second objective of Part III. The hypothesis just advanced of the atomised colonial society is based on the knowledge accrued from the falsification of the three alternative concepts, those depicting the society as hierarchical, as class-divided, or as a collection of local communities. It is possible that this knowledge alone is enough to support the hypothesis. But as it might not be, two additional methods have been devised to demonstrate it. The first method will show that atomisation has a greater power to explain the real problems of the ideal society—loneliness, drunkenness, interpersonal conflict— than any other theory. This will be the subject of Chapter VII. The second method will demonstrate that five mechanisms placed upper limits on the chaos of the minimally organised society, and that these mechanisms were a predictable consequence of the atomisation itself. This will be the subject of Chapter VIII.

Drawn from life by W.F.Gordon
4, 3, 86

At home
Tree 11ft wide & 5 ft high inside & 1 Chain
long to live in: Akitio

A colonial eccentric, 1886. A hermit near Eltham lived in a hollow
totara log and gathered fungus and cocksfoot seed for a living.
Alexander Turnbull Library

CHAPTER VII

Frontier Chaos

Loneliness

The circumstances that led to what colonists thought was good about New Zealand society—the insignificance of demeaning paternalism, class divisions, pressure for conformity—could not help but generate loneliness. What removed New Zealand from these Old World evils also engendered loneliness: transience, the dearth of kinsfolk, the inaccessibility of voluntary organisations, the small population and extreme dispersal of settlement, the paucity of communications, the solitary nature of much work, the high rate of material independence, the newness of settlement, and so on. The few critics of the society were aware that one or another of these factors deprived individuals of social contact; sometimes the link was seen even by the admirers, who were not conscious of how inseparable it was from the things they praised about the new land. One settler reminiscing about a trip he made around the East Cape in 1892, suddenly remembered how few of his friends now dwelt there, and was drawn to comment, 'Alas! that the course of colonial acquaintanceships should be so often rudely severed by the removal to a distant county of one or both the attached friends, perhaps never again to meet.'[1] Particular occupations were notorious for the social isolation they imposed—gumdiggers, waggoners, mailmen tended to operate alone, as did goldminers sometimes, and shepherds most of all: 'A shepherd's life is a terribly lonely one. . . . Every day is alike—work, food, earth and sky—and they live in a dull dreamless sleep, as it were. They feel themselves simply an atom of life in a lifeless world, and they have no hope or ambition.'[2] The largest volume of complaints emanated, however, from geographically isolated households. The famous Edinburgh agronomist, Robert Wallace, warned of the loneliness of the settler's life in 1891, as did Arthur Clayden in his glowing advice-book of 1879.[3] Captain and Mrs Fergusson, who occupied the Opouriao Valley near Whakatane in 1875, soon returned to Auckland after 'Tiring of the solitude'. On the evening before he set out on a six weeks' trip to Wellington, Robert Langdon, a Wairarapa runholder, commented in his diary in 1856, 'Very wet today. Mrs L. very lonely.' Mrs Tripp of Mount Peel station found in the 1850s that she was so in need of human companionship that she feared she would forget her own language, and to assuage her fear she made herself learn the whole of Keble's *Christian Year*.[4]

In many instances, the sense of desperation came from people who were not alone but lived with the same small group of people day after day. William Pember Reeves vividly portrayed the appalling monotony of his life when in the mid 1870s he worked as a cadet on a sheep-station near Ashburton, where he had the company of just the manager, a man-cook, and the ploughman's wife who came in every morning to tidy up. In the 1870s Mrs Caverhill of Highfield station in the Amuri felt in dire need of social stimulation despite the presence of a cook, two maids, a nursemaid, her children, husband, and the station-hands, although it was worse when the cook went away or the maids had resigned and new ones had not been hired.[5] The journal kept by Sarah Courage, a wife of another runholder closer to Christchurch, at Leithfield, is filled with melancholy observations about her loneliness: 'having not a soul to exchange ideas with from morning to night', 'How I did long to hear a noise of some sort', 'I felt so terribly alone', 'I felt the dullness and monotony of our lives very keenly at times', 'My mind would yield helplessly to the influence of the hour, and despondency—that hated spirit— would be an inseparable companion all the way home'; yet she had the company of her husband, a maid, a cook, and a groom, and often went to church. The precursor of suburban neurosis also hit Ellen Timms, the wife of an English rural labourer working on an Ashburton sheep-station, who, according to an acquaintance, 'does not like the country, it is lonely where they are'.[6] The spirits of back-country women often fell to their lowest point when for various reasons their husbands were away from the house. Writing in 1866 from her Canterbury sheep-run, Lady Barker commented upon the dullness of life when her husband was in Christchurch; she could 'get on very well' all day with all her chores to occupy her mind, but at night when the servants went to bed the house became quiet and silent and 'a horrible lonely eerie feeling comes over me; the solitude is so dreary, and the silence so intense, only broken occasionally by the wild, melancholy cry of the weka'. Mrs Elizabeth Mackay, the wife of a runholder in the Rakaia Gorge in the 1860s, discovered 'The loneliness was terrible, especially when at mustering time all the men were camped for days on the high country'.[7] Often mingled with this sense of depression was a fear of being attacked by strangers. Mrs Adams of Marlborough recalled in graphic detail an event 'One dark night' in the late 1850s when she was alone in the house with her baby and toddler:

to my horror, a knock came to the door. It was useless to open it. I had neither bed nor food to offer, and as it was the back door I knew it was not one of our neighbours. I think my blood froze. Knock again. I crept on all fours to the bedroom lest my shadow should be seen. What a night! I was sure it was a tramp else he would have spoken, and I feared he might break the tiny window and murder us all. Round and round the cottage tramped the footsteps, now stopping, now continuing. No light inside or out, no moon, no stars.[8]

On the other side, single, transient men felt just as desolate. George Walker, who moved from Taranaki to the Thames goldfields in 1869, moaned in his letters about his boredom, the unsatisfactory nature of his friends, his restlessness, the quarrels he had at different lodgings, his general low morale, the fact that there was 'not a lady friend or a house where you could visit and feel at home'.[9]

Loneliness also features as a reason for the high turnover of servants and labourers in rural areas and the creation of all sorts of ancillary problems. During the 1880s Thorne Seccombe's father milked over 100 cows on the East Cape to produce cheese for the Auckland market; in 1888 'the share-milkers began to complain that the isolation was more than they could stand, and sought to abrogate their agreement to remain in their employment for three years'; the agreement was broken, litigation ensued; a succession of share-milkers then came and went. Henry Sewell noted in 1854 that in Akaroa 'it is impossible to get Servants . . . they don't like solitudes, and people consequently have to wash their own clothes, scour their own floors. . .'. Between 1864 and 1872 (approximately) Sarah Courage employed a succession of 10 sets of household staff, including four maids and two married couples.[10]

Sometimes loneliness resulted not from the absence of society but from the fact that with such a small range of people living in each settlement, they mixed only at the cost of much mutual embarrassment, so incompatible were their interests and backgrounds. During the 1870s a Rangitikei runholder decided to bring the people of the district together by opening up his house to everyone each weekend. 'It was not, however, everyone who could be at ease in this atmosphere of unaffected gaiety and natural good manners. To such a one nothing could be said or done directly to hurt his feelings but he would soon realise he was a misfit, and he could not ride the pace, and would retire.' Awkwardness also arose when relative strangers met and one unwittingly insulted the other. When Pember Reeves worked on the Ashburton sheep run, an itinerant Nonconformist parson visited who took 'us from our clothing, to be barbarians' and dropped 'a tract or two in corners of the room'; finding this offensive, Reeves in revenge showered the man with his knowledge of abstruse points of theology, a retaliation which had the desired effect, 'As I was going to bed I observed the good man stealthily resuming his tracts and slipping them into his pocket'—but it did nothing to cure Reeves's sense of isolation for the man was 'intelligent' and Reeves otherwise would have enjoyed his company.[11]

The lack of friends and social stimulation also manifested itself in the survival techniques employed. One adjustment can be seen in family life. Lady Barker noticed that there seemed 'to be a greater amount of real domestic happiness out here than at home', 'homes seem to be thoroughly happy ones', which she attributed to 'the want of places of public amusement'; 'A married man is an object of envy to his less fortunate brethren, and he appears anxious to show that he appreciates his good fortune'. Charles Hursthouse scorned the suggestion that an immigrant was without friends in New Zealand by saying that if married, the newcomer had his wife and children as company—'*these* are his nearest and dearest friends, and *these* always go with him'; family life in New Zealand was sufficiently varied and interesting to make up for the dearth of 'sports and pleasures, such things as public amusements, sights, theatres, and raree-shows'.[12] Statements of this kind must, of course, be treated with care since the Arcadian preconceptions disposed writers to romanticise family life. Furthermore, they clash with the views of many historians who have found that the colonial family was under stress, as suggested by the long periods lower-class men often spent working away from home, the apparently large incidence of deserted families and neglected children, as well as cases of family violence perpetrated by drunken husbands.[13] On the other side, however, the evidence of family desertion and neglected children nearly always comes from moralists and the authorities in charge of charitable bodies, who had every interest in exaggerating these problems in order to broadcast the dominant ideology, to make plain through negative definition that the proper norm was self-reliance.[14] Certainly many women applying for charitable aid were classified as 'deserted', but it is not known what this meant—whether husbands had left the family permanently or temporarily or whether the wife was covertly receiving support from the husband while he was away. No doubt drunken men often brutalised their wives and children; but the idea that this was typical is not supported by a correlation analysis over a more extended period: from 1853 to 1930 the number of adult women per 100,000 general population, with all the nine provincial districts treated simultaneously, has a *negative* association with the amount of spirits and beer consumption, drunkenness convictions, and petty violence convictions proportionate to the general population.[15] (See the table of correlations in the appendix attached to this chapter.)

If there were potent forces generating stresses and strains in family life, there were as many, perhaps more, producing cohesion. In a land where formal and informal social services and amenities were scarce or unavailable, the family's capacity to support, protect, and entertain its members would have expanded commensurately in importance. For the lack of other sources of welfare, household heads who were manual workers could ill afford to alienate their dependants, so vital was the unpaid labour of wives and children in the productive activities on the household land, so vital were the cash contributions of older children to family income when the principal breadwinner's earning powers faded with old age or poor health.[16] In the absence of organised recreations, country families had no choice but to organise their own diversions such as picnics, hunting, fishing, boating, music-making, parlour-games (all extensively recorded in colonial memoirs).[17] Mutual aid, which in societies with strong social bonds flowed between the immediate family and somebody outside it (a friend, neighbour, relation, employer), in an atomised society had to be found within the family itself. This accords with two English investigations during the 1950s—one by Elizabeth Bott and the other by Willmott and Young—which showed that parents who had been geographically mobile and no longer belonged to informal support networks were more disposed to be emotionally close and share domestic duties than the parents who had not moved and were still integrated into the informal support networks of the surrounding community.[18] Probably the tendency over the whole late 19th century for completed families to be larger than their equivalents in England and Wales was an adaptive response to the weaknesses of New Zealand society. Large families were more able than smaller ones to act as a surrogate society, to satisfy the needs of its members for companionship, material welfare, recreation.[19]

Various systems of hospitality also evolved to mitigate loneliness. Rural households developed the most advanced system. To attract and facilitate visits from far-away friends and neighbours, they went to great lengths to be able to accommodate them. This affected expenditure priorities and left its mark on rural architecture. The first call upon the discretionary income of the successful was to add another room or to construct a new, spacious house with many rooms. In 1883 W. S. Young, for example, built a home at Otakeho, in Taranaki, containing a 'Big Room' which could act as a dance floor or be divided in half by curtains of green serge for family use. The purpose of the 'Big Room' was to enable the home to become the centre of hospitality for the whole district, an idea which the family had picked up earlier in reaction to their 'lonely years at Kaipara' when their house was too small for entertaining.[20]

Obviously, however, these institutional adjustments were not enough, for contemporaries resorted to all sorts of ploys to keep up their morale, to keep the greyness at bay. A favourite compensation was gardening, especially for women. The educated often escaped through reading books. T. S. Mannering, an Amuri runholder, said that although he was often alone, his 'three or four books read and re-read' kept his mind off his socially undernourished life. Frederick Weld in his *Hints to Intending Sheep Farmers in New Zealand* counselled that such 'accomplishments as poetry and music' were 'invaluable', for 'in moments of gloom and despondency' they 'diverted and aroused' the mind 'from its morbid state by their cheerful and soothing influence'. Ernest Molesworth, an early settler in Opotiki County, who lived alone, acquired an alarm clock which played 'the Absent-minded Beggar' to keep him company. In 1893 Edward Tregear claimed in a government publication on labour in New Zealand that settlers' wives knew that 'housework, cooking, and washing for a family, if properly carried out, prevent any idleness or *ennui* from visiting the household'. Sarah Courage wrote that one of her consolations was her diary: 'I looked upon it as a confidential friend, wherein I could describe my pleasures and sorrows, with observations on my friends and acquaintances which struck me at the time.' Conversations with strangers about English cricket and politics seem to have lessened the strain of social intercourse. Arthur Clayden in 1879 recommended, as an antidote to the 'unavoidable loneliness of a settler's life . . . far away from human habitation', making a virtue out of necessity by communing with nature. H. H. Miller, one of the first pioneers in Apiti during the 1880s, said that, contrary to the impression that 'bush life must of necessity be a lonely depressing one', he maintained his mental stability by taking an interest in the bird life and because the hard physical work gave him long, refreshing sleeps at night, the latter point being quite consistent with modern psychiatric evidence. J. Adam in 1876 said that the best way to cope with the problem was 'by a busy life' and by engaging in 'an extensive correspondence about men and things' to one's 'parents, friends, and relatives' to engender the comforting illusion that these people were actually present and that one was actually conversing with them. While working in the Otago back-country in the 1870s Henry Scott found that shepherds compensated for their lack of human companions by developing close ties with their dogs.[21]

An even better method of coping with loneliness, apparently, was to read letters from former associates back 'Home'. The function of this was to allow settlers to live vicariously in a community, to feel as if they were engaging in its gossip and rituals, to act out in their imaginations the relationships that were forbidden to them by the new desocialised environment. Sarah Courage remembered: 'How eagerly we used to look forward to news from the outer world in those times, as indeed we still do. Every trifling episode of their everyday lives, which one's relations or friends think of no moment, will provide us with fresh thoughts and perhaps conversation for many a day here in the country, where life is such a blank.' Reading the 'home mails' was a momentous event, one of the half dozen or so things most colonists cited in their reminiscences to convey their sense of the frontier past. In B. E. Baughan's poem, 'Early Days', the receipt of letters from 'home' was exciting enough to warrant a stanza of its own:

An' sometimes, oh! a letter.—Then 'twas 'get the slush-lamp, quick'. . . .
An' then we'd hush an' settle down quiet round the hearth
For to hear o' green Kent country, an' the old side of the earth.
Uncle listen'd interested, Father with a frown;
Mother used to listen with her head bow'd down.

In some cases, settlers shared their letters from home with their
few friends and neighbours, attempting, it seems, to make believe
that their former and present associates were members of the same
group, and their affiliations were richer than they actually were.[22]
Many colonists tried to forget they were lonely by collecting various
mementoes symbolising their former old-world companions. Everyday
contact with these objects was supposed to stimulate remembrance
and offset the new land's inability to sustain real forms of association.
Especially important were photographs of loved ones and their
surroundings at 'Home'; W. J. Cox, an unmarried casual labourer,
treasured the snapshots sent to him of his brother's baby, his mother's
house, his mother, and the countryside surrounding the home of his
brother in Cox's native Wiltshire. Also important were ornamental
garden plants. It was recorded of women pioneers in Feilding during
the late 1880s that most 'soon had gardens, and their bright beds
of flowers, grown from cuttings and seeds sent by friends "outside",
provided them with fragrant memories of friendly faces that seemed
so far away'. A poem, 'The Gardener in Exile', by a former pioneer,
discusses each English flower in her garden and links it to the friends
and kin back in the Old World: 'All the plants with pretty names',
'All the flowers with lovely faces', 'Lilies that look softly up', 'Every
well-remembered scent / To bring the exiled heart content.' The
same point was made in a novel published in 1939 on early Hawke's
Bay. The heroine has a grove of peach trees, 'aliens in the virgin
bush, akin in their isolation to Ned and herself, they became to her
not merely trees but friendly, sentient comrades. Recalling the orchard
in Devon at first, they had been a breath of Home; now they had
a calendar of incidents which endeared them to her, ordinary little
memories of an ordinary life. . .'.[23]
Mentioned too as a surrogate for social participation was the reading
of English newspapers and magazines—*Punch, The Field, Illustrateds,
Bailey's Sporting Magazine*, and so forth. This activity allowed a mental
escape from a socially arid world into one of community events,
celebrations, recreations, and endless opportunities to chat, exchange
opinions and ideas. Some settlers even decorated their walls with
these papers, literally surrounding themselves with representations

of social life. 'If our home friends could only realise', Sarah Courage wrote, 'how much pleasure they give us by sending papers and magazines so regularly, they would feel themselves amply repaid for their trouble', and in the same context she added, 'I am naturally of a sociable disposition, and, after all, solitary confinement in paradise would scarcely be better than the same fate on earth.'[24] The strong tendency of colonists to cling to old-world cultural forms, epitomised by their habit of calling England 'Home', has been misunderstood. It was not the outcome of 'immaturity', a neurotic response to an alien environment, a manifestation of a provincial mentality. Instead it was a natural reaction to the dearth of associations—colonists remained emotionally tied to the Old World because their atomised society could not satisfy the human need for gregariousness. They revered their imported cultural forms not for their own sake but because these represented social interactions that had once been enjoyed at 'Home' and that New Zealand took a long time to duplicate. Colonists were understandably fond of 'Home' because the word (for an initial period at least) was a metaphor for the social situations and intimates missing in the new land.[25]

So far the evidence that loneliness was extensive has been drawn from the statements by the literate and educated, chiefly back-country women. The bulk of lower-class men and the inarticulate, in town and country, expressed and compensated for their loneliness through excessive drinking. Colonial drunkenness had many causes and was a complex problem, as we shall see later; without doubt, however, loneliness and drunkenness were connected in several ways. In the first place, alcohol was used to blot out the psychic pain of social isolation. In early Opotiki a young Welsh teacher, appointed to Kutarere school, 'found life very lonely . . . one of the sad cases only too common in those days. Weak, and fond of drink, he had been sent to New Zealand in hopes of a cure, but it was surely the worst course to take', to send a 20-year-old so far away from home and friends, and the unfortunate fellow drowned after a drinking binge.[26] In the second place alcohol was used to break down the barriers that separated people and prevented intimacy in an atomised society. In the places where it was drunk—pubs and drinking shanties— there were always other people to talk to. It helped to loosen tongues, remove the inhibitions between strangers. One drinking convention, 'shouting', could usually be relied upon to buy 'instant' friendships or social acceptance. 'Shouting' was a primitive system of hospitality whereby one person bought drinks for another, or others.[27] Its advantage in a society of strangers was that it obliged whoever was bought a drink to converse and be friendly with the donor. 'Shouting', however, led to immoderate consumption, partly because a large group of men was often thus purchasing a friendship, and partly because there was no logical end to it. For one man to refuse to buy the next round of drinks was to spurn the companionship and invite a hostile response.

The visibility of social derelicts in the colony was likewise a symptom of loneliness. It was argued earlier that mass poverty did not exist in New Zealand. This does not mean, of course, that there was no poverty at all; a formal system of charitable aid evolved to care for widows, deserted families, and, towards the end of the century, a growing proportion of elderly men. But men who could not work, had no savings, and were without friends or relations to support them, missed the slender safety net of charitable aid. Newspaper court reports on vagrancy cases brought these derelicts into public view. In January 1879 William Percy appeared before the Wellington Magistrate's Court charged with having no visible means of support. On information received, two constables discovered Percy, 'An emaciated-looking being', living in a cave in Lyall Bay; he had nothing on but a shirt, there were no possessions in the cave but some empty bottles and a kerosene tin, and he was feeding off shellfish and stewed moss and seaweed. The accused explained that he had 'chopped his hand' about two years ago; he was mending his clothes when the constables arrived; he was 'in the habit of collecting bottles and mushrooms, which he sold. He occasionally caught fish. He had been living in the cave for about six weeks, and had no doubt he could continue to support himself by these means, as there were plenty of people in the district who would buy from him.' In another case in the same year a householder in Kaitoke was awakened one night by the noise of an intruder. The householder confronted the burglar and the two fought until the offender was overpowered. In explanation, the intruder told his intended victim that he was 'Jim Hart, the bushranger' and he had wanted food and clothes. In evidence, the constable said that on the previous day he saw the prisoner preaching on the railway wharf in Upper Hutt. His real name was John Rosemergy. The prisoner told the magistrate that he had a past history of fits but he was not a lunatic.[28]

Perhaps the most problematic symptom of loneliness is the wealth of anecdotes about people who failed to cope psychologically with their solitude or became strange, and the existence of colloquialisms describing those who were thought peculiar in mind and habit, especially if they worked or lived alone. Such people were commonly labelled 'hatters'; to 'go silly', to be 'bush ratty', to suffer from 'bush fright', were likewise popular terms.[29] What is problematic about this sort of evidence is that the perception of abnormality invariably has a subjective element, particularly in a society where the lack of social interaction is bound to throw up widely varying notions of what constitutes unusual behaviour. It could be argued, furthermore, that it is in the very nature of anecdotes to highlight the peculiar. On the other side, there is ample clinical and experimental evidence to suggest that people exposed to social isolation become mentally disturbed,[30] and it makes intuitive sense to believe that those unused to the company of others (strangers especially) could become shy, and that the solitary would lose track of social conventions and be prone to eccentricity (or greater eccentricity). The anecdotes also have an authentic ring to them. Of those collected so far, none concern people who were regarded as strange because they belonged to weird sects, bizarre cults, extreme political movements. They focus consistently on the peculiarities of individuals or families— abnormality without a social context. This is what should be the case; for if we postulate that the colony suffered from bondlessness, then it follows that strange behaviour would have taken individual, not group, form. The dearth of opportunities for association would have prevented outsiders from seeking one another out, from coming together to express their idiosyncratic view of the world through their own groups. For example, the Studholmes of Te Waimate recalled visiting a family of indigents in the 1880s and finding that the children were 'as wild as deer, for they saw few strangers, and looked on us as queer beasts, watching every move we made. . . . For a joke we would look round suddenly, and the children would nearly fall. down with fright. . . .' In 1882 W. D. Hay, thinking back to his life on the Kaipara, observed that people in the 'bush' were initially shy when they met strangers, for unlike towns-people they were unaccustomed to society. The shyness of men working on high-country stations struck Mona Anderson in a later period. Thorne Seccombe recalled the eccentricity of a sheep-station manager, a Mr Callighan, a bachelor and 'real wild Irishman with a long black beard . . . who used to swear "like a trooper"', who had such a 'complex' about women that he would never go into a place if one were there; once when chided for being so shy and for his 'complex' he replied '"Bah,— I never had a mother—I was suckled on a door-nob."' Sarah Courage

remembered a shepherd her husband employed who claimed he was
visited twice a week by a lady wearing white kid gloves accompanied
by her two daughters who, after talking a while, would go away,
'Up the hill, . . . always up the hill'; the man was well educated
and sensible enough on other matters but never wavered in his
statement about the ladies. Another story about mental breakdowns
caused by loneliness features a series of teachers at Te Teko, a sole-
charge school in the Ureweras near Whakatane. After it was opened
in 1891, the first teacher, Mr Crene, soon asked for a transfer to
get away from 'this purgatory with sandflies'. The second teacher,
appointed in 1896, did well until the 'climate and the sandflies' affected
his wife's health and 'her mind collapsed entirely'; she was placed
in an asylum in Auckland, and he, worried about his wife, 'became
a changed man', and retired from the service at the end of the year.
The next teacher who was appointed did not turn up at the school.
The 'sandflies and the climate' then 'wore through the stern reserve'
of the fourth master and his wife: she had a nervous breakdown,
was admitted to an asylum, he worried about her and left the school.
His replacement appeared to run the school effectively for a while
until 'the sandflies and the climate' affected his wife's health,
'necessitating her taking six months' leave of absence until her health
improved'. With the teacher after that the pattern repeated itself:
the 'sandflies and the climate' affected his spouse's health and she
was continually on the verge of a nervous breakdown.[31]

Drunkenness

From two comparative standpoints a *prima facie* case can be made
that colonial New Zealand was gripped by a particularly severe
drinking problem. One is that the number of convictions per 100,000
adult males for drunkenness was far higher in New Zealand than
in England and Wales. In the three years 1860–2 the mean number
of convictions per 100,000 adult males as given in the mid-period
census was 71 per cent less in England and Wales than in New
Zealand; in 1870–2 the English rate was 65 per cent less; in 1880–
2, 34 per cent; in 1890–2, 23 per cent; only by the mid 1890s were
the rates for the two countries about the same.[32] Extreme caution
is necessary in interpreting this gap; until it is analysed further we
cannot say whether there was actually more drunkenness in New
Zealand or greater public visibility or more active policing. At the
very least, however, New Zealand's higher recorded rate contradicts
the impression given by the 'insider's view' that the colony had escaped

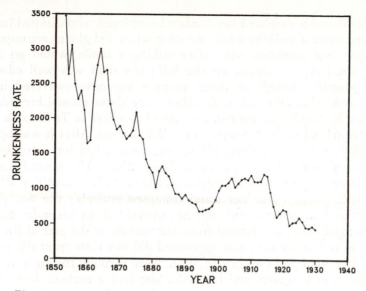

Fig. 7.1. Drunkenness rate (convictions per 100,000 population)

the need for institutionalised repression of such evils. Another comparative indication of the drinking problem is that in relation to the subsequent era in New Zealand (1900–1930), the number of summary convictions per 100,000 of general population in the colonial era was astronomical. From Figure 7.1 it can be seen that from the 1850s to 1930 the conviction rate moved in a series of progressively shallower waves. The highest was at the beginning of the recorded period, in 1853, with almost 3,500 convictions per 100,000 people, the next came in the mid 1860s with 3,000 convictions per 100,000, the third hit in the mid 1870s with over 2,000 convictions per 100,000. Between these historical peaks were two deep troughs, one bottoming out in 1860 with 1,640 convictions per 100,000 and the other in 1872 with about 1,700 convictions per 100,000. From the late 1870s to the 1890s the rate dropped rapidly, reaching its lowest 19th-century point at fewer than 700 convictions per 100,000 in 1895. Although it rose from then on until 1914, this last wave was the weakest, just exceeding 1,200 convictions per 100,000 at its apex in 1914; thereafter it continued to fall, sinking to its lowest point historically by 1930, a third below the most depressed rates in the 19th century (the mid 1890s). Consideration of possible reasons for the high colonial rates will show that atomisation is the best fundamental explanation.

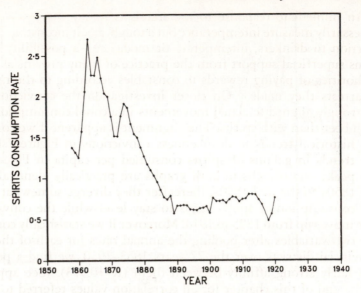

Fig. 7.2. Spirits consumption rate (gallons per capita)

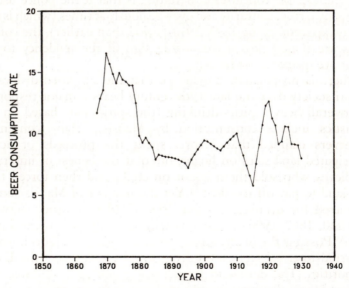

Fig. 7.3. Beer consumption rate (gallons per capita)

Note: The interpolation of missing data for the beer consumption rate on a provincial basis has smoothed the plot between Census periods, especially after 1895.

An immediate response to the trends is to say that they do not necessarily measure intemperance but a tough, albeit inconstant official reaction to drinkers, intemperate or moderate—a possibility which gains superficial support from the practice of many provincial police authorities of paying rewards to constables according to the number of arrests they made.[33] On closer investigation the conviction rate is strongly aligned to actual movements in alcohol consumption, less with beer than with spirits. The alignment is apparent if we compare the historical trends in drunkenness convictions in Figure 7.1 with the trends in gallons of spirits consumed per capita in Figure 7.2: the peaks and troughs in both graphs are practically identical from the 1850s to the mid 1890s; thereafter they diverge somewhat when the consumption of spirits tends to stay level while the convictions rate moves up from 1895 to 1914. Moreover if we statistically correlate the two variables after pooling the annual rates for each of the nine provincial districts over the 77 years 1853–1930, we find a positive and fairly strong affinity between them (R=+0.573). (See appendix at the end of this chapter for all correlation values referred to.) The same procedure applied to drunkenness and the gallons of beer consumed per capita yields a much smaller co-efficient (R=+0.153). The inescapable conclusion, therefore, is that if the police used their power of arrest arbitrarily and over-zealously at times (which is actually more apparent in the 1895–1914 period than earlier), the conviction rates are nonetheless a reasonable sign of the tendency to imbibe excessive quantities of hard liquor.

There is no persuasive evidence that the supposed dislocation of Maori society over the late 19th century bears a major responsibility for overall heavy spirits drinking (the spirits data based on import statistics include consumption by Maoris). Many contemporary observers claimed that Maoris spent the proceeds of actual or anticipated land sales on liquor, often at the behest of unscrupulous publicans who sold them liquor on credit and then forced them to sell land to pay off the debt.[34] Yet the number of Maoris summarily convicted for drunkenness per 100,000 Maoris varied between 99 and 440, 1862–1900, which was trifling compared to the European rate.[35] Possibly the Maori rates were lower because Maori intoxication occurred in tribal areas away from the surveillance of the European authorities. The dominant impression given by historians, though, is that Maori drinking usually took place during visits to the town and was strongly associated with prolonged land court hearings there: hence it should have been as evident as European debauchery was to the authorities and as susceptible to policing.[36] This being so, it is likely that Maoris did not in relative terms purchase as much liquor as Europeans and that their contribution to spirits consumption was comparatively slight.

Unpersuasive, too, is the hypothesis that the hard drinking was an intrinsic element in a Pakeha 'macho' code. Giving the hypothesis superficial support is the fact that the proportion of adult men convicted for drunkenness was many times greater than the female proportion (in 1872, for example, the rate for adult females was just over a quarter of the men's). The model, however, does not square with the rapid long-term reduction in drinking and drunkenness from the mid 1870s onwards. Normative codes generally change slowly since they are maintained and enforced by peer-group pressure, and the individual group-members who score well on the value system have every incentive to defend it in order to preserve the things which award them status. The big slump in drinking after the mid 1870s, therefore, implies that the previous era of high inebriation was the result of little, if any, male peer-group pressure. Certainly the proportion of people—males aged 21 to 40—most likely to belong to 'macho' peer-groups fell over the last two and a half decades of the 19th century. Yet if drunkenness convictions and spirits consumption are controlled for this demographic shift by giving them a population base of males aged 21 to 40, the rates still decline strongly from the 1864 peak to 1895, by 51 per cent in the case of drunkenness and 54 per cent in the case of spirits consumption (as against falls on a general population base of 77 per cent and 73 per cent respectively).[37]

To be sure, there was one male sub-culture in New Zealand that did have a remarkable love for hard liquor, rum especially—Imperial troops. They must have contributed heavily to aggregate spirits consumption when it crested in the early 1860s. Yet brandy, not rum, was the most popular spirit for most of the early 1860s and brandy was the preferred spirit of the civilian population.[38] Furthermore, although the presence of Imperial troops was most significant during the years of peak spirits drinking (1861–6), consumption by historical standards was still astronomical in 1869–1875, when almost no troops, with the exception of one regiment (1869–70), were stationed in the country.

What must be taken more seriously as a longer-term structural factor is prosperity. Zehr in a study of crime in 19th-century France and Germany has found a strong statistical linkage between prosperity and drunkenness, as have Gatrell and Hadden in their survey of crime in 19th-century Britain. The theory is that when the purchasing power of the working classes rose, they could afford to buy more liquor and were thus more disposed to intemperance, while reductions in aggregate working-class real income had the reverse effect.[39] Superficially, New Zealand conforms to the model in that spirits consumption per 100,000 general population peaked during the affluent gold-rush period of the 1860s while the late-century slump in drunkenness coincided with the so-called 'Long Depression'. It seems improbable, however, that common living standards fell sufficiently during the 1880s and early 1900s to account for the sharpness with which the spirits indicator slumped. Indeed, it is doubtful if there was any decline in workers' per capita real incomes at all over the whole period. It is also anomalous that the spirits trend from 1895 to 1908 failed to pick up significantly when economic growth was far more rapid than during the 'Long Depression'. By the 1920s consumption of spirits per head was far lower than it had been up to the 1880s, although it is reasonable to believe that real wages were higher by the 1920s than before 1880. Underlining the weakness of the alleged relationship between prosperity and drunkenness is that over the long term (from 1853 to 1930), the drunkenness rate per 100,000 general population had only a slight, positive correlation with two other proxy measures of economic well-being, namely, the value of imports and exports per 100,000 general population (the correlation here is for all nine provincial districts treated simultaneously). Besides, the logic of the argument is dubious. Low or sliding real incomes could theoretically push up liquor intake, rather than depress it, by creating despair and by encouraging the poor to divert their spending away from relatively high-priced consumer goods to alcohol, which was cheaper item for item because it could be bought in tiny quantities at a time.

A modified prosperity argument assumes that the reason unmarried adult males were the heaviest drinkers was that they had no dependants to support. Having thus the largest margin of discretionary spending, they could afford to spend more on drink than any other social category. The pattern of initial high rates of drinking followed by long-term decline from the mid 1870s can by this argument be attributed to simple demographic changes. The disproportionately large number of these 'at risk' males from the 1850s to the 1870s pushed up the overall incidence of drinking, while from the mid 1870s the shrinking relative size of this category pulled the incidence down. Such a possibility, however, accounts for a tiny fraction of the 19th-century variations. Converting gallons of spirits into a rate per unmarried male aged over 20 (non-Maori), we find that the ratio fell from 14.5 gallons in 1874 (the first Census to specify marital status by age) to 5.3 gallons in 1896, or by almost 64 per cent, as against a decline in gallons per head of general population by 68 per cent between the same years.[40]

Another possible explanation is that consumption was linked to the real price of alcohol—as that went down, it stimulated drinking, as it rose, consumption declined. Unfortunately the only available price index for alcohol (covering the wholesale price of brandy, beer, port, claret and whisky) does not commence until 1877. But if it was a downward movement in real alcohol prices which fuelled the excessive spirits drinking before 1877, then the reverse should apply to the period after 1877 when consumption rapidly shrank. At first sight the hypothesis seems to be confirmed by the general tendency of the alcohol price index to climb by about 12 per cent from 1877 to 1895 (in contrast to the general index for 45 wholesale items which went down by 35 per cent), mainly as a result of rising excise duty. However, statistical tests of the connection between spirits consumption per 100,000 European males aged 21–40 and the alcohol price index over the period 1877–95 give no support for the possibility that consumption was sensitive to price.[41]

Many 'supply-side' explanations also have their difficulties. It is doubtful if the evil sprang from a shortage of readily available, hygienic, non-alcoholic refreshments, which forced the large body of men engaging in intense physical exertion to slake their thirsts with alcohol. Brian Harrison has given much weight to this argument in his study of alcohol abuse in early Victorian England.[42] New Zealand's water supplies were obviously far less polluted than those of an industrialising and densely populated Britain. Furthermore, all colonials carried their own tea-making utensils and tea was brewed in vast quantities, but this did not stop alcoholic drinks from being popular as well. It is doubtful, too, if the large number of hotels and drinking establishments—the sheer accessibility of liquor—was an important engine of intemperance. The first effective measure restricting the sale of alcohol was not imposed until the 1881 Licensing Act;[43] if the rates of spirits consumption and drunkenness convictions diminished for the remainder of the century as access to liquor diminished, it must also be remembered that the long-term falls were well advanced by 1881, showing markedly since the mid 1870s. Then there are the two supply-side arguments put forward by A. E. Dingle to account for alcohol abuse in early colonial Australia.[44] He maintains, firstly, that the general scarcity of consumer goods forced men to waste money on drink because there was little else to spend it on; and secondly, that liquor expenditure was directed overwhelmingly to spirits rather than beer (which was inherently less intoxicating) because importers found spirits cheaper to ship and distribute than beer, and indigenous beer production took time to develop. These arguments are applicable to New Zealand but with critical reservations. According to Dingle's figures (which are for the 19th century), beer and spirits switched places over time in both New South Wales and Victoria, with beer becoming more popular than spirits, a change which the easing of the constraints on beer production and distribution can logically explain. Yet in 19th-century New Zealand beer and spirits were not inversely related over time. As Figure 7.3 shows, beer consumption slid between 1870 and the mid 1890s, during nearly all of which period spirits consumption crashed too. In other words, beer drinking failed to rise despite the growth of the indigenous beer industry, which in turn implies that the peak consumption of spirits before the mid 1870s was influenced less by the shortage of beer than by some other condition or conditions. The first argument Dingle advances—that men bought liquor because they had little else to buy—may fit Australia but its explanatory power weakens (without disappearing) when applied to New Zealand. In this colony men certainly had other items they could purchase and were urged to purchase with their spare cash, namely, real property. No doubt many men preferred to spend money on booze rather than land, but Dingle's supply-side model does not tell us why men should deviate from the respectable normative code so frequently and in such large numbers.

This leads us to the fundamental explanation for colonial New Zealand's great thirst, albeit not the sole explanation: the atomised state of the society. Statistical investigation of spirits consumption per head of general population and drunkenness convictions per 100,000 general population shows that both have a strong and positive relationship over the long term (1853–1930) with three indicators of a deficient social organisation: the ratio of adult males to adult females (a proxy measure of kinship density), the proportion of the overseas born in the general population (assumed to be one of the most disaffiliated elements in the colony), and the ratio of dwellings of one and two rooms to total dwellings (employed as a proxy measure

of transience and new areas of settlement).[45] The appendix at the
end of the chapter gives the correlation values. The correlation and
factor analyses employed in the investigation were based on pooled
data drawn from each of the nine provincial districts (termed hereafter
the global analysis); thus the covariance between excessive drinking
and the indicators of atomisation holds true across time as well as
space. The interconnection between the five circumstances on a colony-
wide basis is highlighted when the graphs in Figures 7.1 and 7.2
(drunkenness convictions and spirits consumption) are matched with
those for the three explanatory variables in Figures 7.4, 7.5, and
7.6. All five indicators peak before the mid 1870s and thereafter
slump quite dramatically. However, as a strong correlation is a
necessary but not a sufficient condition for a cause-and-effect
relationship, we must now establish that the link between under-
organisation and drunkenness was not simply a coincidence. To do
this, we will advance several reasons why up to the end of the 1870s
the peak levels of the former pushed up the latter to its highest
recorded rates; the decline of both from the 1880s onwards will be
the subject of the next chapter.

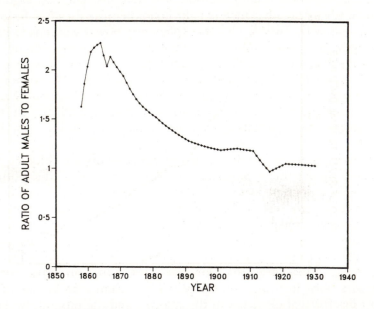

Fig. 7.4. Ratio of adult males to adult females

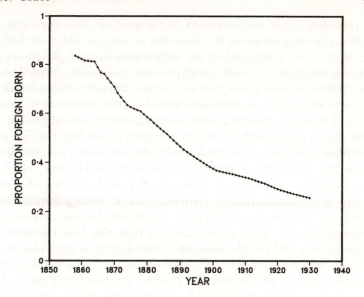

Fig. 7.5. Proportion of foreign born

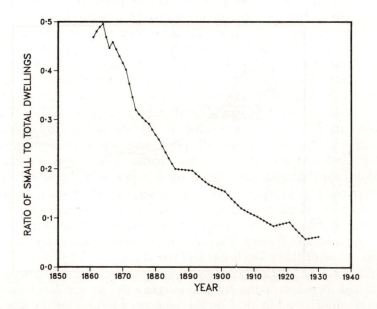

Fig. 7.6. Ratio of small (1–2 rooms) to total dwellings

In the first place, as noted before, if we accept that New Zealand was a socially impoverished society for a long period then it follows that there would have been an inclination for people to resort to alcoholic bingeing to block out the loneliness and monotony of their lives. In the second place, a few contemporaries acknowledged that the members of the vast and heterogeneous floating labour-force were strongly tempted to engage in feverish but erratic drinking bouts since this was the only pastime the colony offered them. In their general disaffiliated condition, the pub was usually the sole place where they could stay when migrating between jobs, relax, find (temporary) companionship, and spend their free time and money. The most common form of entertainment—the self-made family variety—was denied to them either because, if married, they frequently lived away from home or because, if single, they had no kin. Their residential instability meant they had no neighbouring houses to visit; and the location of their work-sites in the backblocks and in new areas, as well as their long hours of work, cut them off from voluntary organisations and respectable commercial amusements, which, anyway were few and far between. Of course they could attend a local festival— a race-day or an A. and P. Show—but the liquor stalls set up for these occasions were just as likely as the pubs to entice them to 'down their cheques', 'go on the burst'.[46] Describing the vices of 'bushmen or up-country men', 'Hopeful' wrote in 1887 that they led a 'solitary and isolated life for months and months together as stock-drivers and shepherds', enduring a life of 'extreme solitude—weeks and months pass without their seeing a fresh face'; after their wages accumulate, they 'come to town to waste it, and this they do in the most reckless way imaginable, and chiefly on *drink*'. The *Timaru Herald* in 1874 expressed horror at the 'dangerous and offensive condition' of the average roadside 'pot-house' where transient workers stayed and had nothing to do but drink: 'The rooms are murky, uninteresting places; not a book or a paper is to be found; there is scarcely a place to sit down in; quiet, or retirement, is out of the question; there is no garden, or outdoor place of any sort, where idle men can go. The whole establishment seems to be made purposely so wretched and forlorn, that an unfortunate sojourner in it must drink or die of sheer loneliness and boredom.'[47]

The large and varied boarding-house population in the towns was attracted to pub-drinking for similar reasons. As the *New Zealand Times* editorialised in 1877 on the paucity of leisure for the working classes, 'Many of them are single men, living in crowded dwellings, and uncomfortable lodgings from which they are glad to escape to the public house, which is their only "club" as matters stand here at present.' The *Evening Post*, referring to the same problem, stated that 'Unmarried men, working at trades and living in lodgings, stand sadly in need of some respectable place of resort where they could read books, magazines, and newspapers in a comfortable room'; without this facility they could do nothing but frequent hotels and drink and play billiards. Generalising from her observations of Christchurch, 'Hopeful' claimed that 'Another great temptation to drink, is the want of social amusements and places to go to'; there was not the 'same amount of social intercourse in the Colonies as at home, where different families from the same locality visit each other'; the large class of young men from all social grades living in boarding houses without home comforts could only pass away the time in the public house or billiard parlour.[48]

Finally, in its most atomised state up to the mid 1870s the colony could not rely upon group and communal pressure to deter and prevent excessive drinking. Although thrift and, by implication, sobriety were believed to be essential personal attributes, a multitude of individuals were free to violate this social code because they had little or no connection to groups and networks and therefore could not be informally disciplined.

Interpersonal Violence

Contemporary and retrospective idealisations of New Zealand as a society relatively free of crime and conflict are belied by official data on crimes of violence. Compared to Britain, supposedly *the* conflict-ridden society, New Zealand had consistently more homicide charges per 100,000 adult males from 1872 (the point at which the Justice Department in New Zealand started compiling court data on homicides) to some time after 1914. Charges for woundings per 100,000 adult males generally ran at a higher rate in New Zealand from 1871 (when their compilation started too) until after 1914; and the charges for common assault per 100,000 adult males far exceeded the English from 1853 (when their tabulation commenced) through to the 1880s.[49] To be sure, it is usually impossible to tell whether cross-cultural variations in the known rates of most crimes represent actual differences or dissimilarities in police efficiency, public attitudes to particular offences, and methods of classifying crime statistics. A large amount of most crime is 'invisible'—unreported to the police and unrecorded in the crime statistics—and thus dissimilarities between the crime rates of two countries may simply reflect the possibility that the 'invisible' quantum as a proportion of actual offences is lower or higher in one country than the other. This stricture generally holds true for common assault, a minor offence so broadly defined that perceptions of its occurrence are bound to vary widely. But it does not hold true for homicide, which, being regarded in almost all societies as the most serious offence, is subject to the least amount of under-reporting and under-recording; and it is only partly true for woundings, which by their very nature are highly reportable.[50] Furthermore, the similarities between the New Zealand and the English judicial systems and definitions of offences reduce the likelihood that the New Zealand court statistics categorised homicides and woundings in a sufficiently divergent manner to account for the considerable and persistent disparities between the respective homicide and wounding rates. Woundings in New Zealand as a mean for the five years 1872–6 proportionate to adult males in the mid-period census were 28.5 per 100,000; in England and Wales during 1869–73 the rate was 12.9. For the period 1909–13, the New Zealand rate was 11.6; the English, 7.1. In the case of homicide, the New Zealand rate was 8.2 per 100,000 in the first five-year period; the English, 5.0; and in the second, 5.1 and 1.9 respectively.[51]

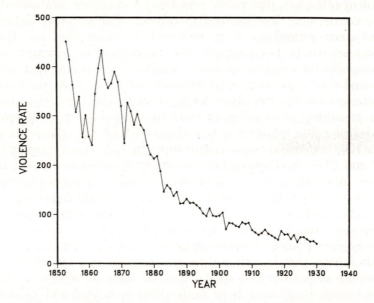

Fig. 7.7. Violence rate (convictions per 100,000 population)

In comparison with the next period, 1900–1940, the colonial era also stands out as being marked by conflict. This is illustrated by the trends in a composite index of summary convictions for petty violence, predominantly common assault, with a small proportion of assaults against the police and aggravated assaults, along with small numbers of a wide variety of other offences against the person, such as minor sexual offences.[52] From Figure 7.7 it can be seen that the number of summary convictions per 100,000 general population collapsed dramatically from the mid 1870s to the mid 1880s, and continued to fall, though less quickly, right to 1930. Thus by 1926–30 the rate had dropped by about 87 per cent from the years 1862–68. There are three basic reasons, moreover, why we can be confident that these recorded rates paralleled the actual trends in violence and that the 19th century was an appreciably more physically aggressive era than the 20th, even though such minor assaultive crimes are not generally a reliable indication of actual trends.[53] First, the long-term decline is consistent with the fall in the more serious violence offences, homicides and woundings, which are much less susceptible to variable reporting habits. Second, there is no evidence that the apparatus of control moved in the same direction as the recorded trends—that the police became less willing and able to apprehend violent offenders, that public sensitivity to violence diminished, that the courts were less inclined to convict, that statutory definitions and court procedures were reshaped, so decreasing the flow of summary trials. For example, the proportion of common assault charges in the magistrates' courts which led to convictions fluctuated around the 52 per cent mark between 1853 and 1900, then steadily increased until it was about 80 per cent by the late 1930s; charges for assaulting, obstructing, or resisting the police—a fairly sensitive index of public willingness to collaborate with the police—as a rate per 100,000 general population dropped by 76 per cent between 1876–80 and 1936–40. Third, it can reasonably be assumed that the trends were minimally distorted by errors and sudden changes in reporting practices, since the rate of petty violence correlates strongly with several variables commonly linked with violent behaviour—a point discussed shortly. This is not to say, it must be emphasised, that at any given point convictions equate with the real number of offences.

It is true that by using a general population base for the petty violence conviction rate we have taken no account of the age and sex transformations in New Zealand between 1853 and 1930 which decreased the proportion of people most at risk of fighting. Even so, if we control for these transformations by adopting an adult male population base, or a base comprised of males aged 21 to 40, we find that the yawning gap between the 19th-century and the 20th-century rates is narrowed but not substantially. Between the quinquenniums of 1862–6 and 1926–30, the rate on a young male base drops by 74 per cent, on an adult male base by 84 per cent, and on a general population base by 87 per cent.[54]

The possibility that the existence and decline of a 'macho' male sub-culture accounts for the trends in petty violence has been examined and discarded in Chapter V, as has domestic stress. Correlation analyses of other possible causes reveal that these have little explanatory value over the long term (1853–1930), when the nine provincial districts are treated simultaneously (the 'global analysis'). The appendix at the end of the chapter gives the correlation values. For example, the correlation coefficient between the violence rate and the annual rate of population growth is too low to allow us to postulate that the stresses of over-population were behind assaultive behaviour— such a connection has been found in 14th-century England.[55] The analysis indicates, too, that young males (aged 21–40) were only slightly more inclined towards violent behaviour than all adult males, which is in accord with the experiences of three older societies (France, Germany, the United States) but not with western society as a whole since 1945.[56] Further, the analysis shows that there was a negligible or negative affinity between urban and industrial growth and the violence rate. Such a pattern corroborates many recent studies of 19th- and early 20th-century England, Germany, America, and France, contradicting the pessimistic view so widespread during the Industrial Revolution that the rise of new industrial and urban ways of life produced social breakdown, increasing every kind of deviance.[57] Moreover, during the peak period of interpersonal conflict—the 1850s to the 1870s—industrial development and urbanisation were so inchoate that it is quite improbable they had anything to do with the peaks. The weak global correlations between petty violence convictions and the proportion of Maoris in the population suggest, too, that the wars of the 1860s failed to condition the residents of disturbed areas to use private coercion as a means of resolving disputes; they also confirm that, whatever else they did, Europeans did not over the long term (1853–1930) rely on the assault laws to impose their hegemony upon Maoris. Taranaki, the province that bore the brunt of the fighting during the wars, had per capita rates of violence well below the national during nearly all the 1860s (with the key exception of 1865) and generally far below the national over the whole period 1853–1930. Another war-torn province, Auckland, although mostly having rates in excess of the national from 1853 to 1930, dipped below the national over the 1860s. Hawke's Bay, the third province involved in the wars, showed no consistent pattern, with rates mainly below the national from 1857 to 1877, and usually higher rates thereafter.[58] It should be added that the data excluded Maori petty violent convictions up to 1911; as a rate per 100,000 Maoris, they are equal to a tiny fraction of the European from the point at which they were first recorded in 1871 to about 1906; obviously they were propelled by a mechanism that was quite different from the European.

The gold-rushes of the 1860s would appear to be a more likely source of petty violence. Otago, for example, had rates of petty violence that in five years out of 10 exceeded the national rate, 1862–1871. Another goldmining province, Westland, had rates in nearly every year many times higher than the national rate not just in the late 1860s but from the 1860s to 1930. Nelson's rate was well above the national during its main rushes period, 1867–1873. Yet the pattern is not consistent enough to suggest that gold-rushes alone induced abnormally high rates of fighting. The number of convictions per capita were below the national rate in the Auckland Province throughout the 1860s and did not rise above it until 1872, despite the Thames rush from 1867 onwards. Wellington, which was never the scene of gold discoveries, had generally higher rates than the national all the way from 1853 to 1930; in fact its mean rate over these years was the highest of all the provincial districts. Furthermore, the 1850s, which saw very few gold discoveries on the scale of the 1860s, experienced recorded levels of violence which, proportionate to population, were not much different from those of the succeeding decade.

What the global analysis does bring out, however, is the strong statistical relationship between the violence rate and the rate of drunkenness (convictions, in both cases, per 100,000 population) where the correlation coefficient is +0.702. The correlation coefficient between the violence rate and the objective measure of drinking, spirits consumption (gallons per capita), was even higher at +0.756. The strength of the association is not at all surprising. A host of other studies of violence in other societies, ranging from 13th-century England to 17th-century England to East Africa in the 1950s, confirm the truism, derived from empirical research and experience, that alcohol, by reducing inhibitions and self-restraint, engenders impulsive violence.[59]

Having said that, it also must be observed that a good proportion of the violent altercations that reached the courts do not appear to have been pothouse brawls or triggered by liquor. For example, a study of the petty violence coming before the Wellington Magistrate's Court over the three years 1870–72, shows that in only 69 of the 192 appearances can a link with alcohol be established (that is, the assailant was also charged with drunkenness, the event took place in a hotel, the magistrate commented on the involvement of alcohol). For 62 of the remaining 86 offences it is clear that violence was instrumental not expressive.[60] It was a means of power used to resolve differences, for example, between employers and employees when wages were not paid, between neighbours when stock strayed, between sellers of goods and dissatisfied customers, between shopkeepers and absconding debtors, and between those involved in accidents to establish who was at fault.[61] The reason violence was resorted to so frequently as a way of settling disputes over rights and obligations is implied by the results of the global analysis. The violence rate has the strongest correlations with the variables measuring atomisation—with the proxy measure of scanty kinship ties, the proportion of persons who were overseas-born, and with the surrogate measure of extreme transience and new areas of settlement (the appendix at the end of the chapter gives these correlation values).

The first reason an atomised society was a source of violence was that people did not interact sufficiently to understand one another's intentions and motives. Weak groups and networks were unable to establish uniform understanding of natural rights. True, the Old World had bequeathed a consensus about certain basic values. But as there was so little social contact, assumptions often varied sharply from person to person on a multitude of particularities. For example, John Hall took up land in the new settlement of Greytown during the 1850s. Finding that his section lacked suitable timber trees, he went over to a neighbouring vacant section and started to split up fallen logs into posts and rails. He took it for granted that as bush fires had left the plain covered in fallen logs, these were common property. However, the absentee-owner, whom Hall had never met before, by coincidence returned to his section and, seeing Hall cutting up a log, demanded the return of the wood. A quarrel ensued. What aggrieved Hall was that the neighbour, despite having all the timber he needed on the place, would not sell the wood to Hall nor compensate him for his effort. The neighbour, for his part, brought an opposing concept to the question. The log was on his land and therefore it was his right to dispose of it as he wanted. Not having met and mixed with Hall before, he did not share his understanding that since it was a burnt log, a waste-product—and such a common one— it could be claimed by anyone. Hall had violated his rights by taking his wood. A few days later Hall found the posts and rails 'lying on the road' and without hesitation started carrying them home— and brought matters to a head.

But before we got the last load away, my friend was there in a great rage, flourishing a small tomahawk over my head, and doing a war dance. He wanted me instantly to carry them all back; but I thanked him for carrying them so far for me, pointed out that we had split them, and that he had carried them on the road. I again offered him payment.

Fortunately, the neighbour did not strike Hall but went to a Wellington magistrate to take out a summons; 'he vowed that I shall pay for them dearly'.[62] At the court hearing Hall pleaded guilty, and although fined £1 was not ordered to pay costs.

Atomisation also led to violence (both instrumental and alcohol-triggered) by leaving a gap in the chain of restraint running from individual conscience to the formal sanctions of the law. The missing section was social pressure. The behaviour of people belonging to no groups and networks, or on their margins, was not checked by gossip, criticism, ridicule, and ostracism. Conformity was not rewarded by approval, affection, and companionship. Enjoying none or few of the advantages of reciprocity, they had nothing or little to lose by acting anti-socially. Hence, although a strict moral code was inherited from the Old World, there was not enough social discipline to stop individuals from deviating from it. In turn the unleashing of egotistical desires led to excessive drinking and dishonest and dishonourable behaviour. Excessive drinking triggered drunken brawls. Dishonest and dishonourable behaviour gave rise to frictions and grievances, which spilt over into bloodshed when the aggrieved resorted to violence in an attempt to win redress.

What, to some extent, supports the hypothesis is that a few contemporaries had a glimmering of what was wrong, though seldom did they admit or see that it was the other side of Arcadianism, and even more rarely connect it to the prevalence of violence. Soon after entering a Dunedin law firm, C. W. Richmond commented in 1862 that 'our outgoings are large and we run considerable risk—

so much business has now to be done with unsubstantial strangers from the neighbouring Colonies—of making bad debts'.[63] Thomas Arnold in 1849 recorded hearing a complaint that in New Zealand people readily broke faith whereas in England a man was as good as his word; Arnold agreed, saying that 'custom and the opinion of . . . neighbours have much less influence upon [people] when moved out of their old haunts, and taken to the other side of the world.'[64] Sir George Grey wrote in 1849 that 'temptations to irregularity are so strong'; people are 'separated from their former neighbours and their relatives' and consequently, 'there are perhaps greater facilities for carelessness and irregularity than there would be in England'.[65] Alexander Bathgate, reflecting on the presence of 'Ne'er do weels' in the colony wrote that 'To such there are more temptations here than at home, and none of the restraints which the presence and opinions of friends always exercise'.[66] The arch-critic of the social pattern, 'Hopeful', discussing 'some of the vices or crimes most common in the Colonies', explained (without referring specifically to violence) that 'in the Colonies there is but little of the *home* feeling so strong and prevalent *at home*—no attachment to place, locality, or friends'; whereas in England people did have these attachments and thus possessed 'every incentive to respect themselves and to be respected by the class and neighbourhood where they have been so long known', in the Colonies 'there are no associations or memories of that kind' and consequently 'there is not the same check or restraint there.'[67] Consistent with these observations is the fact that extreme transients constituted the largest single element charged with violent offences of all kinds. Two separate studies of those charged before the Wellington Magistrate's Court (1870–22, 1896–9) show that about half were not listed in either electoral rolls or street directories. Possibly, the rolling stones were picked on by the police; on the other hand, the brief stay each spent in a locality was a natural inducement to trouble-making, since it allowed him to calculate that he would escape its consequences. One of the Wellington cases in 1872 involved a publican who assaulted a 'swell' attempting to leave town owing £7. A Central Otago story features a storekeeper, William Theyers, during the gold-rushes. The discovery of gold on the West Coast in 1865 led to the exodus of Otago miners; Theyers found that quite a number of the men moving away owed him money and had no apparent intention of paying him back; in response Theyers rode after every absconding debtor and thrashed the man until he paid up, and the practice made him a terror to defaulters.[68]

The victims of these isolated, transient offenders were frequently themselves the same kind of people. This was a third reason a deficient society bred violence. They could of course go to the police and the courts and demand redress. But they could not go to their friends, kin, neighbours, and other associates and ask them to intervene, to remonstrate with the offender, coax him to make restitution, threaten to exclude him from the benefits of community life.

This point is underlined by looking at how things are managed in societies with stronger links. Much historical research on deviance and conflict in pre-modern societies emphasises how often disputes were settled outside the legal system through the peace-making role of an informal conciliator.[69] This was usually a local person known to both parties, a mutual friend, neighbour, employer, priest, landlord or the like. What impelled such intervention was the criss-cross of local allegiances. In the close-knit village or tribal setting the prospective peace-maker was likely to be attached to both parties in a conflict and therefore had an in-built incentive to restore the peace so as to avoid taking sides and betray one set of loyalties for the sake of another. Sometimes the antagonists would be compelled to accept mediation by their social superiors. Often the rest of the community brought strong pressure on them in order to maintain communal solidarity in the face of external enemies and to prevent the society from being divided by enduring animosities. By contrast, in colonial New Zealand, individuals had few if any interconnected ties, and hence little of this amateur peace-making machinery would have existed. For want of it, there was nothing to prevent disagreements from accumulating, multiplying, or escalating. Self-help violence was heavily relied on to resolve conflicts.

The argument so far has been that the high incidence of interpersonal violence up to the 1880s was not just a consequence of the colonial love of hard liquor. It was also driven by grave deficiencies in the social machinery of informal communication, deterrence, prevention, conciliation. Support for this thesis comes from a somewhat unexpected quarter, trends in the rates of civil litigation, a topic that will take up the rest of the chapter.

Civil Litigation

If it is assumed that violence, as a means of attaining an objective,

was a rational if crude adaptation to the scarcity of the informal
community methods of handling disputes, then it should follow that
the same scarcity gave rise to a great deal of civil litigation. The
logic is not immediately obvious. Lawyers presume that if a society
offers sufficient opportunities for taking civil remedies (which the
colony obviously did, as we shall see), then the aggrieved will have
no cause to exercise violent remedies of their own. The logic,
furthermore, cuts against the studies by historians of older societies
which show violent and litigious behaviour inversely related over
time; as a society becomes more civilised and develops a litigious
culture, violence is given up in favour of suing as a method of settling
disputes.[70] The lawyer's model, however, takes no account of the
effectiveness or otherwise of the 'middle-range' (or informal)
processes of dispute prevention, containment, and mediation.
Although the conventional historical model does take these processes
into account, it is not applicable to colonial New Zealand, where
the required framework barely existed up to the 1880s. It follows
that people with grievances sought redress through litigation as well
as violence.

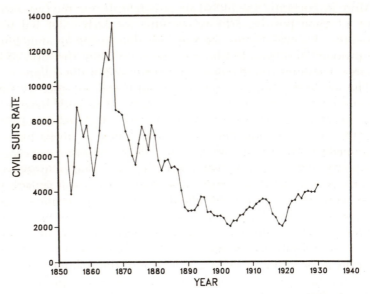

Fig. 7.8. Civil suits rate (suits tried per 100,000 population)

The evidence that instrumental violence and litigation were symptoms of the same thing—the inadequacy of the 'middle-range' or informal social mechanisms of control—is overwhelming. By comparing the graphs in Figures 7.7 and 7.8 it can be seen that the national rate of convictions for petty violence per 100,000 general population followed much the same course between 1853 and 1930 as the national rate of civil suits tried and disposed of each year in the magistrates' courts per 100,000 general population. Both are far higher in the 19th century than between 1900 and 1930. Both are at their highest before the 1880s and diminish sharply thereafter. The recording of violence commences in 1853 at a peak never thereafter exceeded, whereas the civil suits rate has its peak in 1867, but they tend to move up and down together over the same years over the decade; they both fly up in the early 1860s, fall in the late 1860s and rise again in the early 1870s to another secondary peak. From 1876 violence begins its long-term slide; that for civil suits is not obvious until 1880; each drops markedly until 1900, from which point they tend to diverge somewhat, with violence continuing to decline, civil suits showing stronger fluctuations but ending in 1926–30 at one third of the peak in 1864–8.

More importantly, the global analysis reveals that the two variables have a strong positive affinity not only for each other but for the measures of atomisation—the ratio of adult males to adult females, the proportion of people who were born overseas, the ratio of small to large dwellings (see the appendix at the end of the chapter).

The structural similarity of civil suits and violence is further underlined by global analysis which shows they both have a weak or a negative relationship with indicators employed to test other possible causes of inter personal conflict. Most of these have been examined previously. The ones that have not are measures of economic prosperity, change and growth, namely, the value of imports and exports per capita, their year-to-year change rates and growth rates. They were placed in the correlation matrix to determine whether suing was related to the possible rise of bad debts and bankruptcies during recessions and depressions, to the novelty of economic situations in a pioneer setting, to the pace of economic development (which has been found to have a link with the volume of litigation in 16th-century Castile).[71] The measures were employed, too, to ascertain how far per capita prosperity or deprivation and misery stimulated violence; for there is some evidence that in late 19th-century England and in mid-19th-century France and Germany economic growth stimulated violence.[72] Yet irrespective of how average per capita economic conditions have been expressed, they have minimal capacity to explain trends in suing and violence (which is not to say that over the whole colony and/or in some of the provinces there may not be a linkage over the short term).

Five case-studies on civil suits indicate that they had much in common with violence.[73] Firstly, that so few of the suits were settled out of court is indirect evidence of a shortage of informal mediators. In older, past societies disputes were taken to court as a last resort to pressure the other side to settle informally; in most instances the pressure was successful and the dispute would then be settled out of court with the use of an informal conciliator.[74] Only two of the 204 civil cases in the Wanganui Magistrate's Court were disposed of through out-of-court settlements during the years 1871, 1873–5, 1875–7; 36 of the 464 cases in the Wellington Magistrate's Court, 1866–8; 16 of the 254 in the Hokitika Magistrate's Court in early 1871; 45 of the 740 in the Wellington Magistrate's Court, 1870–2. Secondly, there is some evidence that cases of violence and civil suits overlapped. An investigation of the 192 cases of criminal violence and 740 cases of civil suits before the Wellington Magistrate's Court 1870–2 shows that 206, or one fifth, of the combined cases involved people who featured in both types of actions.[75] Thirdly, the overwhelming majority of suits were instrumental; vexatious litigation was almost non-existent—just five of the 740 complaints in Wellington 1870–2 (for example) were counter-suits.[76] In this respect the intention behind the action was comparable to a sizeable minority of the violence cases. Fourth, just as some of the issues in the violence cases were economic, so were those for the vast majority of complaints; they were chiefly brought to recover bad debts (owing to shopkeepers, tradesmen, landlords) and secondarily for damages over breaches of contract (usually price or performance) and failure to pay wages. An infinitesimal number of the suits were for defamation—for example, only one of the 204 in Wanganui 1871–77, none of the 740 in Wellington 1870–2.[77] This might say something about the laws on defamation; it also suggests that in a society of transients and loose relationships, people did not have to worry about losing face and reputation in the 'community'. What gives some support to this latter possibility is that in 17th-century New England and 16th- and 17th-century England—societies of close-knit village communities—libel actions between neighbours flew thick and fast.[78]

Yet the comparability of violence and litigation should not be exaggerated. The social identity of those involved was quite dissimilar without being mutually exclusive. The plaintiffs in civil suits tended disproportionately to be businessmen and the settled (shopkeepers, merchants, tradesmen, hoteliers), while the defendants tended to be disproportionately manual workers (including miners in mining districts) and transients. With violence cases, however, the Wellington study (1870–2) reveals that there was no class bias. The fraction of offenders who were middle-class was not significantly different from the fraction of middle-class victims; the proportion of manual worker offenders was not significantly different from that for manual worker victims. The same lack of bias is true of transients. Why litigation should be class-biased, and violence not, is not yet known.

APPENDIX

Correlation Matrix for Violence rate, Drunkenness rate, Spirits Consumption rate, Civil Suits rate and other Variables for the period 1853–1930

(Nine Provinces analysed simultaneously, maximum of 702 observations)

Variables	Violence Rate	Drunkenness Rate	Civil Suits Rate	Spirits Consumption Rate	Beer Consumption Rate
Violence Rate	1.000	0.702	0.678	0.756	0.350
Drunkenness Rate	0.702	1.000	0.436	0.573	0.153
Civil Suits Rate	0.678	0.436	1.000	0.722	0.298
Spirits Consum. Rate	0.756	0.573	0.722	1.000	0.628
Beer Consum. Rate	0.350	0.152	0.298	0.628	1.000
4	0.299	0.441	0.173	0.068	-0.305
8	-0.767	-0.551	-0.680	-0.742	-0.243
9	0.658	0.427	0.505	0.568	0.310
10	0.507	0.315	0.556	0.677	0.454
11	-0.677	-0.397	-0.527	-0.457	-0.117
Masculin	0.667	0.401	0.626	0.659	0.339
18	-0.254	-0.044	-0.145	-0.016	0.129
21	0.653	0.477	0.673	0.693	0.460
24	0.735	0.397	0.664	0.721	0.420
27	0.373	0.092	0.402	0.504	0.361
24/27	0.746	0.434	0.635	0.690	0.375
38	0.180	0.285	0.212	0.612	0.219
39	-0.094	-0.036	0.095	0.311	0.078
Baltrade	0.078	0.222	-0.026	0.021	-0.209
40	-0.172	-0.093	-0.104	0.057	0.126
41	-0.484	-0.199	-0.453	-0.352	0.158
42	0.451	0.209	0.308	0.680	0.461
43	0.332	0.357	0.207	0.450	0.108
44	0.310	0.309	0.295	0.414	0.026
GR3	0.117	0.181	0.128	0.244	-0.052
GR38	-0.045	0.082	-0.190	-0.008	0.005
GR39	0.042	0.003	0.057	-0.040	-0.056
Δ38	-0.084	0.023	-0.222	-0.047	-0.023
Δ39	-0.083	-0.004	-0.128	-0.146	-0.049

Notes:
A fuller discussion of the correlation analysis and its methodology can be found in M. Fairburn & S. J. Haslett, 'Violent Crime in Old and New Societies: A Case Study Based on New Zealand 1853-1940', *Journal of Social History*, Fall 1986, which gives the preliminary results of a much larger statistical study of violent crime in New Zealand. The values in the matrix above differ slightly from those in the earlier article (mostly in relation to the beer variable) because of corrections to the raw data.

The provinces embraced by the analysis were Auckland, Taranaki, Hawke's Bay, Wellington, Nelson, Marlborough, Canterbury, Westland, Otago (including Southland).

European = Non-Maori.

Most correlations are significantly different from zero at greater than 99.9 per cent probability, even allowing for the non-normal data distribution. The exceptions are the correlations with GR3, GR38, GR39, Δ38, Δ39 that tend to have significance levels greater than .10; as a consequence these correlations must be treated with caution.

Except where stipulated, data were compiled from *Census of New Zealand*, 1858–1936; annual *Statistics of New Zealand*, 1853-1920; and specialised volumes of the annual statistics 1921+.

Missing values have been interpolated using linear interpolation.

Annual Rate of Change for a variable in a given year is defined as the difference between that variable in the given year and its value in the previous year. Growth rate of a variable in a given year is defined as the difference between the variable in the given year and its value in the previous year, all divided by the value for the previous year.

Some variables (e.g., violence and drunkenness rates) are also expressible as rates per 100,000 of population. Correlations between variables are unaffected by such changes to units of measurement.

Population Bases
(i) For violence rate, drunkenness rate, civil suits rate, proportion of New Zealand-born Europeans, proportion Irish-born, annual rate of population growth, the base was the European population up to 1911, and the Europeans plus Maoris thereafter.

(ii) For proportion of Maori population and exports per capita, the base was the Maori and European populations combined.

(iii) For immigration and emigration rates, the base was the European population.

(iv) For import rates, beer consumption per capita and spirits consumption per capita, the base was an aggregate of Europeans, Maoris, and Imperial troops and their families.

(v) For all other variables, the base was the European population. Maori and European populations were interpolated from the Census data 1858+; European population figures before 1858 are the Registrar-General's.

Explanation and Description of Variables
Violence rate. Summary Convictions for Assault 1853–1871, plus Summary Convictions for Offences Against the Person, 1872–1930, rate per capita. No missing values. Maoris are unavoidably included in the convictions line from 1872 to 1930. Sexual offences have been culled out from 1911 to 1930.
Drunkenness rate. Summary Convictions rate per capita, 1853–1930, Maoris excluded 1853–71, included thereafter along with convictions for habitual drunkards; probation orders excluded; like violence, no missing values.
Civil suits rate. Civil Suits tried and disposed of in the Magistrates' Courts, 1853–1930, rate per capita. Maoris excluded 1853–71 and included thereafter; like violence rate and drunkenness, there were no missing values.
Spirits consumption rate. Spirits, gallons consumed, per capita. Data, 1857–1920, calculated from revenue figures and duty rates on spirits imports at the various ports.
Beer consumption rate. Beer, gallons consumed, per capita. Aggregates beer imports, 1867-1930 (calculated on the same basis as spirits) plus gallons domestically manufactured 1867 onwards; the joint data for some provinces from 1895 were split using adult males in the provinces concerned as the rate.
4. Proportion of total population who are Maori. Data from 1858.
8. Proportion of total population who are New Zealand-born Europeans. No data for Westland until 1871.
9. Proportion of total population who are Irish-born. No data for Westland until 1871.
10. Proportion of total population who are European adult males. The 1916 figures were for ages 20 and over, otherwise 21 and over; Westland for 1867 from electoral districts.
11. Proportion of total population who are European adult females. Notes as for variable 10.
Masculin. The ratio of adult males to adult females.
18. Proportion of total population who are European and urban. 1858–64 were for provincial capitals including Lyttelton, 1867 was for chief towns plus towns and townships, 1871–4 for centres with 500 people or more, 1878–81 for 'certain cities, boroughs, and townships', thereafter for boroughs and town districts.
21. Proportion of total population who are young European males (aged 21–40 years). 1916 for ages 20–40, Westland in 1867 from the electoral districts.
24. European Dwellings 1–2 rooms, per capita. Data from 1861 onwards; up to 1911 includes huts and dwellings of canvas, thereafter private inhabited dwellings including tenements; 1936 excludes canvas and temporary dwellings.
27. European total dwellings, per capita. Notes as for variable 24.

24/27. The ratio of dwellings of 1–2 rooms to total dwellings.

38. Imports, £ per capita. Aggregated from the various ports, no missing values. No allowance for changes in the price level.

39. Exports, £ per capita. Notes as for variable 38.

Baltrade. Balance of trade, £ per capita. Exports £ per capita minus imports per capita.

40. Manufacturing horse power per capita. Data from 1867.

41. Proportion of total population who are manufacturing employers. Notes as for variable 40.

42. Police manpower, per capita. 1878–86 from the Census, thereafter aggregates of local manpower figures in Department Reports to *AJHR* for census years.

43. Immigration per capita. Aggregates of the various ports, 1853–1930, no missing values.

44. Emigration per capita. Notes as for variable 43.

GR3. Annual rate of growth of the European (non-Maori) population.

GR38. Annual rate of growth of imports (£ per capita).

GR39. Annual rate of growth of exports (£ per capita).

$\Delta 38$. Imports (£ per capita), annual change rates.

$\Delta 39$. Exports (£ per capita), annual change rates.

The death of atomisation. York Road Creamery, Midhurst, 1904. The mushrooming of dairy factories from about the late 1890s helped reduce social isolation in rural areas. Factory production of butter or cheese created more opportunities for organised leisure because it removed from the home the time-consuming chore of churning cream and making butter. Also the daily ritual of delivering the cream or whole milk to the local factory allowed the men (though not apparently their womenfolk) to rub shoulders much more often in a single setting. *Alexander Turnbull Library*

CHAPTER VIII

Constraints on Chaos

COLONIAL theorists believed that New Zealand's minimal social organisation and ample opportunities to obtain 'competencies' saved the new land from Old World problems—hierarchy, class conflict, oppressive status conformity. In Part II it was argued that they were broadly correct in their belief. On that point the Arcadian formula did equate with the reality. We saw in the last chapter, however, that the minimal social organisation and (more indirectly) the ample opportunities for personal autonomy created other problems of a different type—loneliness, drunkenness, and interpersonal conflict. New Zealand secured itself from collective enemies on one front at the price of being infiltrated by individualised enemies on the other. The central fallacy of the 'insider's view' was its Arcadian premise `that material dearth combined with excessive social organisation was the source of all social evils. Inversion of the premise led to the equally fallacious assumption that the key to the solution of human problems was material amelioration. It was not realised that material improvement in a social vacuum would breed loneliness, departure from hitherto accepted norms of behaviour, and an intolerable amount of friction. It was wrongly supposed that conflict and crime within society were mostly caused by poverty and social injustice—by a hierarchical or class-based society. All that was necessary for social virtue and goodwill was ample social and economic opportunity. People would somehow be able to satisfy their gregarious instincts without being bound to powerful means of association and conformity. The lesson of New Zealand experience is that Arcadianism is a fallacy. It is impossible to have a society of extreme individualism and order and harmony simply on the basis of material abundance. The result is chaos. Paradise is inherently flawed.

These, however, were not the only inaccuracies in the 'insider's view'. This chapter will indicate that various mechanisms in this quasi-Arcadia limited the scale of its real problems, and that most of these mechanisms contradicted other essential features of the 'insider's view'. An underlying theme in the chapter is that the things which helped society to cope with its problems of atomisation were predictable outcomes of atomisation itself. They represent further evidence that bondlessness was central to colonial life.

The Limits of the Chaos
The evidence that the chaos had upper limits is perhaps best exemplified by the violence. Despite the lack of social restraints, homicide each year averaged about two per 100,000 general population over the period 1872–1900.[1] This figure is bad viewed historically in New Zealand terms but it was quite modest compared to the rates from which other societies have suffered. Medieval England was beset by an estimated homicide rate of around 20 per 100,000; a rate of four or so per 100,000 was typical of 16th- and early 17th-century England; modern America (1966–70) has a rate of around seven per 100,000.[2] Drunkenness is a further example. It is true the problem was appalling, but what has to be explained is why it was not worse, considering the inability to enforce taboos and the virtual absence of alternative recreation and means of socialising. And although loneliness was widespread, it is significant that it did not produce a much larger crop of personality disorders.[3]

Atomisation Also Restrained Violence
The looseness of the colony's social ties had a paradoxical effect. Although generating much interpersonal conflict, it simultaneously prevented worse. There are two reasons why this was so. Neither of them contradicts Arcadianism, but this provides no reason for saying that the Arcadian prescription was successful: the incidence of violent crimes was still worse than England's, the usual colonial point of reference.

First of all, the foot-loose character of the population probably brought many disputes to a peaceful end by physically separating the antagonists.[4] It might even be argued that, if close personal relationships raise the emotional temperature of disputes and give opponents personal ammunition to fire at each other, then the generally superficial nature of interpersonal ties in the colony must have had the reverse effect, diminishing the frequency of the kinds of conflict originating from hurt feelings, jealousy, and the like— factors that prevail in modern homicide.[5]

In the second place, a singular advantage of the loose social ties was that they precluded the emergence of a 'dangerous class' or 'classes'—collectivised working-class crime and protest on a large scale—as well as every other kind of collective disorder, political or criminal (the reason for the latter will be spelt out shortly). The advantage of loose ties to the state was that it was never seriously confronted by organised resistance to its authority from Europeans, and this enabled it to give greater attention to the problems of drunkenness and interpersonal conflict. Individual deviancy, troublesome as it was, did not lead to the collapse of civil society. By its very nature it had no overt or implicit political objective; and since it was not accompanied by collective disorder the resources of the state were not overstretched. A coincidence of individual crime and collective disorder was the nightmare of governments elsewhere over the 19th century, and rightly so, for in places like Bengal it did result in the wholescale breakdown of civil society.[6] Inspector Broham of the Auckland Armed Constabulary implicitly acknowledged that individual deviancy was far less threatening to the state than collective disorder or the two simultaneously, when he reported to his Commissioner in 1873, 'From crime of grave character, the district, I am glad to say, enjoys an immunity equal to any other part of the Colony. Organized gangs of highwaymen or burglars are unknown; the crimes that are committed are usually the work of individuals acting singly. . .'.[7] True, the state at times had to face Maori rebellions as well as European crime, but even that did not bring civil breakdown—partly because the state was able to call upon the superior resources of the Imperial Government to repress the troubles.

Transiency, geographical isolation, the ideology of extreme individualism, kinlessness, meagre leisure opportunities, the newness of settlement, the prevalence of the 'masterless individual' and all the other forces of social isolation may have stunted the growth of beneficial associations, but they had the same effect on violent groupings or on patterns of association conducive to social strife. To be sure, the remarkable degree of social harmony in European New Zealand was not simply the product of bondlessness; also working in the same direction were the high level of material satisfaction, the relatively small proportions (compared to Australia and the United States) of ethnic minorities in the Pakeha population, the accessibility of government, received traditions of respectable behaviour, and the power of the state. Moreover the tiny population would itself have lowered the chance of collective disorders involving violence. But the thinness of interpersonal relationships was a large if paradoxical factor.[8]

In contrast to more cohesive societies, the colony was immune to almost every type of collective conflict. Whereas lynchings and killings on the American frontier were often organised by local communities to stamp out troublemakers, New Zealand had no known slayings of this kind. Local communities were usually too fragmented to produce mobs of a size to do a lynching.[9] Whereas, too, in older societies powerful bonds often oblige individuals to aid their friends, kin, or clients in pursuing feuds, few victims of an offence in New Zealand had associates they could rely upon to help them take private retribution.[10] The atomisation of the colony likewise saved it from most forms of criminal violence; New Zealand experienced very little banditry, large-scale robbery, brawls involving more than two participants, or the bloody clashes between, for example, poachers or smugglers and the authorities that disturbed the peace in 18th-century rural England.[11] The things that produced loneliness also prevented the colony from being disrupted by rebellions, revolutions, internal wars, or border skirmishes. Although the Anglo-Maori wars of the 1860s appear to be the exception to this rule, their capacity to instill violent habits was restricted by the fact that outsiders, 'Imperial troops', conducted the bulk of the fighting. As a result of the weak bonding mechanisms, parliamentary politics were often virulent in the early provincial period; but factions never had the power bases they needed to intimidate or physically attack their rivals. Perhaps Auckland politics from 1853 to 1858 came closest to bloodshed, but this was a unique situation in the colony, for one set of antagonists (the Constitutional Association) was able to call upon the support of a large segment of the voting population—the military settlers of the garrison towns. The tension soon dissipated when the two principal leaders of the other side (the Progress Party) left the colony, taking with them the personal basis of the power of their grouping.[12]

Finally, colonial society was very rarely affected by the confrontational style of popular protest—the politically motivated riot, the aggressive street demonstration, vigorous picketing during a strike, organised industrial sabotage. New Zealand was comparable in population size and occupational composition to her sister colonies across the Tasman. Yet it produced nothing like the scale, frequency, and intensity of physical confrontations during strikes suffered by Australia (said by its historians to be a remarkably stable society). For example, there were no incidents like the 1894 Queensland shearers' strike with its 175 arrests, two woundings, the burning of the steamer *Rodney*; or the riot at Circular Quay in Sydney which led to 15 arrests during the 1890 Maritime Strike. New Zealand's worst year of industrial unrest (1890) was also Australia's; but where this occasioned 94 court sentences for crowd disorder in Australia there were apparently none in New Zealand.[13] A crucial reason for New Zealand's freedom from this source of collective violence was the absence of a strong social organisation from which an indigenous tradition of popular protest—peaceful or otherwise—could take root. As social networks were so shallow and the population so small and scattered, there were few communities, certainly none of a reasonable size, from which radical leaders could recruit a stable mass following. Without a 'crowd' to drive it, protest was scarce and fleeting and its principals were forced to adopt a policy of extreme circumspection. The contrast here is with Maori society which, as exemplified by the Ringatu movement or Te Whiti's stand at Parihaka, was able to resist the authorities vigorously and repeatedly because it possessed a tribal structure from which a resistance movement could be drawn. Typifying the Pakeha's weak tradition of protest were the unemployment demonstrations held during the 1880s— the one-off public meetings and/or street processions, which, apart from their infrequency, were notable for their absolute respect for constituted authority, exemplified by their formality, their strict observance of the law, the fact that they usually included members of the local élite, and were concluded with a presentation of a petition to officialdom.[14] Even the so-called 'Fenian riots' on the West Coast in 1868 conformed substantially to this pattern, although the authorities were greatly frightened by them. The 'riots' largely consisted of peaceful processions and mock funerals intended to express solidarity with three Fenians who had been executed in Manchester. The one disturbance came at Addison's Flat when Orangemen provoked trouble at a Roman Catholic dance; yet this caused nothing more than 10 shillings' worth of damage and injuries requiring 12 inches of sticking plaster, so estimated the Commissioner of the Nelson South-West Goldfields.[15]

The virtual absence of collective disorder kept down the incidence of colonial violence in two ways. For one thing—quite obviously—it made an infinitesimal contribution to the reported and actual incidence of total violence. In a statistical sense this is important, for in most societies the blows struck during civil strife are recorded in the statistics of homicide, assaults on police, and woundings, and are not separately categorised. For another, it had a positive educational effect—it stifled the growth of what Wolfgang and Ferracuti have termed a 'sub-culture of violence'.[16] People were not conditioned to value or tolerate private violence, or taught to use it by witnessing or participating in the vicious behaviour of lynch-mobs, feuding groups, bandits, rebels, revolutionaries, or aggressive protest movements. When a deputation of trade unionists met the Premier during the 1890 Maritime Strike, the Premier had only to make an oblique reference to the 'news of scenes down south which looked very bad' to have the unionists fall over themselves, assuring the Premier 'that they had heard nothing of it', that 'they did not think these disturbances were caused by Unionists', that they 'might rather be put down to larrikinism', that 'what the Unions themselves had got to fear was disorderly people', 'would at once disown them' and 'do their best to bring them to justice'.[17]

Chaos is Limited Through Artificial Devices

Apart from the tendency of atomisation itself to limit the violence it caused, the chaos of the atomised society was restricted through four artificial—totally unArcadian—devices: beneficent government action; repressive government action; anxious self-repression; the emergence of informal social mechanisms of control. These will be examined in turn and their contradictions of Arcadia specified.

Beneficent Government Action

From Part I it will be remembered that according to the contemporary view, the natural abundance of New Zealand allowed individuals to rise in the world unaided by any organisation or collective except the immediate family. There was such a wealth of opportunities that people did not need social contrivances 'to get on'; all they needed was the appropriate personal qualities.

In reality, however, a great deal of 'getting on' was promoted and facilitated by the state—a large-scale organisation, a social contrivance. Its massive public works schemes generated jobs; its provision of roads and railways allowed settlers to make capital gains from the rising value of their land; its assisted immigration schemes brought thousands of people to Arcadia in the first place; its energetic activity as New Zealand's largest landlord, landowner, land-agent was a crucial factor in making proprietorship widely accessible. These interventionist tendencies, which aided and abetted the private pursuit of property, had arisen long before the Liberals came to power in 1890; even so, during the 1890s their pace, scale, and complexity were expanded, especially in the areas of land reform (with the subdivision of the large estates and the provision of cheap loan money to settlers), and of industrial reform (with Industrial Conciliation and Arbitration and the regulation of factory conditions).

The capacity to form a state apparatus in an atomised society originated during the Crown Colony period, 1840–52, when its essential shell was established by two coherent organisations, the Imperial Government and the New Zealand Company (and its affiliates). By the end of this period, the colony had acquired a settled core of large landowners who were equipped with sufficient leisure to manage the key lawmaking and administrative institutions themselves; and on this foundation the powers of the state grew, facilitated by a comparatively large revenue base, copious borrowing of overseas finance, and the recruitment of skilled technicians and bureaucrats from overseas.

In part its growth was stimulated by the imagery of New Zealand as an ideal society, for this led to irresistible public demands for state assistance when the satisfaction of these expectations faltered or were frustrated. In part, too, its growth was necessitated by atomisation. André Siegfried, a French visitor at the turn of the century, acknowledged this by writing 'when a colonial finds himself face to face with some difficulty, it is almost always to the State that he first appeals. To what else indeed should he turn?'

In the early days of a colony there is usually little co-operation between the immigrants; the Government is often the only bond which unites them, and some time is necessary before natural groupings are formed. The Government is thus brought by the force of circumstances to perform functions, which in the old countries would lie within the province of private initiative.[18]

The lack of such groupings, Siegfried went on to say, also meant that there were no organised interests, as there were in old countries, capable of resisting the expansion of the state's functions.[19]

Each amenity organised by the state helped to keep the lid on frontier chaos or to mitigate it; in many instances the benefits did not emerge until the last two decades of the century or beyond 1900. Thus the formation of the Public Trust Office (1872), and the gradual establishment of the Torrens system of registering the titles to land, prevented disputes from arising from two specific issues: in the first instance from the mismanagement of trusts and in the second from ambiguous land deeds.[20] Assisted immigration initially added to the number of bondless immigrants; but by swelling the population of the colony, it eventually increased the population density and lessened the geographical isolation of households in rural districts. The development of public services, roads, bridges, railways, although lagging behind the spread of settlement and giving a fillip to transience, eventually helped to overcome isolation. Likewise the promotion of land settlement for a long period fostered both the scattering of the population and geographical isolation; but the greater concentration on closer land settlement from the 1880s, especially the policy of subdividing the large estates under the Liberals, eventually gave rural people more neighbours. The state had to take responsibility for the provision of primary schooling because the churches lacked the resources to do so (a contrast with the situation in the Old World). A rise in literacy enabled solitary people to learn something of the world through the things they read, the most important of which, for the purpose of social contact, were local newspapers. The national system of primary education implemented under the 1877 Act must have gone some way in providing a common experience. To the extent to which they attended, school children were exposed to the same rote learning, the same severe classroom discipline, the same syllabus. The growth of government entailed the expansion of the civil service, which (though its branches often employed only one person) was a major source (one of the few) of work-place associations.[21] The Industrial Conciliation and Arbitration Act of 1894, by protecting trade unions registered under the Act, was the first step towards the regularisation and shortening of working hours, which freed manual workers to take part in organised leisure.

Repressive Government Action

In classical Arcadia there is no need for a repressive state or for other artificial social restraints. In the New Zealand version, although it was not denied the colony had a repressive state apparatus, it was believed that the maintenance of good morals did not rely on it. New Zealand's freedom from major crime and disorder sprang fundamentally from the spontaneous and self-interested responses by individuals to the wholly positive influences in an opportunity-rich environment.

This naive optimism was contradicted not only by the reality of major deviance (as we saw) but also by the insecurity the authorities felt in the face of it. The insecurity expressed itself in the promptness with which the organs of formal repression were placed in the areas most at risk of turmoil, the territory just opened up for settlement. The period when the frontier expanded most dramatically—the 1850s to the 1880s—saw an equally dramatic leap in the number of resident magistrates' courts and police stations. The number of magistrates' courts grew from 19 in 1853–6 to 155 in 1880, of which only eight were located in the early, 1853–6 settlements.[22] The new province of Hawke's Bay started life in 1858 with one police station (Napier); four additional ones were scattered through the province by 1867. There were 18 stations in the Auckland province in 1865, 11 more than in 1849. Fear of Maori rebellion was responsible for some of this increase, but plainly it was not the only factor since the proliferation was just as marked in the South Island. Whereas Otago had five police stations in early 1861, it had 40 by the end of 1863, only five of which were in Dunedin; Canterbury's four police stations of 1854 were still in the same places in 1865 but 15 others, dispersed all over the province, had been added, including six in Westland. Southland began its life as a separate province (1861) with one police station in Invercargill, but by 1863 had established four more well beyond the confines of Invercargill, besides several one-man rural stations.[23] Wardens' courts, an official system of controlling the goldfields, were just as rapidly established in places where gold had been discovered, the warden often doubling as a magistrate and senior police official. The wardens' courts were empowered to register new claims. Copied from Australia, the system was introduced by the central government in 1858 in response to the tumult at the Golden Bay diggings, New Zealand's first major gold-rush.[24]

Policing systems were of a bewildering diversity and changeability. This was partly a reflection of the varied constitutional forms in New Zealand between 1840 and the 1870s. The first professional police forces, under magisterial direction, were introduced by Captain Hobson in 1840; these were supplanted by Governor Grey's Armed Police Forces between 1846 and 1853; Grey's forces were inherited by the provincial governments. In 1867 the central government, on the withdrawal of Imperial troops, formed an Armed Constabulary, which was shared by Auckland Province (1870); finally in 1876–7 the provincial forces and the Armed Constabulary were merged into a centrally commanded national force. In large measure, however, the complexity of policing systems was a manifestation of the state's extraordinary adaptation and sensitivity to the complexities of the colony's disorder. Broadly speaking, two models of professional policing were followed in a variety of combinations, often rapidly changed. One was the London Metropolitan Police model. This emphasised close surveillance of the likely trouble-spots and trouble-makers through frequent and regular patrols, and aimed at deterring trouble by creating a fear of the certainty of apprehension. Such forces in New Zealand were often (before 1876–7) under local magisterial authority, and were mainly employed in the more peaceful regions and periods (such as the late 1850s and after 1876–7). The other model, copied from the Irish Constabulary, was (with the exception of Grey's Armed Police Forces) imported to New Zealand by police officials whom several of the provincial governments recruited from Victoria, Australia. It was a militarised, aggressive, form of policing, under central direction. It focused more on quelling disorder once it had broken out. Based on this model were Grey's Armed Police Force and the later Armed Constabulary (for the purpose of crushing rebellious Maori tribes), and some of the provincial police forces, notably Otago and Canterbury (intended to suppress the hordes of unruly miners). For a country which imagined it did not have a significant law-and-order problem (within European society) comparatively large sums were spent on policing; it was common for an eighth or more of the budget of provincial governments to be spent on their forces.[25] Even more anomalous was the alacrity with which some forces adopted new techniques to help in their battle against crime. For example, the Otago police from 1861 received regular intelligence from the Australian police authorities about the movements across the Tasman of wanted and suspected criminals. Four of the provincial police forces published on a regular basis *Police Gazettes*, circulars containing intelligence about criminal matters, which were sent to police stations within their respective provinces as well as to the heads of police elsewhere in New Zealand. Some forces established specialised branches for particular operations such as detective work, gold convoys, and harbour work.[26]

Finally, the state was ever ready to expand its repressive capabilities. In a series of moves (the most important being an Order-in-Council of 1864) it took over from the victims of crimes the responsibility for prosecuting offenders in the courts. It defined new offences (the licensing laws are a good example of this) and toughened the received body of English criminal law. An example of this was the widening of the vagrancy laws. Otago in 1861 passed a Vagrancy Ordinance which empowered a J.P. to imprison anyone who 'shall not give a good account of his means of support'; Canterbury followed suit in 1867; Auckland planned to before the central government brought down its own measure in 1866.[27]

It is unlikely that the elaboration of formal institutions of law and order actually deterred drunkenness and violence. Persons engaging in these offences are not usually inhibited by the fear of detection and punishment.[28] Yet the police must have stopped many brawls before they reached the vicious stage. In addition, the ability to litigate at the petty level must have stopped the escalation of at least some disputes into violent confrontations. The huge volume of complaints was a general expression of confidence in the capacity of the judicial system to rectify grievances. There is good anecdotal evidence that gold-rush locations suffered far more from physical conflicts over claims before wardens' courts were introduced than after.[29] Finally, the vigour with which the state repressed vagrancy was essential to the processes of self-repression, the third device placing an upper limit on frontier chaos.

Anxious Self-Repression
The 'insider's view' imagined that settlers were driven to cultivate the work ethic not by fear of the penalties for not being good, but by the certainty that the acquisition of property was the inevitable reward for moral living.

The facts do not support this view. Helping to contain frontier chaos was the anxiety at least some individuals felt about deviating from the imported normative code. Maintaining the anxiety was a symbolic figure, the vagrant, known colloquially as the 'loafer', or 'swagger' if found in a rural setting. He was the colonial demon, its 'folk devil', to use the phrase coined by the criminologist, Stanley Cohen, to describe the public hysteria or 'mad panic' over the Mods and Rockers in England during 1964.[30] Vagrant phobia is apparent in nearly every linguistic context where vagrancy is mentioned. Rarely is the vagrant a figure of pity. He is often used to epitomise the terrors of a slide in the social scale.[31] Sometimes he is portrayed as a political threat.[32] Sometimes malice and negligence were imputed to swaggers, leading to blame for damage to or destruction of rural property, gates left open, fired haystacks and buildings.[33] The most common image of the loafer is of his indolence and drunkenness, his 'shiftless' character, his refusal to support himself; all of these compel him, guided by his animal cunning, to live off other people, to be a predator. Later in the century the Liberals blamed the same dark forces for stirring up trouble amongst the unemployed.[34]

The popular revulsion against vagrancy is also revealed in the use made of it to stigmatise people, to abuse, to offend, to censure. Writing to C. W. Richmond on 9 January 1858, Archdeacon Octavius Hadfield referred to an unpleasant and aggressive Maori as 'a drunken lying vagabond'. When Henry Sewell, an early Canterbury settler, considered publishing his journal later in life, he edited it, crossing out all the sections he thought might be defamatory or personally offensive— including the word 'vagabond' used to convey the rapacity of a land grabber.[35]

There is some evidence too that the word vagrant and its variants were the colony's most popular shaming words, labels that corrected and controlled. An English traveller, E. W. Elkington, observed that the 'loafer' 'is the one that stings more than any other, and every man who doesn't work, be he rich or poor, is termed a loafer and is the butt of the public'. W. D. Hay, reminiscing about his pioneering days in the Auckland region, commented that although status boundaries were very open, 'only one man *may* be scouted by any one, and that is the loafer'. The term 'to loaf' was a favourite expression, suggesting idleness, unproductive time, an excess of free time.[36]

At first sight it is difficult to see how these reactions could arise in a society to which we have attributed strong atomistic tendencies. If loafers were 'scouted', made the 'butt of the public', then by implication there was a greater organisational capacity to inculcate and impose norms than our theory allows. But the difficulty can be resolved by postulating that the aversion to vagrancy was carried over from the old society, that immigrants came to New Zealand already trained to react against vagrancy, and that the persistence of these attitudes in the new society did not require much institutional reinforcement. In England over the 16th and 17th centuries wanderers and outsiders were used as the scapegoats for a variety of social problems; in the 18th century, transients were grossly over-represented in the ranks of those indicted for theft. Throughout the 19th century, vagrants were firmly placed by officialdom and by middle-class propaganda in the 'dangerous class(es)' and set in opposition to the industrious, the respectable, the pious. Local newspapers gave prominence to the court cases of tramps having past convictions; in mid century, campaigns were waged against begging; the police employed extensions of the Vagrancy Act to keep the poor under close supervision, coercing the under-employed and the suspiciously employed; and even when more sympathetic views emerged towards the end of the century these did not encompass acceptance of vagrant values or lifestyle. In rural communities (from which New Zealand drew most of its working-class immigrants) official hostility towards vagrancy coincided with an age-long popular intolerance towards strangers, especially itinerant strangers.[37]

Certainly, social interaction in the adopted country was, for the most part, too weak by itself to develop a collective consciousness about vagrancy or anything else. But immigrants had been conditioned to see the world in a predetermined fashion. When they met and mixed in the colony they had been mentally programmed by the parent country to classify and judge one another on anti-vagrant principles. The 'scouting' of loafers was thus a reflex action. It occurred spontaneously when colonists met and mixed, even though the impulse behind it did not and could not originate from these (largely) superficial interactions.

This ethos was reinforced by the high priority the police and the courts gave to arresting and convicting—to labelling—vagrants. This has already been noticed during the provincial period. When the new national police force was established in 1876–77 its rule number five (of 17 maxims) instructed the men to 'watch narrowly all persons having no visible means of subsistence and suppress vagrancy'. The term 'criminal vagrant' became the police commissioner's favourite expression for the trouble-maker. When reporting to their superiors, local police inspectors were increasingly prone to typify criminal elements as lazy, idle itinerants, strangers to the locality, with an abiding dislike of work.[38] The courts likewise paid special attention to vagrancy—in the last 30 years of the century they convicted over 70 per cent of the cases coming before them, a rate that was consistently and substantially higher than for any other category except drunkenness.[39]

Signals against vagrancy were also transmitted by rural households. If lacking the resources to grant overnight hospitality to wayfarers, they turned them away, rationalising their violation of the rural code by declaring that the supplicants were 'loafers'.[40] Equally strong messages came from charitable institutions, who applied the

distinction between the 'deserving' and the 'undeserving' poor so
energetically that it is likely the needy would never have bothered
to apply for relief despite their patent inability to fend for themselves.[41]

The 'moral panic' over vagrancy, given these diffuse forms of
communication, tended thus to burn steadily over a long period rather
in an explosion of hysteria. We can trace its course by looking at
the volume of vagrancy cases in the courts. Before the gold-rushes,
throughout the 1850s, only about 10 or so convictions a year were
handed down by magistrates — just over two per 10,000 people.
From 1861, the onset of the gold discoveries, the number climbed,
peaking at 1,384 summary convictions in early 1879, or 29 per 10,000
population. It rose from the thirteenth most common crime in the
1850s to the third. Thereafter the long-term tendency was for the
rate to fall, mainly as a result of an amendment to the 1866 Vagrancy
Act in 1881 which abolished habitual drunkenness as a definition
of the offence, but also as an indirect result of the long-term tendency
for atomisation to diminish.[42]

Three circumstances suggested to colonials that they had a massive
vagrancy problem. The first was that although immigrants could have
imported a host of deviant stereotypes from the metropolitan society
and transplanted them to their adopted country, in fact most of these
were left behind or given far less significance in the new country.
This stemmed partly from the persistent belief of colonists that their
new society had avoided most of the Old World's problems, including
crime or at least serious crime. Also, a lot of the English images
of deviancy were not adaptable to the realities of the new environment.
For example, the English ideas of the mob, of the habitual criminal,
and of an organised criminal class all implied collective or organised
trouble-making, and did not fit European New Zealand. Their
irrelevance heightened the awareness of vagrancy—it did not have
to compete with them for public attention.

The second circumstance was that so many men were technically
vagrants, according to one of the provisions in vagrancy legislation,
in that they frequently (albeit temporarily) had no visible means
of support. Responsible for this was the irregularity inherent in
colonial employment, the habit of bingeing, the refusal of charitable
organisations to help the able-bodied poor, and the limited ability
of transients to aid one another.

The third circumstance was the difficulty of deciding who exactly
were vagrant. Although in a technical sense a large core of the colony's
many roving men were not vagrants, in outward appearance and

condition they were often indistinguishable from them. Only the few professional swaggers who stuck to a regular beat were capable of being accurately identified. In housing, diet, dress, speech it was largely impossible to pick out the 'loafer' from other foot-loose men or even from the more settled. For example, swaggers either slept in the open, or in the single-room 'swagger's hut' maintained by the larger sheep stations, or in unoccupied shacks; but 'sleeping rough' was just as much the practice of shepherds, drovers, gumdiggers, pioneer landholders.[43] Swaggers ate mutton, damper, black tea with raw sugar prepared on an open fire, and had no butter; this primitive diet was general to the rural work-force, though not to the larger and longer-established landowners. In 1887 William Pember Reeves wittily described 'the usual fare at up-country stations' as 'damper, mutton, and tea; tea, and damper, and mutton; mutton, and damper, and tea'.[44] Although in theory swaggers, without culture or education, could be distinguished by accent and vocabulary, in practice this distinction broke down for the reason, contemporaries averred, that some swaggers were remittance men—educated 'ne'er-do-wells' from the old society.[45] The greatest source of ambiguity was in dress. Swaggers were invariably described as wearing thick boots, moleskin trousers, a blue (crimean) shirt, and cabbage-tree hat.[46] From all accounts this was also the working costume of the majority of the adult male population.[47] It is true that the idealising tendencies in the literary sources make such claims suspect—contemporaries wanted to believe that New Zealand had abolished the artificial symbols of status exhibited in fashions and finery. Yet the submissions by several clothing and boot manufacturers and merchants to the 1912 Royal Commission on the Cost of Living implicitly and unwittingly support the literary sources; the submissions claimed that in comparison with 10 or 20 years earlier, the demand for moleskin trousers and 'blucher' boots had noticeably dropped in favour of fashionable, finer, more varied and expensive articles.[48] Moreover, the number of times the police arrested people on vagrancy charges, or civilians laid complaints against vagrants, only to find in court that the accused were 'respectable persons' and were not convicted, also demonstrates the equality of dress and the widespread confusion it generated as to who was a dreaded loafer and who was not. In 1864 a Nelson mechanical engineer was arrested for 'suspicious behaviour' while taking a midnight stroll, only to be released later by another constable who saw he was 'respectable'. When John Morrison, a station owner in the Wairarapa, had several apparent loafers arrested in 1894 for taking food when

he refused them hospitality, the police subsequently testified in court
that 'the men were of a respectable class' and they were discharged.[49]
   Together the three circumstances created a climate of insecurity.
They focused attention on a single deviant type, they fostered an
impression that many people could belong or did belong to the type,
and laid the individual open to the danger of being suspected or
actually accused of being the type. No one wanted to be thought
of as vagrant: people therefore had good cause to feel anxious. They
struggled vigorously to distance themselves from this awful possibility.
Their struggle was not assisted by the colony's shortage of consumer
commodities, and the taboo on conspicuous spending, for these put
a ban on the external declaration of respectability. Without this aid,
the struggle was deflected to the inner person—the moral qualities
prescribed as essential for success—and to the object that these
qualities were supposed to attain, a 'competency'. In a good many
instances the struggle obviously failed; the penchant for drunkenness
suggests that. Nonetheless the high rate of proprietorship and the
fact that drunkenness as a problem had a certain upper limit also
imply that in a good many other instances the struggle succeeded.
The fear of being identified as a 'loafer' would have induced more
men than would otherwise have been the case to force themselves
to be thrifty, industrious, and persevering—despite their social
isolation, their loneliness, their lack of friends and acquaintances
willing to praise them for their adherence to the inherited puritan
code. The Wairarapa casual labourer, W. J. Cox, puritanical and
fastidious in his habits, confessed in his diary after a long spell of
joblessness, 'The end of the year finds me badly off and no hope
as far as I can see of any thing better [.] I am since Wednesday
last living on the charity of Mrs Stanger [his landlady] and I cannot
do that many more days so shall have to take my swag on my back
and become a vagrant with little hope of ever getting out of the
wretched life.'[50]

The Emergence of Associational Machinery

Although contemporaries quite accurately claimed their society was
minimally organised, after about 1880 this claim becomes increasingly
less true with the decline of atomisation, a process that was not
completed until approximately the 1920s.
   The strongest force behind the change in its initial stages was
the demographic shifts which followed a sharp reduction in the annual
rate of immigration. Fewer newcomers were absorbed into a larger

existing population. Over the 20 years 1861–80, the country received 391,000 new arrivals, equal to 395 per cent of the 1861 population; by contrast, over the succeeding 20 years, 1881–1900, the 346,900 new arrivals were equal to 71 per cent of the 1881 population.[51] Apart from the fact that the size of the 1881 base population was about five times greater than the base in 1861, the immigration rate slowed because the colony did less to attract immigrants. In 1879 the government abruptly ended a free migration scheme which from its introduction in 1873 had brought in some 100,000 people. The Australian colonies experienced more buoyant economic conditions than New Zealand and proved more appealing to British emigrants. At the same time the New Zealand economy was no longer in a boom state; the succession of stimuli from the 1850s to the 1870s, which had enticed hordes of immigrants, had run their course and economic growth slowed as a consequence.

The slump in the rate of immigration diminished the relative size of some of the population categories most prone to social isolation. First of all, it meant that the colony contained proportionately fewer people who had just lost the greater part of their circle of acquaintances back in the Old World but had not been in the colony long enough to replace them. On top of this, the slump reduced the relative size of the young unattached adult male component of the population— the category most predisposed to transience.[52] Lastly, the slump allowed the natural agencies of birth, death, and ageing to yield an increasingly normal demographic structure. This in turn expanded the network of kinship ties, as former immigrants and their offspring aged, married, bore children, so producing cousins, nephews, aunts, grandparents.

Complementing these trends was the slower advancement of the frontier. For example, whereas the area of land in occupied holdings rose by an average of about 709,000 acres a year from 1874 to 1881, the rise was about half that figure (382,000 acres on a yearly average) between 1881 and 1901.[53] The number of one- and two-roomed shacks and tents, after ballooning from 10,500 in 1861 to 26,500 in 1867, slipping by 7000 during the early 1870s, and rising again to 25,000 in 1881, fell slowly from that point onwards.[54] The frontier moved less rapidly after 1880 because it now centred on the North Island bush zone which, until the full impact of refrigeration, yielded lower returns and was therefore less alluring to settlers (and the people of other countries) than goldmining in the interior and pastoralism on the tussock plains had been from the 1850s to the 1870s. The slower movement of the colonising fringe had the effect of steadily increasing the proportion of people inhabiting the longer established settlements. This would also have reduced the share of the population with the least association with others. This, and the growing population density in older localities, were probably the major causes of the expanding membership of churches and lodges over the last two decades of the century. They were also responsible for the fall in the estimated proportion of people living in geographically isolated households, apparent in almost every census from 1878 to the turn of the century.

Furthermore, at least some connective tissue would have developed from the spread of primary schooling and the rising proportion of people going to work outside the home. The latter is impossible to measure completely since official work-place statistics covered only a limited number of sectors. But it is a reasonable surmise given the sharp decline in the relative amount of mining employment (where there was little separation of home and work-place) and the relative growth of factory and white-collar employment between 1871 and 1901.

With the onset of all these stabilising forces the society generally headed in the direction of the 'Littledene' model, though the scale and pace probably varied a great deal from place to place. The average locality grew closer and closer towards the intensely cohesive, undifferentiated, rural community H. C. D. Somerset found in Oxford, Canterbury, over the late 1920s and 1930s. The third alternative construct of colonial social organisation, discussed in Part II, eventually came to pass, even in the larger towns and the four main centres. This is not to say that the historians who have applied the 'Littledene' model to the colonial past are right after all. Probably their views have been influenced by the tightly integrated towns and rural districts they grew up in during the inter-war period or during the 1940s and 1950s. By 1900, however, the dominant social organisation was still a long way from being a patchwork of Littledenes. The demographic imbalances that contributed so much to the fragmentation of the society before 1880 had diminished sharply, but they still existed. The tendency of a rural dwelling to be sited miles away from its nearest neighbour declined from 1881 to 1901— but almost a third of the total population remained in this state by 1901, and road transport and communications were still almost as primitive as they were 30 years earlier. Although a lot of the impetus behind extreme transience had disappeared, the rate of turnover of households in any given locality continued to be much higher than it was from 1900 to 1939 (with the exception of the 1916–20 era). More important than anything else, the influx of women, children, and manual workers into voluntary organisations (especially those related to sport), and the over-organisation of leisure, which Somerset noticed in 'Littledene', were yet to come.

The receding of atomisation after 1880 had the effect of delivering colonial society from its earlier turmoil; in fact it was the primary limit on chaos. As the membership and binding power of associations grew, so too the associational machinery of control expanded. For one thing, the greater frequency and regularity of social interaction meant that fewer people were driven to intoxication out of a desperate need to escape loneliness; and hotels diminished in importance as meeting and entertainment places. There was less need for people to rely on personal violence to rectify grievances; many more of them now had a circle of friends and acquaintances and kin they could appeal to, to deter and correct transgressors through adverse gossip and the denial of favours. Standards of behaviour would have become increasingly uniform and less ambiguous; as 'gossip chains' linked more and more individuals, producing a body of uniform perceptions, there was less likelihood of fights and litigations being caused by unpredictable behaviour and divergent interpretations of rights and obligations. The new circles of friends and kin could mediate and conciliate as well as deter and correct. The overall frequency of disputes would have been reduced as well as the proportion of those that escalated; which would diminish the need to resort to the law and physical coercion to rectify injustices.

A major by-product of the growing social ties from 1880 to 1900 was the rise of WCTU (the Women's Christian Temperance Union), formed in 1885, and the New Zealand Alliance in 1886. Both sought legislative suppression of the worst evils, the drinking habits of the 'Lords of Misrule'.

The irony about both movements is that their ability to mobilise mass support arose some time after the peak in frontier unruliness; as we noted earlier, both consumption of spirits and conviction rates for drunkenness and petty violence began long-term declines in the mid 1870s. Yet the WCTU's mass support was not evident until it engaged in its ambitious campaign of petitions for women's suffrage in 1891, 1892, and 1893—which resulted in the collection of a huge number of women's signatures (10,000, 20,000, 30,000 respectively, the last representing a quarter of the adult female population). It is true that a medley of anti-drink societies existed before 1880; by direct lobbying of individual members of parliament they helped to produce the 1881 licensing act, the first significant attempt to control the hours and days of liquor sales and ban liquor purchases by children. But the arousal of mass electoral opinion as a technique to obtain legislative change did not start until the Alliance was formed.[55] This pressure resulted in the licensing act of 1893, which granted voters the right at every general election to vote for the continuance, reduction, or abolition of the liquor trade within each electorate. Further attempts by the Alliance to mobilise opinion led 12 electorates to go dry from 1894 to 1908, secured legislative provision for a triennial referendum on prohibition in 1910, and almost won national prohibition at the poll in 1911.

The considerable time lag between the peak of alcohol problems (as well as general turmoil) and the mass mobilisation against them is directly attributable to the condition of social bonding. Before, approximately, 1880 women were too few and too thinly spread to be capable of being drawn into petition campaigns in the way they were in 1891, 1892, and 1893. In fact, the reason why the WCTU circulated petitions rather than inducting women formally into its organisation (which had only about 500 members throughout the 1880s and 1890s) was that ordinary women did not have the leisure or the habits of association to be 'joiners', but they were sufficiently concentrated in towns and factories to enable the WCTU, through systematic door-knocking, as small as membership was, to collect the signatures of such a big proportion. The anti-drink societies before the 1880s were not able to mobilise electoral opinion because most people belonged to none of the associations which could have acted as bridges between moralisers and electorate. When, however, the affiliations within society expanded after 1880, the moralisers had steadily increasing links with the electorate.

Even though the two movements did not initiate the decline in unruliness, they would have certainly strengthened the downward momentum once it got under way. As the bonded section of the society grew, the WCTU and the Alliance could rely on their respective members and supporters to communicate their moralising messages through the expanding web of networks. People newly affiliated, in consequence, had little chance of evolving a normative code that did not centre on respectable values, that prescribed or permitted drunkenness or rough behaviour. Existing associations, in addition, were persuaded to commit themselves more firmly to the values of respectability and enforce them with greater vigour, penalising more severely the members who transgressed them.

Why then did the 'wowsers' seek legislative suppression of drinking? Why could they not leave the moderation of drinking habits to the work of informal social pressures, which were obviously very effective? One reason was that a large, bondless element in society still existed by 1900; it was not swayed by informal pressures; consequently the law had to be applied to force it to be good. Another reason is that 'wowserism' took on a life of its own. An increasing proportion of the common people demanded that access to alcohol be restricted or barred, not so much because alcohol abuse was actually a problem or because they sought to control the working classes as because anti-drink opinion was what their groups expected them to display.

*. . . A land wherein
thou shalt eat bread without scarceness; thou
shalt not lack anything in it.*

Twentieth-century images of Arcadia: from the frontispiece of *New Zealand or
Ao-Tea-Roa* by James Cowan (1908). The top photograph visualises New Zealand's
tranquillity; the one below its ordered abundance. The original caption is a
quotation from Deuteronomy on Canaan, the promised land. Over the 19th century
this was a standard metaphor for New Zealand as an Arcadian ideal society. The
custom of calling New Zealand a 'land of milk and honey' persisted well into the
20th century. Harvest scenes, like the one below of densely packed rows of wheat
stooks, were once a common subject for descriptive works on New Zealand,
postcards, and other printed ephemera.

CHAPTER IX

Friends or Enemies?

W E have seen in the last two chapters that in practice colonial society contradicted fundamental aspects of its Arcadian self-image. Our conclusion will suggest how it dealt with these discrepancies.

Some of the anomalies were obscured. The period of the worst interpersonal conflict (from the 1850s to the 1870s) coincided with the Anglo-Maori Wars. Concentration on the latter probably diminished consciousness of the former. In addition, although on a per capita basis the incidence of homicides, assaults, litigations was relatively high, in absolute terms the number was small, and this in consequence lessened appreciation of the magnitude of the problems. Also, Pakeha society's comparative freedom from organised or collective bloodshed and turmoil helped to foster the illusion that it was comparatively free from all kinds of disorder. In Western Europe the reverse tended to occur. In those societies dramatic outbreaks of working-class riot and disturbance (especially in times of political tension) fuelled 'moral panics' about order problems which in turn excited public apprehension and awareness about all the other kinds of deviance practised by the poor.[1]

The contradiction between the libertarianism of Arcadia and the reality of state repression and self-repression was accommodated by a tendency to imagine that some people had a congenital predisposition for deviance. In this respect, colonists borrowed from a well-developed body of ideas in the metropolitan society, expressed most explicitly by Cesare Lombroso and Henry Mayhew, postulating that deviants were born, not made, that they constituted a separate race, physically definable by their physiognomy, phrenology, craniology, and that they possessed a special set of inborn habits.[2] In his famous description of London's 'nomadic tribes', its street folk, the *Lumpen-proletariat* from whom the criminal class was recruited, Mayhew wrote,

The nomad . . . is distinguished from the civilized man by his repugnance to regular and continuous labour—by his want of providence in laying up a store for the future—by his inability to perceive consequences ever so slightly removed from immediate apprehension—by his passion for stupefying herbs and roots, and . . . for intoxicating fermented liquors— by his extraordinary powers of enduring privation—by his comparative insensibility to pain—by an immoderate love of gaming . . . —by his love of libidinous dances—by the pleasure he experiences in witnessing the suffering of sentient creatures—by his delight in warfare and all perilous sports—by his desire for vengeance—by the looseness of his notions as to property—by the absence of chastity among his women, and his disregard of female honour . . . his rude idea of a Creator, and the utter absence of all appreciation of the mercy of the Divine Spirit.[3]

Nineteenth-century New Zealand yielded almost no theoretical writing on crime (a consequence of the smugness induced by Arcadianism).[4] Even so we can tell that this body of ideas influenced colonial sensibility by the language used to represent the 'loafer', the folk-devil. For example, an English immigrant in 1887 accounted for the bingeing habits of the extreme transient by writing,

we must not condemn this class too much, running riot in this way is only the outcome of Nature and natural feeling . . . he takes his pleasure in a very animal way, but then his life rather partakes of that nature; and also, as a rule, this class of men are grossly ignorant, therefore their only idea of relaxation is drinking, noisy music, etc.[5]

Sometimes it was the shape of the head that drew comment. To indicate that a remittance man, who had become a drunken bushman, was potentially capable of reversing his degeneration, W. K. Howitt, in his reminiscences, stated that the man had 'a fine classical head'. E. W. Elkington, who knocked about as a swagger and then found a permanent position on a sheep station, was told by its owner that he was surprised Elkington wanted to go back on the road again because he 'had a respectable face'. Sarah Courage, a runholder's wife, claimed that when work seekers came to the door, one could 'tell at a glance' the 'bonafide seekers of work', the 'decent looking men' from the 'loafers', the 'lazy, shiftless, improvident, good-for-nothing fellows, who will not work when it is offered to them'. In his adventure story, *Wild Will Enderby*, Vincent Pyke, who was familiar with the craniological theories of the British anthropologist, J. C. Pritchard, described a young man who had run wild: 'he had so allowed his hair to encroach upon his face in the customary bush fashion, that the more indicative features, such as the mouth and chin, were entirely concealed from observation'. A New Zealand colonist who visited the Victorian gold-fields in the mid 1850s said of the roving population, their 'state of unfixedness is an insuperable bar to any effective measures of good. It is impossible to civilise nomadic tribes.' Edward Tregear, the Secretary of Labour, recommended in the early 1890s that a centre be established for the indefinite incarceration of the 'incurably vagrant atoms of population'. More indirectly, the biological origins of the 'loafer' were suggested by his characterisation through the items he gathered, hunted and collected in his unimproved back-country habitat (a parallel tendency ran through Mayhew's description of London's nomadic tribes). For example, William Satchell in his gumfields novel, *The Land of the Lost*, compared the gumdigger to the ecological process that made the gum itself: 'this is where all the wrecks of the earth are drawn up to rot'.[6]

One function of this biological explanation of the deviant (or the most deviant-prone) was to distance the society from the problem in its midst. Suggesting that the 'loafer' was a product of inferior genes implied that something independent of the society—biology— was responsible for his deficiencies. It was thus possible to continue to believe that New Zealand was an ideal country. If certain individuals failed to respond to the colony's beneficent environment, then the Arcadian prescription was not at fault; rather the blame lay with innately poor quality of character.[7]

Another function was to allow the state to enlarge its apparatus of coercive law to suppress the loafer, without seeming to contravene Arcadian principles. The visualisation of the 'loafer' as a lesser breed of man put him outside Arcadia's moral community. His exclusion justified the enlargement of coercive control since the control was not directed at the Arcadians themselves. In 1894 C. W. Richmond said he wanted more stringent application of the law against sales of liquor to bingeing men; they were the 'lowest of our working classes, mostly born in Europe' who spent the 'enormous wages they receive whilst work is plentiful at shearing time and harvest, in a few days at the public houses'; then penniless, they leave their wives

unprovided for, appeal for state aid as 'the unemployed', and wander
the country living off free rural hospitality.[8] The language here is
reminiscent of another type of ideal society, the Land of Cockaygne,
likewise an abundant rural country, but inhabited by, among others,
the Lords of Misrule, individuals having no innate moral sense,
possessed of insatiable, coarse appetites.

The biological imagery also functioned to disguise the source of
self-repression, namely the fear of being a vagrant. The idea that
the possibly vagrant self belonged to an inferior species was so
demeaning that any identification with the vagrant had to be locked
away in the unconscious mind. The struggle to distance oneself from
the vagrant therefore was an unconscious struggle (except for those
who had been repeatedly stigmatised by the courts as vagrants; they
probably carried such a strong sense of self-degradation that they
struggled no more).

The contradiction between the self-image of a society that did not
need social restraints and the reality of growing socially enforced
control was not fully appreciated because of the persisting belief that
widespread ownership of real property lay at the heart of New
Zealand's social and political stability. In 1924 William Massey, the
Prime Minister, stated that 'He wanted to have every man become
the owner of the house he occupied. . . . If they were able to do
that, they would have VERY MUCH LESS OF THIS BOLSHEVISTIC NON-
SENSE'. A. Leigh Hunt, a town-planning enthusiast, proclaimed in
1919, 'if a decent man is unable to secure a home for himself and
his family he is likely to become Bolshevik in his ideas and a menace
to the community'. G. W. Russell, the Minister of Internal Affairs
in the 1919 National Government, asserted that 'Revolution and
anarchy are not bred in the houses of men who have happy homes
and delightful gardens'. W. D. S. Macdonald, another Cabinet Minister
in 1919, declared that 'much of the industrial unrest and dissatisfaction
of the miners may be attributed to the sordidness of their housing-
conditions and the monotony of their home life'. Typical too was
the justification for state aid to workers to purchase their own homes:
'The man who has a stake in the country will usually take a sane
view of things, and will not be in the same danger of running to
extremes as he would be if he had no interests in the home in which
he lived.' Such views were a straight continuation of William
Rolleston's comment in 1879, 'that the greatest teacher of morality
was the possession of land', and subsequently they informed the
National Party's concept of New Zealand as a 'property-owner's

democracy'. The point about these comments is not that they are wrong—widespread ownership of real property has had a powerful if not conservative effect in keeping 20th-century New Zealand stable—but that they overlook the fact that New Zealand's patterns of association (exemplified by 'Littledene') have been just as important in achieving these results. In the early 20th century many of the advocates of state aid to workers to buy their own houses did see the associational dimension, but only in a distinctly negative light. Such aid, they observed, would remove the working man's family from the inner city to the suburbs, from a place where the family was in danger of mixing with undesirable elements, to a place where no such danger existed because of the greater isolation. What they failed to understand was it was not the spatial isolation that eliminated the 'danger' but the different pattern of associations the move entailed. It brought the family among respectable middle-class people as neighbours and as fellow members of clubs and societies.[9]

The tension between the Arcadian self-image of a minimally organised society and the diminishing reality was also eased by the rhetoric employed to describe the benefits of 'joining', belonging to the team, 'fitting in'. The rhetoric in large part seems to have been derived from the secondary schools. They borrowed the concept of 'sportsmanship' from the English public schools and disseminated it in New Zealand.[10] An article in *The Wellingtonian*, the Wellington College magazine, of 1895 on the benefits of rugby epitomised what 'sportsmanship' meant.[11] The list of benefits included 'self-reliance', 'endurance', 'courage under difficulties', 'self-control', 'the check on morbid desires and sensations', 'good temper under trying circumstances': the same qualities that colonials had always linked to obtaining an 'independency'. The list of benefits, however, also included different qualities: 'confidence in comrades', 'aptness to act with others for the good of all, and not from selfishness', 'quick response to calls of duty instead of lethargic habits'; in other words, rugby taught collaboration, mutuality, the primacy of the group over the individual. By mixing the old ethic of extreme individualism with the different ethic of collectivism, the code of 'sportsmanship' suggested that the two were compatible if not complementary. The individual could belong to a team, be subjected to its informal group pressures, yet not lose individuality. Associations taught individuals how to obtain 'independencies'.

The remaining contradiction was between the growing dependence of the individual on state assistance and the belief that in Arcadian

New Zealand individuals 'got on' without requiring a strong social organisation to help them. In the 19th century, the contradiction was at its most glaring in 1891, when the Liberals came to power in response to the popular clamour for social justice and legislated vigorously in favour of the small settler and worker in opposition to the interests of the most wealthy. The rise of the state (especially under the Liberals) represented a shift in the Arcadian paradigm, but it was not a fundamental shift. The Arcadian premise remained: popular belief in New Zealand as a place of natural abundance continued to be as strong after 1890 as before. Edward Tregear, a socialist and first head of the Labour Department, wrote in an article on 'Labour in New Zealand' published in a series of *Official Year-Books* over the 1890s, 'There can be little doubt that as a field of labour New Zealand offers exceptional advantages. The average climate permits of work being done in the open air all the year round, and a large area of the country is fertile. The mineral wealth of the islands is almost inexhaustible, and the geographical position of the colony offers a commercial future of the highest promise.' In 1890 a bitter opponent of the Liberals and 'state socialism', Scobie Mackenzie, wrote to a New Zealand friend, while on a visit to Australia, that the 'magnificence of our climate, every Australian admits', the 'capacity for carrying on agricultural pursuits is equally unquestioned'; the gold-mining industry 'is only in its infancy with us'; the colony 'was destined to be the great rivals of New. South Wales in the production of coal'; and it stood second to New South Wales in pastoral pursuits 'with great advantages of climate over that Colony'. In a pamphlet written for the Department of Tourist and Health Resorts in 1908, James Cowan pointed out that vast areas of fertile land lay waiting to be occupied, praised the marvellous climate, and concluded by saying, the 'development of the Dominion's immense underground wealth has hitherto been chiefly confined to gold and coal; but it has practically every known mineral hidden away in the mountains, only waiting for men and money to work them'. The Crown Lands Department in 1902 and 1903 engaged in a 'searching examination' of the less accessible areas of Crown land to determine whether it could increase the supply of land for settlement. Although the results of the 'searching examination' led the Department to acknowledge that most of the area was unsuitable for agriculture and pastoralism, it claimed that 'It was safe to assume' that these tracts 'may nevertheless prove rich in minerals, and are certainly immensely valuable owing to the extent and diversity of the significant and unique scenery and natural wonders with which New Zealand is endowed'. The representation of New Zealand as a place of natural plenty persisted into the 1920s and 1930s, despite the problems of the soldier-settler in the 1920s and the 1930s Depression. The famous preamble to the Labour Party's Election Manifesto of 1935 declared: 'The Objective of the Labour Party is to utilise to the maximum degree the wonderful resources of the Dominion'.[12]

The Liberals then, did not posit their reforms on a bleak perception of the resource base, on a Utopian premise, that New Zealand was a place of natural dearth and that the power of the state had to be expanded to limit the resulting frustration of material appetites. At the same time, however, the Liberals did not consistently draw Arcadian conclusions from the Arcadian premise. The essential ambiguity of their position was revealed when John McKenzie, the Minister of Lands, in a debate on the Lands for Settlements Bill of 1894, justified the compulsory acquisition of the large estates on the ground that the state had a duty to redistribute a scarce resource for the good of the whole community. 'Here we are in this colony', he said, 'with a population less than three-quarters of a million of people, and we already find a scarcity of land for people to settle upon'; he intimated that the problem was Malthusian in origin— 'the number of people who are anxious to obtain homes for themselves is every year increasing', while the area of Crown lands 'is diminishing'. Then in the next breath he negated the Malthusian element. Land was not inherently scarce; the defect lay in the absence of state controls, which allowed the greedy (the large estate owners) to take more than they needed. With the proper state controls, 'We could in this country, with comfort and ease, settle at the very least five millions of people'.[13] What is revealing about McKenzie's analysis is its blend of Utopianism and Arcadianism. The premise is not Utopian but Arcadian in that he assumes (finally) that the frustrated aspirations of people for land did not stem from an inherent over-population in relation to resources. But he does mention that the inability of people to satisfy their proprietorial appetites has come from the laissez-faire application of Arcadianism—the greedy have not been institutionally checked and they have monopolised land resources. McKenzie's analysis epitomises the Liberal view that the distributional mechanism of Arcadianism was flawed. The earlier 'labourer's paradise' notion had assumed that only the 'virtuous' would 'get on' and that privilege, power, and other social contrivances were irrelevant to the process. It had not allowed for the possibility that such contrivances (imported from the Old World) did in fact allow property accumulation well in excess of virtue and created an aristocracy of unmerited wealth. Accordingly, one thrust of the state experiments in the Liberal period was directed at rectifying the allocative deficiencies of past Arcadianism. The Land and Income Tax Act of 1891, the Lands for Settlement Act of 1894 (and subsequent amendments) and the lease-in-perpetuity were all designed to break up the large estates and prevent individuals with superior social capital from ever again destroying equality of opportunity. Another thrust had as its objective the containment and mitigation of the social problems arising from defective allocation (the factory and trade-union legislation)—and this, too, was Utopian, not Arcadian. The most important thrust of state socialism, however, was to provide the landless and the small settler with greater equality of opportunity— by advancing them cheap mortgage money, giving them easy access to Crown land, vigorously servicing their districts with roads and bridges—which also was Utopian, not Arcadian.

Two things, however, emphasised Arcadian continuity, in addition, that is, to the assumption that natural abundance sustained state activity. The first was the actual intimacy between the state and the individual and the simplicity of the state's organisation. Politicians (including cabinet ministers) were highly approachable, extremely sensitive to public opinion, and (after 1890) from typically colonial backgrounds. The bureaucracy was unsophisticated in form, amateurish in its procedures, staffed by the ordinary and the improvisory. The state, that is, was not an authoritarian, monolithic, élite, abstract force in the Utopian tradition. The second influence flowed from an ambiguity in the original idea of the 'labourer's paradise'. As was noted in Part I, the propertyless man advanced in the 'labourer's paradise' through the creation by abundant nature of ample opportunities, which excited him to develop the personal requisites to convert 'natural' opportunities into his private property. Within this framework there is no mention of state aid. The reason for its omission is an ambiguity in the significance of the personal requisites. On the one side, their possession is the *instrument* for property acquisition; on the other, their possession signifies that the individual *deserves* to acquire property. Virtue in the first meaning is the mental and physical effort that converts natural abundance into private property; virtue in the second meaning is the moral justification for the possession of the property itself. The two meanings are in fact quite different, but in the 'labourer's paradise' schema they were thought to be synonymous, from which it is reasonable to deduce that contemporaries thought they were one and the same. As a consequence of the ambiguity, whenever people were helped by the state to acquire property they were able to believe that it was their virtue that was responsible for the acquisition, not the state's action. They took the moral meaning of virtue (that they deserved to possess property fashioned from natural abundance) and equated it with both meanings, instrument as well as desert. Contemporaries were thus able to believe that their efforts, not the state's assistance, had converted the natural abundance into their property. The confusion was always present whenever politicians urged the government to do more of something to foster 'self-reliance' (which in present-day language is called 'private enterprise'). To ensure that the country progresses, said one parliamentarian in 1905 during a debate on the Workers' Dwellings Bill, 'there is only one effective way . . . and that is by placing the best possible machinery at our disposal on the land [i.e. state assistance], enabling the thrifty and industrious to make the best possible use of their opportunities, and giving the working men and women of the towns a chance of bettering their condition by striking out for themselves in the country'.[14]

As a result of its social past New Zealand possessed six powerful agencies of social and political stability by 1900. It had a very high rate of ownership of real property, a strong state apparatus, an increasingly close-knit community embracing people from different strata, a uniform normative code, a strong system of self-repression, a smug belief that the country was some sort of rural ideal society of extreme individualists. Its stability, in other words, was derived from a mix of principles, Arcadian, Perfect Moral Commonwealth, Utopian. These forces of stability should be on the agenda when the social history of 20th-century New Zealand is written.

Retrospect

IN a dual sense the atomised society is a world we have lost. As a living entity it vanished by the 1920s after starting to decay from the 1880s. It is also something we are not aware of; for it plays no role in our present historical thinking, in our view of the past, of where we came from.

The disappearance of the atomised society does not explain why we are not conscious that it once existed. Other European societies have a longer history than ours, a history that led them to evolve and change shape many times, yet they are far more aware of what they once were. Pakeha New Zealanders today may know Europeans were living in New Zealand between the 1850s and 1880s. A few may even think this was a formative stage in their history. But they cannot identify the salient features of European society during this period or even the characteristics of the next stage in our past (1880–1900), when atomisation began to die. On suitable occasions I ask people what impressions they have of settler society. I also ask new batches of students taking courses in New Zealand colonial history to list three things which define European social life before 1900. I have, in addition, made a concerted effort to watch the film versions of the settler social pattern, to read historical novels purportedly set in the same context, to browse through the non-fiction literature about it ranging from popular coffee-table books to modest works on local history written by amateur historians. What I have found is that none of these sources thinks settler society was atomised or uses words which remotely suggest this. None thinks of it as a time of extreme individualism. Few single out the forces that generated atomisation. Seldom do they mention any of its symptoms, the combination of weak interpersonal relationships, comparatively high material living standards, a high incidence of loneliness and individual licence, a low incidence of collective or institutionalised social problems.

There are all manner of possible reasons why modern New Zealand culture has no sense of this crucial stage in our past. One possibility we can safely reject is that Pakehas are not interested in their history and are ignorant of important historical events. For instance, most Pakehas can say that the 'Maori Wars' or the Treaty of Waitangi occurred in the 19th century. The odds are that they know when their forebears came to New Zealand or when their locality was first settled. They probably have an idea that it was a rural, pioneering country without modern technology. In varying degrees they will have stored in their minds all kinds of images and facts about the 19th century, for example that George Grey was a Governor, that Edward Gibbon Wakefield was a founder of particular settlements, that women won the right to vote in 1893, and so on. Moreover, interest in colonial history has grown phenomenally over the last decade or so, as has the propagation of popular knowledge about it. More New Zealand history is taught at schools and universities than when I was young. Museums have mounted exhibitions of artefacts and old photographs. Reproductions of colonial paintings and books on colonial art attract enthusiastic buyers and the wealthy and not-so-wealthy pay high and rising prices for originals. Movements dedicated to the preservation of old buildings have sprung up and angry demonstrators sometimes greet the demolition of edifices which 20 years ago were regarded as having no historical value. Many of the works of fiction and description written during colonial times have been republished and apparently enjoy a ready market. Pakeha New Zealanders are well-informed about many aspects of their past and they certainly do not dismiss it; on the contrary they are fascinated by it and their curiosity in recent years seems insatiable.

Nor can our failure to identify the atomised past be attributed to the alien nature of its ideology. The irony here is that present-day ideology was formed during the phase of atomisation, although we do not realise that this phase existed. We are not aware that the definition by colonists of the sort of society New Zealand is and should be is their legacy to us, and that their social aspirations are also ours. We still believe that New Zealand is a country blessed with a rich stock of 'natural advantages'; witness, for example, how often our political parties affirm this cliché in their propaganda at general elections. Now, as then, we draw upon Arcadian allusions when characterising New Zealand as inherently pure and wholesome, ideal for healthy, outdoor living, relaxed, easy-going, free of the social problems of older societies. These problems have increased since the 19th century, for they now include environmental pollution and nuclear weapons; but we still believe, as the colonists did, that what distinguishes New Zealand is its freedom from deference and subservience, from class hostilities (unless these be imported by 'pommy' trade unionists), and from the snobbery governing status conventions and rigidities. We have certainly broadened the settler notion of the requisites for 'getting on': more emphasis today is given to enterprise, innovation, and education; no longer do we hold that only thrift and industry are needed for individual success. Yet we still believe that rewards should be proportionate to effort, that acquisition should be an individualistic activity, that when reaching adulthood children should make their own way without parental aid and the advantage of privilege. In addition the idea of the rewards of endeavour has remained the same. The traditional goal prescribed for the working man was the acquisition of a 'competency', social independence based on landed property. In today's New Zealand young working-class couples aspire to own a single-unit suburban home of their own, and a surprisingly high proportion of wage-earners still aspire to own a little business, to be their own bosses. In the 19th century New Zealand was projected as a property-owners' paradise, where business people and the middle classes generally enjoyed a risk-free environment for wealth-making. We find the same attitude today reflected in the cost-plus mentality and the clamour for government protection and subsidy. In sum, we have derived from 19th-century ideology our egalitarian ethic: we see New Zealand as a country where abundant natural resources offer limitless opportunities for individual acquisition and a guarantee of social equality.

It is, however, quite likely that atomisation as the central attribute of 19th-century settler society has escaped our attention because our social organisation is now so different. From the 1920s to the 1960s the social organisation can best be characterised as a large collection of powerful and intimate local communities superimposed upon which were the multiple institutions of central government and nationwide sectional interest groups. Recently this social organisation has begun to change, with the intensive local community being replaced by larger, more anonymous associations. Despite the change in form New Zealand society is as highly organised as it was from the 1920s to the 1960s. So familiar are we with strong social bonding that we automatically assume that Pakeha society was always like this, and we are unable to imagine a time when it was not.

Reinforcing this tendency is the fact that colonists themselves deliberately and unconsciously concealed many of the realities about their own condition. Colonists wanted to believe their society was ideal. They did not expect Arcadia to generate chaos. As material optimists, they were genuinely convinced that an environment full of opportunities for material acquisition and self-betterment would necessarily lead to moral improvement, contentment, social harmony, and social equity. Moreover, their desire to boost New Zealand's virtues in order to attract a sufficient flow of immigrants and capital necessary for 'development' led them to be intolerant of social criticism and to discourage objective social analysis. Seldom therefore did they discuss their atomised condition, which meant in turn that they failed to devise a language to express it. None of this, of course, has helped us understand them. They left us no mythology about atomisation because the undesirable facets of atomisation were the inadmissible truths about themselves.

Finally, what has prevented us from conceptualising this lost world is the ambivalence we must feel towards its realities. Consider these again, remembering that they are inseparable: unfettered individualism; a comparatively high standard of living; high rates of loneliness, drunkenness, and interpersonal conflict; a low propensity for group or organised conflict and status competition. We, like the colonists, think that some of these things are ideal. We dream of leading a life of unfettered individualism, in a reasonable standard of comfort, without fear of collective disharmony or status anxiety. This to us is paradise. It is Arcadia. So attracted are we to this vision of the good life, that it is hard for us to appreciate that inextricably linked to it are a set of unacceptable costs and painful experiences: of loneliness, of being under constant threat from the unpredictable and violent behaviour of other people, of unbridled drunken licence, of superficial relationships, of too little community. As it is so difficult for us to confront this unpleasant fact, I suspect we have unconsciously suppressed the knowledge that 19th-century New Zealand proves that Arcadia cannot permanently solve the problem of unhappiness.

There is no good life to look forward to, no possibility of heaven on earth. For every desirable social feature, there is always an unintended bad consequence. Not unnaturally we want to remain ignorant of this; accordingly we have averted our eyes from what is plain to see. New Zealand's experience during the colonial period demonstrates that the real enemy of the Arcadian ideal society is Arcadia itself.

References

Abbreviations

AEHR	*Australian Economic History Review*
AJHR	*Appendices to the Journal of the House of Representatives*
ATL	Alexander Turnbull Library
C&L	V.A.C. Gatrell, B. Lenman, G. Parker (eds), *Crime and the Law: the Social History of Crime in Western Europe since 1500*, London, 1980
HR	*Historical Review; Journal of the Whakatane and District Historical Society Inc. New Zealand*
HN	*Historical News*
HS	*Historical Studies*
JIH	*Journal of Interdisciplinary History*
LH	*Labour History*
NZJH	*New Zealand Journal of History*
NZPD	*New Zealand Parliamentary Debates*
NZYB	*New Zealand Official Year-Book*
P&P	*Past and Present*
PS	*Political Science*
SH	*Journal of Social History*
VUW	Victoria University of Wellington
WDFU	Women's Division of the New Zealand Farmers' Union

Note: In references to the New Zealand Parliamentary Debates the first number refers to the year, the second to the volume, and third and subsequent numbers to the page(s).

Introduction

1. A. de Tocqueville, *Democracy in America* (New York, 1966 edn); F. J. Turner, *The Frontier in American History* (New York, 1948 edn); C. M. H. Clark, *A History of Australia, III, The Beginning of an Australian Civilization, 1824-1851* (Melbourne, 1979).
2. K. R. Popper, *The Open Society and its Enemies*, 2 v., 3rd ed. (rev.), (London, 1957), especially i, ch. 10.

Part I: Prologue

1. *The Tempest*, II,i. For discussion of early European views of the New World as Arcadia see L. Marx, *The Machine in the Garden : Technology and the Pastoral Ideal in America* (London, 1964), chs 2 & 3; L. T. Sargent, 'Utopianism in Colonial America', *History of Political Thought*, IV, 3, 1983; V. L. Parrington, *American Dreams: a Study of American Utopias* (Providence, 1947); B. Smith, *European Vision and the South Pacific, 1768-*

1850: a Study in the History of Art and Ideas (Oxford, 1960). For the 18th-century European idea of the abundance of the legendary 'Southern Continent', see H. T. Fry, *Alexander Dalrymple (1737-1808) and the Expansion of British Trade* (London, 1970), ch. 5; and D. Mackay, 'British Interest in the Southern Oceans 1782-1794', *NZJH*, 3, Oct. 1969.

2. See e.g., C. Lansbury, *Arcady in Australia: the Evocation of Australia in Nineteenth-Century English Literature* (Melbourne, 1970); R. Ward, *The Australian Legend* (Melbourne, 1977), pp.250-2; Clark, *A History of Australia*, III, pp.230-1, 237-8, 243-4.

3. R. Dalziel, *The Origins of New Zealand Diplomacy; the Agent-General in London 1870-1905* (Wellington, 1975), pp.154-5.

4. J. Hector, *Handbook of New Zealand*, 3rd ed. rev. (Wellington, 1883); Dalziel, *Agent-General*, pp.154-5.

5. A. E. Woodhouse (ed.), *Tales of Pioneer Women Collected by the Women's Institutes of New Zealand* (Christchurch, 1940), p.142; J. Hall, *Experience of Thirty Years in the Provincial District of Wellington* (Wellington, 1884), p.5; E. M. Story (ed.), 'Our Fathers Have Told Us: Stories of Settlers Collected in New Zealand', MS typescript, ATL, p.354; C. Erickson, *Invisible Immigrants; the Adaptation of English and Scottish Immigrants in Nineteenth-Century America* (Coral Gables, Fla, 1972), pp.34-35 & p.491, fn. 75, has found very few references to emigrant guidebooks in her survey of private letters written from the United States by English and Scots immigrants, and claims they had minimal influence upon the views of intending emigrants. This does not seem to fit the New Zealand experience. References to such guides by colonists occur more frequently in New Zealand sources. New Zealand's very short history as an immigrant society by the mid 19th century gave intending emigrants access to far fewer colonists who could tell them about the realities of colonial life.

6. H. Scott, *Reminiscences of a New Chum in Otago (New Zealand) in the Early 'Seventies* (Timaru, 1922), p.14; extracts of petition in R. M. Allan, *Nelson; a History of Early Settlement* (Wellington, 1965), p.187; Sale in *AJHR*, C-4, 1905, 1024; Atkinson letter in G. H. Scholefield (ed.), *The Richmond-Atkinson Papers*, 2 v., (Wellington, 1960), i, p.157; *Labourers' Union Chronicle*, 29 Nov. 1873, quoted in R. Arnold, *The Farthest Promised Land: English Villagers, New Zealand Immigrants of the 1870s* (Wellington, 1981), p.51.

7. 'Hopeful', *'Taken In'; Being a Sketch of New Zealand Life* (London, 1887, repr. Christchurch, 1974), pp.182-3.

8. Lansbury, *Arcady*, pp.154-67 points to the transformations brought by Lawson *et al.* though with strong qualifications; Clark, *A History of Australia*, iii, pp.315-6; G. Davison, 'Sydney and the Bush: an Urban Context for the Australian Legend', *HS*, 18, 1978, pp.191-209.

9. J. Adam, *Twenty-five Years of Emigrant Life in the South of New Zealand*, 2nd ed. (Edinburgh, 1876), p.26.

10. E.g., J. Gorst, *New Zealand Revisited; Recollections of the Days of My Youth* (London, 1908), p.53; Hochstetter in J. Buller, *New Zealand: Past and Present* (London, 1880), pp.132-5; quotation from an American visitor in Taranaki in J. Cowan, *Settlers and Pioneers* (Wellington, 1940), p.90.

11. J. C. Davis, *Utopia and the Ideal Society: a Study of English Utopian Writing 1516-1700* (Cambridge, 1981), ch. I. Also see Northrop Frye, 'Varieties of Literary Utopia' in F. E. Manuel (ed.), *Utopias and Utopian Thought* (Boston, 1966).

Chapter 1: Natural Abundance

1. Especially his *New Zealand, or Zealandia, the Britain of the South*, 2 v. (London, 1857). Reference from here on is to the subsequent edition, *New Zealand the 'Britain of the South': with a chapter on The Native War, and Our Future Native Policy*, 2nd ed. (London, 1861), pp.140, 145, 153.

2. D. Kennedy, *Kennedy's Colonial Travel. A Narrative of a Four Years' Tour Through Australia, New Zealand, Canada, etc* (London, 1876), p.219, also see p.221.
3. Buller, *Past and Present*, p.116.
4. P. Robinson, 'Dunedin to Christchurch in 1888', in *The New Zealand Reader* (Wellington, 1895), pp.226-33.
5. Quoted in Hursthouse, *New Zealand*, p.93.
6. Quoted in J. Rutherford, *Sir George Grey, K.C.B., 1812-1898: a Study in Colonial Government* (London, 1961), p.554.
7. *Evening Post*, 3 Jan. 1889, first editorial.
8. S. Butler, *Erewhon or Over the Range* (1872, repr. Auckland 1973), pp.22-23.
9. Hector, *Handbook*, pp.13-14.
10. Quoted in Hursthouse, *New Zealand*, p.193.
11. Thomson quoted by Hursthouse, *New Zealand*, pp.67, also 69-72. Thomson's data first appeared in a learned journal 'On the Influences of the Climate of New Zealand in the Production of Disease among Emigrants from Great Britain', *The Medico-Chirurgical Review*, 74, 1850. The statistics were updated and published in Thomson's *The Story of New Zealand*, 2 v. (London, 1859, repr. 1974), i, pp.320-3; Thomson's data were also cited, e.g., by T. H. Braim, *New Homes: The Rise, Progress, Present Position and Future Prospects of . . . New Zealand . . .* (London, 1870), p.369; I. R. Cooper, *The New Zealand Settlers' Guide, a Sketch of the Present State of the Six Provinces. . .* (London, 1857), pp.12-14.
12. Swainson quoted in Hursthouse, *New Zealand*, p.64.
13. Hursthouse, *New Zealand*, pp.59, 63-64, 75-79, 85, 93-94, 193, 345.
14. Braim, *New Homes*, pp.363-4.
15. J. Vogel (ed.), *The Official Handbook of New Zealand. . .* (London, 1875), *passim*.
16. Robinson quoted in Buller, *Past and Present*, p.103; J. Bathgate, *New Zealand, its Resources and Prospects*, new rev. ed., (London, 1884), pp.24, 49.
17. A. Simmons, *Old England and New Zealand . . .* (London, 1879), pp.30, 42, 63, 65, 70, 102-3.
18. A. Clayden, *The England of the Pacific . . .* (London, 1879), pp.12, 14.
19. Arnold, *Farthest Land*, pp.91-93.
20. Quoted in Arnold, *Farthest Land*, pp.80, 92.
21. W. K. Howitt, *A Pioneer Looks Back: Days of Trials, Hardships and Achievements* (Auckland, 1945), pp.13, 188-9, 201; Hursthouse, *New Zealand*, pp.83, 231; W. D. Hay, *Brighter Britain or Settler and Maori in Northern New Zealand*, 2 v. (London, 1882), i, p.232; A. Saunders, *New Zealand, its Climate, Soil, Natural and Artificial Productions . . .* (London, 1868), p.7; letter to Hursthouse in Hursthouse, *New Zealand*, pp.78-79. Also Thomson, *Story of New Zealand*, pp.66-67.
22. J. Cowan, *The Old Frontier . . .* (Te Awamutu, 1922), p.85. See also e.g., Howitt, *A Pioneer*, p.223; Woodhouse (ed.), *Pioneer Women*, p.85; Story (ed.), 'Our Fathers', pp.103, 105, 364; William Rolleston to Robert Rolleston, 18 Apr. 1882, quoted in W. D. Stewart, *William Rolleston; a New Zealand Statesman* (Christchurch, 1940), p.163; A. Drummond (ed.), *The Thames Journals of Vicesimus Lush 1868-82* (Christchurch, 1975), p.188; Saunders, *New Zealand*, p.11.
23. Hursthouse, *New Zealand*, p.234. See also e.g., W. D. McIntyre (ed.), *The Journal of Henry Sewell 1853-7*, 2 v. (Christchurch, 1980), i, p.325; Hay, *Brighter Britain*, i, p.223.
24. Hursthouse, *New Zealand*, p.87; Hector, *Handbook*, p.7; Simmons, *Old England*, p.42; Woodhouse (ed.), *Pioneer Women*, p.85.
25. Howitt, *A Pioneer*, pp.223-4.
26. A. Briggs, 'The Human Aggregate' in H. J. Dyos & M. Wolff (eds), *The Victorian City— Images and Realities*, 2 v. (London, 1973), i.; R. Taylor, *The Past and Present of New Zealand; with its Prospects for the Future* (London, 1868), p.vi; Hursthouse, *New Zealand*, p.338.
27. Hursthouse, *New Zealand*, p.390; *Evening Post*, 3 Jan. 1889, first editorial.

Chapter II: The Labourer's Paradise

1. Cooper, *Settlers' Guide*, p.9.
2. Hursthouse, *New Zealand*, p.255.
3. R. B. Paul, *New Zealand, As It Was and As It Is* (London, 1861), pp.56-57.
4. Braim, *New Homes*, p.17.
5. A. Bathgate, *Colonial Experiences; or Sketches of People and Places in the Province of Otago, New Zealand* (Glasgow, 1874), pp.44-45.
6. Buller, *Past and Present*, p.142.
7. Quoted in W. Gisborne, *The Colony of New Zealand; its History, Vicissitudes and Progress* (London, 1888), p.345.
8. Ward in *NZPD*, 1894, 85, 692; Buller, *Past and Present*, p.128; R. Taylor, *Te Ika A Maui, or New Zealand and its Inhabitants* (London, 1855), pp.458, 462.
9. Arnold, *Farthest Land, passim*.
10. Quoted in Arnold, *Farthest Land*, pp.296-7.
11. Clayden, *England of the Pacific*, p.8.
12. Simmons, *Old England*, pp.92-94.
13. *AJHR*, 1905, C-4, Peake, 905; Johnston, 1433; Register, 1456; Agar, 610. See also evidence from A. J. Curry of Blenheim, representing a building workers' union, 1455; W. H. Hampton of the Wellington Trades and Labour Council, 1284, 1289; W. H. Westbrook of the Wellington Trades and Labour Council, 1316; J. S. Myers of the Political Labour League, 530; Alexander Osbourne, a bookbinder, 1293; J. Bunting, a Waiau labourer, 554; C. H. Hansen, a Pawaho labourer, 528-9; R. Gee, a Rakaia house-painter, 516; J. Griffiths, a modeller and carver, 1344; J. Wood, a Fendalton carpenter, 618-9; W. Daniel, a Lyttelton wharf labourer, 587; W. Lundon, a labourer, 417-8. Also comments by the president of the Canterbury Trades and Labour Council quoted in Gorst, *Recollections*, p.64; A. Métin, *Socialism without Doctrine* (1908, repr. Chippendale, 1977), pp.148, 153-5.
14. See e.g., Clayden, *England of the Pacific*, pp.8, 21; immigrants' letters cited in Adam, *Twenty-five Years*, p.145 ff.; Jane Maria Richmond, general letter, 24 Sept. 1853, in Scholefield (ed.), *Richmond-Atkinson*, i, p.134; Arnold, *Farthest Land*, pp.32, 34, 45, 156-7; Thomas Arnold to Mrs. Arnold, 22 Dec. 1848, in J. Bertram (ed.), *New Zealand Letters of Thomas Arnold The Younger* (Auckland, 1966), pp 99-100.
15. Simmons, *Old England*, pp.37, 43-44, 60-61, 75-78, 88-89.
16. Hay, *Brighter Britain*, i, p.6.
17. Buller, *Past and Present*, p.137.
18. Saunders, *New Zealand*, p.46; Buller, *Past and Present*, p.92; Hay, *Brighter Britain*, i, pp.56, 59. See also e.g., E. Hodder, *Memories of New Zealand Life* (London, 1862), pp.57-58.
19. Hursthouse, *New Zealand*, p.255.
20. McIntyre (ed.), *Sewell*, i, p.227; E. B. Fitton, *New Zealand: its Present Condition, Prospects and Resources* . . . (London, 1856), p.286; Cooper, *Settlers' Guide*, p.9; Hodder, *Memories*, pp.63-64; Braim, *New Homes*, pp.18-19; Adam, *Twenty-five Years*, p.132; Clayden, *England of the Pacific*, p.9; Hay, *Brighter Britain*, i, p.55; J. Bathgate, *Resources and Prospects*, pp.104-5; Gisborne, *The Colony*, pp.345-6.
21. I. A. McLaren, 'Secondary Schools in the New Zealand Social Order, 1840-1903', unpublished Ph.D. thesis, VUW, 1965, p.272 *et passim*.
22. See e.g., Clayden, *England of the Pacific*, pp.15-16, 17-18.
23. Adam, *Twenty-five Years*, p.33; Cooper, *Settlers' Guide*, pp.5-6; J. Bathgate, *Resources and Prospects*, p.21; Hursthouse, *New Zealand*, p.397; Clayden, *England of the Pacific*, p.10; Fitton, *Prospects and Resources*, p.270; Taylor, *Te Ika*, p.461.
24. Taylor, *Te Ika*, p.462.
25. The stage-by-stage process is implied by E. Tregear, 'Labour in New Zealand', *NZYB*, 1893, pp.218-9; Braim, *New Homes*, pp.17-18; Buller, *Past and Present*, pp.131-2; Gisborne,

The Colony, pp.345-6; E. Jones, *Autobiography of an Early Settler in New Zealand* (Wellington, 1933), p.70; Simmons, *Old England*, pp.93-94; J. Bathgate, *Resources and Prospects*, p.105; and in Holloway's report on New Zealand summarised by Arnold, *Farthest Land*, pp.92-93.

26. W. Satchell, *The Land of the Lost* (1902, repr. Auckland, 1971), p.207; Hochstetter, quofed in Buller, *Past and Present*, pp.132-5. Also Thomson, *Story of New Zealand*, ii, p.312.

Chapter III: The Middle-Class Paradise

1. Letter 23 Mar. 1870 in Scholefield (ed.), *Richmond-Atkinson*, ii, p.300.
2. Saunders, *New Zealand*, p.47.
3. Cooper, *Settlers' Guide*, p.151.
4. J. B. Bennett, 'Statistics of New Zealand—Introductory Memorandum', *Statistics of New Zealand*, 1858, vi-vii.
5. F. Fuller, *Five Years' Residence in New Zealand; or, Observations on Colonization* (London, 1859), p.242; Hursthouse, *New Zealand*, p.407; Saunders, *New Zealand*, pp.40-41; Adam, *Twenty-five Years*, p.77; *Evening Post*, 7 Jan. 1879, editorial; Buller, *Past and Present*, p.93; J. Bathgate, *Resources and Prospects*, pp.22-23, 99; R. Stout, *Notes on the Progress of New Zealand for Twenty Years, 1864-1884* (Wellington, 1886), pp.13-15; W. P. Reeves, *The Long White Cloud Ao Tea Roa*, 4th ed. (London, 1956), pp.183, 273. On anxiety by Victorians about crime and disorder also see W. E. Houghton, *The Victorian Frame of Mind* (Oxford, 1957), pp.54-58.
6. Stout, *Notes on the Progress*, p.16; J. Bathgate, *Resources and Prospects*, p.100.
7. Fuller, *Five Years' Residence*, pp.242, 264.
8. C. W. McMurran, *From New York to New Zealand; or, The New Century Trip* (Wellington, 1904), p.132.
9. Saunders, *New Zealand*, p.45.
10. Buller, *Past and Present*, p.93.
11. *NZPD*, 1879, 32, 581; Governor Grey to Earl Grey, Auckland, 15 Mar., 1849, in *Great Britain. Parliamentary Papers—Papers Relating to New Zealand 1847-50, Colonies New Zealand 6* (Shannon, 1969), pp.56-57.
12. Saunders, *New Zealand*, p.46.
13. Hay, *Brighter Britain*, i, pp.6, 26-38.
14. Braim, *New Homes*, pp.12-13.
15. Hursthouse, *New Zealand*, pp.385-6, 387, 393, 406. The reality of status anxiety to the middle classes in Victorian England has been established by J. A. Banks, *Prosperity and Parenthood: a Study of Family Planning among the Victorian Middle Classes* (London, 1954).
16. Clayden, *England of the Pacific,* pp.10-11.
17. Hursthouse, *New Zealand*, pp.385-7.
18. R. Wallace, *The Rural Economy and Agriculture of Australia and New Zealand* (London, 1891), p.vii.
19. Cooper, *Settlers' Guide*, p.6; Atkinson letter in Scholefield (ed.), *Richmond-Atkinson*, i, pp.325-6.
20. Cooper, *Settlers' Guide*, p.27; Fitton,' *Prospects and Resources*, p.271; Hursthouse, *New Zealand*, pp.408-9; Hodder, *Memories*, p.51.
21. Hay, *Brighter Britain*, i, pp.6, 34.
22. Hursthouse, *New Zealand*, p.387; Cooper, *Settlers' Guide*, pp.27-28; Mary-Ann Martin to Mrs Owen, 8 Aug. 1862, in Sir Robert Owen Correspondence 1817-1855, British Museum, Add. MSS, 39954, v. ii, f.410-12 (I am obliged to Dr James Belich for this reference); Harriet Gore Browne to Emily Richmond, 16 Oct. 1861, in Scholefield (ed.), *Richmond-Atkinson*, i, pp.723-4; Hay, *Brighter Britain*, i, pp.34-37; L. G. D. Acland, *The Early Canterbury Runs*, 4th ed. (Christchurch, 1975), pp.140-1, 186, for stories of runholders mistaken for swaggers because of similar clothing.

23. Hodder, *Memories*, pp.54, 63-64.
24. Hursthouse, *New Zealand*, p.406; Buller, *Past and Present*, p.92; Hay, *Brighter Britain*, i, p.123.
25. Buller, *Past and Present*, pp.140-1. See also J. Bathgate, *Resources and Prospects*, p.107; Hursthouse, *New Zealand*, p.400; Jones, *Autobiography of an Early Settler*, p.65.

Chapter IV: A Hierarchical Society?

1. The best anthropological literature on vertically bonded societies and their manifestations includes E. Gellner and J. Waterbury (eds), *Patrons and Clients in Mediterranean Societies* (London, 1977); J. Boissevain, *Friends of Friends; Networks, Manipulators and Coalitions* (Oxford, 1974). For historical case-studies see L. Stone, *The Crisis of the Aristocracy, 1558-1641* (Oxford, 1965); M. Bloch, *Feudal Society*, 2nd ed. (London, 1962), pp.145 ff; A. Blok, *The Mafia of a Sicilian Village, 1860-1960; a Study of Violent Peasant Entrepreneurs* (Oxford, 1974); H. Hess, *Mafia and Mafiosi: the Structure of Power* (Westmead, 1973); for sociological treatment see H. Newby, *The Deferential Worker: a Study of Farm Workers in East Anglia* (London, 1977).
2. W. B. Sutch, *The Quest for Security in New Zealand, 1840-1966* (Wellington, 1966); *Poverty and Progress in New Zealand: a Reassessment* (Wellington, 1969).
3. Sutch, *Quest for Security*, pp. 27, 33, 41, 62, 65, 140.
4. Sutch, *Quest for Security*, p. 27; also p.140.
5. Sutch, *Quest for Security*, chs. 3 & 4; p.63.
6. J. Martin, 'Whither the Rural Working Class in Nineteenth-Century New Zealand?', *NZJH*, 17, Apr. 1983, p.42.
7. E.g., Rutherford, *Grey*, pp.585-6; W. J. Gardner, *The Amuri; a County History* (Culverden, 1956), p.184, for meddling by Mrs Caverhill in the lives of her servants. See also Arnold, *Farthest Land*, pp.266-7.
8. S. Eldred-Grigg, *A Southern Gentry: New Zealanders Who Inherited the Earth* (Wellington, 1980).
9. Eldred-Grigg, *Southern Gentry*, pp.117, 118; see also 121.
10. Eldred-Grigg, *Southern Gentry*, pp.118, 126.
11. Eldred-Grigg, *Southern Gentry*, pp.118, 121, 146.
12. 'Hopeful', *'Taken In'*, p.119.
13. S. Courage, *Lights and Shadows of Colonial Life, Twenty-six Years in Canterbury, New Zealand* (1896, repr. Christchurch, 1976), p.20. See also journal entry 6 Dec. 1876 by Vicesimus Lush in Drummond, *The Thames Journals of Vicesimus Lush 1868-82*, p.183.
14. According to the 5 April 1891 Census, there were 584 holdings over 5,000 acres and 6151 persons enumerated as salary and wage-earning runholders, graziers, sheep or cattle farmers, stock riders, drovers, shepherds, pastoral labourers, etc.
15. P. Horn, *The Rise and Fall of the Victorian Servant* (Dublin, 1975), p.23.
16. Eldred-Grigg, *Southern Gentry*, p.89; Stone, *Crisis of the Aristocracy*, pp.187, 211-14, 584-5. Eldred-Grigg's figure, moreover, seems to be overstated: for the whole of New Zealand in 1901 there were only 311 households employing three or more servants as against 895 land-holdings larger than 5,000 acres.
17. A. L. Beier, *Masterless Men: the Vagrancy Problem in England 1560-1640* (London, 1985), p.23.
18. C. Wilson, *England's Apprenticeship, 1603-1763* (New York, 1965), p.231; C. M. Cipolla, *Before the Industrial Revolution; European Society and Economy, 1000-1700*, 2nd ed. (London, 1981), pp.13-19.
19. M. F. Chilton, 'The Genesis of the Welfare State: A Study of Hospitals and Charitable Aid in New Zealand, 1877-92', M.A. thesis, University of Canterbury, 1968, p.44; M. Tennant, 'Indigence and Charitable Aid in New Zealand, 1885-1920', PhD. thesis, Massey University, 1981, pp.179, 181, 182, 185 (fn. 18); D. A. Hamer (ed.), *The Webbs in New Zealand 1898* (Wellington, 1974), p.53.

20. On Latin America, see e.g., R. M. Morse, 'The Heritage of Latin America' in L. Hartz, *The Founding of New Societies, Studies in the History of the United States, Latin America, South Africa, Canada, and Australia* (New York, 1964).

21. Data calculated from C. Toynbee, 'Class and Social Structure in Nineteenth-Century New Zealand' in D. Hamer (ed.), *New Zealand Social History: Papers for the Turnbull Conference on New Zealand Social History*, Aug. 1978 (Auckland, n.d.), p.75.

22. The 62 per cent rate of manual workers has been taken from P. Meuli, 'Occupational Change and Bourgeois Proliferation', M.A. thesis, VUW, 1977. The alternative figure of 66 per cent is from C. Toynbee, 'Class and Mobility in Nineteenth Century New Zealand', M.A. thesis, VUW, 1979. Toynbee's figure has been extrapolated from the 1881 Census tabulations on occupations; Meuli's from a combination of the tabulations on occupations and occupational status in the 1896 Census, which, being less coarse-grained, allows more of the non-manual categories (employers, self-employed, the salaried) to be excluded.

23. 'Returns of Expenditure by Working-Men', *AJHR*, H-10, 1893, 40-50. The evidence that the Bureau of Industries conducted the survey in 1892 is indirect, namely that the Bureau was established in May 1891 and the results of the survey were not published by the Department of Labour until 1893 as part of its report on its activities the previous financial year. Eight hundred schedules were sent out in small parcels of four to 12 each to inspectors of factories, trade union secretaries, and bureau agents with letters asking them to hand the schedules to working men who would be likely to make reliable returns. There were 146 schedules returned 'of which some were imperfect'; probably because of these imperfections only 106 were published in *AJHR*.

24. M. Fairburn, 'Why did the New Zealand Labour Party fail to win office until 1935?', *PS*, 37, Dec. 1985, p.121, Table 6.

25. C. Cook & J. Stevenson, *The Longman Handbook of Modern British History, 1714–1980* (Harlow, 1983), p.115.

26. In 1896 New Zealand had 8.2 land-holdings over one acre for every 100 persons; New South Wales in 1897 had 4.9 of one acre and over per 100 persons; South Australia in 1891 had 6.2 of one acre and over per 100 persons; Victoria in 1891 had 5.3 over one acre per 100 persons; Western Australia had 2.9 of one acre and over per 100 persons in 1901. Raw data taken from T. A. Coghlan, *A Statistical Account of the Seven Colonies of Australasia, 1897-8* (Sydney, 1898), p.510; *Census of Victoria*, 1891, Part 8, Table 2; *Official Yearbook of the Commonwealth of Australia, 1901-8*, no. 2, 1909, pp.349-351.

27. Linda Oliver, 'Survey of "Working Class" Landowners in the Wellington Land District, 1853-1860', Hist. 316 research essay, VUW, 1984; Steven Watters, 'Applicants for Crown Land in the Wellington Land District, 1886-1888', Hist. 316 research essay, VUW, 1984; C. Moore, 'The Residential and Occupational Composition of those Applying for Crown Land in the Wellington Land District 1891-1911', B.A. (Hons) History research paper, VUW, 1976; R. Hambling, 'Selectors of Crown Land in the Wellington Land District', B.A. (Hons) History research paper, VUW, 1977.

28. Gross domestic product estimates in current prices taken from G. R. Hawke, 'Towards a Re-Appraisal of the "Long Depression" in New Zealand 1879-1895', Typescript, VUW Economics Department, 1975, p.23, Table 6. The data were converted to per capita rates using the annual December population estimates for the non-Maori general population in the *NZYB*; the resulting figures were adjusted into constant prices on the basis of the wholesale price index in J. W. McIlraith, *The Course of Prices in New Zealand* (Wellington, 1911), p.68, Table 4A.

29. The Valuer-General defined urban freeholders as all freeholders with land in boroughs and town districts and freeholders of land of less than 5 acres in counties; and rural freeholders as freeholders of county land holding 5 acres and over; freeholders with both rural and urban land were counted as rural owners. Data on land-holdings enumerated by the Census exclude Crown Pastoral Leases, and come from J. D. Gould, 'The Occupation

of Farm Land in New Zealand, 1874–1911, A Preliminary Survey', *Business Archives and History*, Aug. 1965.

30. For a parallel argument see M. B. Katz, *The People of Hamilton, Canada West: Family and Class in a Mid-Nineteenth-Century City* (Cambridge, Mass., 1975), pp.78-80.

31. Data were compiled by D. Beaglehole, 'Geographical Mobility: Wellington, 1880–1890', B.A. (Hons) History research paper, VUW, 1982. Her study is based on systematic sampling of Wellington's 3,467 households in 1880, the sample size being 368. This is larger than the aggregate in Table 5.2 since the latter excluded people whose identity was ambiguous. The material cited here is taken from her Appendix VII.

32. Monckton letter to a Tonbridge newspaper quoted in D. Joblin, *The Colonial One: Lorna Monckton of Newstead* (Christchurch, 1975), p.42; Fitton, *Prospects and Resources*, pp.216, 254; *AJHR*, 1895, H-6, 1.

33. M. Boyd, *City of the Plains; a History of Hastings* (Wellington, 1984), p.70.

34. D. Hamer, 'Towns in Nineteenth-Century New Zealand' in D. Hamer (ed.), *New Zealand Social History*, pp.9-10.

35. D. Du Pontet, 'Opotiki from 1884 to 1918', *HR*, 15, Aug. 1967, p.136.

36. 'Hopeful', *'Taken In'*, p.109. Also pp.10, 157, 158. For examples of demands for a Saturday half-day by railwaymen for gardening purposes, see *NZPD*, 1887, 57, 13, and by wharf labourers see *NZPD*, 1896, 96, 101.

37. The bias can be determined very roughly by comparing the representation of each occupation in the sample with the representation of the same occupation in the 1891 Census (male wage-earners only). The comparison, however, overstates the bias since the sample was for household heads while the occupations tabulated in the Census were both household heads and persons living in the households of others. It is reasonable to believe that household heads were a higher proportion of male manual workers in urban than in rural areas, given the failure of rural employers to provide housing for married employees. The occupations substantially over-represented in the sample were artisans 27 per cent; factory workers 12.5 per cent; building trades 11.5 per cent; shop trades 7 per cent. Under-represented were workers in the primary sector — miners, gum-diggers, farm workers, etc., 18 per cent. The distributions of labourers (12 per cent), storemen/shop assistants (5 per cent), railway employees (4 per cent), carters (3 per cent) were similar to those in the Census.

   The main bias in the sample is geographical, with almost 80 per cent drawn from the South Island.

   Demographically the sample seems, broadly, to reflect the age and sex structure of the colony. The ratio of adult males to adult females in the sample was 60:40 (as opposed to 56.13:43.71 in the 1891 Census). Of the dependent population aged under 21, those under five were 31.4 per cent (25.3, 1891 Census); five and under 30.0 per cent (26.2); 10 and under 15, 24.5 per cent (24.7); 15 and under 21, 14.1 per cent (23.7).

   The size of dwellings in the sample differs substantially from the 1891 Census, with a greater fraction of smaller dwellings and a smaller fraction of larger, something to be expected given the sample only embraced 'working-men' heads of households. Houses with two or fewer rooms, 11.3 per cent (18.2, 1891 Census); three to four rooms, 54.7 per cent (33.8); five to six rooms, 30.1 per cent (26.5); seven and above, 4.7 per cent (20.1).

38. These conclusions have been derived from a close analysis of each of the schedules tabulated in the 'Returns of Expenditure by Working-Men', pp.40-50.

39. See R. Arnold, 'The Virgin Forest Harvest and the Development of Colonial New Zealand', *New Zealand Geographer*, 32, Oct. 1976, p.122-3.

40. The best overall evidence for this is that over the late 19th century there were considerably more (as much as a third) landholdings designated in the Census than persons enumerated in the same source as farmers, market gardeners, fruit-growers, hop-growers, wine-growers, horticulturists, runholders (graziers, sheep or cattle farmers), dairy farmers.

41. See R. Dalziel, 'The Colonial Helpmeet; Women's Role and the Vote in Nineteenth-Century New Zealand', *NZJH*, 11, Oct. 1977.

42. Calculated from Census, 1896. The female domestic servants were those under exactly that category (Class II, sub-order 2,1), p.299; the total breadwinners' base, p.281.
43. See appendix to M. Fairburn, 'Local Community or Atomised Society? The Social Structure of Nineteenth-Century New Zealand', *NZJH*, 16, Oct. 1982.
44. See Fairburn, 'Social Mobility and Opportunity in Nineteenth-Century New Zealand', *NZJH*, 13, Apr. 1979.
45. C. Money, *Knocking about in New Zealand* (1871, repr. Christchurch, 1972), *passim*.
46. A. H. Reed, *The Gumdigger; the Story of Kauri Gum* (Wellington, 1948), p.76.
47. See e.g., Hay, *Brighter Britain*, i, p.51; Simmons, *Old England*, p.93; Arnold, *Farthest Land*, p.337.
48. Data taken from M. Arnold, 'Wage Rates, 1873 to 1911', Department of Economics Discussion Paper no. 11, April 1982, VUW, p. 18, Table 4.
49. V. A. C. Gatrell, 'The Decline of Theft and Violence in Victorian and Edwardian England', in *C & L*; D. Hay, 'War, Dearth and Theft in the Eighteenth Century: the Record of the English Courts', *P&P*, 95, May 1982; D. Philips, *Crime and Authority in Victorian England; the Black Country, 1835-1860* (London, 1977), pp.144-6; H. Zehr, *Crime and the Development of Modern Society: Patterns of Criminality in Nineteenth-Century Germany and France* (London, 1976), pp.43-57; J.A. Sharpe, *Crime in Seventeenth-Century England; a County Study* (Cambridge, 1983), pp.198-210; B. Hanawalt, *Crime and Conflict in English Communities, 1300-1348* (Cambridge, Mass., 1979), pp.242 ff; O.H. Hufton, *The Poor of Eighteenth-Century France, 1750-1789* (Oxford, 1974), ch. 9; I. A. Cameron, *Crime and Repression in the Auvergne and the Guyenne, 1720-1790* (Cambridge, 1981); P. N. Grabosky, L. Persson, S. Sperlings, 'Stockholm: the Politics of Crime and Conflict, 1750 to the 1970s' in T. R. Gurr, P. N. Grabosky, R. C. Hula, *The Politics of Crime and Conflict. A Comparative History of Four Cities* (Beverly Hills, 1977), p.310.
50. Dwellings of one–two rooms (including tents) as a percentage of total dwellings (including tents) were calculated from the Census, 1874-1901 (exclusive of Maori dwellings).

	North Island	South Island
1874	23.76	36.67
1878	21.97	33.28
1881	20.56	29.33
1886	16.16	22.42
1891	15.81	20.13
1896	15.96	17.67
1901	13.89	15.94

Although the South Island had a consistently greater proportion of dwellings with one–two rooms than the North, this still does not suggest the index is a reliable measure of the distribution of poverty. (1) The South Island provinces with the highest percentages were always the gold-producing ones, suggesting that the index reflects the transient miner population not poverty. (2) The proportion of dwellings of one–two rooms to the total has a negligible correlation with two key indicators of general prosperity, yearly exports and imports (£ per head), when the nine provinces are analysed simultaneously for the period 1853–1930 (with exports R = -0.042, with imports R = +0.056). Data compiled by M. Fairburn and computed by S. J. Haslett. (3) As demonstrated in chapters V and VII, the distribution of small dwellings was powerfully associated with new areas of settlement and certain demographic abnormalities (disproportionately large proportions of adult males and of the foreign-born).

51. (a) Dwellings three-four rooms in size as a percentage of total dwellings (including tents) were calculated for the Census, 1874–1901 (exclusive of Maoris).

	North Island	South Island
1874	36.82	32.80
1878	38.04	33.82
1881	37.41	36.12

1886	35.14	35.75
1891	32.66	34.84
1896	28.88	31.47
1901	27.46	29.80

(b) Dwellings with five rooms or more as a percentage of total dwellings (including tents) were calculated from the Census, 1874–1901.

	North Island		South Island
1874	37.93		28.71
1878	38.62		30.37
1881	40.89		33.27
1886	47.54		39.19
1891	49.75		44.21
1896	54.30		50.38
1901	58.20		53.99

The indices above take no account of the possibility that while the overall housing stock improved the number of persons occupying each dwelling rose. By dividing the non-Maori population into total dwellings (including tents) for the North and South Islands combined, we find that the average number of people to a house did rise from 4.88 in 1874 to 5.16 in 1886. But this was only a slight increase in the occupancy rate, of about 6 per cent 1874–86; thereafter, furthermore, the rate fell consistently between every census, to 5.05 (1891), 4.97 (1896), and 4.86 (1901).

52. The indices for 1877–1900 are in *AJHR*, 1891, B-6 and *AJHR*, 1900, H-9. See chapter VII for the argument that the modification in drinking habits and the declining proportion of single men were mostly responsible for the sharp falls in beer and spirits consumption per head.

53. R. J. Campbell, '"The Black Eighties"—unemployment in New Zealand in the 1880s', *AEHR*, 16, Sept. 1976, p.69.

54. See P. Gibbons, '"Turning Tramps into Taxpayers"; the Department of Labour and the Casual Labourer in the 1890s', M.A. thesis, Massey University, 1970, *passim*.

55. Campbell, '"The Black Eighties"', pp.68, 71, 77.

56. Between 1874 and 1896 the fraction of women engaged in the broad Domestic category of the occupational Census fell over the same period from 59 to 43 per cent. The real rates of wages for domestic servants increased faster than those for other wage-earner categories. Occupational data calculated from 1874 and 1896 Censuses; real wages from M. Arnold, 'Wage Rates', pp.17, 20, 24.

57. Analysis of individual cases in 'Returns of Expenditure', *AJHR*, 1893, H-10, 40-50.

58. The assumption that 3s. to 4s. (without 'found') were the rock-bottom daily rates of pay for single men in the worst years of the 1880s until the 1890s is based on the fact that unemployed single men were offered these rates on central and local government relief works in such years; see Campbell, '"The Black Eighties"', pp. 75-76. The cost of living and earnings of the average gumdigger come from the Report of the Kauri-Gum Industry Inquiry Commission, *AJHR*, 1893, H-24, 11, 12.

Chapter V: A Class-Divided Society?

1. 'Social Class in Nineteenth-Century New Zealand' in D. Pitt (ed.), *Social Class in New Zealand* (Auckland, 1977); 'The "Working Class" in New Zealand', *NZJH*, 8, Apr. 1974; *A History of Otago* (Dunedin, 1984) especially ch. 8. That Olssen appears of late to be retreating from the position summarised here is apparent from his 'The Origins of the Labour Party: a Reconsideration', *NZJH*, 21, Apr. 1987, p.83. J. H. Angus, 'City and Country, Change and Continuity, Electoral Politics and Society in Otago, 1877–93', 2 v., unpublished Ph.D. thesis, University of Otago, 1976.

2. Olssen, 'Social Class', pp.34-35; *History of Otago*, pp.92, 105; Angus, 'City and Country', i, pp.51, 59ff, 660-1.
3. Olssen, 'Social Class', p.35.
4. Olssen, 'Social Class', p.35; also *History of Otago*, pp.91-92, 94, 103.
5. Olssen, 'Social Class', pp.34, 36; also *History of Otago*, pp.104-5.
6. Olssen, 'Social Class', p.37. Also *History of Otago*, pp.107-9; his fullest account of the *Otago Workman* is in 'The "Working Class". . .', pp.50-59.
7. Olssen, 'Social Class', p.38.
8. Olssen's impressionistic evidence, fullest in 'Social Class', pp.33-35, is principally drawn from G. M. Stedman, 'The South Dunedin Flat: a Study in Urbanisation 1849-1965', M.A. thesis, Otago University, 1966. His reliance on the quantitive evidence produced by Angus is made plain in *History of Otago*, p.251, fn. 38.
9. Angus, 'City and Country', ii, p.38, Table 1:31.
10. M. Pearson, 'Residential Segregation and the Labour Vote in New Zealand Towns, 1925', B.A. (Hons) research paper in History, VUW, 1986. Data on Christchurch South kindly provided by Donna Leong; on Wellington Central by Lynne Dellow; Wellington South by John Aratinimos; Wellington East by D. A. Booth; Eden by P. Manins—all of whom were Hist. 316 students. Data available from author on request.
11. Angus, 'City and Country', ii, pp.37, Table 1:30.
12. It should be noted that the correlations for the nine-boroughs of Otago/Southland are much stronger: for Labour's share of the vote and ratio of houses with four to those with six rooms Rs = 0.71; for Labour's share of the vote and average number of persons to a room Rs = 0.57 (to be significant at the 0.05 level the Rs for nine matched pairs needs to be .60). As two of the three non-Dunedin boroughs were in Invercargill, the implication of the nine-borough analysis is that the link between 'differentiation' and class-consciousness was possibly far stronger in Invercargill than in Dunedin, thus pulling up the correlation values for the whole nine. But it would be unwise to conclude that the nine-borough analysis demonstrates a causal link between working-class radicalism and working-class sub-culture. (a) A strong correlation does not necessarily imply cause and effect. (b) The housing/voting correlations are ambiguous: they may not measure the effect of differential association but varying perceptions by individuals of their self-interests according to the type of housing tenure they hold. (c) He does not tell us whether housing conditions were worse in the other 28 boroughs of Otago/Southland which did not put up Labour candidates.
13. *History of Otago*, pp.91-92, 103.
14. See H. Roth, *Trade Unions in New Zealand, Past and Present* (Wellington, 1973), p.10 and Table I, p.168.
15. K. Moriarty, 'The Rise of the Masses', B.A. (Hons) research paper in History, VUW, 1976, pp.18-19, 24-27, Appendix I; Olssen, 'Social Class', p.37.
16. The *Otago Daily Times* of June 1890 quoted a figure of 10,000 (cited in Olssen, *History of Otago*, p.110). Assuming a ratio of one wage and salary earner (male and female) to 4.222 of Dunedin's inhabitants (the national ratio of all wage and salary earners to the non-Maori population enumerated in the 1891 census), then the 10 boroughs of greater Dunedin would have had 11,344 male and female wage and salary earners.
17. See estimates on trade union membership for New South Wales and Victoria in J. Rickard, *Class and Politics; New South Wales, Victoria and the Early Commonwealth, 1890-1910* (Canberra, 1976), pp.314-5, Appendix B.
18. Métin, *Socialism Without Doctrine*, pp.55-71; R. Markey, 'New Unionism in Australia, 1880-1900', *LH*, no. 48, May 1985; R. Ward, *A Nation for a Continent: the History of Australia 1901-1975* (Richmond, 1977), *passim*.
19. B. Gustafson, *Labour's Path to Political Independence: the Origins and Establishment of the New Zealand Labour Party 1900-19*, (Auckland, 1980), p.13, lists seven manual worker M.H.R.s: Tanner and Sandford (Christchurch), Pinkerton, Earnshaw, Millar (Dunedin), Buick (Wairau), Kelly (Invercargill). Roth, *Trade Unions*, p.18, has an identical

list. Neither list includes J. F. Arnold, a boat-clicker, elected to the House for Dunedin in 1899; on the other side, Millar, a former merchant marine officer, should not be considered a manual worker yet is included in both lists.

20. Payment of M.H.R.s is from A. H. McLintock (ed.), *An Encyclopaedia of New Zealand*, 3 v. (Wellington, 1966), i, p.851; the classification of constituencies from L. Lipson, *The Politics of Equality; New Zealand's Adventures in Democracy*, (Chicago, 1948), Table II, p.178; and the 60 to 70 per cent rate of manual representation from analyses of electoral rolls by D. J. Morgan, Caroline Holden, Cathy Swanson (all Hist. 316 students, data in author's possession).

21. Roth, *Trade Unions*, pp.9-10.

22. J. W. Scott, *The Glassworkers of Carmaux: French Craftsmen and Political Action in a Nineteenth-Century City* (Cambridge, Mass., 1974), pp.86-87.

23. S. Thernstrom, *The Other Bostonians: Poverty and Progress in the American Metropolis, 1880-1970* (Cambridge, Mass., 1973), pp.231-2; see also Katz, *The People of Hamilton*, pp.112-4.

24. See Fairburn, 'The New Zealand Labour Party and 1935', p.115; and Tables 1 & 2 in B. Hall, D. Thorns, B. Willmott, 'Community Formation and Change: A Study of Rural and Urban Localities in New Zealand', Dept. of Sociology, University of Canterbury, working paper 4, Sept. 1983, p.115.

25. W. P. Reeves, *State Experiments in Australia and New Zealand*, 2 v. (London, 1902), i, pp.31-32; ii, pp.200, 218-9.

26. Bertram (ed.), *Thomas Arnold*, pp.150-1.

27. 'Hopeful', *'Taken In'*, pp.140-2, 144-6, 148, 153ff.

28. E.g., J. Graham, 'Settler Society' in W. H. Oliver (ed.), *The Oxford History of New Zealand* (Oxford & Wellington, 1981), writes on p.113: 'Settler mobility was a notable feature of the adjustment and establishment years, though not all of the movement within the colony was voluntary', and goes on to list its causes (earthquakes, armed conflict in the North Island, the gold discoveries); but then contradicts herself on p.119: 'Such was the difficulty of communications that settlers moved little between communities during the first decade of colonization.'

29. For assertions of this kind see e.g., Olssen, 'Social Class', p.39; W. J. Gardner, 'New Zealand Regional History: General and Canterbury Perspectives', *HN*, 41, 1980, p.2.

30. See Beaglehole, 'Geographical Mobility: Wellington, 1880-1890'; R. Henderson, 'Communities under Threat? Some Effects of the Great Depression in the Manawatu Region', B.A. (Hons) History research paper, VUW, 1984, pp.50-53.

31. E.g., Katz, *The People of Hamilton*, ch. 3; Thernstrom, *The Other Bostonians*, Table 9.1, p.222; D. H. Doyle, *The Social Order of a Frontier Community: Jacksonville, Illinois, 1825-70* (Chicago, 1978); R. Doherty, *Society and Power: Five New England Towns, 1800-1860* (Amherst, 1977); C. Griffen, 'Workers Divided: The Effect of Craft & Ethnic Differences in Poughkeepsie, New York, 1855-1880' in S. Thernstrom & R. Sennett (eds), *Nineteenth-Century Cities* (New Haven, 1969). For good summary articles of the North American studies see P. F. Bourke, 'A Note on the Study of Mobility', *Australia 1888*, Bull. No. 4, May 1980; S. Thernstrom and P. R. Knights, 'Men in Motion: Some Data and Speculations about Urban Population Mobility in Nineteenth-Century America', *JIH*, I, Autumn 1970; D. Parkerson, 'Internal Migration: Research Themes and New Directions', *O.A.H. Newsletter*, August 1983.

32. See Bourke, 'The Study of Mobility', p.57.

33. 'Hopeful', *'Taken In'*, pp.153-4.

34. Simmons, *Old England*, p.38.

35. Bertram (ed.), *Thomas Arnold*, pp.60-61, 237-8.

36. M. A. Barker, *Station Life in New Zealand* (1870, repr. Auckland, 1973), p.110. For other examples of extreme or moderately extreme transients occupying one- or two-roomed shacks see S. Butler, *A First Year in Canterbury Settlement* (London, 1863); J. A. Lee, *Roughnecks, Rolling Stones & Rouseabouts with an Anthology of Early Swagger*

Literature (Christchurch, 1977), pp.24ff, 32, 39-41; W. Satchell, *The Land of the Lost; a Tale of the New Zealand Gum Country*, (1902, repr. Auckland, 1971); L. J. Kennaway, *Crusts. A Settler's Fare Due South* (London, 1874); Scott, *Reminiscences of a New Chum*, pp.15, 26; T. Seccombe, 'Pioneering Days at Orete Point. . .', *HR*, 11, Mar. 1963, p.15. In 1921 the Registrar General wrote, 'There are in general relatively more of the smaller dwellings in the country than in the towns. The disparity in one-roomed dwellings is due to the number of temporary camps of those engaged in road and other public-works construction, outlying huts belong [*sic*] to stations, small week-end whares, and so forth.' *Census of New Zealand*, 1921, 'Dwellings', p.14.

37. See Gibbons, '"Turning Tramps into Taxpayers"', pp.73-88.
38. G. A. Wood, 'The 1878 Electoral Bill and Franchise Reform in Nineteenth Century New Zealand', *PS*, 28, July 1976, p.54; Angus, 'City and Country', i, p.686.
39. *NZPD*, 1878, 28, 607-8.
40. *NZPD*, 1895, 87, 377 (Smith). See also comment along similar lines by Maslin, same page.
41. See B. Conradson, 'Politics and Penury: County and Province, 1868–76' in P. R. May (ed.), *Miners and Militants: Politics in Westland 1865–1918* (Christchurch, 1975), especially p.27. Also P. May, 'Politics and Gold: the Separation of Westland, 1865–7', in *Miners and Militants*, pp.17-18.
42. See e.g., Doherty, *Society and Power*, pp.36-41; Katz, *The People of Hamilton*, pp.123-5.
43. Letter quoted in Adam, *Twenty-five Years*, p.146.
44. Information on police from R. Hill, private communication to the author; comparatively high rate of transience by senior bureaucrats is apparent in many local studies on transience, e.g. Beaglehole, 'Geographical Mobility: Wellington, 1880–1890', p.36; for turnover of school teachers in new areas see R. Arnold, 'The Wellington Education Board, 1878–1901: Grappling with Educational Backwardness and Advancing Settlement', *Australia and New Zealand History of Education Society Journal*, 6, Spring 1977, 44; for lack of accommodation for married hands on sheep stations, see 'The Royal Commission on the Cost of Living', *AJHR*, 1912, H-18, 126, 134, 172-3; Stewart, *Rolleston*, p.54; on domestic servants see e.g., McIntyre (ed.), *Sewell*, i, p.443; on Presbyterian clergy, see the analysis of parish registers by P. K. Daube, 'A Pioneer Church . . .', Hist. 316 research essay, VUW, 1984, p.18.
45. Fitton, *Prospects and Resources*, pp.291-2. The transitoriness of milling settlements is noted by Hamer, 'Towns in Nineteenth-Century New Zealand', pp.7-8.
46. This seasonal pattern was recorded in the *Journal of the Department of Labour*, published monthly, from information collected by the Department's local agents.
47. *AJHR*, 1893, H-10; J. Bradshaw, *New Zealand As It Is* (London, 1883), p.253; Gibbons, '"Turning Tramps into Taxpayers"', pp.44-45.
48. Census, 1921, 'Drift of Population', p.39.
49. 'Hopeful', '*Taken In*', pp.141-2.
50. William Orchard to his sister(?), Melbourne, 20 June 1876, Helston Museum, Cornwall, quoted in G. Davison, 'The Dimensions of Mobility in Nineteenth-Century Australia', *Australia 1888*, Bull. 2, Aug. 1979, pp.19-21.
51. Hursthouse biography in J. Bassett, *Sir Harry Atkinson 1831-1892* (Auckland, 1975), p.80; Wain biography in Story (ed.), 'Our Fathers', pp.318-26; 'Mr. George Pain's Story', Pain Collection, MS Papers 1740, Folder I, ATL.
52. On produce consumed at the home see e.g., J. Cowan, *Settlers and Pioneers* (Wellington, 1940), pp.46-48; *NZPD*, 1879, 34, 699 (Atkinson), 748 (George); Bassett, *Atkinson*, p.84; Barker, *Station Life*, p.111; Woodhouse (ed.), *Pioneer Women*, pp.85, 91, 104; J. A. Thomson, *The Taieri Aliens and Related Families* (Dunedin, 1929), p.58. On the clamour for amenities to attract population for a larger local market, see Hamer, 'Towns in Nineteenth-Century New Zealand'. The art of 'making do' by small settlers is illustrated in Woodhouse (ed.), *Pioneer Women*, pp.89, 305-14. One of the most common second-occupations for farmers, shearing, is discussed by R. Arnold, 'Yeomen and Nomads:

New Zealand and the Australian Shearing Scene, 1886–1896', *NZJH*, 18, 1984. The shortage of cash is typified by the accounts in WDFU, *Brave Days; Pioneer Women of New Zealand* (Wellington, 1939), pp.226, 240.

53. Beaglehole, 'Geographical Mobility', Table 5:1, p.45, found that of the Wellington household heads (1880-90) owning land valued between £1 and £499, transients were 19.5 per cent of those with titles only in the city, 20 per cent of those with titles both in Wellington and outside it, 42 per cent of those with titles outside Wellington only. Of the owners with land valued between £500 and £999 transients were eight per cent of those with titles in Wellington only, 11 per cent of those with titles in Wellington and elsewhere, a third of those with titles outside Wellington only. Of the owners with land valued at £1,000 and over, the pattern was less clear-cut: transients were 23 per cent of those with land in Wellington only, 11 per cent of those with titles in Wellington and elsewhere, one quarter of those with titles outside Wellington city.

54. K. Sinclair (ed.), *A Soldier's View of Empire; the Reminiscences of James Bodell, 1831-92* (London, 1982), pp.180, 210.

55. T. K. Hareven, *Family Time and Industrial Time: the Relationship between the Family and Work in a New England Industrial Community* (Cambridge, 1982).

56. Thernstrom and Knights, 'Men in Motion', 35; Doyle, *The Social Order of a Frontier Community*, pp.101-2.

57. E. J. Hobsbawm's essay 'The Tramping Artisan' is in his *Labouring Men; Studies in the History of Labour* (London, 1964), pp.34-63.

58. See e.g., the essays by C. Winslow, 'Sussex Smugglers', and D. Hay, 'Poaching and the Game Laws on Cannock Chase', in D. Hay *et al.*, *Albion's Fatal Tree. Crime and Society in Eighteenth-Century England* (Harmondsworth, 1975). The concept of 'primitive rebels' originated from E. J. Hobsbawm, *Primitive Rebels: Studies in Archaic Forms of Social Movement in the 19th and 20th Centuries* (Manchester, 1959).

59. J. O. C. Phillips, 'Mummy's Boys: Pakeha Men and Male Culture in New Zealand' in P. Bunkle & B. Hughes (eds), *Women in New Zealand Society* (Auckland, 1980), pp.221, 222. In his latest contribution to the subject, *A Man's Country? The Image of the Pakeha Male—A History* (Auckland, 1987), Phillips has moved towards the author's position by downplaying the strength of male associations through 'mateship', saying that it was more a relationship of convenience, abbreviated by transience. This modification in the argument has injected a fundamental contradiction into the thesis, for he still maintains that mateship groupings produced a powerful and lasting 'culture' or normative code. How can loose and weak groupings sustain a powerful culture when by definition they lack the informal sanctions of group-life to do so?

60. Ward, *Australian Legend*.

61. S. A. Frogley, 'Thieves of Wellington: A Study of Theft in the District of Wellington 1865–1867', B.A. (Hons) research essay in History, VUW, 1985, Appendix 1; P. M. Todd, 'The Crime of Vagrancy in Wellington 1875–76', B.A. (Hons) research essay in History, VUW, 1986, attached appendices; P. M. Todd, 'Vagrancy in Nineteenth-Century Canterbury Province New Zealand', Hist. 316 Research Essay in History, VUW, 1985, appendix; C. Daley, 'Interpersonal Conflict in Colonial New Zealand: A Study of Violence and Civil Litigation in Wellington, 1870–1872', B.A. (Hons) research essay in History, VUW, 1986, p.20. Todd, 'Crime of Vagrancy in Wellington', found that joint offending by females was far more frequent than by males.

62. Hannawalt, *Crime and Conflict in English Communities*, p 187-8. Beier, *Masterless Men*, Table V, p.218.

63. Information kindly provided to the author by Tony Walzl. The sample was drawn from all cases in the years 1876, 1878, 1880, 1883, 1885, 1888, 1890.

64. Returns of Persons Drowned in New Zealand, *AJHR*, 1870, 1875, 1877, 1881, 1882, 1883, 1884, 1885, 1888. Analysis by W. Stagg, 'Death by Drowning', Hist. 316 research essay, VUW, 1983, p.12.

65. Letters quoted in Lee, *Roughnecks, Rolling Stones and Rouseabouts*, p.36; R. Gilkison,

Early Days in Central Otago . . . (Dunedin, 1930), p.159. See also J. G. Wilson, *Road to Porangahau and Notes on Land Settlement* (Napier, 1962), p.46.

66. Markey, 'New Unionism in Australia'; also D. H. Clune, 'The State Labor Party's Electoral Record in Rural New South Wales 1904-1981', *LH*, 47 (Nov. 1984).

67. D. T. Macnaughton, 'The New Zealand Shearers' Union and the Crisis in the Shearing Industry 1910-1916', *Auckland University Historical Society Annual*, 1971; J. D. Salmond, *New Zealand Labour's Pioneering Days* (Auckland, 1950), p.44.

68. 'Returns of Expenditure by Working-Men', *AJHR*, 1893, H-10; *Statistics of New Zealand*, 1888 and 1900, Benevolent and Orphan Asylums, Ages of inmates; M. Tennant, 'Elderly Indigents and Old Men's Homes 1880-1920', *NZJH*, 17, Apr. 1983.

69. T. Cooper, *A Digger's Diary at the Thames 1867* (Dunedin, 1978), p.17.

70. Gilkison, *Early Days*, pp.141, 191-2; Scott, *Reminiscences of a New Chum*, p.47; T. Seccombe,' . . . The Seccombe Story, part 3, *HR*, 12, Mar. 1964, p.4; W. J. Cox, Diaries,' ATL, *passim*.

71. M. E. Wolfgang & F. Ferracuti, *The Subculture of Violence; towards an Integrated Theory in Criminology* (London, 1967).

72. R. Hill, *Policing the Colonial Frontier: the Theory and Practice of Coercive Social and Racial Control in New Zealand, 1767-1867* (Wellington, 1986), pp.563, 606; D. Burton (ed.), *Confessions of Richard Burgess. The Maungatapu Murders and Other Grisly Crimes* (Wellington, 1983); estimate of bushranging population in G. Boxall, *History of the Australian Bushrangers*, (1899, repr. Harmondsworth, 1974), p.384.

73. On the reliance of the Kelly gang on a local and regional network see D. Morrissey, 'Ned Kelly's Sympathisers', *HS*, 18, 1978; E. J. Hobsbawm, *Bandits* (London, 1969), pp.39, 46.

74. Scott, *Reminiscences of a New Chum*; extract from J. W. Reed's autobiography in Reed, *The Gumdigger*, pp.80-97. Another example of this type is E. W. Elkington; see his *Adrift in New Zealand* (London, 1906), pp.116-7.

75. *AJHR*, 1895, H-6, 1. The mixed composition of the gangs under the cooperative system is from H. J. H. Blow, 'The Co-operative System of Public Works', *NZYB*, 1894, pp.234-42, cited by P. J. Gibbons, 'Some New Zealand Navvies; Co-operative Workers, 1891-1912', *NZJH*, 11, Apr. 1977, p.67.

76. *Statistics of New Zealand*, 1914, p.28 for years 1861-1870 inclusive.

77. Olssen, 'Social Class', p.29; WDFU, pp.58, 101 (also 54-55); R. Arnold, 'The Opening of the Great Bush, 1869-1881', unpublished Ph.D. thesis, VUW, 1971, pp.124, 190; Eldred-Grigg, *Southern Gentry*, p.52.

78. Hodder, *Memories*, pp.63ff.

79. W. J. Barry, *Past & Present and Men of the Times* (Wellington, 1897), *passim*.

80. These patterns have been extracted from the discursive observations in Money's reminiscences, *Knocking about in New Zealand*, *passim*.

81. Macnaughton, 'The New Zealand Shearers' Union'.

82. 'It is a common thing in the farming districts for men to come along the road, especially in harvest and shearing time, to call over the fence to the farmer, asking for work, and to start at once', *NZPD*, 1886, 55, 562 (Sutter).

83. J. C. Andersen, *Jubilee History of South Canterbury* (Auckland, 1916), p.135; Reeves, *State Experiments in Australia and New Zealand*, i, pp.31-32, made the same point.

84. D. McKee Wright, 'While the Billy Boils' in A. E. Woodhouse (ed.), *New Zealand Farm and Station Verse 1850-1950* (Christchurch, 1950); W. J. Cox, Diaries, ATL, entries for period 1891-3; Scott, *Reminiscences of a New Chum*, who may also have been in partnership with four miners for a few weeks at the digging (p.61); Elkington, *Adrift in New Zealand*, pp.116-129; H. Brownlie, ' "Without Work, Nothing": A Study of the Changing Attitudes Towards the Swagger in the 1890s', Long Essay for Postgraduate Diploma of Arts in History, Otago University, 1980, Appendix E. See also the letter from an ex-swagger in Lee, *Roughnecks*, pp.32-34; E. McLay, *Stepping Out: a History of Clutha County Council* (Dunedin 1977), pp.372-3.

85. For examples of hostile reception by less wealthy rural settlers to swaggers, see comments by the Labour Department's local agents, *AJHR*, 1897, H-6, 21; 1896, H-6, 20. For examples of the fear felt by women and children see J. N. W. Newport, *Footprints: the Story of the Settlement and Development of the Nelson Back Country Districts* (Christchurch, 1962), p.395; McLay, *Stepping Out*, pp.372-3.
86. See the comment on this by Elkington, *Adrift in New Zealand*, p.129.
87. This is suggested by Brownlie, ' "Without Work, Nothing" . . .', pp.87-92.
88. Burton (ed.), *Confessions*, pp.130, 143-4.

Chapter VI: A Society of Cohesive Local Communities?

1. See e.g., Gardner, 'New Zealand Regional History: General and Canterbury Perspectives', p.2; E. Olssen, 'Towards a New Society' in Oliver (ed.), *The Oxford History*, pp.256-7; Angus, 'City and Country', i, pp.76, 110ff.
2. Arnold, *Farthest Land*, p.357; the same theme also underlies his 'The Opening of the Great Bush'.
3. W. H. Oliver, *Towards a New History?*, 1969 Hocken Lecture (Dunedin, 1971), pp.19-20. See also his 'New Zealand about 1890', unpublished Macmillan Brown Lectures, 1972.
4. Olssen, 'Towards a New Society', pp.256-7. See also his 'Truby King and the Plunket Society: An Analysis of a Prescriptive Ideology', *NZJH*, 15, (1981), p.3; his 'Social Class', pp.35, 39, and with A. Levesque, 'Towards a History of the European Family in New Zealand', in P. G. Koopman-Boyden (ed.), *Families in New Zealand Society* (Wellington, 1978), p.3, where reference is made to the 'considerable communal supervision' of married couples (except for those in the outback).
5. Sandra Bugg, 'Public Festivals in the Nineteenth Century: The Wellington Regatta', Hist. 316 research essay, VUW, 1982.
6. Bassett, *Atkinson*, pp.2-8; Hall, Thorns, & Willmott, 'Community Formation and Change', pp.2-4.
7. K. Arensberg & S. Kimball, *Family and Community in Ireland*, 2nd ed. (Cambridge, Mass., 1968); M. Young & P. Willmott, *Family and Kinship in East London* (London, 1957).
8. This is based on a close study of the footnotes provided for each of the 106 cases in the 'Returns of Expenditure by Working-Men'.
9. See L. Stone, *The Family, Sex and Marriage in England, 1500-1800* (London, 1977), pp.148-9.
10. *AJHR*, 1880, H-6, 2 (Dr. Skae); 1871, H-10, 11; 1882, H-9, 12.
11. MacGregor in *AJHR*, 1887, H-9, 1; 1888, H-9, 2, cited by Tennant, 'Elderly Indigents and Old Men's Homes', p.4.
12. Immigration rate calculated from the returns in *Statistics of New Zealand*.
13. T. J. Archdeacon, *Becoming American; an Ethnic History* (New York, 1983), Table V-2, p.112, gives decennial rates from 1820-29 to 1890-99 which vary between a high of 12.1% and a low of 1.3%. By comparison, the rates in New Zealand between 1861-70 and 1891-1900 varied between 199% and 31%.
14. T. A. Coghlan, *A Statistical Account of the Seven Colonies of Australasia, 1895-6* (Sydney, 1896), p.50; Archdeacon, *Becoming American*, p.142. New Zealand overseas-born data calculated from the Census, excluding Imperial troops and their families.
15. P. Smith, *As a City Upon a Hill: the Town in American History*, (Cambridge, Mass., 1966), ch. 2.
16. Pieced together from Hursthouse, *New Zealand*, p.429; Cowan, *Settlers and Pioneers*, pp.31ff; D. McGill, *The Other New Zealanders* (Wellington, 1982), *passim*.
17. *NZPD*, 1880, 36, 70.
18. Calculated from the data in the Census 1867 and 1891 for non-Maori population exclusive of Imperial troops and their families.

19. Immigration data from McLintock (ed.), *Encyclopaedia of N.Z.* ii, p.133.
20. Arnold, *Promised Land*; J. Morris, 'The Assisted Immigrants to New Zealand, 1871–79; A Statistical Study', M.A. thesis, University of Auckland, 1973.
21. For erosion of kinship ties by geographical mobility in other societies, see Stone, *Family, Sex and Marriage*, pp.146-8; M. Young & P. Willmott, *Family and Class in a London Suburb* (London, 1960), chs. 2, 4, 5, 6.
22. McIntyre (ed.), *Sewell*, i, p.443; H. R. Richmond to C. W. Richmond, April 1851, in Scholefield (ed.), *Richmond-Atkinson*, i, p.89 (though note that according to Bassett, *Atkinson*, p.10, the local socialising of the Richmond/Atkinson clan increased substantially from 1856); Rhoda Coote, diary 1853-1867, ATL, typescript, quoted in A. G. Bagnall, *Wairarapa; an Historical Excursion* (Masterton, 1976), p.513; Story (ed.), 'Our Fathers', p.442; Barker, *Station Life*, p.39; extract from W. P. Reeves's unpublished autobiography in K. Sinclair, *William Pember Reeves: New Zealand Fabian* (Oxford, 1965), pp.41-45; Robert Petch Papers 1876–1882, Micro MS349, ATL, quoted in Graham, 'Settler Society', in Oliver (ed.), *Oxford History*, p.125; 'Hopeful', '*Taken In*', pp.147, 167; Courage, *Lights and Shadows*, p.240.
23. Diary of W. B. Matheson, MS, 1886-1939, ATL; Diary and Papers of Duncan MacRae, MS MACR, 1898-1949, ATL; both analysed by G. Blackshaw, 'The Diaries of W. B. Matheson and D. MacRae', Hist. 316 research essay, VUW, 1982.
24. Howitt, *A Pioneer*, p.190.
25. Andersen, *Jubilee History of South Canterbury*, p.138; W. D. Stewart (ed.), *The Journal of George Hepburn* (Dunedin, 1934), p.137; Hay, *Brighter Britain*, i, pp.209, 219-20.
26. Gardner, *The Amuri*, pp.355-6.
27. R. Dalziel, 'The Politics of Settlement' in Oliver (ed.), *Oxford History*, pp.96-97; Angus, 'City and Country', i, pp.277-81, 357-8.
28. See e.g., Young & Willmott, *Family and Kinship in East London*.
29. The idea of the school as the centre of the local community can be seen e.g., in Arnold, 'The Opening of the Great Bush', pp.250, 580-2. School enrolments and attendance figures from A. E. Campbell, *Educating New Zealand* (Wellington, 1941), pp.44, 90. Also see, D. McKenzie, 'Reluctantly to School' in *Education and Social Structure: Essays in the History of New Zealand Education* (Dunedin 1982); C. McGeorge, 'School Attendance and Child Labour 1890–1914', *HN*, May 1983.
30. See e.g., D. Denoon, *Settler Capitalism: the Dynamics of Dependent Development in the Southern Hemisphere* (Oxford, 1983), pp.73, 226; Gardner, 'New Zealand Regional History', p.1; R. Arnold, 'The Dynamics and Quality of Trans-Tasman Migration, 1885–1920', *AEHR*, 26, Mar. 1986, p.2.
31. '. . . in many cases the size of the borough is very great compared with the population, [and] a large number of the inhabitants [are] engaged in rural or mining pursuits', Census, 1886, Report p.10. See also Hamer, 'Towns in Nineteenth-Century New Zealand', p.9; P. J. Gibbons, *Astride the River: a History of Hamilton* (Christchurch, 1977), pp.106-8.
32. E.g., Hall, Thorns, Willmott, 'Community Formation and Change', p.43, have found that the average section in Fendalton in 1880 was 1.58 hectares; 1885, 0.57 hectares; 1890, 0.49 hectares; 1895, 0.51 hectares. See also advertisements for suburban housing in local newspapers.
33. See e.g., Census, 1886, Table XX, pp.23ff.
34. Census, 1896, Report p.16.
35. Quoted in Stewart, *Rolleston*, p.146.
36. See Arnold, 'The Opening of the Great Bush', pp.38-39, 512. The Land Acts of 1885 and 1892 which instituted the Special Settlement Associations expressly permitted selectors under these schemes to postpone residence and the rate of absenteeism was in fact high (see *AJHR*, 1893, C-1, 4, 78).
37. Hursthouse, *New Zealand*, p.201; letter cited in Arnold, *Farthest Land*, p.300; Bagnall, *Wairarapa*, p.256 also pp.297-300; H. H. Miller, 'Bush Pioneering Days', *HR*, 7, Sept. 1959, pp.59-60; *NZYB*, 1921-22, p.560.

38. Arnold, 'The Opening of the Great Bush', pp.104, 512; Bagnall, *Wairarapa*, pp.292-300; *New Zealand Town-Planning Conference and Exhibition* . . . (Wellington, 1919), p.189; McLintock (ed.), *Encyclopaedia of NZ*, iii, p.93.

39. H. C. D. Somerset, *Littledene: a New Zealand Rural Community* (Wellington, 1938).

40. Church attendance figures taken from the Census and made into a percentage using the population estimates (non-Maori) for the December year. Their reliability is discussed by H. Jackson, 'Churchgoing in Nineteenth-Century New Zealand', *NZJH*, 17, Apr. 1983, pp.46-47. Jackson is also the source for the higher rates in England, Wales, Scotland, Victoria, New South Wales and South Australia, though he employs different population bases to show this for Victoria and New South Wales; Somerset, *Littledene*, p.49.

41. Friendly Society and Lodge membership figures for New Zealand taken from *AJHR*. Australian rates calculated from tabulation of 'Total Adjusted Members' in D. Green & L. Cromwell, *Mutual Aid or Welfare State: Australia's Friendly Societies* (Sydney, 1984), p.217, with male breadwinner base from Census of Victoria in *Papers Presented to Parliament*, Session 1893, Legislative Assembly, ii, p.236. English and Welsh figures calculated from F. E. Huggett, *A Dictionary of British History, 1815-1973* (Oxford, 1974), p.111.

42. Raw figures on membership of the volunteers from *Statistics of New Zealand*. P. Grimshaw, *Women's Suffrage in New Zealand* (Auckland, 1972), p.109. Data on public libraries, mechanics' institutes and all other literary and scientific institutions from Census 1874, 1878, 1881, 1891, 1896 (no data furnished in 1886 and 1901), with the rates per 100 adult males 21 and over (non-Maori) being 9.89 at the highest point and 8.63 at the lowest.

43. Raw figures tabulated in *NZYB*, 1926, pp.823-5. Taking children out of the raw figures reduced the winter participation rate to nine per cent and the summer rate to 14 per cent.

44. S. Fisk, 'Friendly Societies in New Zealand 1840-1900 . . .', Hist. 316 research paper, VUW, 1979, p.5; A. B. Thompson, *Adult Education in New Zealand* (Wellington, 1945), ch. 2; G. Nadel, *Australia's Colonial Culture; Ideas, Men and Institutions in Mid-Nineteenth Century Eastern Australia* (Melbourne, 1957); A. Head, 'Mechanics' Institutions in Early Victoria', B.A. (Hons) thesis, University of Melbourne, 1979.

45. B. Howard, 'Changing Social Composition in Wellington Rugby, 1879 to 1939', B.A. (Hons.) History research paper, VUW, 1981; N. Beckford, 'Working Class Participation in Wellington Club Cricket, 1878-1940', B.A. (Hons) History research paper, VUW, 1981; N. Swindells, 'Social Aspects of Rugby Football in Manawatu from 1878 to 1910', B.A. (Hons) History research paper, Massey University, 1978.

46. T. Brooking, 'New Zealand Farmers' Organisations and Rural Politics in the late Nineteenth and Early Twentieth Centuries', *HN*, 41, 1980, pp.9-13.

47. Andersen, *Jubilee History of South Canterbury*, pp.488, 492, 598, 600; A. P. C. Bromley, *Hawera District Centenary: Hawera: An Outline, of the Development of a New Zealand Community* (Hawera, 1981), pp.40, 156, 263, 245-6; Gibbons, *Astride the River*, pp.39, 48, 49; Boyd, *City of the Plains*, pp.13, 47, 50, 56, 57, 152-3; S. W. Grant, *Havelock North; from Village to Borough, 1860-1952* (Hastings, 1978), pp.17, 29, 30, 36, 38; Gardner, *The Amuri*, pp.232-43.

48. McLintock (ed.), *Encylopaedia of NZ*, ii, p.840.

49. Data on one- and two-roomed dwellings taken from Census.

50. The assumption behind this estimated percentage is that only the territory in the following boroughs and counties in 1881 had been settled by 1850 (pop. figures in brackets): Auckland b. (16,664), Parnell b. (3,529), Onehunga b. (2,217), Bay of Islands c. (2,184), Waitemata c. (4,522), Eden c. (17,593), Manukau c. (10,274), New Plymouth b. (3,310), Wanganui b. (4,646), Wellington b. (20,563), Masterton b. (2,241), Greytown b. (1,048), Hutt c. (7,858), Wairarapa East c. (1,475), Wairarapa West c. (5,759), Blenheim b. (2,107), Nelson b. (6,764), Marlborough c. (4,680), Waimea c. (7,535), Collingwood c. (1,643), Akaroa b. (611), Lyttelton b. (4,127), Christchurch b. (15,213), Sydenham b. (8,460), Akaroa c. (4,020), Dunedin b. (24,372), Roslyn b. (2,875), Caversham b. (3,989), Mornington

b. (2,886), Maori Hill b. (1,136), St Kilda b. (773), Sth Dunedin b. (2,796), N. E. Valley b. (2,754), West Harbour b. (1,213), Waikouaiti c. (6,661), Peninsula c. (2,425). Total = 210,923.

51. Somerset, *Littledene*, chs. 3 to 5, and appendix, pp.99-100.

52. *State of Religion and Morals, 1894*, General Assembly Proceedings, cited in Daube, 'A Pioneer Church', p.29.

53. The over-representation of women as church members can be reasonably inferred from the fact that women had greater access to churches: proportionately more women than men dwelt in the urban areas, which had a greater share of churches than the rural. Sunday school data taken from successive Censuses, 1874–1901; the trend was an upward one from 1871, with the exception of the period 1886–91. The church and the Sunday school were not the only voluntary organisations for women and children before the 1890s. But the few others were tiny in number and membership. Intensive newspaper research for Wellington over the 1883 year has uncovered only two formal groupings expressly for women: the Ladies' Christian Association (which ran a charitable agency, the Home for Destitute and Friendless Women) and the Ladies' Working Society; and seven expressly for children: The Terrace and Karori School Cricket Clubs, and five lodges with Juveniles' Temples, all of which may well have catered only for the older age groups, adolescents. A few, microscopic, groupings almost certainly had mixed memberships (men and women), for example, the Choral Society, the Amateur Dramatic Club, and Fine Arts Association. See M. Reilly, 'Wellington Unofficial Organisations . . .', Hist. 412 extended essay, VUW, 1979.

54. Data obtained through systematic counting of sports results in the *Evening Post*. I am indebted to Kerry Robinson for this information.

55. Howard, 'Changing Social Composition in Wellington Rugby'; Beckford, 'Working-class Participation in Wellington Club Cricket'; Swindells 'Social Aspects of Rugby Football in Manawatu'; J. Durrand, 'The Wellington Working Men's Club and Literary Institute . . .', B.A. (Hons) research essay in History, VUW, 1984.

56. Chilton, 'The Genesis of the Welfare State'.

57. Fall in working hours calculated from data in *NZYB*, 1936.

58. *NZYB*, 1894, p.220; 1898, p.299; 1899, pp.312-3; 1939, p.716.

59. This and the following references have been drawn from a long series of parliamentary debates on the eight-hour day, 1882–1901. *NZPD* 1887, 57, 347; 1889, 64, 225; 1897, 97, 497-8; 1901, 116, 312; 1887, 57, 346.

60. *NZPD*, 1887, 57, 13; 1882, 41, 171; 1884, 49, 28; 1889, 64, 222; 1882, 41, 171.

61. *NZPD*, 1887, 57, 345; 1896, 96, 102; 1897, 97, 498.

62. *NZPD*, 1892, 75, 444; 1882, 41, 172; 1889, 64, 223; 1897, 97, 492.

63. *NZPD*, 1896, 96, 101, 271; 1901, 116, 312, 319.

64. Bagnall, *Wairarapa*, p.476; *NZPD*, 1889, 64, 222.

65. *NZPD*, 1897, 97, 492; 1896, 96, 107, 269, 271; 1892, 75, 445; 1887, 97, 494, 497, 498; 1886, 55, 564; 1889, 64, 217; 1896, 96, 267; 1885, 52, 197-8; 1892, 75, 447-8; 1882, 42, 381; 1884, 49, 23, 24; 1885, 52, 196; 1886, 55, 559; 1889, 64, 222; 1892, 77, 175; 1900, 113, 323; 1901, 116, 487; 1882, 42, 383; 1884, 49, 23, 24, 27; 1886, 55, 559, 564; 1889, 64, 217, 222, 223.

66. *NZPD*, 1889, 64, 224; 1897, 97, 497, 499; Sutch, *Poverty and Progress*, pp.95, 111; *NZYB*, 1919, pp.913-5.

67. Explicit mention of the differences within a locality are *NZPD*, 1886, 55, 565; *NZPD*, 1887, 57, 347 (for variations in the hours of Wellington factories); 1896, 96, 106 (where it was claimed that in Dunedin most occupations were on a 45-hour week except the railway workshops and one or two firms).

Part III: Prologue

1. J. Demos, *A Little Commonwealth: Family Life in Plymouth Colony* (London, 1970), pp.3, 5; P. Smith, *As a City Upon a Hill*, chs. 1 & 2; B. Bailyn, *The Peopling of British North America; an Introduction*, (New York, 1986), pp.11-15; A. G. L. Shaw, *Convicts & the Colonies* . . . (London, 1966), ch. 5, pp.215-6, 212, and *passim*. G. Rudé, *Protest and Punishment: the Story of the Social and Political Protesters Transported to Australia 1788-1868* (Oxford, 1978), pp.157-8.

Chapter VII: Frontier Chaos

1. M.E.T., 'Round the East Cape in 1892', reprinted in *HR*, 20, Nov. 1972, p.104.
2. Quotation from Courage, *Lights and Shadows*, p.100. See also Scott, *Reminiscences of a New Chum*, pp.37-38; Tregear, 'Labour in New Zealand', p.221; Barker, *Station Life*, p.72; 'Hopeful', '*Taken In*' p.144.
3. Wallace, *Rural Economy*, p.225; Clayden, *England of the Pacific*, p.20.
4. H. D. London, 'The Opouriao Estate', *HR*, 13, June 1965, pp.82-3; R. Langdon, 'Diary', 22 May 1856, quoted in Bagnall, *Wairarapa*, p.513; Woodhouse (ed.), *Pioneer Women*, p.243.
5. Extract from Reeves's unpublished and unfinished autobiography in Sinclair, *William Pember Reeves*, pp.41-44; Gardner, *The Amuri*, pp.183-4.
6. Courage, *Lights and Shadows*, pp.33-34, 42, 49, 53-54, 60, 101-2, 181-2, 234; quoted in Arnold, *Farthest Land*, p.275.
7. Barker, *Station Life*, pp.81-2; WDFU, *Brave Days*, p.247.
8. Quoted in WDFU, *Brave Days*, p.219.
9. Letters 10 May 1869 and 29 March 1870 in Drummond (ed.), *The Thames Journals of Vicesimus Lush*, p.260.
10. T. T. Seccombe, 'Pioneering Days at Orete Point . . .', *HR*, 11, Mar. 1963, pp.13, 14, 17, 18; McIntyre (ed.), *Sewell*, p.443; Courage, *Lights and Shadows, passim*.
11. Arnold, 'Great Bush', pp.348-9; extract from Reeves's autobiography in Sinclair, *William Pember Reeves*, p.43.
12. Barker, *Station Life*, p.59; Hursthouse, *New Zealand*, pp.403, 408.
13. See e.g., Olssen & Levesque, 'Towards a History of the European Family', pp.3, 4; Sutch, *Quest for Security*, pp.51-52, 61.
14. See W. H. Oliver, 'The Origins and Growth of the Welfare State' in A. D. Trlin (ed.), *Social Welfare and New Zealand Society* (Wellington, 1977), pp.6-10.
15. As a rebuttal of the argument above, it could be maintained that the rate of petty violence convictions is a woefully deficient measure of domestic violence. It is, after all, a well-known fact that in every society most domestic violence is hidden from the public and is rarely reported to the police, let alone dealt with by the courts. Two factors, however, suggest that the petty violence rate was a broadly accurate indication of the movements in the rates of actual domestic violence even though it must have grossly under-represented the actual amount of it. (1) The per capita rate of alcohol consumption is itself a good proxy measure of the trends in the actual rate of domestic violence. Studies across a wide range of societies have shown that excessive alcohol consumption goes along with a high propensity for interpersonal violence—in any context, inside the house or outside it. Thus the negative R between the rate of alcohol consumption (spirits especially) and the proportion of women suggests that the rate of alcohol-driven domestic violence was inversely related to the proportion of women in the population, i.e., over time and space, the greater the density of women, the weaker was the tendency for alcohol-driven domestic violence. The only alternative interpretation for this negative correlation is to say that drinking at home increased as the proportion of women rose and as the general rate of alcohol consumption fell. But given that colonial husbands were more

inclined to drink in pubs than at home and given the aversion of colonial women to the practice of men drinking inside the home, this alternative does not seem likely. (2) Over the long term the rate of petty violence moves in the same direction as two other indicators of interpersonal violence: woundings and homicides. The petty violence rate plummets from the late 1870s to 1940, the rate of woundings drops less sharply but strongly all the same from 1896–1900 to 1936–40, as does the rate of homicides from 1901–5 to 1936–40 (see the Fairburn and Haslett article referred to in the appendix). Woundings and homicides, being highly visible and reportable offences, are accurate measures of trends in actual interpersonal violence. If the actual rate of domestic violence moved against the petty violence rate downward trend, it should therefore have increased the risk of woundings and homicides and thus pushed up these rates in the long term or at least prevented their fall. The magnitude of the downward movement in the rate of homicides and woundings implies, then, that the rate of domestic violence went down over the long term along with the rate of petty violence convictions.

16. The best objective evidence of the critical nature of children's contributions to the family economy is the comments by school inspectors and others on child labour and its effect on school attendance (see McKenzie, 'Reluctantly to School'; also McGeorge, 'School Attendance and Child Labour 1890–1914'; see too the detail in the 1892 Department of Labour survey of working men's expenditure).

17. See e.g., A. Mulgan, *The Making of a New Zealander* (Wellington, 1958), p.26; Woodhouse (ed.), *Pioneer Women*, p.268.

18. E. Bott, *Family and Social Network: Roles, Norms, and External Relationships in Ordinary Urban Families* (London, 1957), pp.67-95, 103, 106, 122, 132-3; Young & Willmott, *Family and Class in a London Suburb*, chs. 3-6.

19. See data in M. G. Vosburgh, 'The New Zealand Family and Social Change: Trend Analysis', occasional papers in Sociology and Social Welfare No. 1, VUW, 1978, p.57a (Table 33). For the effect of the frontier in expanding family functions see also M. D. Campbell, 'The Evolution of Hawke's Bay Landed Society, 1850–1914', Ph.D. thesis, VUW, 1972, p.242.

20. L. Young, *Father and Son; a Young Saga* (Christchurch, 1976), pp.169-70. See also 'Mrs. Withers' Story' in Story (ed.), 'Our Fathers', pp.442-3.

21. Woodhouse (ed.), *Pioneer Women*, pp.54, 62, 65, 83, 131, 268; T. S. Mannering cited in Gardner, *The Amuri*, p.104; Weld quoted in Fitton, *Prospects and Resources*, p.273; D. Du Pontet, 'Early Days in the Waiotahi Valley', *HR*, 12, June 1964, p.68, Tregear, 'Labour in New Zealand', pp.223-4; Courage, *Lights and Shadows*, p.61; D. Du Pontet, 'Opotiki as a Young Girl First Saw It', *HR*, 22, Nov. 1974, p.06; Clayden, *England of the Pacific*, p.20; H. H. Miller, 'Bush Pioneering Days', *HR*, 7, Sept. 1959, pp.67-68; Adam, *Twenty-five Years*, p.41; Scott, *Reminiscences of a New Chum*, pp.37-38.

22. Courage, *Lights and Shadows*, p.95; Baughan verse in Woodhouse (ed.), *Pioneer Women*, p.214. See also Howitt, *A Pioneer*, p.181.

23. W. J. Cox, Diaries, ATL, entries 20/1/1900, 7/11/1897, 7/1/1902, 25/3/1909; Woodhouse (ed.), *Pioneer Women* pp.131-2; 'The Gardener in Exile' by M. A. B. Latter, quoted in Auckland Lyceum Club, *Silhouettes of the Past: a Century Ago* (Auckland, 1939), p.198; B. McCarthy, *Castles in the Soil* (Wellington, 1939), p.5.

24. Howitt, *A Pioneer*, p.181; Mulgan, *Making of a New Zealander* p.31; Courage, *Lights and Shadows*, pp.95, 115.

25. Mulgan, *Making of a New Zealander*, p.25 noted that the singing of 'Home Sweet Home' brought tears into the eyes of many, while Courage, *Lights and Shadows*, p.204 observed that at one function an offer to sing 'Home Sweet Home' was declined as being too touching. Significant, too, is Mulgan's comment that at every Christmas dinner in Katikati there was a toast to 'Absent Friends' at which point the thoughts of all the elders went across the world to 'Home'. It is likely that by the early 20th century the term 'Home' had become disconnected from its initial meaning, and had evolved into a general reference to Britain.

26. D. Du Pontet, 'Opotiki as a Young Girl First Saw It', HR, 22, Nov. 1974, pp.020-021.
27. The earliest reference I have to the use of the word in New Zealand is in 1874 by Bathgate, Experiences, p.90.
28. Evening Post, 25 June 1879; 6 May 1879.
29. For examples of the use of these terms see H. H. Miller, 'Bush Pioneering Days', HR, 7, Sept. 1959, p.68; V. Pyke, The Story of Wild Will Enderby (1873, repr. 1974), p.95; D. Du Pontet, 'Early Days in the Waiotahi Valley', HR, 12, June 1964, p.68; R. Finlayson, Tidal Creek (Sydney, 1948), pp.107-8.
30. See e.g., discussion in S. Worchel & J. Cooper, Understanding Social Psychology, rev. ed. (Homewood, 1979), pp.561-9.
31. Studholme quoted in Eldred-Grigg, Southern Gentry, p.122; Hay, Brighter Britain, i, p.111; M. Anderson, A River Rules My Life (Wellington, 1965), p.192; T. Seccombe, 'Pioneering Days at Orete Point', HR, 11, June 1963, pp.93-94; Courage, Lights and Shadows, p.100; F. K. B., 'A History of Te Teko School', reprinted in HR, 13, June 1965, pp.73-75.
32. New Zealand drunkenness data taken from Statistics of New Zealand and population data from Census. Data for England and Wales were taken from V. A. C. Gatrell & T. B. Hadden, 'Criminal Statistics and their Interpretation', in E. A. Wrigley (ed.), Nineteenth-Century Society: Essays in the Use of Quantitative Methods for the Study of Social Data (Cambridge, 1972), p.391, Table II; data on adult male population in England and Wales from B. R. Mitchell & P. Deane (eds), Abstract of British Historical Statistics (Cambridge, 1962), p.12. The comparison is slightly overstated, for the adult male population for England and Wales is those aged 20 and over while the New Zealand base is for ages 21 and over. The New Zealand population base excludes Maoris; the conviction data exclude Maoris 1853-71 and include them thereafter.
33. Hill, Policing the Colonial Frontier, pp.571 & 620 (Otago), p.641 (Canterbury), pp.923, 932 (Auckland).
34. See discussion of this in M. P. K. Sorrenson, 'Land Purchase Methods and their Effect on Maori Population, 1865-1901', Journal of the Polynesian Society, 14, 3, 1956.
35. Data on summary convictions taken from Statistics of New Zealand; the Maori population base comes from the Census, the intercensal values being obtained through linear interpolation.
36. Sorrenson, 'Land Purchase Methods'.
37. For the general population (incl. Maoris and Imperial Troops) spirits consumption fell from 2.240 gallons per head in 1864 to 0.612 in 1895; drunkenness convictions (with general population excluding Maoris and Imperial Troops) from 2997.58 per 100,000 in 1864 to 680.46 in 1895. On a base of males aged 21 to 40 (exclusive of Maoris and Imperial Troops) spirits consumption dropped from 9.712 gallons a head in 1864 to 4.434 in 1895; drunkenness convictions from 9569.2 per 100,000 in 1864 to 4653.6 in 1895.
38. Data on brandy and rum are from the import statistics in Statistics of New Zealand. Only in 1860 and 1861 did colonists drink more rum than brandy, 1860-1869.
39. Zehr, Crime and the Development of Modern Society, pp.96-102; Gatrell & Hadden, 'Criminal Statistics and their Interpretation', in Wrigley (ed.), Nineteenth-Century Society, pp.369-71.
40. Gallons of spirits consumed per head of general population declined from 1.905 in 1874 to 0.607 in 1896 (Maoris and Imperial Troops included in the population base).
41. The actual yearly amount of spirits consumed (1877-95) was converted into a per capita rate using non-Maori males aged 21-40 as the population base. Two tests were applied to see how far the rates were related to the real price of alcohol: one was the Spearman rank-order correlation, the other the Pearson simple correlation. The Spearman test yielded an Rs of 0.14 (significant at the 0.54 level); the Pearson an R of -0.46 (significant at the 0.04 level). The non-normal distribution of the data and the small number of observations throw doubt on the result of the Pearson test, leaving the Spearman with its low Rs and poor significance level as the better test. Alcohol price index from McIlraith,

The Course of Prices; spirits data from *AJHR*, 1897, H-9, and *Statistics of New Zealand*, 1877; males 21-40 from Census, missing values for intercensal years being estimated with linear interpolation.

42. B. Harrison, *Drink and the Victorians: the Temperance Question in England 1815-1872*, (London, 1971), pp.37-39.

43. Sutch, *Poverty and Progress*, p.138.

44. A. E. Dingle, '"The Truly Magnificent Thirst": an Historical Survey of Australian Drinking Habits', *HS*, 19, Oct. 1980.

45. The model has been advanced by M. Fairburn & S. J. Haslett in an article, 'Violent Crime in Old and New Societies: A Case Study. Based on New Zealand 1853-1940', *SH*, Fall 1986.

46. See e.g., the description of the debauchery at a Northland race-meeting in Satchell, *Land of the Lost*, ch. 13.

47. 'Hopeful', *'Taken In'*, pp.144-5; *Timaru Herald*, 9 February 1874, quoted in Andersen, *Jubilee History of South Canterbury*, pp.473ff. See also E. R. Bayliss, *Tinwald, a Canterbury Plains Settlement* (Timaru, 1970), p.189.

48. *New Zealand Times*, 5 July 1877, and *Evening Post*, 27 June 1877, cited in Durrand, 'The Wellington Working Men's Club and Literary Institute . . .'; 'Hopeful', *'Taken In'*, pp.147-8.

49. See Fairburn & Haslett, 'Violent Crime in Old and New Societies', p.117, fn. 6. Data on common assault for England and Wales are calculated from Gatrell, 'The Decline of Theft and Violence', pp.358-9, Table A5, with the population base of males aged 20 and over from Mitchell & Deane, *Abstract of British Historical Statistics*, p.12.

50. See Gatrell's argument in 'The Decline of Theft and Violence', p.292.

51. Fairburn & Haslett, 'Violent Crime in Old and New Societies', p.117, fn. 6.

52. For a full description of this index see Fairburn & Haslett, 'Violent Crime in Old and New Societies', pp.96, 119, fn. 20.

53. These tests have been adapted from Gatrell, 'The Decline of Theft and Violence', pp.251, 289-93. Fuller application of them is in Fairburn & Haslett, 'Violent Crime in Old and New Societies'.

54. On a general population base, summary convictions for violence per 100,000 go from a mean of 381.07 in 1862 to 47.81 in 1926-30; on a male 21-40 base, from 1283.99 in 1862-6 to 338.93 in 1926-30; on an adult male base, from 1002.01 in 1862-4 to 159.69 in 1926-30.

55. L. Stone, 'Interpersonal Violence in English Society 1300-1980', *P&P*, 101, Nov. 1983, p.31.

56. Zehr, *Crime and the Development of Modern Society*, pp.104-5, 115-8, 168, 171; E. H. Monkkonen, *The Dangerous Class: Crime and Poverty in Columbus, Ohio, 1860-1880* (Cambridge, Mass., 1975), pp.81ff.

57. E.g., Gatrell, 'The Decline of Theft and Violence';. Zehr, *Crime and the Development of Modern Society*; Monkkonen, *The Dangerous Class*; R. Lane, *Violent Death in the City: Suicide, Accident, and Murder in Nineteenth-Century Philadelphia* (Cambridge, Mass., 1979).

58. The rates for Taranaki, Auckland and Hawke's Bay (as well as for all the other provinces) were compiled and analysed by M. Fairburn & S. J. Haslett.

59. See e.g., Gatrell & Hadden, 'Criminal Statistics and their Interpretation' in Wrigley (ed.), *Nineteenth-Century Society*, pp.369-71; J. B. Given, *Society and Homicide in Thirteenth-Century England* (Stanford, 1977) ch. 10; P. Bohannan, 'Patterns of Murder and Suicide' in P. Bohannan (ed.), *African Homicide and Suicide* (New York, 1967), p.257; Zehr, *Crime and the Development of Modern Society*, pp.98-99, 173-6; Sharpe, *Crime in Seventeenth-Century England*, p.131.

60. C. Daley, 'Interpersonal Conflict in Colonial New Zealand: A Study of Violence and Civil Litigation in Wellington, 1870-1872', B.A. (Hons) History research paper, VUW, 1986.

61. Of the remaining 24 cases, 18 were familial (where jealousy or some other pent-up emotion may have been the cause, so should perhaps be excluded from the instrumental category), five were previous court cases, one had sexual jealousy as its stated cause.

62. Hall, *Thirty Years*, pp.12-14.

63. C. W. Richmond to T. Richmond, 7 Apr. 1862, in Scholefield (ed.), *Richmond-Atkinson*, i, p.755.

64. T. Arnold to J. Arnold, 22 November 1849 in Bertram (ed.), *Thomas Arnold*, p.158.

65. Governor Grey to Earl Grey, Auckland, Mar. 15, 1849, in *British Parliamentary Papers— Papers Relating to New Zealand 1847-50*, pp.56-57.

66. Bathgate, *Experiences*, p.167.

67. 'Hopeful', *'Taken In'*, pp.140-1.

68. Daley, 'Interpersonal Conflict in Colonial New Zealand', pp.26, 41; S. Bartlett, 'Crime 1896, 1897', Hist. 316 research essay, VUW, 1984; Gilkison, *Early Days in Central Otago*, pp.111-2.

69. See e.g.; M. J. Ingram, 'Communities and Courts: Law and Disorder in early Seventeenth-Century Wiltshire' in J. S. Cockburn (ed.), *Crime in England 1550-1800* (London, 1977); J. A. Sharpe, 'Enforcing the Law in the Seventeenth-Century English Village', and B. Lenman & G. Parker 'The State, the Community and the Criminal Law in Early Modern Europe' in *C&L*; S. G. Reinhardt, 'Crime and Royal Justice in Ancien Régime France: Modes of Analysis', *JIH*, 13, Winter 1983; R. L. Kagan, *Lawsuits and Litigants in Castile, 1500-1700* (Chapel Hill, 1981), pp.18-19 and *passim*.

70. See e.g., Stone, *Crisis of the Aristocracy*, pp.240-2; Kagan, *Lawsuits and Litigants*, pp.xxi-xxii, but cf. p.136; J. J. Beattie, 'The pattern of Crime in England 1660-1800', *P&P*, 62, Feb. 1974, p.70.

71. For Castile, see Kagan, *Lawsuits and Litigants*.

72. Zehr, *Crime and the Development, of Modern Society*, pp.96-102; Gatrell and Hadden, 'Criminal Statistics and their Interpretation' in Wrigley (ed.), *Nineteenth-Century Society*, pp.369-71.

73. Daley, 'Interpersonal Conflict in Colonial New Zealand'; R. Shires, 'Civil Litigation in Nineteenth Century Wellington', Hist. 316 research essay, VUW, 1985; J. Cunninghame, 'Litigation in the 19th Century: Hokitika—A Case Study', Hist. 316 research essay, VUW, 1985; R. Palairet, 'Litigation in Wanganui in the 1870s', Hist. 316 research paper, 1984.

74. See e.g., J. A. Sharpe, '"Such Disagreement Betwyx Neighbours"; Litigation and Human Relations in Early Modern England' in J. Bossy (ed.), *Disputes and Settlements: Law and Human Relations in the West* (Cambridge, 1983), p.174.

75. Daley, 'Interpersonal Conflict in Colonial New Zealand', p.39.

76. Daley, 'Interpersonal Conflict in Colonial New Zealand', p.36.

77. Daley, 'Interpersonal Conflict in Colonial New Zealand', p.36; Palairet, 'Litigation in Wanganui in the 1870s'.

78. Demos, *A Little Commonwealth*, pp.49-51, 138-9; Sharpe, '"Such Disagreement Betwyx Neighbours". . . ', p.172.

Chapter VIII: Constraints on Chaos

1. See Fairburn & Haslett, 'Violent Crime in Old and New Societies', p.92, Table 1d.

2. Given, *Society and Homicide in Thirteenth-Century England*, p.36, Table 2; Stone, 'Interpersonal Violence in English Society 1300-1980'; D. Archer & R. Gartner, *Violence and Crime in Cross-National Perspective* (New Haven, 1984).

3. A rough indication of this is the apparently moderate suicide rate constructed by P. Luke, 'Suicide in Auckland, 1848-1939', M. A. thesis, Auckland University, 1982, Appendix I, p.217. This is not an adequate index, however, for it does not control for demographic changes—the rate is based on the general population over the 19th century, when demographic changes were comparatively intense and sudden. Also Luke makes little

attempt to assess the impact on the index of the under-reporting of suicides, which would appear to be most common before the 1880s.

4. Given, *Society and Homicide*, pp.206ff, sees this as a factor in restricting the rate of medieval homicide.

5. Wolfgang and Ferracuti, *The Subculture of Violence*, pp.266-7; M. P. Baumgartner, 'Social Control in Suburbia' in D. Black (ed.), *Towards a General Theory of Social Control*, 2 v. (Orlando, Florida, 1984), i.

6. See D. Philips, '"A New Engine of Power and Authority": the Institutionalisation of Law-Enforcement in England 1780-1830' in *C&L*, for a discussion of how fears of unbridled crime and collective disorder in early 19th-century England led to a transformation in the state's mechanism of repressive coercion; see also A. Silver, 'The Demand for Order in Civil Society: a Review of Some Themes in the History of Urban Crime, Police, and Riot' in D. J. Bordua (ed.), *The Police: Six Sociological Essays* (New York, 1967). For America see R. M. Brown, 'Historical Patterns of American Violence' in H. D. Graham & T. R. Gurr (eds), *Violence in America: Historical and Comparative Perspectives* (Beverly Hills, 1979). On Bengal, consult R. C. Hula, 'Calcutta: the Politics of Crime and Conflict, 1800 to the 1970s' in Gurr, Grabosky, Hula, *The Politics of Crime and Punishment*.

7. *AJHR*, 1873, H-14, 16.

8. This point has been shaped by the many writings on collective protest by Charles Tilly, who maintains that social organisation, while not in itself a 'cause' of collective violence, allows it to happen and determines the form it takes. See e.g., his 'Collective Violence in European Perspective' in Graham & Gurr (eds), *Violence in America*; C. Tilly & E. Shorter, *Strikes in France, 1830-1968* (London, 1974); C. Tilly *et al.*, *The Rebellious Century, 1830-1930* (Cambridge, Mass., 1975).

9. R. Maxwell Brown, 'The History of Vigilantism in America', in H. J. Rosenbaum & P. C. Sederberg (eds), *Vigilante Politics* (Pittsburgh, 1976).

10. See the case-studies and associated discussion in Wolfgang & Ferracuti, *The Subculture of Violence*, pp.279-282.

11. See e.g., C. Winslow, 'Sussex Smugglers' and D. Hay, 'Poaching and the Game Laws on Cannock Chase' in Hay *et al.*, *Albion's Fatal Tree*.

12. See R. Stone, 'Auckland Party Politics in the Early Years of the Provincial System, 1853-58', *NZJH*, 14, Oct. 1980.

13. R. B. Walker, 'Violence in Industrial Conflicts in New South Wales in the late Nineteenth Century', *HS*, 22, Apr. 1986.

14. See Campbell, ' "The Black Eighties" '.

15. R. P. Davis, *Irish Issues in New Zealand Politics, 1868-1921* (Dunedin, 1974), pp.13-15, 18-19.

16. Wolfgang & Ferracuti, *Subculture of Violence*.

17. Minutes of the meeting dated 1 Sept. 1890 in Scholefield (ed.), *Richmond-Atkinson*, ii, pp.561, 563.

18. A. Siegfried, *Democracy in New Zealand*, tr. E.V. Burns (London, 1914), p.54.

19. Siegfried, *Democracy in New Zealand*, pp.48, 50, 55.

20. Lipson, *Politics of Equality*, pp.145-6; G. R. Hawke, *The Making of New Zealand: an Economic History* (Cambridge, 1985), p.25.

21. Lipson, *Politics of Equality*, pp.157-8.

22. Numbers of Resident Magistrates' Courts taken from the lists of courts in the justice statistics, *Statistics of New Zealand*, 1853-8, 1880.

23. Hill, *Policing the Colonial Frontier*, pp.262-7, 915-7 (Auckland), 513, 896 (Hawke's Bay), 539-40, 601-3 (Otago), 471-2, 666 (Canterbury), 693, 706 (Southland).

24. Hill, *Policing the Colonial Frontier*, p.513.

25. Hill, *Policing the Colonial Frontier*, pp.300, 416, 493. In the Provincial period, the two largest forces, in Otago and Canterbury, peaked at about 158 and 108 respectively, pp.608, 682.

26. Hill, *Policing the Colonial Frontier*, pp.562-3; also e.g., p.557 (permanent detective force in Otago), pp.662ff (gold-escort services in Canterbury), p.909 (water-police in Auckland).

27. I am obliged to Richard Shires for the information on the replacement of private prosecutions by the machinery of State prosecution. Hill, *Policing the Colonial Frontier*, pp.566, 681-2, 926-7. Also G. P. Curry, 'Vagrancy', L.L.M. thesis, VUW, 1971.

28. See e.g., Gatrell, 'The Decline of Theft and Violence', p.300.

29. See e.g., Gilkison, *Early Days in Central Otago, passim*.

30. S. Cohen, *Folk Devils and Moral Panics: the Creation of the Mods and Rockers* (New York, 1980).

31. E.g., Hall, *Thirty Years*, p.29, uses the term to describe the prospect, after a series of personal misfortunes, of eviction from his house.

32. E.g., J. C. Richmond to C. W. Richmond, 9 Feb. 1860, in Scholefield (ed.), *Richmond-Atkinson*, i, p.516, during the first Taranaki War: 'We shall get a few moveables down to town. We have not only Maoris to fear in case of a rupture but also loafers & vagabonds, black sheep of all sorts with white skins who wd. seek to suck advantage out of our confusion. I am going to get a muster roll of the rogues & vagabonds that as far as possible they may be kept under surveillance & at innocent amusements as militiamen.'

33. See e.g., letter by J. Claridge, *Evening Post*, 4 June 1886; McLay, *Stepping Out*, pp.372-3; Campbill, 'The Evolution of Hawke's Bay Landed Society', p.263; Elkington, *Adrift in New Zealand*, p.120.

34. See quotations in Gibbons, ' "Turning Tramps into Taxpayers". . .', p.88.

35. Archdeacon Hadfield to C. W. Richmond, 9 January 1858, in Scholefield (ed.), *Richmond-Atkinson*, i, p.336; McIntyre (ed.), *Sewell*, i, p.439.

36. Elkington, *Adrift in New Zealand*, p.13; Hay, *Brighter Britain*, i, pp.33,34. Also Paul, *Was and Is*, p.62; Kennedy, *Kennedy's Colonial Travel*, p.165; Adam, *Twenty-five Years*, p.40; Braim, *New Homes*, p.35, noted that the term 'loafer' was a colonial colloquialism.

37. Ingram, 'Communities and Courts'; Beier, *Masterless Men*, pp.3-13; Hay, 'War, Dearth and Theft in the Eighteenth Century'; J. J. Tobias, *Crime and Industrial Society in the 19th Century* (London, 1967) pp.68-77; G. Pearson, *The Deviant Imagination; Psychiatry, Social Work and Social Change* (London, 1975), pp.148-76; D. Jones, *Crime, Protest, Community, and Police in Nineteenth-Century Britain* (London, 1982), ch. 7.

38. The maxims were straight imports from the London Metropolitan Police; M. McConchie, 'The Police View of Crime', Hist. 316 research essay, VUW, 1983.

39. Calculated from the justice statistics in *Statistics of New Zealand*.

40. See e.g., Courage, *Lights and Shadows*, p.201.

41. See Oliver, 'The Origins and Growth of the Welfare State', pp.8-9.

42. Rates calculated from the justice section of the annual *Statistics of New Zealand*. The conviction rate is for Europeans divided by the total European population. The indicator is admittedly crude, partly because the police used the drunkenness laws as an alternative form of control.

43. Descriptions of swaggers in this context include McLay, *Stepping Out*, pp.372-3; Lee, *Roughnecks*, pp.24ff. That other—respectable—elements had the same sort of housing is evident, e.g. from L. J. Kennaway, *Crusts. A Settler's Fare Due South* (London, 1874), *passim*.

44. The primitive diet of swaggers is recorded by the informants in, Lee, *Roughnecks*, pp.25, 38. For runholders see C. W. Adams, *A Spring in the Canterbury Settlement* (London, 1853), p.71; Story (ed.), 'Our Fathers', p.202; Kennaway, *Crusts*, p.59. Reeves's statement is in Bassett, *Atkinson*, p.140.

45. See e.g., McLay, *Stepping Out*, pp.372-3; Newport, *Footprints: the Story of the Settlement and Development of the Nelson Back Country Districts*, p.375; Wilson, *Road to Porangahau*, p.46; E. C. Studholme, *Te Waimate: Early Station Life in New Zealand*, 2nd ed. (Wellington, 1954), pp.216-7.

46. See e.g., Acland, *The Early Canterbury Runs*, pp.139ff; W. H. S. Roberts *et al, History of North Otago from 1853* (Oamaru, 1937), p.122.

47. E.g., Scott, *Reminiscences of a New Chum*, p.21; Pyke, *Wild Will Enderby*, p.6; G. C.

Beale, *Seventy Years In and Around Auckland* (Dunedin, 1937), pp.61-4; Satchell, *Land of the Lost*, p.9; Adams, *A Spring in the Canterbury Settlement*, p.57; Howitt, *A Pioneer*, pp.164-5.

48. *AJHR*, 1912, H-18, 81, 99, 103, 117, 175, 253, 319, 335, 447, 448, 469.
49. Hill, *Policing the Colonial Frontier*, pp.729-30; Bagnall, *Wairarapa*, pp.478-9.
50. W. J. Cox, Diaries, ATL, entry for 31/12/1910.
51. Population base excludes Maoris and Imperial troops.
52. From the first Census that linked marital status with age (1874) to 1901, unmarried males aged over 20 fell from 14.7 to 12.96 per cent of the total population. Males aged 21 to 40 (single and married) dropped from a peak of 31.3 per cent in 1861 to 15.7 per cent in 1901. Population base excludes Maoris and Imperial Troops.
53. Calculated from Gould, 'The Occupation of Farm Land in New Zealand'. The yearly annual figure excludes Crown pastoral leasehold land.
54. Data taken from successive Censuses.
55. Grimshaw, *Women's Suffrage in New Zealand*; P.F. McKimmey, 'The Temperance Movement in New Zealand, 1835-1894', M A thesis, Auckland University, 1968, pp.51-194, gives an excellent account of the shift in strategy by the anti-drinking movement from the mid 1880s towards the mobilising of mass opinion but fails to tie this to the expansion of associative mechanisms over the same period.

Chapter IX: Friends or Enemies?

1. See e.g., Gatrell, 'The Decline of Theft and Violence', pp.270-3.
2. C. Lombroso, *L'Uomo Delinquente* (1876) discussed by I. Taylor, P. Walton, J. Young, *The New Criminology* (London, 1973); H. Mayhew, *London Labour and the London Poor; the Condition and Earnings of Those that Will Work, Cannot Work, and Will not Work*, 2 v. (London, 1864).
3. Mayhew, *London Labour and the London Poor*, i, p.4.
4. T. Y. Wilson, 'New Zealand Prisons 1880–1909: The Administration of Colonel Arthur Hume', M.A. thesis, VUW, 1970, pp.71-75.
5. 'Hopeful', *'Taken In'*, pp.145-6.
6. Howitt, *A Pioneer*, p.165; Elkington, *Adrift in New Zealand*, p.150; Courage, *Lights and Shadows*, p.201; Pyke, *Wild Will Enderby*, p.53 (also pp.6, 44); colonist quoted in Hill, *Policing the Colonial Frontier*, p.542; Tregear quoted in Gibbons, '"Turning Tramps into Taxpayers". . .', p.88; Satchell, *The Land of the Lost*, p.12.
7. A strong inclination to attribute poverty to 'degeneracy' has been noted by Oliver, 'The Origins and Growth of the Welfare State', pp.8-9.
8. Letter from C. W. Richmond to Alice Blake, 29 Mar. 1894, in Scholefield (ed.), *Richmond-Atkinson*, ii, p.598.
9. Massey quoted in *New Zealand Worker*, 27 Feb. 1924; speeches by Hunt, Russell, and MacDonald in *New Zealand Town-Planning Conference and Exhibition*, pp.38, 126, 219; *NZPD*, 1919, 185, 372-3 (Smith); 1879, 32, 581. On the concept of state-promoted workers' housing in the suburbs as a means of social insulation, see e.g, *NZPD*, 1905, 135, 198 (Bollard), 218 (Hanan); 1919, 185, 379 (Glover).
10. The key role of the late-19th-century public schools and grammar schools in spreading popular interest in sport in Britain is discussed by J. Walvin, *Leisure and Society, 1830-1950* (London, 1978).
11. *The Wellingtonian*, 1895, p.7. I am grateful to Janette Cook for this reference.
12. Tregear, 'Labour in New Zealand', p.218. Mackenzie letter quoted in S. MacDonald, *The Member for Mount Ida* (Wellington, 1938), pp.86-87; J. Cowan, *New Zealand or Ao-Tea-Roa (The Long Bright World)* . . . (Wellington, 1908), p.41; *AJHR*, 1902, C-1, ii-iii, and 1903, C-1, i.
13. McKenzie speech cited in W. D. McIntyre & W. J. Gardner (eds), *Speeches and Documents on New Zealand History* (Oxford, 1971), pp.205-6.
14. *NZPD*, 1905, 135, 203 (Hogg).

Bibliography

A. PRIMARY SOURCES

1: PUBLISHED OFFICIAL PAPERS

A Return of the Freeholders of New Zealand, 1882, Wellington, 1884.
Census of New Zealand, 1858–1936.
'Census of Victoria' in *Papers Presented to Parliament*, Session 1893, Legislative Assembly, v. ii.
Great Britain, *Parliamentary Papers: Papers relating to New Zealand 1847–50, Colonies New Zealand*, 6, Shannon, 1969.
New Zealand, *Appendices to the Journals of the House of Representatives*, 1861–1920.
New Zealand, *Journal of the Department of Labour*, 1893.
New Zealand Official Yearbook, 1892–1926.
New Zealand Parliamentary Debates, 1854–1912.
New Zealand Town-Planning Conference and Exhibition: Official Volume of Proceedings of the First New Zealand Town-Planning Conference and Exhibition, Wellington, 1919.
Official Yearbook of the Commonwealth of Australia, 1901–8.
'Returns of Expenditure by Working-Men', *AJHR*, H-10, 1893.
Statistics of New Zealand, 1853–1920.
'The Royal Commission on the Cost of Living', *AJHR*, 1912, H-18.

2: UNPUBLISHED UNOFFICIAL PAPERS

Cox, W. J., Diaries, ATL.
'Mr. George Pain's Story', Pain Collection, MS Papers 1740, Folder I, ATL.
Sir Robert Owen Correspondence 1817–1855, British Museum, Add. MSS. 39954 (notes taken by J. Belich).
Story, E. M. (ed.), 'Our Fathers Have Told Us: Stories of Settlers Collected in New Zealand', ATL.

3: Newspapers

Evening Post, 1876–1900.
New Zealand Herald, 1877–1895.
New Zealand Times, 1878–1888.

4: Books, Articles, Pamphlets, Published Journals, And Diaries

Adam, J., *Twenty-five Years of Emigrant Life in the South of New Zealand*, 2nd ed., Edinburgh, 1876.
Adams, C. W., *A Spring in the Canterbury Settlement*, London, 1853.
Alpers, O. T. J., *Cheerful Yesterdays*, London, 1928.
Andersen, J. C., *Jubilee History of South Canterbury*, Auckland, 1916.
Anderson, M., *A River Rules My Life*, Wellington, 1965.
Auckland Lyceum Club, *Silhouettes of the Past: a Century Ago*, Auckland, 1939.
Ayson, W., *Pioneering in Otago: the Recollections of William Ayson, Set Down in his 97th Year*, Dunedin, 1937.
Barker, M. A., *Station Life in New Zealand*, 1870, repr. Auckland, 1973.
Barlow, P. W., *Kaipara or Experiences of a Settler in North New Zealand*, London, 1888.
Barry, W. J., *Past & Present and Men of the Times*, Wellington, 1897.
Bathgate, A., *Colonial Experiences; or Sketches of People and Places in the Province of Otago, New Zealand*, Glasgow, 1874.
Bathgate, J., *New Zealand, its Resources and Prospects*, new rev. ed., London, 1884.
Beale, G. C., *Seventy Years In and Around Auckland*, Dunedin, 1937.
Berry, J., *New Zealand as a Field for Emigration*, London, 1879.
Bertram, J. (ed.), *New Zealand Letters of Thomas Arnold the Younger with Further Letters from Van Diemen's Land and Letters of Arthur Hugh Clough 1847–1851*, Auckland, 1966.
Boxall, G., *History of the Australian Bushrangers*, 1899, repr. Harmondsworth, 1974.
Bradshaw, J., *New Zealand as it Is*, London, 1883.
Bradshaw, J., *New Zealand of Today*, London, 1888.
Braim, T. H., *New Homes: The Rise, Progress, Present Position, and Future Prospects of each of the Australian· Colonies and New Zealand, Regarded as Homes for all Classes of Emigrants*, London, 1870.
Buller, J., *New Zealand: Past and Present*, London, 1880.
Burton, D. (ed.), *Confessions of Richard Burgess, The Maungatapu Murders and other Grisly Crimes*, Wellington, 1983.
Butler, A. R., *Glimpses of Maori Land*, London, 1886.
Butler, S., *A First Year in Canterbury Settlement*, London, 1863.
Butler, S., *Erewhon or Over the Range*, 1872, repr. Auckland, 1973.
Chamier, G., *A South-Sea Siren*, 1895, repr. Auckland, 1970.
Clayden, A., *The England of the Pacific or New Zealand as an English Middle-Class Emigration-Field*, London, 1879.
Coghlan, T. A., *A Statistical Account of the Seven Colonies of Australasia*, 1895–6, Sydney, 1896.
Coghlan, T.A., *A Statistical Account of the Seven Colonies of Australasia*, 1897–8, Sydney, 1898.

Cooper, I. R., *The New Zealand Settlers' Guide, a Sketch of the Present State of the Six Provinces*, London, 1857.
Cooper, T., *A Digger's Diary at the Thames 1867*, Dunedin, 1978.
Cowan, J., *The Old Frontier . . .*, Te Awamutu, 1922.
Cowan, J., *New Zealand, or, Ao-Tea-Roa (The Long Bright World)*, Wellington, 1908.
Cowan, J., *Settlers and Pioneers*, Wellington, 1940.
Cowan, J., *Tales of the Maori Border*, Wellington, 1944.
Courage, S., *Lights and Shadows of Colonial Life, Twenty-six Years in Canterbury, New Zealand*, 1896, repr. Christchurch, 1976.
Cox, M. (ed.), *On Record. Being the Reminiscences of Isaac Coates 1840-1932*, Hamilton, 1962.
Drummond, A. (ed.), *The Thames Journals of Vicesimus Lush 1868-82*, Christchurch, 1975.
Drummond, A. (ed.), *The Waikato Journals of Vicesimus Lush 1864-8, 1881-2*, Christchurch, 1982.
Elkington, E. W., *Adrift in New Zealand*, London, 1906.
Finlayson, R., *Tidal Creek*, Sydney, 1948.
Fitton, E. B., *New Zealand: its Present Condition, Prospects and Resources . . .*, London, 1856.
Fuller, F., *Five Years' Residence in New Zealand; or, Observations on Colonization*, London, 1859.
Gilkison, R., *Early Days in Central Otago; Being Tales of Times Gone By*, Dunedin, 1930.
Gisborne, W., *The Colony of New Zealand; its History, Vicissitudes and Progress*, London, 1888.
Godley, J. R. (ed.), *Letters from Early New Zealand by Charlotte Godley, 1850-1853*, Christchurch, 1951.
Gorst, J., *New Zealand Revisited; Recollections of the Days of My Youth*, London, 1908.
Grossmann, E. S., *The Heart of the Bush*, London, 1910.
Hall, J., *Experience of Thirty Years in the Provincial District of Wellington*, Wellington, 1884.
Hamer, D. (ed.), *The Webbs in New Zealand 1898*, Wellington, 1974.
Harper, H. W., *Letters from New Zealand, 1857-1911*, London, 1914.
Hay, W. D., *Brighter Britain! or Settler and Maori in Northern New Zealand*, 2 vols, London, 1882.
Hector, J., *Handbook of New Zealand*, Wellington, 1883.
Hewett, E., *Looking Back or Personal Reminiscences*, St. Albans, 1911.
Hodder, E., *Memories of New Zealand Life*, London, 1862.
'Hopeful', *'Taken In', Being a Sketch of New Zealand Life*, London, 1887, repr. Christchurch, 1974.
Howitt, W. K., *A Pioneer Looks Back: Days of Trials, Hardships and Achievements*, Auckland, 1945.
Hursthouse, C., *New Zealand the 'Britain of the South'*, 2nd ed., London, 1861.
Inglis, J., *Our New Zealand Cousins*, London, 1887.
Jones, E., *Autobiography of an Early Settler in New Zealand*, Wellington, 1933.
Kennaway, L. J., *Crusts. A Settler's Fare Due South*, London, 1874.

Kennedy, D., *Kennedy's Colonial Travel. A Narrative of a Four Years' Tour Through Australia, New Zealand, Canada, etc.*, London, 1876.

Lawlor, P., *The House of Templemore*, Wellington, 1938.

Loughnan, R. A., *New Zealand at Home*, London, 1908.

MacDonald, S., *The Member for Mount Ida*, Wellington, 1938.

Mayhew, H., *London Labour and the London Poor*, 2 vols, London, 1864.

McCarthy, B., *Castles in the Soil*, Wellington, 1939.

McIlraith, J. W., *The Course of Prices in New Zealand*, Wellington, 1911.

McIntyre, W. D. (ed.), *The Journal of Henry Sewell 1853-7*, 2 vols, Christchurch, 1980.

McMurran, C. W., *From New York to New Zealand; or, the New Century Trip*, Wellington, 1904.

M. E. T., 'Round the East Cape in 1892', *HR*, 20, Nov. 1972.

Métin, A., *Socialism Without Doctrine*, 1908, repr. Chippendale, 1977.

Miller, H. H., 'Bush Pioneering Days', *HR*, 7, Sept. 1959.

Money, C., *Knocking about in New Zealand*, 1871, repr. Christchurch, 1972.

Mulgan, A., *The Making of a New Zealander*, Wellington, 1958.

Paul, R. B., *New Zealand, as It Was and as It Is*, London, 1861.

Pratt, W. T., *Colonial Experiences; or, Incidents and Reminiscences of Thirty-four Years in New Zealand*, London, 1877.

Pyke, V., *The Story of Wild Will Enderby*, 1873, repr. 1974.

Reed, G. M., *The Angel Isafrel; A Story of Prohibition in New Zealand*, Auckland, 1896.

Reeves, W. P., *The Long White Cloud Ao Tea Roa*, 4th ed., London, 1956.

Reeves, W. P. (ed.), *The New Zealand Reader*, Wellington, 1895.

Reeves, W. P., *State Experiments in Australia and New Zealand*, 2 vols, London, 1902.

Satchell, W., *The Land of the Lost*, 1902, repr. Auckland, 1971.

Saunders, A., *New Zealand, its Climate, Soil, Natural and Artificial Productions, Animals, Birds, and Insects, Aboriginal and European Inhabitants, etc.*, London, 1868.

Scanlon, N. M., *Pencarrow*, London, 1932.

Scholefield, G. H. (ed.), *The Richmond-Atkinson Papers*, 2 vols, Wellington, 1960.

Scott, H., *Reminiscences of a New Chum in Otago (New Zealand) in the Early 'Seventies*, Timaru, 1922.

Seccombe, T., 'Farming at Rewarau, Opouriao District, 1897-1906. The Seccombe Story—Part 3', *HR*, 12, Mar. 1964.

Seccombe, T., 'Pioneering Days at Orete Point, Better Known as Waihau Bay, East Cape. The Seccombe Story—Part 2', *HR*, 11, Mar., June, 1963.

Siegfried, A., *Democracy in New Zealand*, London, 1914.

Simmons, A., *Old England and New Zealand: The Government, Laws, Churches, Public Institutions, and the Resources of New Zealand*, London, 1879.

Sinclair, K. (ed.), *A Soldier's View of Empire; the Reminiscences of James Bodell, 1831-92*, London, 1982.

Somerset, H. C. D., *Littledene: A New Zealand Rural Community*, Wellington, 1938.

Stewart, A. B., *My Simple Life in New Zealand*, London, 1908.

Stewart, W. D. (ed.), *The Journal of George Hepburn*, Dunedin, 1934.

Stewart, W. D., *William Rolleston; a New Zealand Statesman*, Christchurch, 1940.

Stout, R., & Stout, J. L., *New Zealand*, Cambridge, 1911.

Stout, R., *Notes on the Progress of New Zealand for Twenty Years, 1864-1884*, Wellington, 1886.
Taylor, R., *Te Ika A Maui, or New Zealand and its Inhabitants*, London, 1855.
Taylor, R., *The Past and Present of New Zealand; with its Prospects for the Future*, London, 1868.
Thomson, A. S., *The Story of New Zealand—Past & Present—Savage and Civilized*, 2 vols, London, 1859.
Thomson, J. A., *The Taieri Allens and Related Families*, Dunedin, 1929.
Tregear, E., 'Labour in New Zealand', *NZYB*, 1893.
Trollope, A., *Australia and New Zealand*, 2 vols, London, 1873.
Vaile, P. A., *New Zealand*, 2nd ed., London, 1921.
Vogel, J. (ed.), *The Official Handbook of New Zealand*, London, 1875.
Wakefield, E., *New Zealand Illustrated*, Wanganui, 1889.
Wallace, R., *The Rural Economy and Agriculture of Australia and New Zealand*, London, 1891.
WDFU, *Brave Days; Pioneer Women of New Zealand*, Wellington, 1939.
Wise and Co's New Zealand Directory, 1880-81, 1890, 1900.
Woodhouse, A. E. (ed.), *New Zealand Farm and Station Verse 1850-1950*, Christchurch, 1950.
Woodhouse, A. E. (ed.), *Tales of Pioneer Women Collected by the Women's Institutes of New Zealand*, Christchurch, 1940.
Young, L., *Father and Son; a Young Saga*, Christchurch, 1978.

B. SECONDARY SOURCES

1: Books

Acland, L. G. D., *The Early Canterbury Runs*, 4th ed., Christchurch, 1975.
Allan, R. M., *Nelson; a History of Early Settlement*, Wellington, 1965.
Andersen, A. L., *Norsewood: The Centennial Story*, Dannevirke, 1972.
Archdeacon, T. J., *Becoming American; an Ethnic History*, New York, 1983.
Archer, D., & Gartner, R., *Violence and Crime in Cross-National Perspective*, New Haven, 1984.
Arensberg, K., & Kimball, S., *Family and Community in Ireland*, 2nd ed., Cambridge, Mass., 1968.
Arnold, R., *The Farthest Promised Land: English Villagers, New Zealand Immigrants of the 1870s*, Wellington, 1981.
Bagnall, A. G., *Wairarapa; an Historical Excursion*, Masterton, 1976.
Bailyn, B., *The Peopling of British North America; an Introduction*, New York, 1986.
Banks, J. A., *Prosperity and Parenthood: a Study of Family Planning among the Victorian Middle Classes*, London, 1954.
Bassett, J., *Sir Harry Atkinson 1831-1892*, Auckland, 1975.
Bayliss, E. R., *Tinwald; a Canterbury Plains Settlement*, Timaru, 1970.
Beier, A. L., *Masterless Men: the Vagrancy Problem in England, 1560-1640*, London, 1985.
Bell, C., & Newby, H., *Community Studies; an Introduction to the Sociology of the Local Community*, London, 1971.

Bloch, M., *Feudal Society*, 2nd ed., London, 1962.

Blok, A., *The Mafia of a Sicilian Village, 1860-1960; a Study of Violent Peasant Entrepreneurs*, Oxford, 1974.

Boissevain, J., *Friends of Friends; Networks, Manipulators and Coalitions*, Oxford, 1974.

Bott, E., *Family and Social Network: Roles, Norms, and External Relationships in Ordinary Urban Families*, London, 1957.

Boyd, M., *City of the Plains: a History of Hastings*, Wellington, 1984.

Bromley, A. P. C., *Hawera District Centenary: Hawera: an Outline of the Development of a New Zealand Community*, Hawera, 1981.

Cameron, I. A., *Crime and Repression in the Auvergne and the Guyenne, 1720-1790*, Cambridge, 1981.

Campbell, A. E., *Educating New Zealand*, Wellington, 1941.

Cipolla, C. M., *Before the Industrial Revolution; European Society, and Economy, 1000-1700*, 2nd ed., London, 1981.

Clark, A. H., *The Invasion of New Zealand by People, Plants and Animals; the South Island*, New Brunswick, 1949.

Clark, C. M. H., *A History of Australia, III: The Beginning of an Australian Civilization, 1824-1851*, Melbourne, 1979.

Cohen, S., *Folk Devils and Moral Panics: the Creation of the Mods and Rockers*, New York, 1980.

Cook, C., & Stevenson, J., *The Longman Handbook of Modern British History 1714-1980*, Harlow, 1983.

Dalziel, R., *The Origins of New Zealand Diplomacy; the Agent-General in London 1870-1905*, Wellington, 1975.

Davis, J. C., *Utopia and the Ideal Society: a Study of English Utopian Writing 1516-1700*, Cambridge, 1981.

Davis, R. P., *Irish Issues in New Zealand Politics 1868-1922*, Dunedin, 1974.

Demos, J., *A Little Commonwealth: Family Life in Plymouth Colony*, London, 1970.

Denoon, D., *Settler Capitalism: the Dynamics of Dependent Development in the Southern Hemisphere*, Oxford, 1983.

De Tocqueville, A., *Democracy in America*, New York, 1966 ed.

Doherty, R., *Society and Power: Five New England Towns, 1800-1860*, Amherst, 1977.

Doyle, D. H., *The Social Order of a Frontier Community: Jacksonville, Illinois, 1825-70*, Chicago, 1978.

Eldred-Grigg, S., *A Southern Gentry: New Zealanders Who Inherited the Earth*, Wellington, 1980.

Elias, N., & Scotson, I. L., *The Established and the Outsiders—A Sociological Enquiry into Community Problems*, London, 1965.

Erickson, C., *Invisible Immigrants; the Adaptation of English and Scottish Immigrants in Nineteenth-Century America*, Coral Gables, 1972.

Frankenberg, R., *Communities in Britain: Social Life in Town and Country*, Harmondsworth, 1967.

Fry, H. T., *Alexander Dalrymple (1737-1808) and the Expansion of British Trade*, London, 1970.

Gardner, W. J., *The Amuri; a County History*, Culverden, 1956.

Gellner, E., & Waterbury, J. (eds), *Patrons and Clients in Mediterranean Societies*, London, 1977.

Gibbons, P. J., *Astride the River: a History of Hamilton*, Christchurch, 1977.
Given, J. B., *Society and Homicide in Thirteenth-Century England*, Stanford, 1977.
Grant, S. W., *Havelock North; from Village to Borough, 1860-1952*, Hastings, 1978.
Green, D., & Cromwell, L., *Mutual Aid or Welfare State: Australia's Friendly Societies*, Sydney, 1984.
Grimshaw, P., *Women's Suffrage in New Zealand*, Auckland, 1972.
Gustafson, B., *Labour's Path to Political Independence: the Origins and Establishment of the New Zealand Labour Party 1900-19*, Auckland, 1980.
Hanawalt, B., *Crime and Conflict in English Communities, 1300-1348*, Cambridge, Mass., 1979.
Hareven, T. K., *Family Time and Industrial Time: the Relationship between the Family and Work in a New England Industrial Community*, Cambridge, 1982.
Harrison, B., *Drink and the Victorians: the Temperance Question in England 1815-1872*, London, 1971.
Hawke, G. R., *The Making of New Zealand: an Economic History*, Cambridge, 1985..
Hess, H., *Mafia and Mafiosi: the Structure of Power*, Westmead, 1973.
Hill, R., *Policing the Colonial Frontier: the Theory and Practice of Coercive Social and Racial Control in New Zealand 1767-1867*, Wellington, 1986.
Hobsbawm, E. J., *Bandits*, London, 1969.
Hobsbawm, E. J., *Primitive Rebels: Studies in Archaic Forms of Social Movement in the 19th and 20th Centuries*, Manchester, 1959.
Horn, P., *The Rise and Fall of the Victorian Servant*, Dublin, 1975.
Houghton, W. E., *The Victorian Frame of Mind*, Oxford, 1957.
Hufton, O. H., *The Poor of Eighteenth-Century France, 1750-1789*, Oxford, 1974.
Huggett, F. E., *A Dictionary of British History 1815-1973*, Oxford, 1974.
Joblin, D., *The Colonial One: Lorna Monckton of Newstead*, Christchurch, 1975.
Jones, D., *Crime, Protest, Community, and Police in Nineteenth-Century Britain*, London, 1982.
Kagan, R. L., *Lawsuits and Litigants in Castile, 1500-1700*, Chapel Hill, 1981.
Katz, M. B., *The People of Hamilton, Canada West: Family and Class in a Mid-Nineteenth-Century City*, Cambridge, Mass., 1975.
Lane, R., *Violent Death in the City: Suicide, Accident and Murder in Nineteenth-Century Philadelphia*, Cambridge, Mass., 1979.
Lansbury, C., *Arcady in Australia: the Evocation of Australia in Nineteenth-Century English Literature*, Melbourne, 1970.
Laslett, P. & Wall, R. (eds), *Household and Family in Past Time*, Cambridge, 1972.
Lee, J. A., *Roughnecks, Rolling Stones & Rouseabouts*, Christchurch, 1977.
Lenski, G., *Power and Privilege*, London and New York, 1966.
Lipson, L., *The Politics of Equality; New Zealand's Adventures in Democracy*, Chicago, 1948.
Marx, L., *The Machine in the Garden: Technology and the Pastoral Ideal in America*, London, 1964.
McGill, D., *The Other New Zealanders*, Wellington, 1982.
McIntyre, W. D., & Gardner, W. J. (eds), *Speeches and Documents on New Zealand History*, Oxford, 1971.
McLay, E., *Stepping Out: a History of Clutha County Council*, Dunedin 1977.
McLintock, A. H. (ed.), *An Encyclopaedia of New Zealand*, 3 vols, Wellington, 1966.

Mitchell, B. R., & Deane, P. (eds), *Abstract of British Historical Statistics,* Cambridge, 1962.

Monkkonen, E. H., *The Dangerous Class: Crime and Poverty in Columbus, Ohio, 1860-1885,* Cambridge, Mass., 1975.

Nadel, G., *Australia's Colonial Culture; Ideas, Men and Institutions in Mid-Nineteenth-Century Eastern Australia,* Melbourne, 1957.

Newby, H., *The Deferential Worker: a Study of Farm Workers in East Anglia,* London, 1977.

Newport, J. N. W., *Footprints: the Story of the Settlement and Development of the Nelson Back Country Districts,* Christchurch, 1962.

Oliver, W. H. (ed.), *The Oxford History of New Zealand,* Oxford and Wellington, 1981.

Oliver, W. H., *Towards a New History?* 1969 Hocken Lecture, Dunedin, 1971.

Olssen, E., *A History of Otago,* Dunedin, 1984.

Parkin, F., *Class Inequality and Political Order,* London, 1973.

Parrington, V. L., *American Dreams: a Study of American Utopias,* Providence, 1947.

Pearson, D. G., *Johnsonville: Continuity and Change in a New Zealand Township,* Sydney, 1980.

Pearson, G., *The Deviant Imagination; Psychiatry, Social Work and Social Change,* London, 1975.

Philips, D., *Crime and Authority in Victorian England; the Black Country 1835-1860,* London, 1977.

Phillips, J. O. C., *A Man's Country? The Image of the Pakeha Male—A History,* Auckland, 1987.

Pinney, R., *Early Northern Otago Runs,* Auckland, 1981.

Popper, K. R., *The Logic of Scientific Discovery,* rev. ed., London, 1968.

Popper, K, R., *The Open Society and its Enemies,* 2 vols, 3rd ed. (rev.), London, 1957.

Reed, A. H., *The Gumdigger; the Story of Kauri Gum,* Wellington, 1948.

Rickard, J., *Class and Politics; New South Wales, Victoria and the Early Commonwealth, 1890-1910,* Canberra, 1976.

Roberts, W. H. S., *et al, History of North Otago from 1853,* Oamaru, 1937.

Roth, H., *Trade Unions in New Zealand, Past and Present,* Wellington, 1973.

Rudé, G., *Protest and Punishment: the Story of the Social and Political Protesters Transported to Australia 1788-1868,* Oxford, 1978.

Rutherford, J., *Sir George Grey, K.C.B., 1812-1898: a Study in Colonial Government,* London, 1961.

Salmond, J. D., *New Zealand Labour's Pioneering Days,* Auckland, 1950.

Scott, J. W., *The Glassworkers of Carmaux: French Craftsmen and Political Action in a Nineteenth-Century City,* Cambridge, Mass., 1974.

Sharpe, J. A., *Crime in Seventeenth-Century England; a County Study,* Cambridge, 1983.

Shaw, A. G. L., *Convicts & the Colonies—A Study of Penal Transportation . . .,* London, 1966.

Sinclair, K., *William Pember Reeves: New Zealand Fabian,* Oxford, 1965.

Smith, B., *European Vision and the South Pacific, 1768-1858,* Oxford, 1960.

Smith P., *As a City Upon a Hill: the Town in American History,* Cambridge, Mass., 1966.

Stone, L., *The Family, Sex and Marriage in England, 1500-1800*, London, 1977.
Stone, L., *The Crisis of the Aristocracy, 1558-1641*, Oxford, 1965.
Studholme, E. C., *Te Waimate: Early Station Life in New Zealand*, 2nd ed., Wellington, 1954.
Sturma, M., *Vice in a Vicious Society: Crime and Convicts in Mid-Nineteenth-Century New South Wales*, St Lucia, 1983.
Sutch, W. B., *Poverty and Progress in New Zealand: a Reassessment*, Wellington, 1969.
Sutch, W. B., *The Quest for Security in New Zealand 1840-1966*, Wellington, 1966.
Taylor, I., Walton, P., & Young, J., *The New Criminology: for a Social Theory of Deviance*, London, 1973.
Thernstrom, S., *The Other Bostonians; Poverty and Progress in the American Metropolis, 1880-1970*, Cambridge, Mass., 1973.
Thompson, A. B., *Adult Education in New Zealand*, Wellington, 1945.
Tilly, C., *et al.*, *The Rebellious Century, 1830-1930*, Cambridge, Mass., 1975.
Tilly, C., & Shorter, E., *Strikes in France, 1830-1968*, London, 1974.
Tobias, J. J., *Crime and Industrial Society in the 19th Century*, London, 1967.
Turner, F. J., *The Frontier in American History*, New York, 1948 ed.
Walvin, J., *Leisure and Society, 1830-1950*, London, 1978.
Ward R., *A Nation for a Continent: the History of Australia 1901-1975*, Richmond, 1977.
Ward, R., *The Australian Legend*, Melbourne, 1977.
Wilson, C., *England's Apprenticeship, 1603-1763*, New York, 1965.
Wilson, J. G., *Road to Porangahau and Notes on Land Settlement*, Napier, 1962.
Worchel, S., & Cooper, J., *Understanding Social Psychology*, rev. ed., Homewood, 1979.
Wolfgang, M. E., & Ferracuti, F., *The Subculture of Violence*, London, 1967.
Young, M., & Willmott, P., *Family and Kinship in East London*, London, 1957.
Young, M., & Willmott, P., *Family and Class in a London Suburb*, London, 1960.
Zehr, H., *Crime and the Development of Modern Society: Patterns of Criminality in Nineteenth-Century Germany and France*, London, 1976.

2: ARTICLES

Arnold, R., 'The Dynamics and Quality of Trans-Tasman Migration, 1885-1920', *AEHR*, 26, Mar. 1980.
Arnold, R., 'The Virgin Forest Harvest and the Development of Colonial New Zealand', *New Zealand Geographer*, 32, Oct. 1976.
Arnold, R., 'The Wellington Education Board, 1878-1901: Grappling with Educational Backwardness and Advancing Settlement', *Australia and New Zealand History of Education Society Journal*, 6, Spring 1977.
Arnold, R., 'Yeomen and Nomads: New Zealand and the Australian Shearing Scene, 1886-1896', *NZJH*, 18, 1984.
Baumgartner, M. P., 'Social Control in Suburbia' in D. Black (ed.), *Toward a General Theory of Social Control*, 2 vols, Orlando, Florida, 1984, i.
Beattie, J. J., 'The Pattern of Crime in England 1660-1800', *P&P*, 62, Feb. 1974.
Bohannan, P., 'Patterns of Murder and Suicide', in P. Bohannan (ed.), *African Homicide and Suicide*, New York, 1967.
Bourke, P. F., 'A Note on the Study of Mobility', *Australia 1888*, Bull. 4, May 1980.

Briggs, A., 'The Human Aggregate' in H. J. Dyos & M. Wolff (eds), *The Victorian City—Images and Realities*, 2 vols, London, 1973, i.

Brooking, T., 'New Zealand Farmers' Organisations and Rural Politics in the late Nineteenth and Early Twentieth Centuries', *HN*, 41, 1980.

Brown, R. M., 'Historical Patterns of American Violence' in H. D. Graham & T. R. Gurr (eds), *Violence in America: Historical and Comparative Perspectives*, Beverly Hills, 1979.

Brown, R. M., 'The History of Vigilantism in America' in H. J. Rosenbaum & P. C. Sederberg (eds), *Vigilante Politics*, Pittsburgh, 1976.

Campbell, R. J., '"The Black Eighties"—Unemployment in New Zealand in the 1880s', *AEHR*, 16, Sept. 1976.

Clune, D. H., 'The State Labour Party's Electoral Record in Rural New South Wales 1904–1981', *LH*, 47, Nov. 1984.

Conradson, B., 'Politics and Penury: County and Province, 1868–76' in P. R. May, (ed.), *Miners and Militants: Politics in Westland 1865–1918*, Christchurch, 1975.

Dalziel, R., 'The Colonial Helpmeet, Women's Role and the Vote in Nineteenth-Century New Zealand', *NZJH*, 11, Oct. 1977.

Dalziel, R., ' The Politics of Settlement' in W. H. Oliver (ed.), *The Oxford History of New Zealand*, Oxford and Wellington, 1981.

Davison, G., 'Sydney and the Bush: An Urban Context for the Australian Legend', *HS*, 18, 1978.

Davison, G., 'The Dimensions of Mobility in Nineteenth-Century Australia', *Australia 1888*, Bull. 2, Aug. 1979.

Dingle, A. E., '"The Truly Magnificent Thirst": an Historical Survey of Australian Drinking Habits', *HS*, 19, Oct. 1980.

Du Pontet, D., 'Opotiki from 1884 to 1918', *HR*, 15, Aug. 1967.

Du Pontet, D., 'Opotiki as a Young Girl First Saw It', *HR*, 22, Nov. 1974.

Du Pontet, D., 'Early Days in the Waiotahi Valley', *HR*, 12, June 1964.

Fairburn, M., 'Local Community or Atomised Society? The Social Structure of Nineteenth-Century New Zealand', *NZJH*, 16, Oct. 1982.

Fairburn M., 'Social Mobility and Opportunity in Nineteenth-Century New Zealand', *NZJH*, 13, Apr. 1979.

Fairburn, M., 'Why did the New Zealand Labour Party Fail to Win Office until 1935?', *PS*, 37, Dec. 1985.

Fairburn, M., 'Vagrants, "Folk Devils" and Nineteenth-Century New Zealand as a Bondless Society', *HS*, 21, Oct. 1985.

Fairburn, M., & Haslett, S. J., 'Violent Crime in Old and New Societies: A Case Study Based on New Zealand 1853–1940', *SH*, Fall 1986.

F. K. B. 'A History of Te Teko School', *HR*, 13, June 1965.

Frye, N., 'Varieties of Literary Utopia' in F. E. Manuel (ed.), *Utopias and Utopian Thought*, Boston, 1966.

Gardner, W. J., 'New Zealand Regional History: General and Canterbury Perspectives', *HN*, 41, 1980.

Gatrell, V. A. C., & Hadden, T. B., 'Criminal Statistics and their Interpretation', in E. A. Wrigley (ed.), *Nineteenth-Century Society: Essays in the Use of Quantitative Methods for the Study of Social Data*, Cambridge, 1972.

Gatrell, V. A. C., 'The Decline of Theft and Violence in Victorian and Edwardian England', in *C&L*.

Gibbons, P. J., 'Some New Zealand Navvies—Co-operative Workers, 1891–1912', NZJH, 11, Apr. 1977.

Gould, J. D., 'The Occupation of Farm Land in New Zealand, 1874–1911: A Preliminary Survey', Business Archives and History, Aug. 1965.

Grabosky, P. N., Persson, L., Sperlings, S., 'Stockholm: the Politics of Crime and Conflict, 1750 to the 1970s' in T. R. Gurr, P. N. Grabosky, R. C. Hula, The Politics of Crime and Conflict. A Comparative History of Four Cities, Beverly Hills, 1977.

Graham, J., 'Settler Society', in W. H. Oliver (ed.), The Oxford History of New Zealand, Oxford & Wellington, 1981.

Griffen, C., 'Workers Divided: The Effect of Craft and Ethnic Differences in Poughkeepsie, New York, 1855–1880' in S. Thernstrom & R. Sennett (eds), Nineteenth-Century Cities; Essays in the New Urban History, New Haven, 1969.

Hamer, D., 'Towns in Nineteenth-Century New Zealand' in D. Hamer (ed.), New Zealand Social History, Aug. 1978, Auckland, n.d.

Hay, D., 'Poaching and the Game Laws on Gannock Chase' in D. Hay et al., Albion's Fatal Tree. Crime and Society in Eighteenth-Century England, Harmondsworth, 1975.

Hay, D., 'War, Dearth and Theft in the Eighteenth Century: the Record of the English Courts', P&P, 95, May 1982.

Hobsbawm, E. J., 'The Tramping Artisan' in E. J. Hobsbawm, Labouring Men, Studies in the History of Labour, London, 1964.

Hula, R. C., 'Calcutta: the Politics of Crime and Conflict, 1800 to the 1970s' in T. R. Gurr, P. N. Grabosky, R. C. Hula The Politics of Crime and Conflict, Beverly Hills, 1977.

Ingram, M. J., 'Communities and Courts: Law and Disorder in Early Seventeenth-Century Wiltshire' in J. S. Cockburn (ed.), Crime in England 1550–1800, London 1977.

Jackson, H., 'Churchgoing in Nineteenth-Century New Zealand', NZJH, 17, Apr. 1983.

Lenman, B., & Parker, G., 'The State, the Community and the Criminal Law in Early Modern Europe' in C&L.

London, H. D., 'The Opouriao Estate', HR, 13, June 1965.

Mackay, D., 'British Interest in the Southern Oceans 1782–1794', NZJH, 3, Oct. 1969.

Macnaughton, D. T., 'The New Zealand Shearers' Union and the Crisis in the Shearing Industry 1910–1916', Auckland University Historical Society Annual, 1971.

Markey, R., 'New Unionism in Australia, 1880–1900', LH, 48, May 1985.

Martin, J., 'Whither the Rural Working Class in Nineteenth-Century New Zealand?', NZJH, 17, Apr. 1983.

May, P., 'Politics and Gold: the Separation of Westland, 1865–7' in P. R. May (ed.), Miners and Militants: Politics in Westland 1865–1918, Christchurch, 1975.

McGeorge, C., 'School Attendance and Child Labour 1890–1914', HN, May 1983.

McKenzie, D., 'Reluctantly to School', in D. McKenzie, Education and Social Structure: Essays in the History of New Zealand Education, Dunedin, 1982.

Morrissey, D., 'Ned Kelly's Sympathisers', HS, 18, 1978.

Morse, R. M., 'The Heritage of Latin America' in L. Hartz, The Founding of New Societies. Studies in the History of the United States, Latin America, South Africa, Canada and Australia, New York, 1964.

Oliver, W. H; 'The Origins and Growth of the Welfare State' in A. D. Trlin (ed.), *Social Welfare and New Zealand Society*, Wellington, 1977.

Olssen, E., & Levesque, A., 'Towards a History of the European Family in New Zealand' in P. G. Koopman-Boyden (ed.), *Families in New Zealand Society*, Wellington, 1978.

Olssen, E., 'Social Class in Nineteenth-Century New Zealand' in D. Pitt (ed.), *Social Class in New Zealand*, Auckland, 1977.

Olssen, E., 'The Origins of the Labour Party: a Reconsideration', *NZJH*, 21, Apr. 1987.

Olssen, E., 'Truby King and the Plunket Society: An Analysis of a Prescriptive Ideology', *NZJH*, 15, 1981.

Olssen, E., 'The "Working Class" in New Zealand', *NZJH*, 8, Apr. 1974.

Olssen, E., 'Towards a New Society' in W. H. Oliver (ed.), *The Oxford History of New Zealand*, Oxford and Wellington, 1981.

Parkerson, D., 'Internal Migration: Research Themes and New Directions', *O.A.H. Newsletter*, Aug. 1983.

Philips, D., '"A New Engine of Power and Authority": the Institutionalisation of Law-Enforcement in England 1780–1830' in *C&L*.

Phillips, J. O. C., 'Mummy's Boys: Pakeha Men and Male Culture in New Zealand' in P. Bunkle & B. Hughes (eds), *Women in New Zealand Society*, Auckland, 1980.

Reinhardt, S. G., 'Crime and Royal Justice in Ancien Régime France: Modes of Analysis', *JIH*, 13, 1983.

Sargent, L. T., 'Utopianism in Colonial America', *History of Political Thought*, 4, 3, 1983.

Sharpe, J. A., 'Enforcing the Law in the Seventeenth-Century English Village' in *C&L*.

Sharpe, J. A., '"Such Disagreement Betwyx Neighbours": Litigation and Human Relations in Early Modern England' in J. Bossy (ed.), *Disputes and Settlements: Law and Relations in the West*, Cambridge, 1983.

Shepard, P., 'English Reaction to the New Zealand Landscape Before 1850', *Pacific Viewpoint Monograph*, No. 4, Dept. of Geography, VUW, 1969.

Silver, A., 'The Demand for Order in Civil Society: a Review of Some Themes in the History of Urban Crime, Police, and Riot' in D. J. Bordua (ed.), *The Police: Six Sociological Essays*, New York, 1967.

Sorrenson, M. P. K., 'Land Purchase Methods and their Effect on Maori Population, 1865–1901', *Journal of the Polynesian Society*, 14, 3, 1956.

Stone, L., 'Interpersonal Violence in English Society 1300–1980', *P&P*, 101, Nov. 1983.

Stone, R., 'Auckland Party Politics in the Early Years of the Provincial System, 1853–58', *NZJH*, 14, Oct. 1980.

Tennant, M., 'Elderly Indigents and Old Men's Homes 1880–1920', *NZJH*, 17, Apr. 1983.

Thernstrom, S., & Knights, P. R., 'Men in Motion: Some Data and Speculations about Urban Population Mobility in Nineteenth-Century America', *JIH*, 1, Autumn 1970.

Tilly, C., 'Collective Violence in European Perspective' in H. D. Graham & T. R. Gurr (eds), *Violence in America*, Beverly Hills, 1979.

Toynbee, C., 'Class and Social Structure in Nineteenth-Century New Zealand' in D. Hamer (ed), *New Zealand Social History*, Auckland, n.d.
Walker, R. B., 'Violence in Industrial Conflicts in New South Wales in the Late Nineteenth Century', *HS*, 22, Apr. 1986.
Winslow, C., 'Sussex Smugglers', in D. Hay *et al., Albion's Fatal Tree*, Harmondsworth, 1975.
Wood, G. A., 'The 1878 Electoral Bill and Franchise Reform in Nineteenth-Century New Zealand', *PS.*, 28, July 1976.

3: Unpublished Papers, Theses

Angus, J. H., 'City and Country, Change and Continuity, Electoral Politics and Society in Otago, 1877-93', 2 v., Ph.D. thesis, Otago University, 1976.
Arnold, M. N., 'Wage Rates, 1873 to 1911', Dept. of Economics Discussion Paper No. 11, Apr. 1982, VUW.
Arnold, R., 'The Opening of the Great Bush, 1869-1881', Ph.D. thesis, VUW, 1971.
Bartlett, S., 'Crime 1896, 1897', Hist. 316 research essay, VUW, 1984.
Beaglehole, D., 'Geographical Mobility: Wanganui and Turakina 1866-76', Hist. 316 research paper, VUW, 1980.
Beaglehole, D., 'Geographical Mobility : Wellington, 1880-1890', B.A. (Hons) History research paper, VUW, 1982.
Beckford, N., 'Working Class Participation in Wellington Club Cricket 1878-1940', B.A. (Hons) History research paper, VUW, 1981.
Blackshaw, G., 'The Diaries of W. B. Matheson and D. MacRae', Hist. 316 research essay, VUW, 1982.
Brownlie, H., '"Without Work, Nothing": A Study of the Changing Attitudes Towards the Swagger in the 1890s', Long Essay for postgraduate Diploma of Arts in History, Otago University, 1980.
Bugg, S., 'Public Festivals in the Nineteenth Century: The Wellington Regatta', Hist. 316 research essay, VUW, 1982.
Campbell, M. D., 'The Evolution of Hawke's Bay Landed Society, 1850-1914', Ph.D. thesis, VUW, 1972.
Chilton, M. F., 'The Genesis of the Welfare State: A Study of Hospitals and Charitable Aid in New Zealand, 1877-92', M.A. thesis, Canterbury University, 1968.
Cumming, G. B., 'A Comparative Study of the Popularity of Sport in Auckland in 1895 and 1926', Hist. 316 research paper, VUW, 1983.
Cunninghame, J., 'Litigation in the 19th Century: Hokitika — A Case Study', Hist. 316 research essay, VUW, 1985.
Curry, G. P., 'Vagrancy', L.L.M. thesis, VUW, 1971.
Daley, C., 'Interpersonal Conflict in Colonial New Zealand: A Study of Violence and Civil Litigation in Wellington, 1870-1872', B.A. (Hons) History research paper, VUW, 1986.
Daube, P. K., 'A Pioneer Church . . .', Hist. 316 research essay, VUW, 1984.
Durrand, J., 'The Wellington Working Men's Club and Literary Institute . . .', B.A. (Hons) History research essay, VUW, 1984.
Fisk, S., 'Friendly Societies in New Zealand 1840-1900 . . .', Hist. 316 research paper, VUW, 1979.

Foster, A., 'A Survey of Geographical Mobility in New Zealand: Blenheim, Nelson and Greymouth 1875/6–1885/6', Hist. 316 research essay, 1983.

Frogley, S. A., 'Thieves of Wellington: A Study of Theft in the District of Wellington 1865–1867', B.A. (Hons) History research paper, 1985.

Gibbons, P., '"Turning Tramps into Taxpayers": the Department of Labour and the Casual Labourer in the 1890s', M.A. thesis, Massey University, 1970.

Hall, B., Thorns, D., Willmott, B., 'Community Formation and Change: A Study of Rural and Urban Localities in New Zealand', Dept. of Sociology, Canterbury University, working paper 4, Sept. 1983.

Hambling, R., 'Selectors of Crown Land in the Wellington Land District', B.A. (Hons) History research paper, VUW, 1977.

Harkness, M., 'Geographical Mobility in Wellington, 1868–78', Hist. 316 research paper, VUW, 1980.

Hawke, G. R., 'Towards a Re-Appraisal of the "Long Depression" in New Zealand 1879–1895', Typescript, VUW Economics Dept., 1975.

Head, A., 'Mechanics' Institutions in Early Victoria', B.A. (Hons) thesis, University of Melbourne, 1979.

Henderson, R., 'Communities under Threat? Some Effects of the Great Depression in the Manawatu Region', B.A. (Hons) History research paper, VUW, 1984.

Howard, B., 'Changing Social Composition in Wellington Rugby, 1879 to 1939', B.A. (Hons.) History research paper, VUW, 1981.

Luke, P., 'Suicide in Auckland, 1848–1939', M.A. thesis, Auckland University, 1982.

MacBeth, R. B., 'Geographical Mobility in Taranaki, New Zealand, 1878–1889', Hist. 316 research paper, VUW, 1983.

McConchie, M., 'The Police View of Crime', Hist. 316 research essay, VUW, 1983.

McGrath, F., 'An Investigation into the Population Mobility of the Town of Oxford between 1878 and 1949', Hist. 316 research paper, VUW, 1983.

McKimmey, P. F., 'The Temperance Movement in New Zealand; 1835–1894', M.A. thesis, Auckland University, 1968.

McLaren, I. A., 'Secondary Schools in the New Zealand Social Order, 1840–1903', Ph.D. thesis, VUW, 1965.

Meuli, P., 'Occupational Change and Bourgeois Proliferation', M.A. thesis, VUW, 1977.

Moore, C., 'The Residential and Occupational Composition of those Applying for Crown Land in the Wellington Land District 1891- 1911', B.A. (Hons) History research paper, VUW, 1976.

Moriarty, K., 'The Rise of the Masses', B.A. (Hons), History research paper, VUW, 1976.

Morris, J., 'The Assisted Immigrants to New Zealand, 1871–79; a Statistical Survey', M.A. thesis, Auckland University, 1973.

Oliver, L., 'Survey of "Working Class" Landowners in the Wellington District, 1853–1860', Hist. 316 research essay, VUW, 1984.

O'Riley, B., 'A Comparative Study and Insight into Participation in Winter Sport in the Taranaki Province in 1893', Hist. 316 research paper, VUW, 1983.

Ormerod, R., 'The Churches' Response to the Social Problems in Wellington, 1888–1891', B.A. (Hons.) History research paper, VUW, 1984.

Palairet, R., 'Litigation in Wanganui in the 1870s', Hist. 316 research paper, VUW, 1984.

Pearson, M., 'Residential Segregation and the Labour Vote in New Towns, 1925', B.A. (Hons) History research paper, VUW, 1986.

Pegden, J., 'Geographical Mobility of the Levin Area from 1878 to 1929', Hist. 316 research paper, VUW, 1983.

Reilly, M., 'Wellington Unofficial Organizations. . .', Hist. 412 extended essay, VUW, 1979.

Robertson, D., 'Geographical Mobility: Rates of Persistence and Transiency in Masterton 1872–1902', Hist. 316 research paper, VUW, 1984.

Shepherd, J., 'An Analysis of the *Evening Post* in 1878 and 1928', Hist. 316 research paper, VUW, 1982.

Shires, R., 'Civil Litigation in Nineteenth-Century Wellington', Hist. 316 research essay, VUW, 1985.

Shone, P. M., 'Marton: New Zealand Geographical Mobility . . .', Hist. 316 research paper, VUW, 1981.

Stagg, W., 'Death by Drowning', Hist. 316 research essay, VUW, 1983.

Stedman, G. M., 'The South Dunedin Flat: a study in Urbanisation 1849–1965', M.A. thesis, Otago University, 1966.

Swindells, N., 'Social Aspects of Rugby Football in Manawatu from 1878–1910', B.A. (Hons) History research paper, Massey University, 1978.

Tennant, M., 'Indigence and Charitable Aid in New Zealand, 1885–1920', Ph.D. thesis, Massey University, 1981.

Todd, P. M., 'Vagrancy in Nineteenth-Century Canterbury Province New Zealand', Hist. 316 research essay in History, VUW, 1985.

Todd, P. M., 'The Crime of Vagrancy in Wellington 1875–76', B.A. (Hons) History research paper, VUW, 1986.

Toynbee, C., 'Class and Mobility in Nineteenth-Century New Zealand', M.A. thesis, VUW, 1979.

Turney, C. R., 'A Comparative Study of the Rate of Participation in Rugby, Hockey and Soccer in Wanganui . . . in 1896 and 1926', Hist. 316 research essay, VUW, 1984.

Vosburgh, M. G., 'The New Zealand Family and Social Change: a Trend Analysis', Occasional papers in Sociology and Social Welfare No. 1, VUW, 1978.

Watters, S., 'Applicants for Crown Land in the Wellington Land District, 1886–1888', Hist. 316 research essay, VUW, 1984.

Wilson, T. Y., 'New Zealand prisons 1880–1909: The Administration of Colonel Arthur Hume', M.A. thesis, VUW, 1970.

Young, I., 'A comparative Study of the Organised Groups and Clubs of Wellington in 1895 & 1926', Hist. 316 research paper, VUW, 1982.

Index